Search through the complete book in PDF!

- Access the entire *CCIP: MPLS Study Guide*, complete with figures and tables, in electronic format.
- Search the *CCIP: MPLS Study Guide* chapters to find information on any topic in seconds.
- Use Adobe Acrobat Reader (included on the CD-ROM) to view the electronic book.

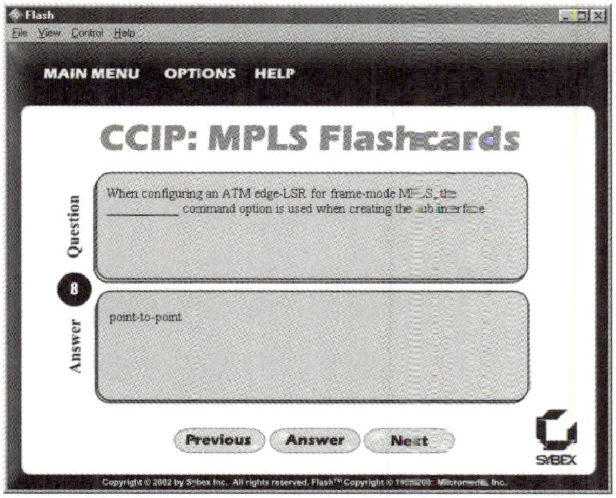

Use the Electronic Flashcards for PCs, Pocket PCs, or Palm devices to jog your memory and prep last minute for the exam!

- Reinforce your understanding of key concepts with these hardcore flashcard-style questions.

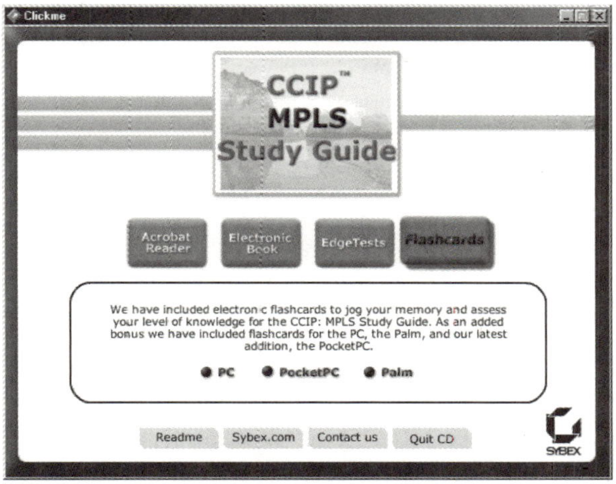

Electronic Flashcards now available for your Pocket PC as well!

- Download the Flashcards to your Pocket PC or Palm device and go on the road. Now you can study for the MPLS exam anytime, anywhere.

SYBEX

CCIP: MPLS Study Guide

Implementing Cisco MPLS Exam (640-910)

OBJECTIVE	CHAPTER
Core MPLS Technologies	
List the features, functions, and benefits of MPLS.	1
Identify suitable applications for MPLS.	1
Describe the underlying concepts of MPLS.	1
Describe frame-mode MPLS and cell-mode MPLS.	2, 3
Describe the concept of MPLS labels, label stack, and different label formats.	1
Describe the label distribution process between LSRs.	2
Describe the loop-detection and prevention mechanisms in MPLS.	3
Frame-Mode MPLS Implementation on Cisco IOS Platforms	
Describe the basic process of CEF switching.	2
Identify the IOS commands and their proper syntax used to configure MPLS on frame-mode MPLS interfaces on IOS platforms.	2
Identify the IOS commands and their proper syntax used to configure advanced core MPLS features (TTL propagation, controlled label distribution) on IOS platforms.	2
Identify the IOS commands and their proper syntax used to configure frame-mode MPLS on ATM PVC on IOS platforms.	3
Identify the IOS commands and their proper syntax used to monitor operations and troubleshoot typical MPLS failures on IOS platforms.	2
Cell-Mode MPLS Implementation on Cisco IOS Platforms	
Identify the IOS commands and their proper syntax used to configure cell-mode MPLS on ATM interfaces on IOS platforms.	3
Identify the IOS commands and their proper syntax used to monitor operations and troubleshoot typical cell-mode MPLS failures on IOS platforms.	3
MPLS VPN Technology	
Identify major virtual private network topologies, their characteristics, and usage scenarios.	4
Describe the differences between an overlay VPN and a peer-to-peer VPN.	4
List the major technologies supporting overlay VPNs and peer-to-peer VPNs.	4, 5
Identify the pros and cons of MPLS VPN implementations in comparison with other peer-to-peer VPN implementations.	6

SYBEX

OBJECTIVE	CHAPTER
MPLS VPN Technology *(Continued)*	
Describe the major architectural blocks of MPLS VPN.	5, 6
Describe the MPLS VPN routing model and packet forwarding.	5
MPLS VPN Implementation on Cisco IOS	
Identify the IOS commands and their proper syntax used to configure virtual routing and forwarding tables.	5, 6
Identify the IOS commands and their proper syntax used to configure Multi-Protocol BGP in MPLS VPN backbone.	5, 6
Identify the IOS commands and their proper syntax used to configure PE-CE routing protocols.	6
Identify the IOS commands and their proper syntax used to configure advanced MPLS VPN features.	8
Identify the IOS commands and their proper syntax used to monitor MPLS VPN operations.	6
Identify the IOS commands and their proper syntax used to troubleshoot typical failures in MPLS VPN implementation.	6
Running OSPF Inside a VPN	
Describe how OSPF operates inside a VPN.	7
Describe the enhanced OSPF hierarchical model.	7
Explain the interactions between OSPF and MP-BGP.	7

SYBEX

CCIP: MPLS

Study Guide

CCIP™: MPLS Study Guide

James Reagan

San Francisco • London

Associate Publisher: Neil Edde
Acquisitions and Developmental Editor: Maureen Adams
Editor: Sarah H. Lemaire
Production Editors: Molly Glover, Mae Lum
Technical Editors: Wade Edwards, Roger Clark Williams
Graphic Illustrator: Tony Jonick
Electronic Publishing Specialists: Rozi Harris, Bill Clark, Interactive Composition Corporation
Proofreaders: Nelson Kim, David Nash, Laurie O'Connell, Yariv Rabinovitch, Nancy Riddiough
Indexer: Ted Laux
CD Coordinator: Dan Mummert
CD Technician: Kevin Ly
Book Designer: Bill Gibson
Cover Designer: Archer Design
Cover Photographer: Andrew Ward, PhotoDisc

Library of Congress Card Number: 2002103170

ISBN: 0-7821-4096-3

Manufactured in the United States of America

10 9 8 7 6 5 4 3 2 1

SYBEX

To Our Valued Readers:

Cisco continues to dominate the internetworking market, and Cisco's range of professional certifications continue to be amongst the most highly respected in the business. Recently, Cisco developed the Cisco Certified Internetwork Professional (CCIP) certification to address the growing needs in the telecommunications and service provider industries for individuals competent in infrastructure or access solutions in a Cisco internetworking environment. Sybex expects the CCIP program to be well received, both by companies seeking qualified technical staff and by the IT training community.

We're proud to have helped thousands of Cisco certification candidates prepare for their exams over the years, and we are excited about the opportunity to continue to provide computer and networking professionals with the skills they'll need to succeed in the highly competitive IT industry.

The author and editors have worked hard to ensure that the Study Guide you hold in your hand is comprehensive, in-depth, and pedagogically sound. We're confident that this book will exceed the demanding standards of the certification marketplace and help you, the Cisco certification candidate, succeed in your endeavors.

As always, your feedback is important to us. Please send comments, questions, or suggestions to support@sybex.com. At Sybex we're continually striving to meet the needs of individuals preparing for IT certification exams.

Good luck in pursuit of your CCNP/CCIP certification!

Neil Edde
Associate Publisher—Certification
Sybex, Inc.

Software License Agreement: Terms and Conditions

The media and/or any online materials accompanying this book that are available now or in the future contain programs and/or text files (the "Software") to be used in connection with the book. SYBEX hereby grants to you a license to use the Software, subject to the terms that follow. Your purchase, acceptance, or use of the Software will constitute your acceptance of such terms.

The Software compilation is the property of SYBEX unless otherwise indicated and is protected by copyright to SYBEX or other copyright owner(s) as indicated in the media files (the "Owner(s)"). You are hereby granted a single-user license to use the Software for your personal, noncommercial use only. You may not reproduce, sell, distribute, publish, circulate, or commercially exploit the Software, or any portion thereof, without the written consent of SYBEX and the specific copyright owner(s) of any component software included on this media.

In the event that the Software or components include specific license requirements or end-user agreements, statements of condition, disclaimers, limitations or warranties ("End-User License"), those End-User Licenses supersede the terms and conditions herein as to that particular Software component. Your purchase, acceptance, or use of the Software will constitute your acceptance of such End-User Licenses.

By purchase, use or acceptance of the Software you further agree to comply with all export laws and regulations of the United States as such laws and regulations may exist from time to time.

Software Support

Components of the supplemental Software and any offers associated with them may be supported by the specific Owner(s) of that material, but they are not supported by SYBEX. Information regarding any available support may be obtained from the Owner(s) using the information provided in the appropriate read.me files or listed elsewhere on the media.

Should the manufacturer(s) or other Owner(s) cease to offer support or decline to honor any offer, SYBEX bears no responsibility. This notice concerning support for the Software is provided for your information only. SYBEX is not the agent or principal of the Owner(s), and SYBEX is in no way responsible for providing any support for the Software, nor is it liable or responsible for any support provided, or not provided, by the Owner(s).

Warranty

SYBEX warrants the enclosed media to be free of physical defects for a period of ninety (90) days after purchase. The Software is not available from SYBEX in any other form or media than that enclosed herein or posted to `www.sybex.com`. If you discover a defect in the media during this warranty period, you may obtain a replacement of identical format at no charge by sending the defective media, postage prepaid, with proof of purchase to:

SYBEX Inc.
Product Support Department
1151 Marina Village Parkway
Alameda, CA 94501
Web: `http://www.sybex.com`

After the 90-day period, you can obtain replacement media of identical format by sending us the defective disk, proof of purchase, and a check or money order for $10, payable to SYBEX.

Disclaimer

SYBEX makes no warranty or representation, either expressed or implied, with respect to the Software or its contents, quality, performance, merchantability, or fitness for a particular purpose. In no event will SYBEX, its distributors, or dealers be liable to you or any other party for direct, indirect, special, incidental, consequential, or other damages arising out of the use of or inability to use the Software or its contents even if advised of the possibility of such damage. In the event that the Software includes an online update feature, SYBEX further disclaims any obligation to provide this feature for any specific duration other than the initial posting.

The exclusion of implied warranties is not permitted by some states. Therefore, the above exclusion may not apply to you. This warranty provides you with specific legal rights; there may be other rights that you may have that vary from state to state. The pricing of the book with the Software by SYBEX reflects the allocation of risk and limitations on liability contained in this agreement of Terms and Conditions.

Shareware Distribution

This Software may contain various programs that are distributed as shareware. Copyright laws apply to both shareware and ordinary commercial software, and the copyright Owner(s) retains all rights. If you try a shareware program and continue using it, you are expected to register it. Individual programs differ on details of trial periods, registration, and payment. Please observe the requirements stated in appropriate files.

Copy Protection

The Software in whole or in part may or may not be copy-protected or encrypted. However, in all cases, reselling or redistributing these files without authorization is expressly forbidden except as specifically provided for by the Owner(s) therein.

I would like to dedicate this book to my wife Maria. Without her never-ending patience and support, this book would have never been written.

Acknowledgments

My thanks go to all the wonderful Sybex staff who worked with me every step of the way in writing this book. Maureen, Molly, Sarah, and Wade, you have my gratitude.

There is no way I could have ever written this book if my wife did not have the patience of Job. Thanks, Maria!

Contents at a Glance

Contents

Introduction

This book is intended to help you continue on your exciting new path toward obtaining your CCNP/CCIP and CCIE certification. Before reading this book, it is important to have at least read the *CCNA: Cisco Certified Network Associate Study Guide*, Third Edition (Sybex, 2002). You can take the CCNP/CCIP tests in any order, but you should have passed the CCNA exam before pursuing your CCNP/CCIP. Many questions in the MPLS exam are based on the CCNA material. However, we have done everything possible to make sure that you can pass the MPLS exam by reading this book and practicing with Cisco routers.

Cisco—A Brief History

A lot of readers may already be familiar with Cisco and what it does. However, those of you who are new to the field, just coming in fresh from your MCSE, or maybe even with 10 or more years in the field but wishing to brush up on the new technology, may appreciate a little background on Cisco.

In the early 1980s, a married couple who worked in different computer departments at Stanford University started up cisco Systems (notice the small *c*). Their names are Len and Sandy Bosack. They were having trouble getting their individual systems to communicate (like many married people), so in their living room they created a gateway server to make it easier for their disparate computers in two different departments to communicate using the IP protocol.

In 1984, cisco Systems was founded with a small commercial gateway server product that changed networking forever. Some people think the name was intended to be San Francisco Systems, but the paper got ripped on the way to the incorporation lawyers—who knows? But in 1992, the company name was changed to Cisco Systems, Inc.

The first product Cisco marketed was called the Advanced Gateway Server (AGS). Then came the Mid-Range Gateway Server (MGS), the Compact Gateway Server (CGS), the Integrated Gateway Server (IGS), and the AGS+. Cisco calls these "the old alphabet soup products."

In 1993, Cisco came out with the amazing 4000 router and then created the even more amazing 7000, 2000, and 3000 series routers. These are still around and evolving (almost daily, it seems).

Cisco Systems has since become an unrivaled worldwide leader in networking for the Internet. Its networking solutions can easily connect users who work from diverse devices on disparate networks. Cisco products make it simple for people to access and transfer information without regard to differences in time, place, or platform.

Cisco Systems' big picture is that it provides end-to-end networking solutions that customers can use to build an efficient, unified information infrastructure of their own or to connect to someone else's. This is an important piece in the Internet/networking-industry puzzle because a common architecture that delivers consistent network services to all users is now a functional imperative. Because Cisco Systems offers such a broad range of networking and Internet services and capabilities, users needing regular access to their local network or the Internet can do so unhindered, making Cisco's wares indispensable.

Cisco answers this need with a wide range of hardware products that are used to form information networks using the Cisco Internetworking Operating System (IOS) software. This software provides network services, paving the way for networked technical support and professional services to maintain and optimize all network operations.

Along with the Cisco IOS, one of the services Cisco created to help support the vast amount of hardware it has engineered is the Cisco Certified Internetworking Expert (CCIE) program, which was designed specifically to equip people to effectively manage the vast quantity of installed Cisco networks. The business plan is simple: If you want to sell more Cisco equipment and have more Cisco networks installed, make sure that the networks you installed run properly.

However, having a fabulous product line isn't all it takes to guarantee the huge success that Cisco enjoys—lots of companies with great products are now defunct. If you have complicated products designed to solve complicated problems, you need knowledgeable people who are fully capable of installing, managing, and troubleshooting them. That part isn't easy, so Cisco began the CCIE program to equip people to support these complicated networks. This program, known colloquially as the Doctorate of Networking, has been very successful, primarily due to its extreme difficulty. Cisco continuously monitors the program, changing it as it sees fit, to make sure that it remains pertinent and accurately reflects the demands of today's internetworking business environments.

Building on the highly successful CCIE program, Cisco Career Certifications permit you to become certified at various levels of technical proficiency, spanning the disciplines of network design and support. So, whether you're beginning a career, changing careers, securing your present position, or seeking to refine and promote your position, this is the book for you!

Cisco's Certifications

Cisco has created new certification tracks that will help you get the coveted CCIE, as well as aid prospective employers in measuring skill levels. Before these new certifications, you took only one test and were then faced with the lab, which made it difficult to succeed. With these new certifications that add a better approach to preparing for that almighty lab, Cisco has opened doors that few were allowed through before. So, what are these new certifications, and how do they help you get your CCIE?

Cisco Certified Network Associate (CCNA) 2.0

The CCNA certification is the first certification in the new line of Cisco certifications, and it is a precursor to all current Cisco certifications. With the new certification programs, Cisco has created a type of stepping-stone approach to CCIE certification. Now, you can become a Cisco Certified Network Associate for the meager cost of the *CCNA: Cisco Certified Network Associate Study Guide*, Third Edition (Sybex, 2002), plus $125 for the test. And you don't have to stop there—you can choose to continue with your studies and select a specific track to follow. The Installation and Support track will help you prepare for the CCIE Routing and Switching certification, whereas the Communications and Services track will help you prepare for the CCIE Communication and Services certification. It is important to note that you do not have to attempt any of these tracks to reach the CCIE, but it is recommended.

Cisco's Installation and Support Track

The Installation and Support track is aimed at the engineer who wants to become an expert of enterprise networks. The engineer will need to show proficiency with LAN and WAN technologies along with the other technologies that predominate enterprise networks. After obtaining the CCNA, the next step is to pursue the CCNP certification. Once you have completed the CCNP, it is time to set your sights on the coveted CCIE Routing and Switching certification.

Cisco Certified Network Professional (CCNP) 2.0

This new Cisco certification has opened up many opportunities for the individual wishing to become Cisco-certified but who is lacking the training, the expertise, or the bucks to pass the notorious and often failed two-day Cisco torture lab. The new Cisco certifications will truly provide exciting new opportunities for the CNE and MCSE who just don't know how to advance to a higher level.

So, you're thinking, "Great, what do I do after I pass the CCNA exam?" Well, if you want to become a CCIE in Routing and Switching (the most popular certification), understand that there's more than one path to that much-coveted CCIE certification. The first way is to continue studying and become a Cisco Certified Network Professional (CCNP). That means four more tests, and the CCNA certification, to you.

The CCNP program will prepare you to understand and comprehensively tackle the internetworking issues of today and beyond—not limited to the Cisco world. You will undergo an immense metamorphosis, vastly increasing your knowledge and skills through the process of obtaining these certifications.

Remember that you don't need to be a CCNP or even a CCNA to take the CCIE lab, but to accomplish that, it's extremely helpful if you already have these certifications.

WHAT ARE THE CCNP CERTIFICATION SKILLS?

Cisco demands a certain level of proficiency for its CCNP certification. In addition to those required for the CCNA, these skills include the following:

- Installing, configuring, operating, and troubleshooting complex routed LANs, routed WANs, and switched LANs, and Dial Access Services.
- Understanding complex networks, such as IP, IGRP, IPX, Async Routing, AppleTalk, extended access lists, IP RIP, route redistribution, IPX RIP, route summarization, OSPF, VLSM, BGP, Serial, IGRP, Frame Relay, ISDN, ISL, X.25, DDR, PSTN, PPP, VLANs, Ethernet, ATM LAN-emulation, access lists, 802.10, FDDI, and transparent and translational bridging.

To meet the Cisco Certified Network Professional requirements, you must be able to perform the following:

- Install and/or configure a network to increase bandwidth, quicken network response times, and improve reliability and quality of service.

- Maximize performance through campus LANs, routed WANs, and remote access.
- Improve network security.
- Create a global intranet.
- Provide access security to campus switches and routers.
- Provide increased switching and routing bandwidth—end-to-end resiliency services.
- Provide custom queuing and routed priority services.

HOW DO YOU BECOME A CCNP?

After becoming a CCNA, the four exams you must take to get your CCNP are as follows:

Exam 640-503: Routing This exam continues to build on the fundamentals learned in the CCNA course. It focuses on large multiprotocol internetworks and how to manage them with filtering, policy-based routing, route distribution, route maps, BGP, OSPF, and route summarization. The *CCNP: Routing Study Guide* (Sybex, 2001) covers all the objectives you need to understand for passing the Routing exam.

Or

Exam 640-900: Building Scalable Cisco Internetworks (BSCI) This exam can be used as a replacement to Exam 640-503: Routing. The BSCI exam covers all of the topics covered in the Routing exam plus coverage of IS-IS and more in-depth coverage of BGP. *CCNP/CCIP: BSCI Study Guide* (Sybex, 2002) covers everything you need to pass the new BSCI exam.

Exam 640-504: Switching This exam tests your knowledge of the 1900 and 5000 series of Catalyst switches. The *CCNP: Switching Study Guide* (Sybex, 2001) covers all the objectives you need to understand for passing the Switching exam.

Exam 640-506: Support This exam tests you on troubleshooting information. You must be able to troubleshoot Ethernet and Token Ring LANs, IP, IPX, and AppleTalk networks, as well as ISDN, PPP, and Frame Relay networks. The *CCNP: Support Study Guide* (Sybex, 2000) covers all the exam objectives you need to understand for passing the Support exam.

Exam 640-505: Remote Access This exam tests your knowledge of installing, configuring, monitoring, and troubleshooting Cisco ISDN and dial-up access products. You must understand PPP, ISDN, Frame Relay, and authentication. The *CCNP: Remote Access Study Guide* (Sybex, 2000) covers all the exam objectives you need to understand for passing the Remote Access exam.

NOTE

If you hate tests, you can take fewer of them by signing up for the CCNA exam and the Support exam, and then take just one more long exam called the Foundation R/S exam (640-509). Doing this also gives you your CCNP—but beware, it's a really long test that fuses all the material listed previously into one exam. Good luck! However, by taking this exam, you get three tests for the price of two, which saves you $100 (if you pass). Some people think it's easier to take the Foundation R/S exam because you can leverage the areas that you would score higher in against the areas in which you wouldn't.

TIP

Remember that test objectives and tests can change at any time without notice. Always check the Cisco website for the most up-to-date information (`www.cisco.com`).

Cisco Certified Internetworking Expert (CCIE) Routing and Switching

You've become a CCNP, and now you have fixed your sights on getting your CCIE in Routing and Switching—what do you do next? Cisco recommends that before you take the lab, you take Exam 640-025: Cisco Internetwork Design (CID) and the Cisco-authorized course called Installing and Maintaining Cisco Routers (IMCR). By the way, no Prometric test for IMCR exists at the time of this writing, and Cisco recommends a *minimum* of two years of on-the-job experience before taking the CCIE lab. After jumping those hurdles, you then have to pass the CCIE-R/S Qualification exam (Exam 350-001) before taking the actual lab.

To become a CCIE, Cisco recommends the following:

1. Attend all the recommended courses at an authorized Cisco training center and pony up around $15,000–$20,000, depending on your corporate discount.

2. Pass the Qualification exam ($300 per exam—so hopefully you'll pass it the first time).

3. Pass the one-day, hands-on lab at Cisco. This costs $1,250 per lab, which many people fail two or more times. (Some never make it through!) Also, because you can take the exam only in San Jose, California; Research Triangle Park, North Carolina; Sydney, Australia; Brussels, Belgium; Sao Paulo, Brazil; Beijing, China; Bangalore, India; Tokyo, Japan; Seoul, Korea; Halifax, Nova Scotia; Singapore; or Johannesburg, South Africa, you might just need to add travel costs to that $1,250. Cisco has added new sites lately for the CCIE lab; it's best to check the Cisco website at `http://www.cisco.com/warp/public/625/ccie/exam_preparation/lab.html` for the most current information.

THE CCIE SKILLS

The CCIE Routing and Switching exam includes the advanced technical skills that are required to maintain optimum network performance and reliability, as well as advanced skills in supporting diverse networks that use disparate technologies. CCIEs just don't have problems getting a job. These experts are basically inundated with offers to work for six-figure salaries! But that's because it isn't easy to attain the level of capability that is mandatory for Cisco's CCIE. For example, a CCIE will have the following skills down pat:

- Installing, configuring, operating, and troubleshooting complex routed LANs, routed WANs, and switched LANs.
- Diagnosing and resolving network faults.
- Using packet/frame analysis and Cisco debugging tools.
- Documenting and reporting the problem-solving processes used.
- Having general LAN/WAN knowledge, including data encapsulation and layering; windowing and flow control, and their relation to delay; error detection and recovery; link-state, distance-vector, and switching algorithms; management, monitoring, and fault isolation.
- Having knowledge of a variety of corporate technologies—including major services provided by desktop, WAN, and Internet groups—as well as the functions, addressing structures, and routing, switching, and bridging implications of each of their protocols.

- Having knowledge of Cisco-specific technologies, including router/switch platforms, architectures, and applications; communication servers; protocol translation and applications; configuration commands and system/network impact; and LAN/WAN interfaces, capabilities, and applications.
- Designing, configuring, installing, and verifying voice-over IP and voice-over ATM networks.

Cisco's Communications and Services Track

The Communications and Support track is aimed at the engineer that wants to become an expert on the service provider side. The engineer will need to show the same proficiencies as the Installation and Support track with more emphasis placed on such technologies as wireless, DSL, Optical, and MPLS. After obtaining the CCNA, the next step is to pursue the CCIP certification. Once you have completed the CCIP, it is time to set your sights on the CCIE Communications and Services certification.

Cisco Certified Internetwork Professional (CCIP)

After passing the CCNA, the next step in the Communications and Services track would be the CCIP. The CCIP is a professional-level certification.

The CCIP will provides you with the skills necessary to understand and tackle the complex internetworking world of the service provider. The skills you will obtain will prepare you to move forward toward the ever-elusive CCIE Communications and Services certification.

WHAT ARE THE CCIP CERTIFICATION SKILLS?

Cisco demands a certain level of proficiency for its CCIP certification. In addition to those required for the CCNA, the required CCIP skills include the following:

- Perform complex planning, operations, installations, implementations, and troubleshooting of internetworks.
- Understand and manage complex communications networks—last mile, edge, or core.

HOW DO YOU BECOME A CCIP?

After becoming a CCNA, you must take two core exams and an elective. The core exams are as follows:

Exam 640-900: Building Scalable Cisco Internetworks (BSCI) This exam takes the material covered in Exam 640-503: Routing and introduces coverage of IS-IS and more in-depth coverage of BGP. The *CCNP/CCIP: BSCI Study Guide* (Sybex, 2002) covers everything you need to pass the new BSCI exam.

Exam 640-905: MCAST + QoS This exam tests your knowledge on multicasting and quality of service for internetworks.

After passing the two core tests, you can choose from the following electives:

Exam 640-910: Implementing Cisco MPLS (MPLS) This exam tests your knowledge on multiprotocol label switching and its implementation. This book covers all the exam objectives.

Exam 640-920: Building Cisco Packet Telephony Networks (PKTEL) This exam tests your knowledge of IP Telephony networks. It will test your knowledge of the voice-over technologies along with monitoring these networks.

Exam 9E0-700: Cisco Cable Communications Specialist This exam will test your knowledge of utilizing cable access technology in internetworks. It will test your theoretical knowledge along with your practical knowledge on cable access technology. This exam will meet the elective requirement for the CCIP and will also provide you with the Cisco Cable Communications Specialist certification.

Exam 640-925: Building Cisco Content Networking Solutions (CN) This exam will test your knowledge on content networking. It will test your knowledge of content routing, switching, caching, edge delivery, and distribution management.

Exam 640-800: Building Cisco DSL Networks (DSLN) This exam will test your knowledge of the DSL access technology. You will be tested on the different types of DSL, along with the implementation of DSL.

Exam 640-915: Building Cisco Metro Optical Networks (METRO) This exam will test your knowledge of optical networking. You will be tested on your knowledge of SONET, DWDM, DPT, and other optical-related technologies.

Security If you choose the security route, you will be required to pass the following four tests to meet your CCIP elective requirement:

- 640-442: Managing Cisco Network Security (MCNS)
- 9E0-571: Cisco Secure PIX Firewall Advanced (CSPFA)

- 9E0-572: Cisco Intrusion Detection System with Policy Manager (IDSPM)
- 9E0-570: Cisco Secure VPN (CSVPN)

Passing these four tests will meet the elective requirement for the CCIP and will also earn you the Cisco Security Specialist (CSS1) certification. The forthcoming *CSS1/CCIP: Cisco Security Specialist Study Guide* from Sybex covers all the exam objectives.

Cisco Certified Internetworking Expert (CCIE) Communications and Services

You have become a CCIP and now you want to pursue the CCIE Communications and Services (C/S). So, what do you do next? The first item you must decide on is the specialty you want to select to pursue for the CCIE C/S. There are eight specialties you can choose from:

- Optical
- DSL
- Dial
- Cable
- Wireless
- WAN Switching
- Content Networking
- Voice

After selecting your specialty, you will need to take the CCIE C/S Qualification exam. The qualification exam is a two-hour, 100-question test. It consists of 50% general knowledge and 50% of your selected specialty. Below is a list of the exam numbers for the different CCIE C/S qualification exams:

- Optical—Exam 350-020
- DSL—Exam 351-022
- Dial—This exam was not available at the time of this writing.
- Cable—Exam 350-021
- Wireless—This exam was not available at the time of this writing.

- WAN Switching—Exam 351-023
- Content Networking—This exam was not available at the time of this writing.
- Voice—This exam was not available at the time of this writing.

To become a CCIE C/S, Cisco recommends the following:

1. Attend all the recommended courses at an authorized Cisco training center and pony up around $15,000–$20,000, depending on your corporate discount.
2. Pass the Qualification exam ($300 per exam—so hopefully you'll pass it the first time).
3. Pass the one-day, hands-on lab at Cisco. This costs $1,250 per lab, which many0 people fail two or more times. (Some never make it through!) Also, because you can take the exam only in Halifax, Nova Scotia, Canada, you might just need to add travel costs to that $1,250. Cisco will be adding new sites to this list so it is best to check `http://www.cisco.com/warp/public/625/ccie/exam_preparation/lab.html` for the most current information.

THE CCIE SKILLS

The CCIE Communications and Services require the individual to possess the same skills necessary for the CCIE R/S with the addition of MPLS and MPLS VPN, plus a specialty. Below is a list of the skills required of a CCIE C/S:

- Installing, configuring, operating, and troubleshooting complex routed LANs, routed WANs, switched LANs, QoS, multicasting, MPLS, and MPLS VPNs.
- Diagnosing and resolving network faults.
- Using packet/frame analysis and Cisco debugging tools.
- Documenting and reporting the problem-solving processes used.
- Having general LAN/WAN knowledge, including data encapsulation and layering; windowing and flow control, and their relation to delay; error detection and recovery; link-state, distance-vector, and switching algorithms; management, monitoring, and fault isolation.

- Having knowledge of a variety of corporate technologies—including major services provided by desktop, WAN, and Internet groups—as well as the functions, addressing structures, and routing, switching, and bridging implications of each of their protocols.
- Having knowledge of Cisco-specific technologies, including router/switch platforms, architectures, and applications; communication servers; protocol translation and applications; configuration commands and system/network impact; and LAN/WAN interfaces, capabilities, and applications.
- Designing, configuring, installing, and verifying voice-over IP and voice-over ATM networks.

Cisco's Network Design and Installation Certifications

In addition to the Network Installation and Support track and the Communications and Services track, Cisco has created another certification track for network designers. The two certifications within this track are the Cisco Certified Design Associate (CCDA) and Cisco Certified Design Professional (CCDP) certifications. If you're reaching for the CCIE stars, we highly recommend the CCNP and CCDP certifications before attempting the CCIE R/S Qualification exam.

These certifications will give you the knowledge to design routed LANs, routed WANs, and switched LANs.

Cisco Certified Design Associate (CCDA)

To become a CCDA, you must pass the DCN (Designing Cisco Networks) test (640-441). To pass this test, you must understand how to do the following:

- Design simple routed LANs, routed WANs, switched LANs, and ATM LANE networks.
- Use network-layer addressing.
- Filter with access lists.
- Use and propagate VLAN.
- Size networks.

TIP The *CCDA: Cisco Certified Design Associate Study Guide* (Sybex, 2000) is the most cost-effective way to study for and pass your CCDA exam.

Cisco Certified Design Professional (CCDP) 2.0

If you're already a CCNP and want to get your CCDP, you can simply take the CID 640-025 test. If you're not yet a CCNP, however, you must take the CCDA, CCNA, Routing, Switching, Remote Access, and CID exams.

CCDP certification skills include the following:

- Design complex routed LANs, routed WANs, switched LANs, and ATM LANE networks.
- Build on the base level of the CCDA technical knowledge.

CCDPs must also demonstrate proficiency in the following:

- Network-layer addressing in a hierarchical environment
- Traffic management with access lists
- Hierarchical network design
- VLAN use and propagation
- Performance considerations: required hardware and software; switching engines; memory, cost, and minimization

What Does This Book Cover?

This book covers everything you need to pass the CCIP MPLS exam. This book does not cover everything there is to know about MPLS and MPLS VPNs, only what is necessary to successfully pass the exam. The material covered in this book serves as a foundation for your later studies in MPLS. It teaches you how to configure and maintain Cisco routers in a large internetwork. Each chapter begins with a list of the topics covered that relate to the CCIP MPLS test, so make sure to read them over before working through the chapter.

Chapter 1, "An Introduction to MPLS," introduces you to the topic of MPLS. Many of the problems in service provider networks and how MPLS can fix them are discussed. In addition, you'll be introduced to the MPLS label, MPLS applications, and basic label-switching operation.

Chapter 2, "Frame-Mode MPLS," reviews traditional Layer 3 routing to get you up to speed for a discussion on frame-mode MPLS. The main topics in this chapter are frame-mode MPLS, label bindings, label-switching operation, and configuration.

Chapter 3, "MPLS and ATM," describes MPLS operation in ATM networks. In this chapter you'll learn about cell-mode MPLS and cell-mode MPLS configuration.

Chapter 4, "VPNs: An Overview," explains point-to-point connections, overlay VPNs, and peer-to-peer VPNs. This chapter covers the basics of pre-MPLS VPNs and discusses the routing and security issues of each.

Chapter 5, "MPLS VPNs," introduces MPLS VPNs. Topics covered include VRFs, route distinguishers, and MP-BGP.

Chapter 6, "MPLS VPNs and RIP," is a continuation of Chapter 5. Topics covered in this chapter include route targets, using RIPv2 as a PE-CE routing protocol, redistribution, and configuration of an end-to-end simple MPLS VPN using RIPv2.

Chapter 7, "MPLS VPNs and OSPF," covers OSPF operation in an MPLS VPN. Topics covered include the super-backbone, the down bit, and the tag field.

Chapter 8, "Advanced MPLS Topics," is a catch-all chapter of topics that aren't listed in the exam outline but are important to know about anyway. In particular, this chapter discusses using static routes for an MPLS VPN, E-BGP, AS-override, and complex VPN topologies.

Each chapter ends with review questions that are specifically designed to help you review the information presented. To really nail down your skills, read each question carefully and take the time to work through the hands-on labs in the chapters.

In addition, Appendix A contains six challenge labs. The challenge labs will test your ability to configure all of the topics covered in this study guide.

Finally, Appendix B, "Service Provider Tag Switching with OSPF and IS-IS," expands upon Chapter 2 by showing you how to configure IS-IS and OSPF as the service provider IGP. In this appendix, a sample network is configured with BGP between the PE and CE routers.

Where Do You Take the Exam?

You may take the exams at any of the Sylvan Prometric or Virtual University Enterprises (VUE) testing centers around the world. For the location of a testing center near you, call Sylvan at (800) 755-3926 or VUE at (877) 404-3926. Outside of the United States and Canada, contact your local Sylvan Prometric Registration Center.

To register for a Cisco Certified Network Professional exam:

1. Determine the number of the exam you want to take. (The MPLS exam number is 640-910.)
2. Register with the nearest Sylvan Prometric or VUE testing center. At this point, you will be asked to pay in advance for the exam. At the time of this writing, the exams are $125 each and must be taken within

one year of payment. You can schedule exams up to six weeks in advance or as soon as one working day prior to the day you wish to take it. If something comes up and you need to cancel or reschedule your exam appointment, contact the testing center at least 24 hours in advance. Same-day registration isn't available for the Cisco tests.

3. When you schedule the exam, you'll get instructions regarding all appointment and cancellation procedures, the ID requirements, and information about the testing-center location.

Tips for Taking Your CCIP Exam

The CCIP MPLS test contains about 70 questions to be completed in about 90 minutes. However, understand that individual tests may vary.

Many questions on the exam have answer choices that at first glance look identical—especially the syntax questions! Remember to read through the choices carefully because "close" doesn't cut it. If you put commands in the wrong order or you forget one measly character, you'll get the question wrong.

Unlike the Microsoft or Novell tests, the MPLS exam has answer choices that are very similar in syntax—although some syntax is dead wrong, it is usually just *subtly* wrong. Some other syntax choices may be right, but they're shown in the wrong order. Cisco does split hairs, and it is not at all averse to giving you classic trick questions.

Also, never forget that the right answer is the Cisco answer. In many cases, more than one appropriate answer is presented, but the *correct* answer is the one that Cisco recommends.

Here are some general tips for exam success:

- Arrive early at the exam center, so you can relax and review your study materials.
- Read the questions *carefully*. Don't just jump to conclusions. Make sure that you're clear about *exactly* what each question asks.
- Don't leave any questions unanswered. They count against you.
- When answering multiple-choice questions that you're not sure about, use a process of elimination to get rid of the obviously incorrect answers first. Doing this greatly improves your odds if you need to make an educated guess.
- As of this writing, the written exams still allow you to move forward and backward. However, it is best to always check the Cisco website before taking any exam to get the most up-to-date information.

After you complete an exam, you'll get immediate, online notification of your pass or fail status, a printed Examination Score Report that indicates your pass or fail status, and your exam results by section. (The test administrator will give you the printed score report.) Test scores are automatically forwarded to Cisco within five working days after you take the test, so you don't need to send your score to them.

How to Use This Book

This book can provide a solid foundation for the serious effort of preparing for the CCIP MPLS exam. To best benefit from this book, use the following study method:

1. Take the Assessment Test immediately following this Introduction. (The answers are at the end of the test.) Carefully read over the explanations for any question you get wrong and note which chapters the material comes from. This information should help you plan your study strategy.
2. Study each chapter carefully, making sure that you fully understand the information and the test topics listed at the beginning of each chapter. Pay extra-close attention to any chapter where you missed questions in the Assessment Test.
3. Complete all hands-on exercises in the chapter, referring back to the material in the chapter so that you understand the reason for each step you take. If you do not have Cisco equipment available, make sure to study the examples carefully.
4. Note the questions that confuse you, and study those sections of the book again.
5. Do the Challenge Labs in this book. You'll find them in Appendix A. The answers appear at the end of each lab.
6. Before taking the exam, try your hand at the two bonus exams that are included on the CD that comes with this book. The questions in these exams appear only on the CD. This will give you a complete overview of what you can expect to see on the real thing.
7. Remember to use the products on the CD that is included with this book. The electronic flashcards and the EdgeTest exam-preparation software have all been specifically picked to help you study for

and pass your exam. Study on the road with the *CCIP: MPLS Study Guide* eBook in PDF, and be sure to test yourself with the electronic flashcards.

> **TIP** The electronic flashcards can be used on your Windows computer or on your Palm device.

8. Make sure you read the Key Terms list at the end of each chapter. The glossary includes all the key terms used in the book, along with a definition of each key term.

To learn all the material covered in this book, you'll have to apply yourself regularly and with discipline. Try to set aside the same time every day to study and select a comfortable and quiet place to do so. If you work hard, you'll be surprised at how quickly you learn this material. All the best!

What's on the CD?

We worked hard to provide some really great tools to help you with your certification process. All of the tools described in this section should be loaded on your workstation when studying for the test.

The EdgeTest for Cisco MPLS Test-Preparation Software

Provided by EdgeTek Learning Systems, this test-preparation software prepares you to successfully pass the MPLS exam. In this test engine, you will find all of the questions from the book, plus two additional bonus exams that appear exclusively on the CD. You can take the Assessment Test, test yourself by chapter or by objective, or take the two bonus exams that appear on the CD.

To find more test-simulation software for all Cisco exams, look for the exam link on `www.lammle.com`.

Electronic Flashcards for PC and Palm Devices

After you read the *CCIP: MPLS Study Guide*, read the review questions at the end of each chapter and study the practice exams included in the book and on the CD. But wait, there's more! Test yourself with the flashcards included on the CD. If you can get through these difficult questions and understand the answers, you'll know you'll be ready for the CCIP MPLS exam.

The flashcards include 150 questions specifically written to hit you hard and make sure you're ready for the exam. Between the review questions, the bonus exams, and the flashcards, you'll be more than prepared for the exam.

CCIP: MPLS Study Guide in PDF

Sybex is now offering the Cisco Certification books on CD so you can read the book on your PC or laptop. The *CCIP: MPLS Study Guide* is in Adobe Acrobat format. Acrobat Reader 4 with Search is also included on the CD.

This will be extremely helpful to readers who travel and don't want to carry a book, as well as to readers who find it more comfortable to read from their computer.

How to Contact the Author

James Reagan works for Reagan Systems (`www.ReaganSystems.com`) in Melbourne, Florida. James can be reached at `James.Reagan@ReaganSystems.com`.

Assessment Test

1. Which IOS command is necessary to globally configure MPLS on a Cisco IOS device?

   A. `ip mpls`

   B. `mpls ip`

   C. `mpls advertise labels`

   D. `tag-switching advertise labels`

2. Overlay VPNs replace ___________.

   A. Full-mesh topologies

   B. MPLS VPNs

   C. Point-to-point connections

   D. Simple VPNs

3. Which of the following OSPF LSA types is generated by an ASBR?

   A. 1 or 2

   B. 3

   C. 4

   D. 5

4. MP-BGP is typically used between which routers?

   A. P routers

   B. CE routers

   C. PE routers

   D. None of the above

5. E-BGP neighbors must be ___________.

   A. Redistributed

   B. Activated

   C. Upgraded

   D. None of the above

6. The LIB is in the ___________.

   A. Control plane

   B. Forwarding plane

   C. Data plane

   D. None of the above

7. Which of the following commands enables VC merge on an ATM-LSR?

   A. `mpls ldp atm vc-merge`

   B. `mpls ip atm vc-merge`

   C. `mpls ip atm vc merge`

   D. `mpls ip atm vc merge`

8. After you associate an interface with a VRF, it ___________.

   A. Shows up in the global routing table

   B. Loses its IP address

   C. Must be activated

   D. None of the above

9. VRF names are ___________.

   A. Not case-sensitive

   B. Locally significant

   C. Global in nature

   D. None of the above

10. With an MP-BGP backbone, PE routers are viewed as __________ routers by CE OSPF routers.

   A. ABR

   B. ASBR

   C. Internal

   D. External

11. What command would you use to display the label bindings on a Cisco IOS device?

   A. `show mpls ip`

   B. `show mpls forwarding-table`

   C. `show tag forwarding-table`

   D. `show mpls labels`

12. Cell-mode MPLS __________ the TLV.

   A. Increments

   B. Decrements

   C. None of the above

13. In the following code snippet, what is the maximum number of routes allowed in the VRF?

```
ip vrf vpn-X
 rd 1000:1
 route-target both 1000:1
 maximum-routes 20 50
```

   A. 1000:1

   B. 20

   C. 50

   D. None of the above

14. In a peer-to-peer VPN, the __________ becomes responsible for routing protocol convergence.

    A. Customer

    B. Service provider

    C. Edge-LSR

    D. PE

15. Customer routers __________ MPLS functionality.

    A. Do need

    B. Do not need

    C. None of the above

16. A GRE tunnel is a __________ VPN technology.

    A. Layer 1

    B. Layer 2

    C. Layer 3

    D. None of the above

17. An LSC communicates with an ATM-LSR on which of the following virtual circuits?

    A. 0/1

    B. 0/6

    C. 0/32

    D. 0/4096

18. For static VRF routes, the next-hop IP address is __________.

    A. Mandatory

    B. Optional

    C. None of the above

19. The FIB is built by __________.

    A. TDP

    B. LDP

    C. CEF

    D. LFIB

20. PE routers support a total of __________ routing processes.

    A. 16

    B. 32

    C. 48

    D. 64

21. In an MPLS-enabled service provider core, P routers need which of the following?

    A. An IGP only

    B. An IGP and BGP

    C. BGP only

    D. BGP and OSPF

22. Which of the following commands is used to configure an export route target?

    A. `route-target both` *`number`*

    B. `route-target export` *`number`*

    C. `route-target` *`number`*

    D. `route target both` *`number`*

23. Which of the following are valid peer-to-peer VPN methods? (Choose all that apply.)

    A. Dedicated router

    B. Full-mesh

    C. Partial-mesh

    D. Shared router

24. Which command do you use to begin the configuration of MP-BGP?

    A. `rd #.#`

    B. `ip vrf` *`vpn_name`*

    C. `address-family vpnv4`

    D. `address-family ipvrf`

25. Which protocol does the IETF version of Cisco's tag switching use to exchange labels between neighbors?

    A. CDP

    B. LDP

    C. TDP

    D. MDP

26. When configuring frame-mode MPLS on an ATM edge-LSR, which of the following command options is used?

    A. `tag-switching`

    B. `mpls`

    C. `point-to-point`

    D. `cell-mode`

27. Which of the following overlay VPN topologies is typically used by financial organizations?

    A. Full-mesh

    B. Partial-mesh

    C. Hub-and-spoke

    D. None of the above

28. Which of the following BGP communities is required for MPLS VPNs?

    A. Standard

    B. Extended

    C. No communities

29. Which of the following commands is used to view the global PE routing table?

A. `show ip route`

B. `show ip route vrf` *`vpn_name`*

C. `show ip route vpnv4` *`vpn_name`*

D. `show ip route` *`vpn_name`*

30. A route from another AS is advertised as an OSPF LSA Type ____________.

A. 1 or 2

B. 3

C. 4

D. 5

Answers to Assessment Test

1. B. The command to enable MPLS on an interface is `mpls ip`. See Chapter 2 for more information.
2. C. Overlay VPNs evolved as a less expensive alternative to point-to-point connections. See Chapter 4 for more information.
3. D. External routes, OSPF LSA Type 5, are generated by ASBRs. See Chapter 7 for more information.
4. C. MP-BGP is configured between edge-LSRs or PE routers. See Chapter 5 for more information.
5. B. E-BGP neighbors must be activated. See Chapter 8 for more information.
6. A. The LIB is a mapping of labels and resides in the control plane. See Chapter 1 for more information.
7. A. To enable VC merge on an ATM-LSR, use the `mpls ldp atm vc-merge` command. See Chapter 3 for more information.
8. B. After you associate an interface with a VRF, it loses its IP address. The IP address needs to be reconfigured. See Chapter 6 for more information.
9. B. VRF names are only applicable for the router on which they are configured. Therefore, they are locally significant. See Chapter 5 for more information.
10. A. With the MP-BGP (OSPF super-backbone), PE routers are viewed as ABRs. See Chapter 7 for more information.
11. B. The command to display label bindings in an MPLS environment is `show mpls forwarding-table`. See Chapter 1 for more information.
12. A. Cell-mode MPLS increments the TLV. Frame-mode MPLS decrements the TTL. See Chapter 3 for more information.
13. B. The first option after the `maximum-routes` command is the maximum number of routes allowed in the VRF. See Chapter 8 for more information.

14. B. In a peer-to-peer VPN, the service provider becomes responsible for routing protocol convergence. See Chapter 4 for more information.

15. B. Customer routers do not need MPLS functionality. An edge-LSR receives an unlabeled IP packet from CE routers and imposes a label. See Chapter 2 for more information.

16. C. A GRE tunnel is a Layer 3 VPN technology. An additional Layer 3 VPN technology is IPSec. See Chapter 6 for more information.

17. C. An LSC communicates with an ATM-LSR over VC 0/32. See Chapter 3 for more information.

18. B. The outgoing interface is mandatory when configuring a static VRF route, but the next-hop IP address is optional. See Chapter 8 for more information.

19. C. Cisco Express Forwarding (CEF) builds the FIB. The FIB resides in the forwarding plane of the MPLS architecture. See Chapter 1 for more information.

20. B. 32 total processes are available. Connected, RIPv2, and BGP all use only one process. OSPF uses a process for each individual VPN. See Chapter 7 for more information.

21. A. LSRs in the core of the network only need an IGP. Packets will be label-switched and not routed. See Chapter 2 for more information.

22. B. To configure an export route target, use the `route-target export` *`number`* command. See Chapter 6 for more information.

23. A, D. The two ways to implement peer-to-peer VPNs are dedicated router and shared router. See Chapter 4 for more information.

24. B. From inside BGP configuration mode, the `address-family vpnv4` command is used to begin the MP-BGP configuration. See Chapter 5 for more information.

25. B. MPLS, the IETF version of Cisco's tag switching, uses LDP to exchange labels between neighbors. See Chapter 2 for more information.

26. C. On an ATM edge-LSR, as the sub-interface is configured, the `point-to-point` command option is applied for frame-mode MPLS. See Chapter 3 for more information.

27. C. A hub-and-spoke topology is often used by financial organizations because they usually have centralized resources that need to be accessed by remote branch offices. See Chapter 4 for more information.

28. B. Extended communities are required for MPLS VPNs. See Chapter 5 for more information.

29. A. To view the global routing table on a PE, the `show ip route` command is used. See Chapter 6 for more information.

30. D. OSPF routes from an external AS are OSPF LSA Type 5. See Chapter 7 for more information.

Chapter 1

An Introduction to MPLS

CCIP MPLS EXAM TOPICS COVERED IN THIS CHAPTER:

- ✓ **List the features, functions, and benefits of MPLS.**
- ✓ **Identify suitable applications for MPLS.**
- ✓ **Describe the underlying concepts of MPLS.**
- ✓ **Describe the concept of MPLS labels, label stack, and different label formats.**
- ✓ **Describe the basic process of CEF switching.**

This chapter will introduce you to the basic technology that you need to become familiar with for a thorough understanding of MPLS. I'll start with a quick review of traditional service provider networks and the challenges of managing them. After that review, I'll introduce you to the basics of MPLS architecture and operation. You'll need a good understanding of the basic MPLS concepts to understand the material in later chapters and to succeed on the MPLS exam.

As an instructor of MPLS, I've found that the best way for someone to learn MPLS is to simply jump right in. This chapter will introduce you to some of the major MPLS topics—it's the baptism by fire into the world of MPLS. Let's get to it.

Service Provider Networks

We're going to begin discussing MPLS not with the technology itself, but with many of the problems it is designed to fix in service provider networks.

To illustrate some of the problems that are experienced by service providers, let's start with a simple service provider network. Figure 1.1 shows four POPs (points of presence): Atlanta, Miami, Orlando, and Raleigh. At each of these POPs, the routers are connected to ATM switches that are fully meshed, creating the core of the service provider network.

Another way to represent the service provider network is to show the POP locations connected to a cloud, as illustrated in Figure 1.2. This representation of the service provider network in Figure 1.2 is logical, compared to the physical topology in Figure 1.1. The cloud is a way to demonstrate the problem faced when integrating ATM- and IP-based routers.

IP and ATM were developed separately and without much regard for each other. The ATM switches are only concerned with moving traffic based on VPI/VCI values of which the IP-based POP routers are unaware. IP-based POP routers are Layer 3 devices, concerned with forwarding packets based on information contained in the packet, of which the ATM switches are unaware.

FIGURE 1.1 Service provider physical topology

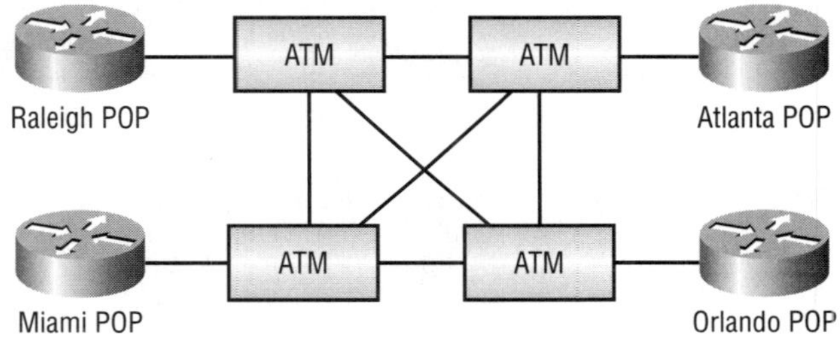

FIGURE 1.2 Service provider logical topology

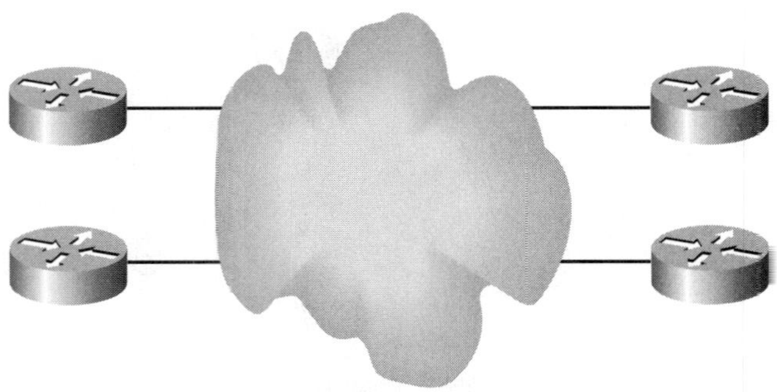

Scalability

Another problem experienced by service providers is scalability. To allow for maximum redundancy and optimum routing, a full mesh of virtual circuits (VCs) must be created, resulting in an overlay. In Figure 1.3, the four POP routers are connected together with a full mesh of VCs. Notice that for four POP routers, six VCs are required.

If two more POP routers are added, as shown in Figure 1.4, a total of 15 VCs are required to provide full-mesh connectivity.

FIGURE 1.3 Full mesh with six virtual circuits

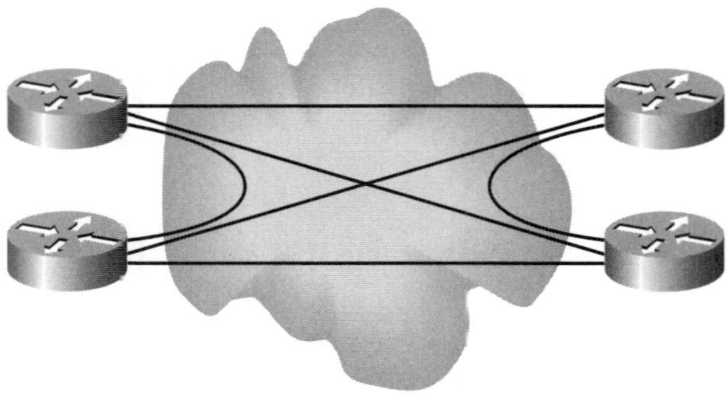

FIGURE 1.4 Full mesh with 15 virtual circuits

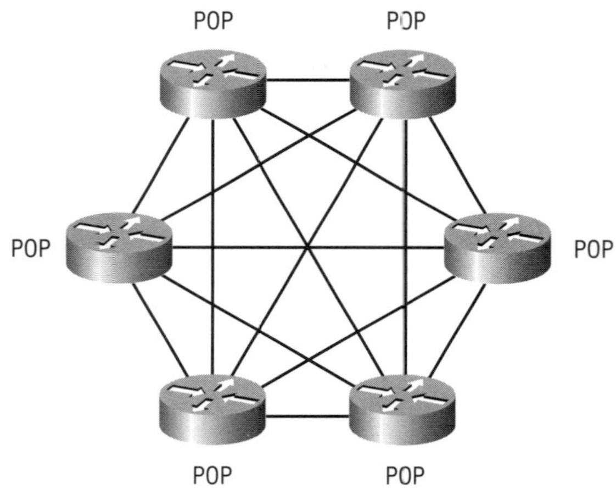

As more and more POP routers are added to this core, more and more VCs will be required to provide a full mesh.

Real World Scenario

The Overlay Model

The big problem with an overlay model, in which the routers are connected in a full mesh through virtual circuits, is that officially it is not scalable. Depending on who you talk to, either an ATM overlay is scalable or an ATM overlay is not scalable. Since this is an exam preparation guide, the official ruling is that an ATM overlay is not scalable.

To illustrate, if you assume that the virtual circuits in question are bi-directional in nature, the following formula calculates the number of virtual circuits required: $n(n-1)/2$, where n is the number of routers. So, if you have four routers and you want full-mesh connectivity, the math to determine the number of required VCs is as follows:

```
4(4-1)/2
4(3)/2
12/2
6
```

If there are six routers connected together, the number of required VCs is 15:

```
6(6-1)/2
6(5)/2
30/2
15
```

As you add more routers, the number of VCs required to implement a full mesh increases exponentially. If there are 100 routers, the total number of bi-directional VCs required is calculated as follows:

```
100(100-1)/2
100(99)/2
9900/2
4500
```

Not only are there scalability problems with the number of VCs required to implement a full mesh, but there are also scalability problems associated with the routing protocols in use in the network. As more and more VCs are created, more and more routers must form adjacencies with one another to ensure redundancy. All of these routers must exchange routing table updates with every router, thus creating a great deal of traffic that is merely updating routing tables. This excessive traffic can utilize significant resources on the routers and slow them down.

Traffic Engineering

The ATM world has a rich feature set that is used for traffic engineering. *Traffic engineering* is simply a process by which traffic is optimized to follow certain paths based on specified requirements. The IP world also has features, although not nearly as extensive as ATM, to provide for traffic engineering. The problem experienced by service providers is how to combine the traffic engineering of IP with the traffic engineering of ATM. Since ATM and IP are totally separate technologies, it is difficult to implement combined end-to-end traffic engineering.

Quality of Service

Both IP and ATM have Quality of Service (QoS) capabilities. The difference between the two has to do with their operation. IP is connectionless and ATM is connection-oriented. Again, the problem experienced by a service provider is how to combine these two different ways of implementing QoS into a firm end-to-end solution.

MPLS Label Stack

Now that you have seen some of the challenges of merging the IP and ATM worlds, it's time to talk about MPLS. MPLS, as a technology, evolved from early attempts to glue the IP world and ATM world together. What we know as MPLS today is, for the most part, a standardized version of Cisco's proprietary tag switching.

The best place to get started with a discussion of MPLS is with the label itself. The MPLS label, or more specifically the *MPLS label stack*, is composed of four octets (32 bits) and is illustrated in Figure 1.5.

FIGURE 1.5 The MPLS label stack

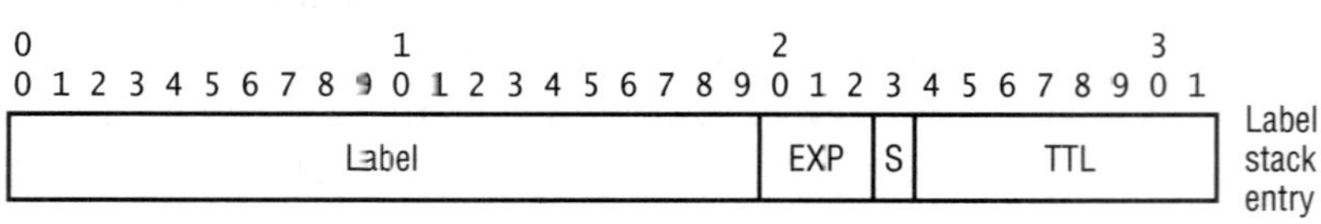

The label is the magic of MPLS, so it is important for you to be familiar with the fields in the MPLS label stack, henceforth referred to as the

MPLS label, or simply the *label*. The fields in the label are as follows:

Label This field is the label itself, and it is 20 bits in length. With 20 bits, there can be over one million labels.

Experimental (EXP) The Experimental (EXP) field is three bits in length and is used to map the standard IP packet ToS (type of service) into the Experimental field for MPLS CoS (class of service).

S MPLS labels can be stacked one on top of the other. The S, or stack bit, is used to indicate the bottom of the stack. A value of 1 in this field indicates the bottom, or last label, of the stack.

TTL The TTL (Time-to-Live) field from the IP TTL (or Ipv6 Hop Limit field) is decremented by 1 and then copied into the MPLS label TTL field. Upon exiting the MPLS network, the MPLS label TTL value is copied back into the IP TTL field. If this field is set to 0, the packet will be discarded. The TTL field is 8 bits in length.

Shim Header

Now that you're familiar with the label, you need to know where it's located. Figure 1.6 shows the placement of the MPLS label.

FIGURE 1.6 MPLS label stack placement

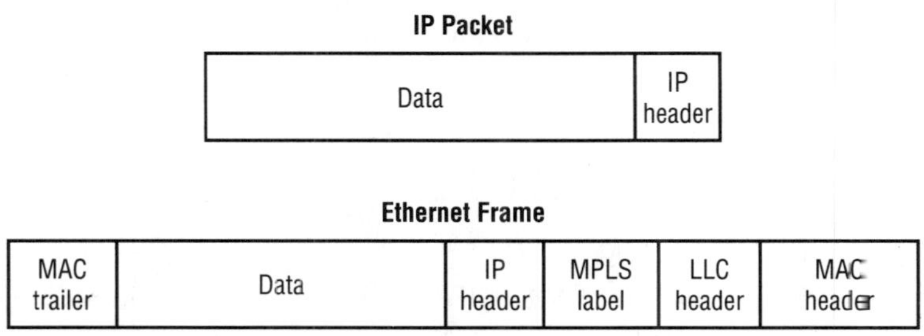

Take a look at Figure 1.6 and find the frame that contains the MPLS label stack. Where is the label? Smack dab between the Layer 2 header and the Layer 3 header. The MPLS label stack is sometimes referred to as a *shim header* because of how it is placed between the Layer 2 header and the Layer 3 payload.

In Figure 1.7, the placement of the MPLS label is shown with a variety of frame-mode encapsulations. Notice in all the frame-mode encapsulations that the placement of the MPLS label remains the same.

FIGURE 1.7 The MPLS label stack with frame-mode encapsulations

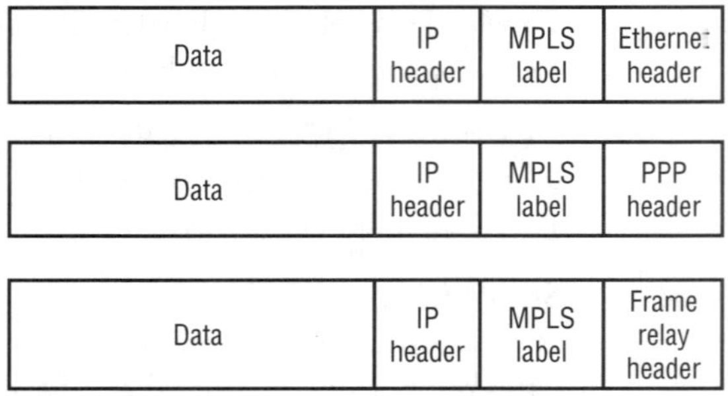

NOTE: The encapsulations discussed in this section are for frame-mode MPLS only. There is another method called cell-mode MPLS that is discussed in Chapter 3, "MPLS and ATM." For now, you need only be concerned with frame-mode MPLS.

As you can see in Figure 1.7, regardless of the frame-mode encapsulation method, the placement of the label does not change. You may recall that the Layer 3 header contains the destination field that is used for Layer 3 routing (forwarding). Because the label comes before the Layer 3 header, the router sees it first. The router can now forward packets based on the MPLS label instead of on the Layer 3 header. We say that in MPLS, IP traffic is *switched* instead of routed.

MPLS Architecture

Now that you know what a label is, let's learn about the MPLS architecture. Whenever I teach MPLS and I start talking about the MPLS architecture, students usually give me that deer-in-the-headlights look. I don't want your eyes to glaze over as you read this section. If you get confused at any time during this section, just repeat to yourself, "Labels are bound to routes in the routing table."

With that said, let me start with an introduction to the MPLS architecture. Essentially, there are two components that make up the architecture of MPLS: control and forwarding.

Control

The *control plane* of the MPLS architecture is responsible for binding a label to network routes and distributing those bindings among other MPLS-enabled routers. Again, repeat to yourself, "Labels are bound to routes in the routing table."

Let's break the function of the control plane down a little bit further. Since labels are bound to network routes, an MPLS-enabled router needs to have a routing table. To get a routing table, you need a routing protocol. (Or you could use static routes, but I don't recommend it.) Now that you have a routing table, you need some way to exchange labels. Why do you need a label-exchanging mechanism? Because labels get bound to routes in the routing table. There are two protocols that are supported by Cisco IOS devices to exchange labels: TDP and LDP.

TDP The *Tag Distribution Protocol (TDP)* is Cisco's proprietary protocol that is used to bind tags (which are the same as MPLS labels) to network routes in the routing table.

LDP The *Label Distribution Protocol (LDP)* is the IETF version of Cisco's TDP. LDP is used to bind labels to network routes. The *label information base (LIB)* is a mapping of incoming labels to outbound labels, along with outbound interface and link information.

Now, repeat to yourself, "Labels are bound to routes in the routing table." (Go ahead. Nobody is watching.)

Real World Scenario

Forwarding Equivalence Class (FEC)

A *forwarding equivalence class (FEC)* is a grouping of IP packets that are treated in the same way. For example, a destination subnet could correspond to an FEC. When I say that labels get bound to routes in the routing table, I'm referring to an IP prefix being the equivalent of an FEC. So, to be specific, labels are bound to FECs.

FECs can be based on a number of criteria, including IP ToS bits, IP protocol ID, port numbers, etc.

Forwarding

An MPLS-enabled router switches IP packets instead of forwarding them traditionally. The forwarding component of the MPLS architecture (known as the *forwarding plane* or *data plane*) is where information created and maintained from the control plane is actually used. Simply put, think of the forwarding plane as being like a big cache. The routing table is built in the control plane and cached in the forwarding plane. For labels, the LIB is built in the control plane, and only those labels in use reside in the *label forwarding information base (LFIB)*. The LFIB is a subset of the LIB.

An additional component that resides in the forwarding plane is the *forwarding information base (FIB)*. The FIB is built by *Cisco Express Forwarding (CEF)*. The FIB is essentially a cached version of the IP routing table that eliminates the need for a route-cache. For Cisco MPLS or tag switching to work, CEF must be enabled.

Real World Scenario

Cisco Tag Switching

Cisco's proprietary tag switching was the precursor of MPLS and is the technology on which the MPLS standard is based.

In Cisco's tag switching, what we refer to as a label is called a *tag*. The architecture of Cisco's tag switching is made up of two main components: the control plane and the forwarding plane. The control plane comprises the following:

- Routing protocol
- Routing table
- Tag exchange using Tag Distribution Protocol (TDP), resulting in the tag information base (TIB)

The forwarding plane is made up of:

- FIB
- tag forwarding information base (TFIB)

The two technologies are virtually identical.

MPLS Label Switching

Until you see MPLS label switching in operation, it may still be all smoke and mirrors. This section runs through a quick and dirty example that shows how MPLS label switching works.

MPLS Network Components

Figure 1.8 illustrates a simple service provider network that we'll use for the example in this section.

FIGURE 1.8 A simple service provider network

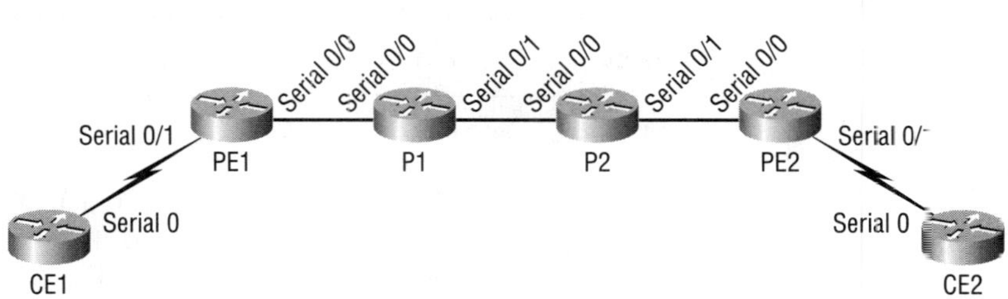

The routers in the network are labeled CE1, PE1, P1, P2, PE2, and CE2. These names are acronyms for:

CE A customer edge (CE) device. This is a router that connects to the customer network and to a service provider.

PE A provider edge (PE) device. This is a service provider piece of equipment that connects to a customer and into the provider (P) network.

P A provider (P) device. This is a service provider piece of equipment that exists entirely in the provider (P) network and only connects to other service provider devices (not to customers).

In addition, the PE and P routers are label switch routers. There are two types of label switch routers:

LSR A *label switch router (LSR)* is a Cisco IOS router/switch that is capable of forwarding packets based on labels. The CE, or customer, devices are not LSRs and can handle regular unlabeled IP packets.

Edge-LSR An *edge label switch router (edge-LSR)* is a more specific term for the PE routers. An edge-LSR is an edge device that is also an LSR. For an MPLS network, this is the device that takes unlabeled IP traffic and imposes, or in MPLS terms, pushes an MPLS label and switches the traffic to the next LSR. The edge-LSR also takes labeled traffic and deposes, or in MPLS terms, pops the label and forwards it to the next hop. A PE device is an edge-LSR in MPLS-based networks.

The network addresses for the provider devices are listed in Table 1.1. The IP addresses of the clients and client connections will be shown in a later example.

TABLE 1.1 Service Provider IP Addressing

Device	Serial 0/0	Serial 0/1	Loopback 0
PE1	192.168.1.10		192.168.1.1
P1	192.168.1.9	192.168.1.14	192.168.1.2
P2	192.168.1.13	192.168.1.18	192.168.1.3
PE2	192.168.1.17		192.168.1.4

RIPv2 and MPLS have been enabled on each of the P and PE devices in Figure 1.8.

Device Output

As you may recall from the MPLS architecture section, I asked you to repeat to yourself, "Labels are bound to routes in the routing table." The only exceptions to this rule are BGP routes. So, you can expand the mantra to, "Labels get bound to subnets in the routing table, with the exception of BGP routes."

In the following output, each network device in the simple network illustrated in Figure 1.8 has both a routing table and labels bound to network routes. As you look at the following device outputs, take a careful look at the IP prefixes in the routing table and then look to find the corresponding label.

The following output shows the RIPv2 routes on PE1:

```
PE1#show ip route rip
... Output Omitted
R 192.168.1.16/30 [120/2] via 192.168.1.21, 00:00:20, Serial0/0
R 192.168.1.4/32 [120/3] via 192.168.1.21, 00:00:20, Serial0/0
R 192.168.1.2/32 [120/1] via 192.168.1.21, 00:00:20, Serial0/0
R 192.168.1.3/32 [120/2] via 192.168.1.21, 00:00:20, Serial0/0
R 192.168.1.12/30 [120/1] via 192.168.1.21, 00:00:20, Serial0/0
```

The following output shows the label mappings on PE1:

```
PE1#show mpls forwarding-table
Local Outgoing  Prefix           Bytes tag Outgoing  Next Hop
tag   tag or VC or Tunnel Id     switched  interface
27    27        192.168.1.16/30 0          Se0/0     point2point
28    28        192.168.1.4/32  0          Se0/0     point2point
29    Pop tag   192.168.1.2/32  0          Se0/0     point2point
30    29        192.168.1.3/32  0          Se0/0     point2point
32    Pop tag   192.168.1.12/30 0          Se0/0     point2point
```

The following output shows the RIPv2 routes on P1:

```
P1#show ip route rip
... Output Omitted
R 192.168.1.16/30 [120/1] via 192.168.1.17, 00:00:27, Serial0/1
R 192.18.1.1/32  [120/1] via 192.168.1.22, 00:00:25, Serial0/0
R 192.168.1.4/32  [120/2] via 192.168.1.17, 00:00:27, Serial0/1
R 192.168.1.3/32  [120/1] via 192.168.1.17, 00:00:27, Serial0/1
```

The following output shows the label mappings on P1:

```
P1#show mpls forwarding-table
Local Outgoing  Prefix           Bytes tag Outgoing  Next Hop
tag   tag or VC or Tunnel Id     switched  interface
27    Pop tag   192.168.1.16/30 0          Se0/1     point2point
28    27        192.168.1.4/32  0          Se0/1     point2point
29    Pop tag   192.168.1.3/32  0          Se0/1     point2point
31    Pop tag   192.168.1.1/32  0          Se0/0     point2point
```

The following output shows the RIPv2 routes on P2:

```
P2#show ip route rip
... Output Omitted
R 192.168.1.1/32 [120/2] via 192.168.1.18, 00:00:27, Serial0/0
R 192.168.1.4/32 [120/1] via 192.168.1.13, 00:00:00, Serial0/1
R 192.168.1.2/32 [120/1] via 192.168.1.18, 00:00:27, Serial0/0
R 192.168.1.8/30 [120/1] via 192.168.1.18, 00:00:27, Serial0/0
```

The following output shows the label mappings on P2:

```
P2#show mpls forwarding-table
Local Outgoing   Prefix           Bytes tag Outgoing   Next Hop
tag   tag or VC  or Tunnel Id     switched  interface
27    Pop tag    192.168.1.4/32 26224     Se0/1      point2point
28    Pop tag    192.168.1.2/32 29568     Se0/0      point2point
30    Pop tag    192.168.1.8/30 0         Se0/0      point2point
31    31         192.168.1.1/32 0         Se0/0      point2point
```

The following output shows the RIPv2 routes on PE2:

```
PE2#show ip route rip
... Output Omitted
R 192.168.1.1/32 [120/3] via 192.168.1.14, 00:00:22, Serial0/0
R 192.168.1.2/32 [120/2] via 192.168.1.14, 00:00:22, Serial0/0
R 192.168.1.3/32 [120/1] via 192.168.1.14, 00:00:22, Serial0/0
R 192.168.1.12/30 [120/1] via 192.168.1.14, 00:00:22, Serial0/0
R 192.168.1.8/30 [120/2] via 192.168.1.14, 00:00:22, Serial0/0
```

The following output shows the label mappings on PE2:

```
PE2#show mpls forwarding-table
Local Outgoing   Prefix           Bytes tag Outgoing   Next Hop
tag   tag or VC  or Tunnel Id     switched  interface
26    31         192.168.1.1/32   0         Se0/0      point2point
27    28         192.168.1.2/32   0         Se0/0      point2point
28    Pop tag    192.168.1.3/32   0         Se0/0      point2point
30    Pop tag    192.168.1.12/30 0          Se0/0      point2point
31    30         192.168.1.8/30   0         Se0/0      point2point
```

Label-Switched Paths

Now let's take a look at the label-switched paths. A *label-switched path (LSP)* is a unidirectional set of LSRs that the labeled packet must flow through in order to get to a particular destination.

Let's say that the user on PE1 wants to ping the loopback address of PE2. So, the user types **ping 192.168.1.4**.

By looking at the labels in the following output of PE1, you can see the outbound label that will be used is 28 and it will be sent out Serial 0/0:

```
PE1#show mpls forwarding-table
Local Outgoing  Prefix           Bytes tag Outgoing  Next Hop
tag   tag or VC or Tunnel Id     switched  interface
27    27        192.168.1.16/30 0          Se0/0     point2point
28    28        192.168.1.4/32  0          Se0/0     point2point
29    Pop tag   192.168.1.2/32  0          Se0/0     point2point
30    29        192.168.1.3/32  0          Se0/0     point2point
32    Pop tag   192.168.1.12/30 0          Se0/0     point2point
```

If a labeled packet of 28 arrives on P1, it will be sent out Serial 0/1 with an outbound label of 27, as the following output shows:

```
P1#show mpls forwarding-table
Local Outgoing  Prefix           Bytes tag Outgoing  Next Hop
tag   tag or VC or Tunnel Id     switched  interface
27    Pop tag   192.168.1.16/30 0          Se0/1     point2point
28    27        192.168.1.4/32  0          Se0/1     point2point
29    Pop tag   192.168.1.3/32  0          Se0/1     point2point
31    Pop tag   192.168.1.1/32  0          Se0/0     point2point
```

If a labeled packet of 27 arrives on P2, it will be sent out Serial 0/1 unlabeled. The `Pop tag`, which you can see from the `show mpls forwarding-table` command on P2, means, "Don't send this traffic as labeled, but instead send it as unlabeled IP traffic." You can think of `Pop tag` as meaning, "The next hop router needs to do a Layer 3 lookup on the packet" or "The next hop router is the destination network or has a connected interface that is in the destination network." The official name for this process is called *penultimate hop popping*.

The word penultimate means "next to last." With penultimate hop popping, the penultimate router in an LSP pops the label and forwards the packet as unlabeled IP to the next hop router.

In this example, the next-to-last router (P2) in the LSP pops the label and forwards the unlabeled packet to its ultimate destination (PE2), as the following output demonstrates:

```
P2#show mpls forwarding-table
Local Outgoing Prefix          Bytes tag Outgoing  Next Hop
tag   tag or VC or Tunnel Id   switched  interface
27    Pop tag   192.168.1.4/32 26224     Se0/1     point2point
28    Pop tag   192.168.1.2/32 29568     Se0/0     point2point
30    Pop tag   192.168.1.8/30 0         Se0/0     point2point
31    31        192.168.1.1/32 0         Se0/0     point2point
```

Figure 1.9 shows the LSP from PE1 to PE2.

FIGURE 1.9 The LSP from PE1 to PE2

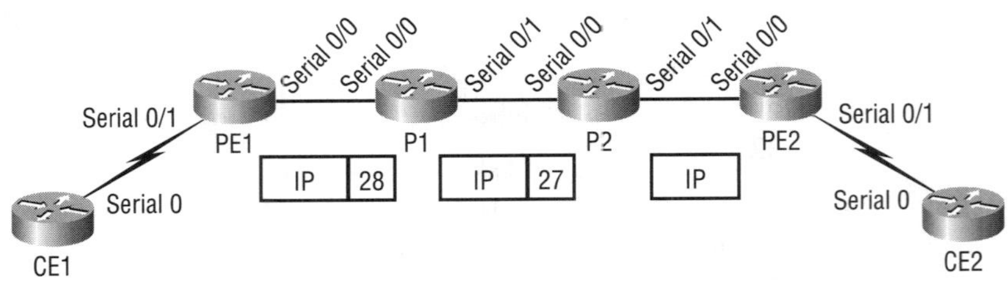

Now let's now see what happens when a user on PE1 wants to ping the loopback address of PE2. The user types **ping 192.168.1.3**.

By looking at the labels of PE1 in the following output, you can see the outbound label that will be used is 29, and it will be sent out Serial 0/0:

```
PE1#show mpls forwarding-table
Local Outgoing Prefix          Bytes tag Outgoing  Next Hop
tag   tag or VC or Tunnel Id   switched  interface
27    27        192.168.1.16/30 0        Se0/0     point2point
28    28        192.168.1.4/32  0        Se0/0     point2point
29    Pop tag   192.168.1.2/32  0        Se0/0     point2point
30    29        192.168.1.3/32  0        Se0/0     point2point
32    Pop tag   192.168.1.12/30 0        Se0/0     point2point
```

If a labeled packet of 29 arrives on P1, it will be sent out Serial 0/1 as an unlabeled IP packet, as you can see in the following output:

```
P1#show mpls forwarding-table
Local  Outgoing    Prefix            Bytes tag  Outgoing   Next Hop
tag    tag or VC   or Tunnel Id      switched   interface
27     Pop tag     192.168.1.16/30   0          Se0/1      point2point
28     27          192.168.1.4/32    0          Se0/1      point2point
29     Pop tag     192.168.1.3/32    0          Se0/1      point2point
31     Pop tag     192.168.1.1/32    0          Se0/0      point2point
```

What about a ping to the Serial 0/0 interface of P2 (192.168.1.13) By looking at the labels of PE1, you can see that the packet will be sent out Serial 0/0 as an unlabeled IP packet, as you can see in the following output:

```
PE1#show mpls forwarding-table
Local  Outgoing    Prefix            Bytes tag  Outgoing   Next Hop
tag    tag or VC   or Tunnel Id      switched   interface
27     27          192.168.1.16/30   0          Se0/0      point2point
28     28          192.168.1.4/32    0          Se0/0      point2point
29     Pop tag     192.168.1.2/32    0          Se0/0      point2point
30     29          192.168.1.3/32    0          Se0/0      point2point
32     Pop tag     192.168.1.12/30   0          Se0/0      point2point
```

Notice that the network in question is 192.168.1.12. Router P1 has a directly connected interface into this network and therefore does not need a labeled packet. Remember that penultimate hop popping is a time saving mechanism.

MPLS Applications

One of the basic principles of MPLS is that packets are switched instead of routed. When a packet enters the service provider network from a customer, it is unlabeled IP. The router at the edge of the service provider network accepts the incoming unlabeled packet and applies a label.

The newly labeled packet follows an LSP through the service provider network and is label-switched, not forwarded. When the packet leaves the MPLS-enabled service provider network, the label is removed and it again becomes an unlabeled IP packet. This process is illustrated in Figure 1.10.

You can see that the label is attached to the packet by the PE1 router as it enters the service provider network and is removed by the PE2 router as it is routed to the customer network.

FIGURE 1.10 The MPLS process

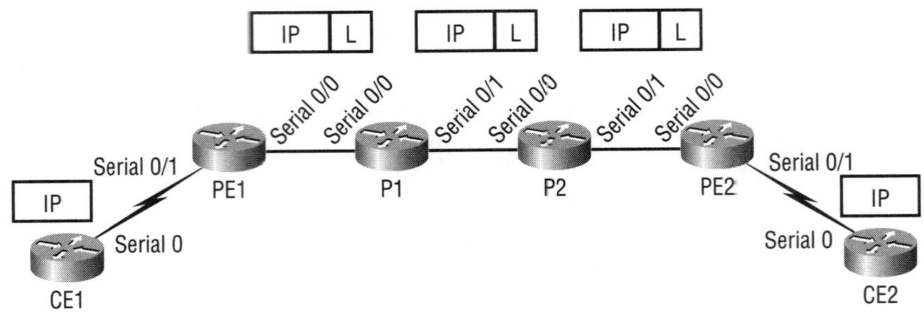

> **NOTE** Figure 1.10 is a logical, and not exact, representation of what happens to an IP packet as it moves through an MPLS-enabled service provider network.

Since packets receive labels at the edge of the network by the edge-LSR, and those labels are used by every LSR in the service provider network to switch traffic, many applications exist for MPLS, such as MPLS virtual private networks (VPNs), traffic engineering, and QoS.

MPLS and ATM

By turning a standard ATM Forum ATM switch into an *ATM label switch router (ATM-LSR)*, it is possible to merge the ATM and IP worlds to provide end-to-end solutions. An ATM-LSR is an ATM switch that is capable of forwarding packets based on labels.

> **NOTE** Chapter 3 provides more detail about implementing MPLS in an ATM network.

Overlay

When an ATM switch is enabled as an ATM-LSR, an overlay between service provider edge devices is no longer necessary. In Figure 1.8, all of the POP routers are edge-LSRs, and all the ATM switches are ATM-LSRs. Since every router in the network is running an Interior Gateway Protocol (IGP) such as Open Shortest Path First (OSPF) or Intermediate System-Intermediate System (IS-IS), POP routers now peer with ATM-LSRs directly instead of with each other in a full mesh.

As packets enter the network as unlabeled IP, the edge-LSR labels the packet and forwards it along the LSP. Figure 1.10 shows the labeled packet as it traverses the service provider network. The actual process is a little more complex than this example illustrates, but I want you to notice two very important areas in Figure 1.10:

- Instead of an overlay, routers are directly connected to ATM-LSRs. Scalability is achieved by eliminating the need for a full mesh of VCs and reducing the numbers of neighbors that must be maintained by a routing protocol.
- In Figure 1.11, packets enter the network as unlabeled IP. In this figure, the edge-LSR is in Raleigh, and it accepts the unlabeled IP packet and applies a label. Each ATM-LSR in the LSP uses the label to move packets.

FIGURE 1.11 MPLS-enabled service provider network

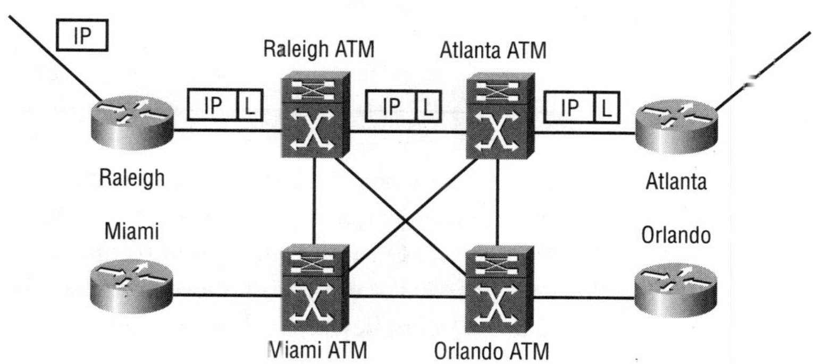

Quality of Service

MPLS addresses QoS by allowing packets to be classified at the network edge. Standard IP packets enter the network at an edge-LSR. The Experimental (EXP) field of the MPLS label stack is used to hold QoS information for use by MPLS-enabled devices along the LSP.

The Experimental field is three bits in size. With three bits, a total of eight values are possible, but only six values are available for QoS. (The remaining two values are reserved for internal network use only.) The default operation is for the IP precedence value to be copied into the EXP field of the MPLS label stack. Table 1.2 shows the mappings of IP precedence to MPLS EXP.

TABLE 1.2 Experimental-to-IP Precedence Mappings

Experimental	IP Precedence	Class
7	7	Reserved
6	6	Reserved
5	5	Real-time
4	4	
3	3	
2	2	
1	1	Best effort

With packets being classified at the network edge, it's easier to provide for enforceable service-level agreements (SLAs). Queuing methods such as WRED and WFQ can be configured to operate using the EXP value in the MPLS label stack. With MPLS, every device in the network can enforce a consistent QoS policy regardless of whether they are routers or ATM switches.

Traffic Engineering

Routing protocols, by their use of metrics, attempt to determine the best (fastest) path for traffic to travel. For example, Figure 1.12 illustrates a simple routed network with various link speeds. In this figure, the objects R1 through R8 represent routers in the network, and the connections OC3 and OC12 represent the speed of the links between them.

FIGURE 1.12 A simple traffic-engineering network

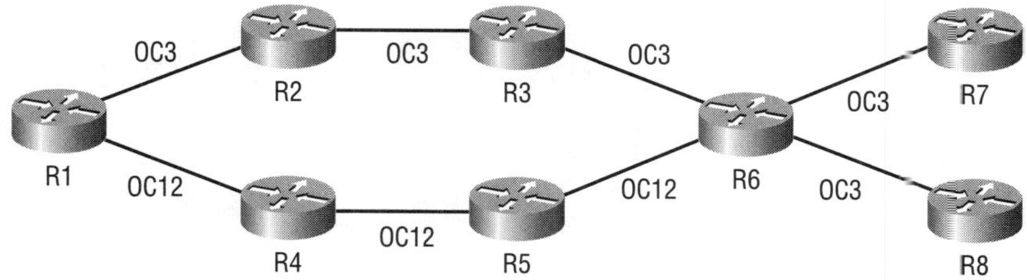

What is the best path for traffic to flow from R1 to R7? If the routing protocol is using bandwidth as a metric, then traffic will follow the path of R1 to R4 to R5 to R6 to R7, as shown in Figure 1.13.

FIGURE 1.13 Traffic flow from R1 to R7

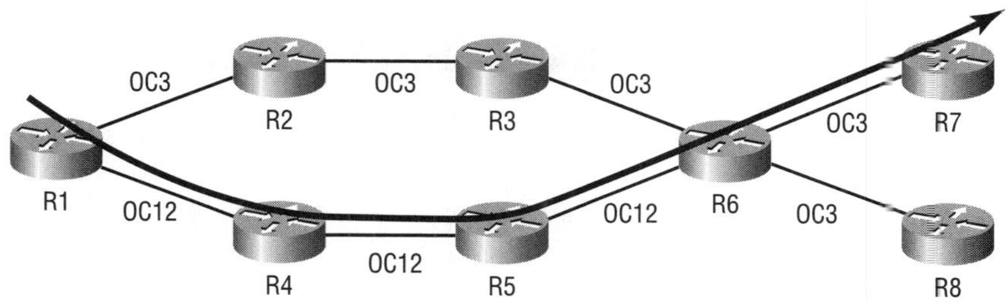

What if traffic is coming from R8 to R1? The best path from the perspective of a routing protocol is from R8 to R6 to R5 to R4 to R1, as shown in Figure 1.14.

FIGURE 1.14 Traffic flow from R8 to R1

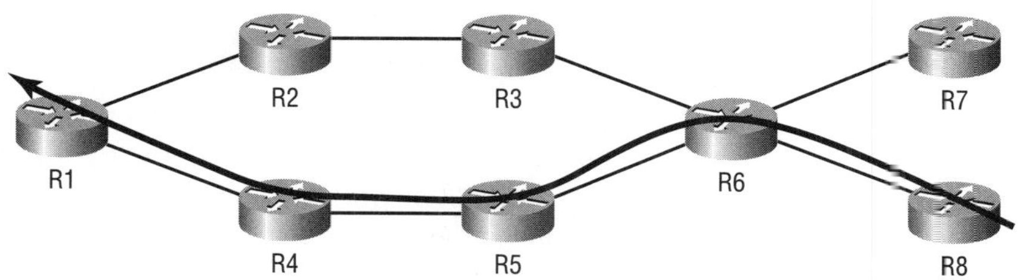

What about traffic coming from R7 destined for R1? Well, when the packet arrives at R6, it is sent along the same path as traffic from R8 to R1. From the routing protocol's perspective, the best path is from R7 to R6 to R5 to R4 to R1, as shown in Figure 1.15.

FIGURE 1.15 Traffic flow from R7 to R1

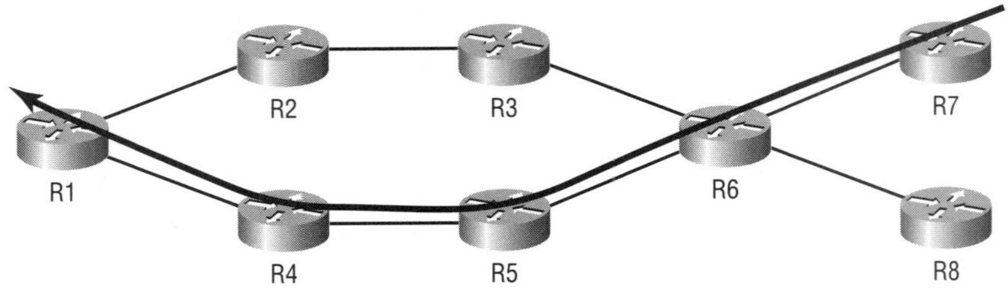

Take a moment and look back at Figures 1.13, 1.14, and 1.15. Which routers are continually traversed regardless of source, destination, or direction? You should notice that R1, R4, R5, and R6 are continually used to move traffic across the network.

Traffic Engineering and Routing Protocols

If you are not a lord-high super-guru of routing, then there are a few issues that you should be aware of. First of all, with all the traffic being sent along the same path, it is possible for those links to become saturated. When a link becomes saturated, packets will be dropped. The alternate path (R1 to R2 to R3 to R4) will not be used.

Routing protocols find the best path to move the packet across the network. Routing protocols such as OSPF and IS-IS, which are used in the core of service provider networks, do not support unequal cost load balancing. In other words, even though there are two possible paths to get across the network, the routing protocol will only use one of them based on the metrics in use.

There is a little magic that you can do with routing protocols to try to make two unequal paths look equal. If the routing protocol has two equal routes across a network, it will load-balance. Be forewarned though: If you dabble in the black art of routing protocol manipulation and try to do this in a large network, it will become too much to manage.

Additionally, you could try to do some special policy-based routing. If you do this on your core routers, it will slow them down. You also might not want the job of managing such a solution.

Which routers are never used to move user traffic across the network? You should notice in Figures 1.13, 1.14, and 1.15 that routers R2 and R3 are simply not used. To illustrate this, Table 1.3 describes the utilization of each of the links in this network.

TABLE 1.3 Link Utilization

Link	Usage
R1 to R4	Utilized
R4 to R5	Utilized
R5 to R6	Utilized
R1 to R2	Not Utilized
R2 to R3	Not Utilized
R3 to R4	Not Utilized

You can see that half of the links that are being paid for are used and half of the links that are being paid for are not being used. This problem is referred to as *the fish*. If you look at Figure 1.16, you can see why it is called the fish.

FIGURE 1.16 The fish

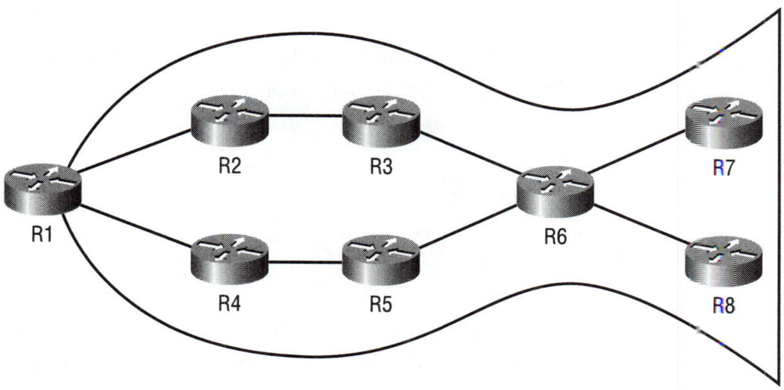

The MPLS solution is to use traffic-engineered tunnels that are made possible with label stacking. Figure 1.17 shows two tunnels. On R6, two tunnels, both with a destination of R1, are configured to load-share. The first tunnel takes a path from R6 to R5 to R4 to R1. The second tunnel follows the path from R6 to R3 to R2 to R1. Since MPLS supports unequal cost load balancing, traffic will be load-balanced now across these two tunnels on a per-packet basis. Tunnels are unidirectional, so a second set of tunnels would need to be set up from R1 to R6 to support traffic flow in the opposite direction from the example. Since tunnels are unidirectional in nature, it's possible for the return tunnel from R1 to R6 to take a completely different path that's based on the tunnel constraints.

FIGURE 1.17 Traffic-engineered network with tunnels

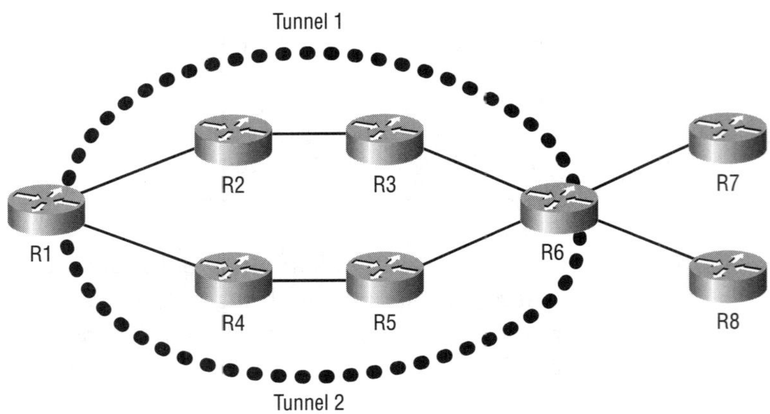

NOTE: Another application for MPLS is VPNs. A discussion of VPNs begins in Chapter 4, "VPNs: An Overview."

Summary

There are many problems experienced by service providers when trying to implement end-to-end solutions using two dissimilar technologies: ATM and IP. MPLS evolved out of early attempts at solutions to glue the IP and ATM worlds together. Cisco's proprietary solution, tag switching, later became standardized into what we now know as MPLS.

Frame-mode MPLS uses a 32-bit label stack, referred to as a shim header, because it is placed between the Layer 2 header and the Layer 3 payload. An MPLS-capable router or switch label-switches packets instead of routing them traditionally.

The MPLS architecture consists of two components: the control plane and the forwarding or data plane. These two components make label switching possible. The control plane binds labels to FECs. With CEF, label switching is made possible in the forwarding plane with the FIB and LFIB.

As packets enter the service provider network, an edge-LSR imposes a label. The label is used by every LSR along the LSP to label-switch the packet. By labeling at the network edge, it is possible to classify packets and implement consistent QoS throughout the network. Traffic engineering is made possible with label stacking.

Exam Essentials

Understand the MPLS label stack. The MPLS label stack is a total of 32 bits. The label itself is 20 bits. The label stack is placed between the Layer 2 header and the Layer 3 payload and is referred to as a shim header.

Know the MPLS architecture. The MPLS architecture is divided into two planes: control and forwarding. The control plane is responsible for binding labels to routes, or more specifically, to FECs. The forwarding plane (also known as the data plane) operates like a big cache by maintaining the FIB and LFIB. The control plane builds the bindings and the forwarding plane actually uses those bindings to switch packets. Don't forget, CEF must be enabled for MPLS to work.

Be able to identify MPLS operation. Packets enter the service provider network as unlabeled IP. An edge-LSR imposes a label and forwards the newly labeled packet to the next LSR along an LSP. Each LSR along the LSP label-switches the packet. The next-to-last router in the path pops the label through a mechanism called penultimate hop popping.

Know MPLS applications. First of all, MPLS changes network design by eliminating the need for an overlay. Performance is improved because packets are switched instead of routed. QoS can be implemented end to end by having an edge-LSR classify packets and map a value to the Experimental (EXP) field of the MPLS label stack. Traffic engineering is made possible through label stacking and traffic-engineered tunnels.

Key Terms

Before you take the exam, be certain you are familiar with the following terms:

- ATM label switch router (ATM-LSR)
- Cisco Express Forwarding (CEF)
- control plane
- data plane
- edge label switch router (edge-LSR)
- forwarding equivalence class (FEC)
- forwarding information base (FIB)
- forwarding plane
- Label Distribution Protocol (LDP)
- label forwarding information base (LFIB)
- label information base (LIB)
- label switch router (LSR)
- label-switched path (LSP)
- MPLS label stack
- penultimate hop popping
- shim header
- Tag Distribution Protocol (TDP)
- traffic engineering

Review Questions

1. What command do you use to display the labels on a Cisco IOS router/switch using MPLS?

   A. `show mpls ip`

   B. `show mpls forwarding-table`

   C. `show tag forwarding-table`

   D. `show mpls labels`

2. How many octets are there in the MPLS label stack header?

   A. 1

   B. 2

   C. 3

   D. 4

3. In frame-mode MPLS, the MPLS label stack resides ___________ and ___________. (Choose two.)

   A. Before the Layer 2 header

   B. After the Layer 2 header

   C. Before the Layer 3 payload

   D. After the Layer 3 payload

4. How many bits make up the label portion of the MPLS label stack?

   A. 3

   B. 16

   C. 20

   D. 32

5. What command do you use to display the labels on a Cisco IOS router/switch using tag switching?

   A. `show ip mpls`

   B. `show mpls forwarding-table`

   C. `show tag forwarding-table`

   D. `show mpls labels`

6. An MPLS-capable router/switch is called a(n) ___________?

   A. LSA

   B. LSR

   C. LRR

   D. TSR

7. Which device in the network only connects to service provider equipment?

   A. P

   B. PE

   C. CE

   D. C

8. Which network device typically imposes the labels?

   A. P

   B. PE

   C. CE

   D. C

9. What is the process of removing a label by the next-to-last router called?

A. Popping

B. Fast switch popping

C. Penultimate hop popping

D. Label disposition

10. Which field of the MPLS label stack is used for Quality of Service (QoS)?

A. Label

B. Experimental

C. S

D. TTL

11. Which of the following is *not* a suitable application for MPLS?

A. Quality of Service

B. Virtual private networks

C. Routing protocol replacement

D. Traffic engineering

12. In MPLS, VPNs and traffic engineering are made possible by ______. (Choose the most appropriate answer.)

A. Label stacking

B. Label popping

C. Label imposition

D. Label switching

13. Cisco's proprietary version of MPLS is called ___________.

A. Multi-protocol tag switching

B. Multi-Protocol Label Switching

C. Tag forwarding

D. Tag switching

14. Which protocol does tag switching use to exchange tags with neighbors?

    A. LDP

    B. LIB

    C. TDP

    D. FIB

15. Which protocol does MPLS use to exchange labels with neighbors?

    A. LDP

    B. LIB

    C. TDP

    D. FIB

16. For MPLS or tag switching to work, __________ must be enabled.

    A. LFIB

    B. LIB

    C. FIB

    D. CEF

17. To indicate the bottom of a stack, the S bit is set to __________.

    A. 0

    B. 1

    C. 2

    D. None of the above

18. An IP prefix is analogous to a(n) __________.

    A. FIB

    B. LFIB

    C. FEC

    D. CEF

19. LSPs are ___________.

A. Unidirectional

B. Bi-directional

C. None of the above

20. An ATM switch that is MPLS-enabled is called a(n) ___________.

A. ATM-LSR

B. Edge-LSR

C. ATMF-LSR

D. Core-LSR

Answers to Review Questions

1. B. The command to display label bindings in an MPLS environment is `show mpls forwarding-table`.
2. D. The MPLS label stack header is 32 bits in total size, or 4 octets.
3. B, C. The MPLS label stack is often referred to as a shim header because it resides between the Layer 2 header and Layer 3 payload.
4. C. The label portion of the MPLS label stack is 20 bits in length.
5. C. The command to display label bindings in a tag-switching environment is `show tag forwarding-table`.
6. B. The correct terminology for an MPLS-capable router/switch is that of a label switch router (LSR).
7. A. Network devices under control of the service provider and that only connect to other provider devices are called P devices.
8. B. Labels enter the service provider network as unlabeled IP. The PE, which is an edge-LSR, imposes a label.
9. C. To improve performance, the penultimate (next-to-last) router in the LSP pops the label and forwards it to the next hop router as an unlabeled packet.
10. B. The Experimental (EXP) field of the MPLS label stack is used for QoS. Packets enter the network as unlabeled IP. An edge-LSR applies the label and can set a value in the Experimental field that is used for QoS by other LSRs.
11. C. The major applications for MPLS are QoS, VPNs, and traffic engineering. An argument could be made that MPLS changes how routing protocols are used by service providers, but MPLS does not replace the need for them.
12. A. The ability to stack labels makes traffic engineering possible in MPLS networks. Label stacking also makes MPLS VPNs possible.
13. D. Cisco's proprietary way of moving tagged packets through a network is called tag switching.
14. C. The proprietary protocol used by Cisco tag switching to exchange tags is Tag Distribution Protocol (TDP).

15. A. The protocol used by MPLS to exchange labels is Label Distribution Protocol (LDP).

16. D. Cisco Express Forwarding (CEF) creates an optimized, "cached" version of the routing table. CEF is a requirement for MPLS and tag switching.

17. B. A value of 1 in this field indicates the bottom, or last label, of the stack.

18. C. An FEC is a grouping of IP packets that are treated the same way. For unicast-based routing, an IP prefix is the equivalent of an FEC.

19. A. A label-switched path (LSP) is a unidirectional set of label switch routers (LSRs) that a labeled packet must flow through.

20. A. The proper term for an ATM switch that is MPLS-enabled is ATM-LSR.

Chapter 2

Frame-Mode MPLS

CCIP MPLS EXAM TOPICS COVERED IN THIS CHAPTER:

- ✓ Identify the IOS commands and their proper syntax used to configure MPLS on frame-mode MPLS interfaces on IOS platforms.
- ✓ Describe the label distribution process between LSRs.
- ✓ Describe frame-mode MPLS and cell-mode MPLS.
- ✓ Identify the IOS commands and their proper syntax used to configure advanced core MPLS features (TTL propagation, controlled label distribution) on IOS platforms.
- ✓ Identify the IOS commands and their proper syntax used to monitor operations and troubleshoot typical MPLS failures on IOS platforms.

Chapter 1, "An Introduction to MPLS," introduced you to the basic operation of MPLS. You learned that with MPLS, packets are switched instead of routed. Unlabeled IP packets enter the service provider network at the edge, and a label is applied. Every label switch router (LSR) in the label-switched path (LSP) uses that label to label-switch the packet.

This chapter will build on what you already know, adding a little more detail. This chapter starts with a review of traditional Layer 3 routing. To really understand MPLS, you need a solid understanding of Layer 3 routing.

After routing, this chapter takes you though frame-mode MPLS step by step in the "Frame-Mode MPLS Working Example" section. This section builds on the concepts introduced in the previous chapter and focuses on the interaction between MPLS and the routing protocols in the network. If you are not comfortable with LSPs, go back and re-read that section of Chapter 1.

Labels and how they are bound to routes are described in greater detail in the "Label Distribution" section. Again, if there are any concepts that you are not totally comfortable with, make sure to re-read Chapter 1's description of labels.

Finally, this chapter will explain troubleshooting and network verification using configurations and output from a simple network.

Routing Review

You might be thinking to yourself, "I don't need to read this section on routing," or "I already know all about routing." Well, you might already know Layer 3 routing, but please read this section carefully anyway. If the ideas discussed here are somewhat new, take the time to really understand everything you're reading. If your routing skills are rusty, you may have difficulty understanding the interaction of MPLS and routing protocols.

So, let's do a quick and dirty review of routing. Figure 2.1 illustrates a simple Layer 3 routed network that you'll use for this review.

FIGURE 2.1 A sample network for Layer 3 routing

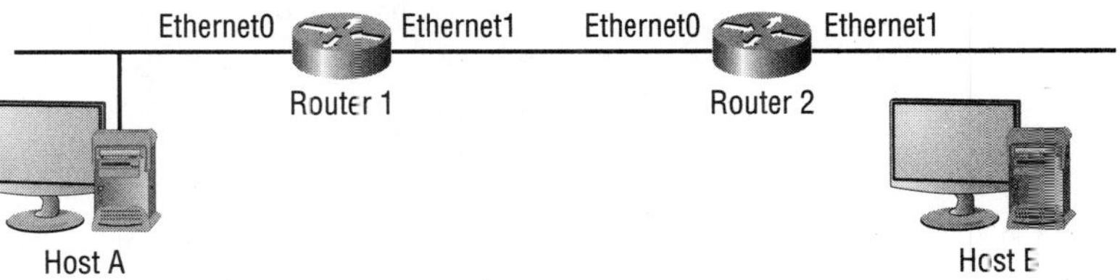

The IP and MAC addresses for each device in Figure 2.1 are listed in Table 2.1 and Table 2.2.

TABLE 2.1 Host Addresses

	Host A	Host B
IP address	192.168.1.10	192.168.3.10
Subnet mask	255.255.255.0	255.255.255.0
Default gateway	192.168.1.1	192.168.3.1
Mac address	AAAA-AAAA-AAAA	BBBB-BBBB-BBBB

TABLE 2.2 Router Addresses

	Router 1	Router 2
IP address (Ethernet0)	192.168.1.1	192.168.2.2
Subnet mask (Ethernet0)	255.255.255.0	255.255.255.0
MAC address (Ethernet0)	1111-1111-1111	2222-2222-2222
IP address (Ethernet1)	192.168.2.1	192.168.3.1
Subnet mask (Ethernet1)	255.255.255.0	255.255.255.0
MAC address (Ethernet1)	3333-3333-3333	4444-4444-4444

To begin this example, let's say that Host A wants to send some packets to Host B. The first thing that Host A does is determine whether Host B is local (on the same subnet) or remote (on a different subnet). Host A, by comparing its network at 192.168.1.0 to that of Host B at 192.168.3.0, can see that the network portions of the IP addresses do not match, meaning that Host B is remote. Host A, now knowing that Host B is remote, puts a frame on the wire destined for the default gateway. Table 2.3 shows the Layer 2 and Layer 3 information as placed on the wire.

TABLE 2.3 Layer 2 and Layer 3 Information from Host A to Router 1

From Host A to Router 1	
Layer 3 source	192.168.1.10
Layer 3 destination	192.168.3.10
Layer 2 source MAC	AAAA-AAAA-AAAA
Layer 2 destination MAC	1111-1111-1111

NOTE As you look over this example, pay close attention to the source and destination IP addresses.

Router 1 knows that the frame is destined for it because it sees its own Ethernet0 MAC address in the destination field in the frame. Router 1 picks the frame up off the wire, discards the Layer 2 information, and looks in the destination part of the Layer 3 header. Router 1, knowing that the packet is destined for network 192.168.3.0, does a Layer 3 lookup and checks its routing table to see if it has an entry for 192.168.3.10. It finds a route to network 192.168.3.0/24 with a next hop of 192.168.2.2 via interface Ethernet1. The following output is the routing table as it exists on Router 1:

```
Router1#show ip route

R 192.168.3.0/24 [120/1] via 192.168.2.2, 00:00:01, Ethernet1
C 192.168.1.0/24 is directly connected, Ethernet0
C 192.168.2.0/24 is directly connected, Ethernet1
```

Router 1 knows that to get to network 192.168.3.0, it needs to send the packet out of Ethernet1 to 192.168.2.2. Router 1 programmatically moves the packet to the outbound Ethernet1 interface, creates a new frame, and places the new frame on the wire. Table 2.4 lists the Layer 2 and Layer 3 information as it is placed on the wire from Router 1 to Router 2.

TABLE 2.4 Layer 2 and Layer 3 Information from Router 1 to Router 2

From Router 1 to Router 2	
Layer 3 source	192.168.1.10
Layer 3 destination	192.168.3.10
Layer 2 source MAC	2222-2222-2222
Layer 2 destination MAC	3333-3333-3333

NOTE: Notice in Table 2.4 that only the Layer 2 source and destination MAC addresses have changed. The Layer 3 information is unchanged.

Router 2 knows that the frame is destined for it because it sees its own Ethernet0 MAC address in the destination field in the frame. Router 2 picks the frame up off the wire, discards the Layer 2 information, and looks in the destination part of the Layer 3 header. Router 2, knowing that the packet is destined for 192.168.3.10, does a Layer 3 lookup and checks its routing table to see if it has an entry for 192.168.3.10. It finds a route to network 192.168.3.0/24 with a directly connected interface of Ethernet1. The following output is the routing table as it exists on Router 2:

```
Router2#show ip route

R 192.168.1.0/24 [120/1] via 192.168.2.1, 00:00:06, Ethernet0
C 192.168.2.0/24 is directly connected, Ethernet0
C 192.168.3.0/24 is directly connected, Ethernet1
```

Router 2 knows that to get to network 192.168.3.0, it needs to go out the directly connected interface Ethernet1. Router 2 programmatically moves the packet to the outbound Ethernet1 interface, creates a new frame, and places the new frame on the wire. Table 2.5 shows the Layer 2 and Layer 3 information as it is placed on the wire from Router 2 to Host B.

TABLE 2.5 Layer 2 and Layer 3 Information from Router 2 to Host B

From Router 2 to Host B	
Layer 3 source	192.168.1.10
Layer 3 destination	192.168.3.10
Layer 2 source MAC	4444-4444-4444
Layer 2 destination MAC	BBBB-BBBB-BBBB

NOTE: Notice in Table 2.5 that the Layer 3 source and destination addresses remain unchanged.

Host B knows that the frame is destined for it because it sees its own MAC address in the destination field in the frame. Host B pulls the frame off the wire and processes the data it contains.

Let's do that one more time just to be thorough. Suppose Host B needs to send something back to Host A. First, Host B determines whether Host A is local or remote. Host B, by comparing its network at 192.168.3.0 to that of Host A at 192.168.1.0, can see that the network portions of the IP addresses do not match, meaning that Host A is remote. Host B, now knowing that Host A is remote, puts a frame on the wire destined for the default gateway. Table 2.6 shows the Layer 2 and Layer 3 information as placed on the wire.

TABLE 2.6 Layer 2 and Layer 3 Information from Host B to Router 2

From Host B to Router 2	
Layer 3 source	192.168.3.10
Layer 3 destination	192.168.1.10

TABLE 2.6 Layer 2 and Layer 3 Information from Host B to Router 2 *(continued)*

From Host B to Router 2	
Layer 2 source MAC	BBBB-BBBB-BBBB
Layer 2 destination MAC	4444-4444-4444

Router 2 knows that the frame is destined for it because it sees its own Ethernet1 MAC address in the destination field in the frame. Router 2 picks the frame up off the wire, discards the Layer 2 information, and looks in the destination part of the Layer 3 header. Router 2, knowing that the packet is destined for network 192.168.1.10, does a Layer 3 lookup and checks its routing table to see if it has an entry for 192.168.1.10. It finds a route to network 192.168.1.0/24 with a next hop of 192.168.2 via interface Ethernet0. The following output is the routing table as it exists on Router 2:

```
Router2#show ip route

R 192.168.1.0/24 [120/1] via 192.168.2.1, 00:00:06, Ethernet0
C 192.168.2.0/24 is directly connected, Ethernet0
C 192.168.3.0/24 is directly connected, Ethernet1
```

Router 2 knows that to get to network 192.168.1.0, it needs to send the packet out of Ethernet0 to 192.168.2.1. Router 2 programmatically moves the packet to the outbound Ethernet0 interface, creates a new frame, and places the new frame on the wire. Table 2.7 shows the Layer 2 and Layer 3 information as it is placed on the wire from Router 1 to Router 2.

TABLE 2.7 Layer 2 and Layer 3 Information from Router 2 to Router 1

From Router 2 to Router 1	
Layer 3 source	192.168.3.10
Layer 3 destination	192.168.1.10
Layer 2 source MAC	3333-3333-3333
Layer 2 destination MAC	2222-2222-2222

Router 1 knows that the frame is destined for it because it sees its own Ethernet1 MAC address in the destination field in the frame. Router 1 picks the frame up off the wire, discards the Layer 2 information, and looks in the destination part of the Layer 3 header. Router 1, knowing that the packet is destined for 192.168.1.10, does a Layer 3 lookup and checks its routing table to see if it has an entry for 192.168.1.10. It finds a route to network 192.168.1.0/24 with a directly connected interface of Ethernet0. The following output is the routing table as it exists on Router 1:

```
Router1#show ip route

R 192.168.3.0/24 [120/1] via 192.168.2.2, 00:00:01, Ethernet1
C 192.168.1.0/24 is directly connected, Ethernet0
C 192.168.2.0/24 is directly connected, Ethernet1
```

Router 1 knows that to get to network 192.168.3.0, it needs to go out the directly connected interface Ethernet0. Router 1 programmatically moves the packet to the outbound Ethernet0 interface, creates a new frame, and places the new frame on the wire. Table 2.8 shows the Layer 2 and Layer 3 information as it is placed on the wire from Router 1 to Host A.

TABLE 2.8 Layer 2 and Layer 3 Information from Router 1 to Host A

From Router 1 to Host A	
Layer 3 source	192.168.3.10
Layer 3 destination	192.168.1.10
Layer 2 source MAC	1111-1111-1111
Layer 2 destination MAC	AAAA-AAAA-AAAA

Host A knows that the frame is destined for it because it sees its MAC address in the destination field in the frame. Host A pulls the frame off the wire and processes the data it contains.

So now that we're done with the review of Layer 3 routing, there were two very important things you should have noticed:

- Throughout the entire process, the source IP address and destination IP address in the Layer 3 header never changes from source device to destination device. Only the Layer 2 information changes from hop to hop.

- At each router between the host devices, the Layer 3 information is checked and a routing determination is made. If a route does not exist for a destination network and there is not a default route, the packet is dropped into the bottomless bit bucket of no return.

Frame-Mode MPLS Working Example

In Chapter 1, you learned about LSPs, penultimate hop popping, and the basics of MPLS. Frame-mode MPLS runs on routers with frame-mode interfaces. Frame-mode MPLS covers just about everything except Asynchronous Transfer Mode (ATM). This section uses the example service provider network illustrated in Figure 2.2 to build upon what you learned in Chapter 1.

FIGURE 2.2 A full service provider network

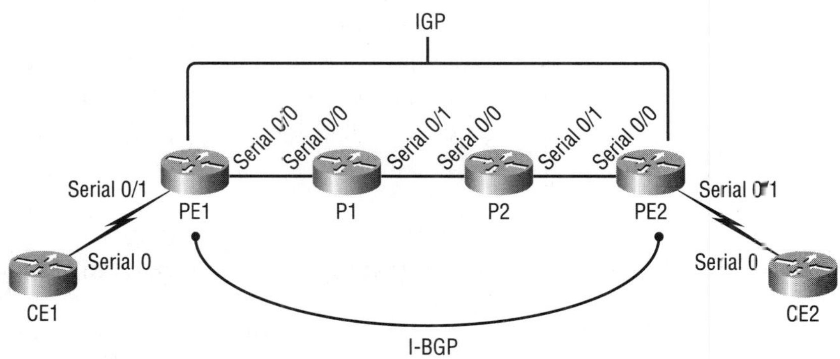

Table 2.9 lists the IP addresses of the service provider devices in Figure 2.2.

TABLE 2.9 Service Provider Network Device Addresses

Device	Serial 0/0	Serial 0/1	Loopback 0
PE1	192.168.1.10	128.107.10.2	192.168.1.1
P1	192.168.1.9	192.168.1.14	192.168.1.2
P2	192.168.1.13	192.168.1.18	192.168.1.3
PE2	192.168.1.17	128.107.10.5	192.168.1.4

Table 2.10 lists the IP addresses of the customer devices in Figure 2.2.

TABLE 2.10 Customer Device Addresses

Device	Ethernet0	Serial 0
CE1	204.134.83.1	128.107.10.1
CE2	209.39.164.0	128.107.10.6

Network Routing Protocol Examples

The use of routing protocols by the devices in Figure 2.2 deserves a little discussion:

CE1 CE1 is configured with a default route out Serial 0 to the service provider network (PE1). CE1 is not an LSR.

PE1 PE1 is configured with a static route for network 204.134.83.0. PE1 is also configured with Border Gateway Protocol (BGP). An I-BGP session is configured between PE1 and PE2. For provider network routing, an Interior Gateway Protocol (IGP) is configured. For the purpose of this example, we'll use the IGP Open Shortest Path First (OSPF). PE1 is an LSR.

BGP Configuration on Provider Edge Devices

If you are not familiar how BGP is going to be implemented, take a look at the configuration of PE1 and PE2. PE1 has the following BGP configuration:

```
router bgp 1
 no synchronization
 bgp log-neighbor-changes
 network 192.168.1.1 mask 255.255.255.255
 neighbor 192.168.1.4 remote-as 1
 neighbor 192.168.1.4 update-source Loopback0
 redistribute static
 no auto-summary
```

This configuration means that PE1 is advertising its loopback address (network 192.168.1.1, mask 255.255.255.255). PE1 has a neighbor, PE2, and they are part of the same autonomous system (neighbor 192.168.1.4, remote-as 1). Whenever PE1 communicates a route to its neighbor, Loopback 0 (192.168.1.1) of PE1 is used as the next hop address (neighbor 192.168.1.4, update-source Loopback 0). Statically entered routes are populated into BGP (redistribute static).

Based on this configuration, a static route is redistributed into BGP and sent to a neighbor router, with the next hop being the Loopback 0 of the originating router.

The configuration of PE2 is as follows:

```
router bgp 1
 no synchronization
 bgp log-neighbor-changes
 network 192.168.1.4 mask 255.255.255.255
 neighbor 192.168.1.1 remote-as 1
 neighbor 192.168.1.1 update-source Loopback0
 redistribute static
 no auto-summary
```

The way that routes are communicated from PE2 to PE1 works the same way that routes are communicated from PE1 to PE2. On PE2, the loopback address (network 192.168.1.4, mask 255.255.255.255) is being advertised. PE2 has a neighbor of PE1, and they are part of the same autonomous system (neighbor 192.168.1.1, remote-as 1). Whenever PE1 communicates a route to its neighbor, the Loopback 0 (192.168.1.4) of PE1 is used as the next hop address (neighbor 192.168.1.1, update-source Loopback 0). Statically entered routes are populated into BGP (redistribute static).

P1 P1 is configured with OSPF for provider network routing. P1 is an LSR.

P2 P2 is configured with OSPF for provider network routing. P2 is an LSR.

PE2 PE2 is configured with a static route for network 209.39.164.0. PE1 is also configured with BGP. An I-BGP session is configured between PE1 and PE2. OSPF is configured as the service provider routing protocol. PE2 is an LSR.

CE2 CE2 is configured with a default route out Serial 0 to the service provider network (PE2). CE2 is not an LSR.

MPLS Step by Step

There is really no better way to learn MPLS than to see it in a step-by-step format. Take all the time you need to read through this section because the information you learn here will be used throughout this book.

Step 1 A host on the 204.134.83.0 subnet wants to send data to a host on the 209.39.164.0 subnet. The host knows that the destination host is remote and places a frame on the wire to its default gateway, which is CE1.

Step 2 Router CE1 receives the frame, discards the Layer 2 information, and does a Layer 3 lookup to see if it has a path to get to the destination network of 209.39.164.0. There is no route in the routing table for the destination network, so the packet is forwarded to PE1 using the default route or the gateway of last resort.

Step 3 Router PE1 receives the packet and does a Layer 3 lookup. PE1 knows about the destination network (it was learned from PE2 through BGP). The next hop address for the remote network is 192.168.1.4 (the loopback address of PE2). Router PE1, being an LSR, inserts a label and forwards the labeled packet to P1.

NOTE

This is a good place to define a few more technical terms of MPLS. You are already familiar with the process of removing a label; it's called *penultimate hop popping*. When a router adds a label, this process is referred to as *pushing* or *label imposition*. Alternately, when a label is removed, this process is sometimes referred to as *popping*. Which direction is the traffic going? The traffic is coming into PE1. PE1 is called an *ingress router*. Since PE1 is an LSR and sits at the network edge (pushing and popping labels), it can be also called an *edge-LSR*.

NOTE

So, if you want really impress someone, you could say that PE1 is an ingress edge-LSR that provides label imposition to traffic entering the service provider network. That and $2.00 will get you a cup of coffee.

Just in case I distracted you with the new technical terms you can use at dinner parties or to impress your co-workers, I'll repeat what happens at PE1.

The Layer 3 header is examined, and PE1 has a BGP route to the destination network. The destination BGP route says that to get to the remote network, send the traffic to the loopback of PE2 (192.168.1.4). PE1 has an LSP to get to the loopback of PE2. A label is pushed on and then sent out to P1.

Step 4 This next part is very important! P1 is only running OSPF. P1 only knows about the internal networks (those networks that start with 192.168.1). P1 does not look at the destination field of the Layer 3 header. P1 does not do a Layer 3 lookup; it simply swaps the label out and forwards it to P2.

Step 5 Router P2 receives the labeled packet. P2 is only running OSPF and just like P1, P2 does no processing based on the Layer 3 information. P2 pops the label and forwards a standard packet to PE2.

Step 6 Router PE2 receives the packet and does a Layer 3 lookup. PE1 knows about the destination network (it was statically entered). The next hop address for the remote network is 128.107.10.6 (the Serial 0 address of CE2). Router PE2 sends that packet to CE2.

> **NOTE** There's just one last technical term you need to know. The packet is leaving the provider network at PE2. PE2 is called the *egress router*. As explained earlier, PE1, where the packet came into the provider network, is called the *ingress router*.

Step 7 CE2 receives the packet and does a Layer 3 lookup. CE2 has a directly connected interface on the destination network and forwards the packet to the destination host.

Figure 2.3 shows the labeled/unlabeled status of the packet as it traverses the network from CE1 to CE2.

FIGURE 2.3 CE1-to-CE2 packet status

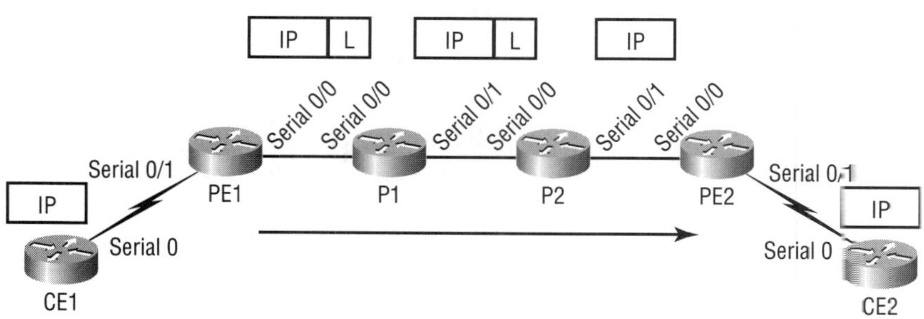

Let's run through the same process but this time in reverse:

Step 1 A host on the 209.39.160.0 subnet wants to send data to a host on the 204.134.83.0 subnet. The host knows that the destination host is remote and places a frame on the wire to its default gateway, which is CE2.

Step 2 Router CE1 receives the frame, discards the Layer 2 information, and does a Layer 3 lookup to see if it has a path to get to the destination network 204.134.83.0. There is no route in the routing table for the destination network, so the packet is forwarded to PE2 using the default route.

Step 3 Router PE2 receives the packet and does a Layer 3 lookup. PE1 knows about the destination network (it was learned from PE1 through BGP). The next hop address for the remote network is 192.168.1.1 (the loopback address of PE1). Router PE2, being an LSR, inserts a label and forwards the labeled packet to P2.

Step 4 P2, running only OSPF, does not look at the destination field of the Layer 3 header and does not do a Layer 3 lookup. P2 simply swaps the label out and forwards it to P1.

Step 5 P1, running only OSPF, does not look at the destination field of the Layer 3 header and does not do a Layer 3 lookup. P2 simply pops the label and forwards it on to PE1.

Step 6 Router PE1 receives the unlabeled packet and does a Layer 3 lookup. PE1 knows about the destination network (it was statically entered). The next hop address for the remote network is 128.107.10.1 (the Serial 0 address of CE1). Router PE1 sends that packet to CE1.

Step 7 CE1 receives the packet and does a Layer 3 lookup. CE1 has a directly connected interface in the destination and forwards the packet to the destination host.

Figure 2.4 shows the labeled/unlabeled status of the packet as it traverses the network from CE2 to CE1.

FIGURE 2.4 CE2-to-CE1 packet status

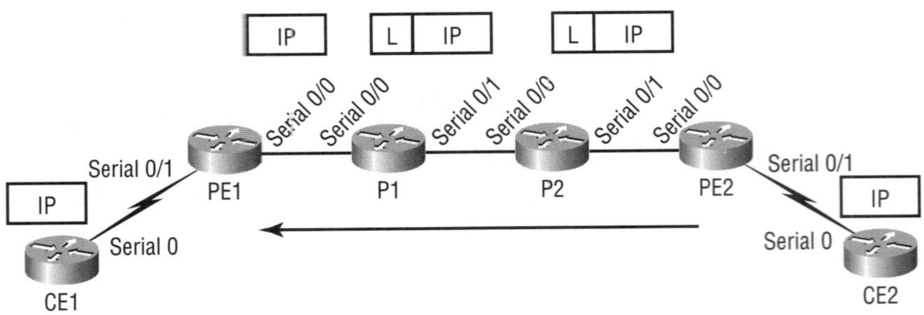

Label Distribution

Since you already know that packets are switched instead of routed, let's look at the details of how labels are exchanged between LSRs. If you remember in Chapter 1, I asked you to repeat to yourself that labels get bound to routes (more specifically, non-BGP routes) in the routing table. This section goes into a little more detail about that operation.

TDP

As you learned in Chapter 1, there are two ways you can implement a switching solution. First, if you have all Cisco equipment, you can use *tag switching*. Tag switching is Cisco proprietary and was the precursor to MPLS. Tag switching relies on *Tag Distribution Protocol (TDP)* to exchange packets between *tag switching routers (TSRs)*.

Once TDP has been configured on an interface, neighbor discovery is automatic. TDP uses UDP broadcast or multicast packets to discover a neighbor. To configure tag switching, *Cisco Express Forwarding (CEF)* must be enabled, and then tag switching must be enabled on the appropriate interface(s). The IOS commands to configure tag switching on a router are as follows:

```
P1#config t
P1(config)#ip cef
P1(config)#tag-switching advertise-tags
P1(config-if)#interface serial 0/0
P1(config-if)#tag-switching ip
```

NOTE You can control which labels are distributed by configuring an access list and associating it with the `tag-switching advertise-tags` command.

Once a neighbor is discovered, TDP uses well-known TCP port 711 to exchange tags with its peer. Just like OSPF or BGP, TDP uses an identifier that is the highest IP address of the configured loopback addresses. If there are no loopback interfaces configured, the identifier is chosen from the highest IP address of all the active interfaces.

To verify that you have established TDP neighbors, use the IOS command `show tag-switching tdp-neighbor`, which produces the following output:

```
P1# show tag-switching tdp-neighbor
Peer TDP Ident: 192.168.1.1:0; Local TDP Ident 192.168.1.2:0
      TCP connection: 192.168.1.1:11004 - 192.168.1.2.678
   State: Oper; PIEs sent/rcvd: 1506/1500; ; Downstream
   Up time: 12:36:08
   TDP discovery sources:
     Serial 0/0
   Addresses bound to peer TDP Ident:
   192.168.1.10       192.168.1.1
```

LDP

Since MPLS came after tag switching, much of its operation is the same as tag switching, and even their configurations are quite similar. However, there are a few differences to note.

MPLS relies on *Label Distribution Protocol (LDP)* to exchange labels with neighboring LSRs. Once LDP has been configured on an interface, neighbor discovery is automatic, just like in TDP. LDP uses UDP broadcast or multicast packets to discover a neighbor. To configure MPLS, CEF must be enabled and then MPLS must be enabled on the appropriate interface(s). The IOS commands to configure MPLS on a router are as follows:

```
P1#config t
P1(config)#ip cef
P1(config)#mpls ip
P1(config-if)#interface serial 0/0
P1(config-if)#mpls ip
```

Just like TDP, LDP provides for automatic neighbor discovery. Once a neighbor is established, TCP port 646 is used to exchange labels. The LDP identifier is chosen in the same method as TDP. To verify LDP neighbor establishment, use the IOS command `show mpls ldp neighbor`, which produces the following output:

```
P1# show mpls ldp neighbor
Peer LDP Ident: 192.168.1.1:0; Local TDP Ident 192.168.1.2:0
      TCP connection: 192.168.1.1:11033 - 192.168.1.2.647
```

```
State: Oper; PIEs sent/rcvd: 8/8; ; Downstream
Up time: 00:02:15
LDP discovery sources:
  Serial 0/0
Addresses bound to peer LDP Ident:
  192.168.1.10  192.168.1.1
```

Assigning Labels

There might be some confusion about how labels are assigned. Almost all of this confusion has to do with downstream and upstream in relation to MPLS terminology.

I'll take a little creative license here and explain these terms like I do in class. In Figure 2.5, there are three routers: R1, R2, and R3. Router R1 advertises a subnet (204.134.83.0) that R2 will learn. R3 will learn the route from R2. Traffic destined for the advertised subnet (204.134.83.0) must eventually get to R1 (the original source of the route). The terms *upstream* or *downstream* are in relation to the flow of user packets, *not* in relation to the flow of a routing update. For example, traffic destined for subnet 204.134.83.0 flows from upstream routers (R2 and R3) to the downstream router (R1). Confused yet?

FIGURE 2.5 Upstream/downstream

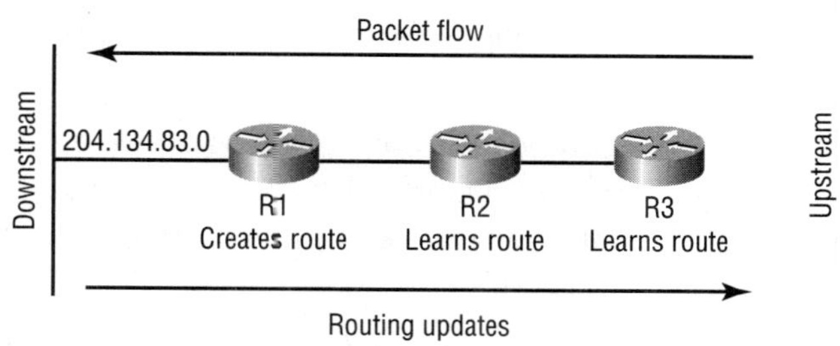

An alternative, and easier, way to think of upstream and downstream is illustrated in Figure 2.6. In Figure 2.6, R1 is at the mouth of the river. R2 and R3 are upstream from R1. The flow of packets, as represented by the ship, is from upstream to downstream. From the perspective of R1, R2 and R3 are upstream. From the perspective of R2, R1 is downstream and R3 is upstream. From R3, R1 and R2 are downstream.

FIGURE 2.6 Upstream/downstream alternative

Now that you can identify upstream and downstream, the way in which labels are bound can make a little more sense. Let's define all the necessary terminology:

Independent control When a new forwarding equivalence class (FEC) appears on an LSR, a label is bound to it immediately and can be advertised to its neighbors at any time. Since there is no waiting on a label from the downstream LSR, it is possible for the upstream LSRs to be label-switching without a complete LSP. *Independent control* provides for the fastest LSP setup and is the control method used by the routers (LSRs).

Ordered control *Ordered control* occurs when an upstream LSR must wait on a label to be received from its downstream LSR. Ordered control takes longer to set up an LSP and is used by MPLS-enabled ATM switches (ATM-LSRs).

Downstream-on-demand *Downstream-on-demand* occurs when an upstream LSR, using the Label Request message, requests a label from its downstream neighbor.

Unsolicited downstream *Unsolicited downstream* occurs when a downstream LSR advertises labels to its neighbors automatically without the need of a Label Request message.

The official way to describe label distribution in frame-mode MPLS is to say that it is independent control with unsolicited downstream. Remember that labels get bound to routes in the routing table. What this means is that a non-BGP route arrives in the routing table (the equivalent of an FEC), and a local label gets bound immediately to it. That local label is advertised to an upstream LSR to be used in sending the labeled packet. What this means in layman's terms is that an LSR will bind a label to an FEC and advertise it to its neighbor without its neighbor having to ask. To provide a little contrast, MPLS in an ATM network uses ordered control with downstream-on-demand.

Troubleshooting and Verification

So far, you've been exposed to the basic concepts of frame-mode MPLS. This section uses a simple network to illustrate device configuration, configuration verification commands, and troubleshooting. For this section, we'll be using the simple network shown in Figure 2.7.

FIGURE 2.7 A simple network

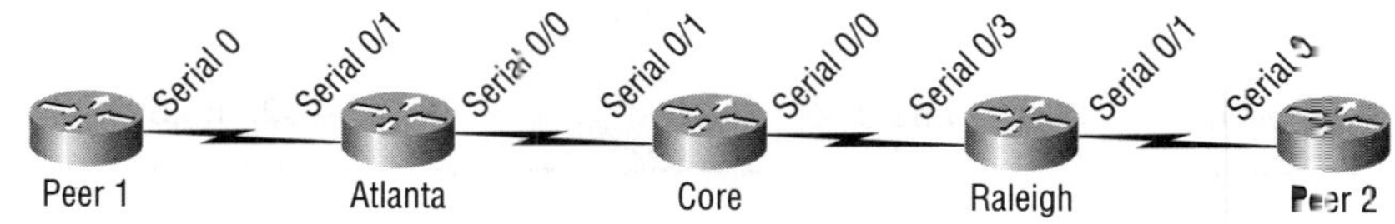

Routing protocol utilization is illustrated in Figure 2.8.

FIGURE 2.8 Routing protocol utilization

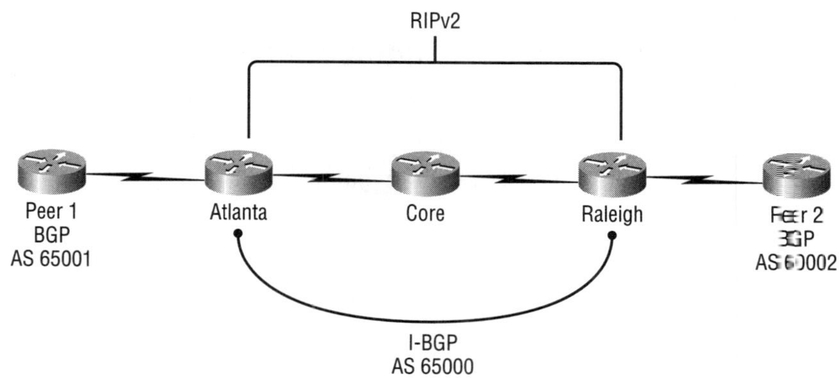

The IP addresses of the CE devices in Figures 2.7 and 2.8 (Peer 1 and Peer 2) are listed in Table 2.11.

TABLE 2.11 Customer Addressing

Device	Loopback 0	Serial 0
Peer 1	192.168.1.1/32	192.168.3.5/30
Peer 2	192.168.2.1/32	192.168.3.10/30

The IP addresses of the three service provider devices in Figures 2.7 and 2.8 are listed in Table 2.12.

TABLE 2.12 Service Provider Addressing

Device	Loopback 0	Serial 0/0	Serial 0/1	Serial 0/3
Atlanta	204.134.83.1/32	204.134.83.5/30	192.168.3.6/30	N/A
Core	204.134.83.2/32	204.134.83.9/30	204.134.83.6/30	N/A
Raleigh	204.134.83.3/32	N/A	192.168.3.9/30	204.134.83.10/30

Device Configuration

The configurations of the Atlanta POP, Core, Raleigh POP, Peer 1, and Peer 2 routers are described in the following sections.

Atlanta Router Configuration

The configuration of the Atlanta POP router is as follows:

```
Atlanta#show running-config
Building configuration...

Current configuration : 1492 bytes
!
version 12.1
service timestamps debug uptime
service timestamps log uptime
```

```
no service password-encryption
!
hostname Atlanta
!
enable password cisco
!
!
!
!
!
memory-size iomem 25
ip subnet-zero
ip tcp synwait-time 5
no ip domain-lookup
!
ip cef
cns event-service server
!
!
!
!
!
interface Loopback0
 ip address 204.134.83.1 255.255.255.255
!
interface Serial0/0
 description *** Link to Core Router ***
 ip address 204.134.83.5 255.255.255.252
 tag-switching ip
 no fair-queue
 clockrate 64000
!
interface Serial0/1
 description *** Link to Peer1 ***
 ip address 192.168.3.6 255.255.255.252
 clockrate 64000
!
```

```
interface Serial0/2
 no ip address
 shutdown
 clockrate 64000
!
interface Serial0/3
 no ip address
 shutdown
 clockrate 64000
!
interface Ethernet1/0
 no ip address
 shutdown
!
interface Ethernet1/1
 no ip address
 shutdown
!
interface Ethernet1/2
 no ip address
 shutdown
!
interface Ethernet1/3
 no ip address
 shutdown
!
router rip
 version 2
 network 204.134.83.0
!
router bgp 65000
 no synchronization
 bgp log-neighbor-changes
 neighbor 192.168.3.5 remote-as 65001
 neighbor 204.134.83.3 remote-as 65000
 neighbor 204.134.83.3 update-source Loopback0
```

```
 neighbor 204.134.83.3 next-hop-self
 no auto-summary
!
ip classless
no ip http server
!
!
!
line con 0
 exec-timeout 0 0
 privilege level 15
 logging synchronous
 transport input none
 ip netmask-format decimal
line aux 0
line vty 0 4
 privilege level 15
 password cisco
 logging synchronous
 login
 ip netmask-format decimal
!
end
```

Core Router Configuration

The configuration of the Core router is as follows:

```
Core#show running-config
Building configuration...

Current configuration : 1249 bytes
!
version 12.1
service timestamps debug uptime
service timestamps log uptime
no service password-encryption
!
```

```
hostname Core
!
enable password cisco
!
!
!
!
!
memory-size iomem 25
ip subnet-zero
ip tcp synwait-time 5
no ip domain-lookup
!
ip cef
cns event-service server
!
!
!
!
!
interface Loopback0
 ip address 204.134.83.2 255.255.255.255
!
interface Serial0/0
 description *** Connection to Raleigh POP ***
 ip address 204.134.83.9 255.255.255.252
 tag-switching ip
 no fair-queue
!
interface Serial0/1
 description *** Connection to Atlanta POP ***
 ip address 204.134.83.6 255.255.255.252
 tag-switching ip
!
interface Serial0/2
 no ip address
```

```
 shutdown
!
interface Serial0/3
 no ip address
 shutdown
!
interface Ethernet1/0
 no ip address
 shutdown
!
interface Ethernet1/1
 no ip address
 shutdown
!
interface Ethernet1/2
 no ip address
 shutdown
!
interface Ethernet1/3
 no ip address
 shutdown
!
router rip
 version 2
 network 204.134.83.0
!
ip classless
no ip http server
!
!
!
line con 0
 exec-timeout 0 0
 privilege level 15
 logging synchronous
 transport input none
```

```
 ip netmask-format decimal
line aux 0
line vty 0 4
 privilege level 15
 password cisco
 logging synchronous
 login
 ip netmask-format decimal
!
end
```

Raleigh Router Configuration

The configuration of the Raleigh POP router is as follows:

```
Raleigh#show running-config
Building configuration...

Current configuration : 1531 bytes
!
version 12.1
service timestamps debug uptime
service timestamps log uptime
no service password-encryption
!
hostname Raleigh
!
enable password cisco
!
!
!
!
!
memory-size iomem 25
ip subnet-zero
ip tcp synwait-time 5
no ip domain-lookup
!
```

```
ip cef
cns event-service server
!
!
!
!
!
interface Loopback0
 ip address 204.134.83.3 255.255.255.255
!
interface Serial0/0
 no ip address
 shutdown
 no fair-queue
 clockrate 64000
!
interface Serial0/1
 description *** Link to Peer2 ***
 ip address 192.168.3.9 255.255.255.252
 clockrate 64000
!
interface Serial0/2
 no ip address
 shutdown
 clockrate 64000
!
interface Serial0/3
 description *** Link to Core Router ***
 ip address 204.134.83.10 255.255.255.252
 tag-switching ip
 clockrate 64000
!
interface Ethernet1/0

 no ip address
 shutdown
!
```

```
interface Ethernet1/1
 no ip address
 shutdown
!
interface Ethernet1/2
 no ip address
 shutdown
!
interface Ethernet1/3
 no ip address
 shutdown
!
router rip
 version 2
 network 204.134.83.0
!
router bgp 65000
 no synchronization
 bgp log-neighbor-changes
 neighbor 192.168.3.10 remote-as 65002
 neighbor 204.134.83.1 remote-as 65000
 neighbor 204.134.83.1 update-source Loopback0
 neighbor 204.134.83.1 next-hop-self
 no auto-summary
!
ip classless
no ip http server
!
!
!
line con 0
 exec-timeout 0 0
 privilege level 15
 logging synchronous
 transport input none
 ip netmask-format decimal
line aux 0
```

```
line vty 0 4
 privilege level 15
 password cisco
 logging synchronous
 login
 ip netmask-format decimal
!
end
```

Peer 1 Router Configuration

The configuration of the Peer 1 router is as follows:

```
Peer1#show running-config
Building configuration...

Current configuration : 914 bytes
!
version 12.1
service timestamps debug uptime
service timestamps log uptime
no service password-encryption
!
hostname Peer1
!
enable password cisco
!
!
!
!
!
ip subnet-zero
ip tcp synwait-time 5
no ip domain-lookup
!
!
!
!
```

```
interface Loopback0
 ip address 192.168.1.1 255.255.255.255
!
interface Ethernet0
 no ip address
 shutdown
!
interface Serial0
 description *** Link to Atlanta POP ***
 ip address 192.168.3.5 255.255.255.252
 no fair-queue
!
interface Serial1
 no ip address
 shutdown
!
router bgp 65001
 no synchronization
 bgp log-neighbor-changes
 redistribute connected
 neighbor 192.168.3.6 remote-as 65000
 no auto-summary
!
ip classless
no ip http server
!
!
line con 0
 exec-timeout 0 0
 privilege level 15
 logging synchronous
 transport input none
 ip netmask-format decimal
line aux 0
line vty 0 4
 privilege level 15
```

```
 password cisco
 logging synchronous
 login
 ip netmask-format decimal
!
end
```

Peer 2 Router Configuration

The configuration of the Peer 2 router is as follows:

```
Peer2#show running-config
Building configuration...

Current configuration : 951 bytes
!
version 12.1
service timestamps debug uptime
service timestamps log uptime
no service password-encryption
!
hostname Peer2
!
enable password cisco
!
!
!
!
!
ip subnet-zero
ip tcp synwait-time 5
no ip domain-lookup
!
!
!
!
interface Loopback0
 ip address 192.168.2.1 255.255.255.255
!
```

```
interface Ethernet0
 no ip address
 shutdown
!
interface Serial0
 description *** Link to Raleigh POP ***
 ip address 192 168.3.10 255.255.255.252
 no fair-queue
!
interface Serial1
 no ip address
 shutdown
!
router bgp 65002
 no synchronization
 bgp log-neighbor-changes
 redistribute connected
 neighbor 192.168.3.9 remote-as 65000
 no auto-summary
!
ip classless
no ip http server
!
!
line con 0
 exec-timeout 0 0
 privilege level 15
 logging synchronous
 transport input none
 ip netmask-format decimal
line aux 0
line vty 0 4
 privilege level 15
 password cisco
 logging synchronous
```

```
 login
 ip netmask-format decimal
!
end
```

MPLS, as you have seen so far, is quite straightforward to configure. MPLS and tag switching need to be enabled both globally and on a per-interface basis. An IGP needs to be running in the core of the network, and BGP needs to be configured between the PE routers.

However, there are many minor problems that can crop up even though MPLS and tag switching are straightforward to configure. The next few sections explain how to deal with and prevent these problems.

IGP Verification

First of all, tag switching or MPLS will not work if an IGP is not configured properly in the service provider core network. In the troubleshooting example, Routing Information Protocol (RIP) version 2 was used as a core IGP. To ensure that RIP is running, use the `show ip route` command with the `rip` option to view only RIP routes on the Atlanta POP, Core, and Raleigh POP routers.

The output of the `show ip route rip` command follows, as executed on the Atlanta POP router:

```
Atlanta#show ip route rip
     204.134.83.0 255.255.255.0 is variably subnetted,
  5 subnets, 2 masks
R       204.134.83.8 255.255.255.252
           [120/1] via 204.134.83.6, 00:00:28, Serial0/0
R       204.134.83.3 255.255.255.255
           [120/2] via 204.134.83.6, 00:00:28, Serial0/0
R       204.134.83.2 255.255.255.255
           [120/1] via 204.134.83.6, 00:00:28, Serial0/0
```

The output of the `show ip route rip` command follows, as executed on the Core router:

```
Core#show ip route rip
     204.134.83.0 255.255.255.0 is variably subnetted,
  5 subnets, 2 masks
```

```
R       204.134.83.1 255.255.255.255
           [120/1] via 204.134.83.5, 00:00:21, Serial0/1
R       204.134.83.3 255.255.255.255
           [120/1] via 204.134.83.10, 00:00:03, Serial0/0
```

The output of the `show ip route rip` command follows, as executed on the Raleigh POP router:

```
Raleigh#show ip route rip
     204.134.83.0 255.255.255.0 is variably subnetted,
  5 subnets, 2 masks
R       204.134.83.1 255.255.255.255
           [120/2] via 204.134.83.9, 00:00:09, Serial0/3
R       204.134.83.2 255.255.255.255
           [120/1] via 204.134.83.9, 00:00:09, Serial0/3
R       204.134.83.4 255.255.255.252
           [120/1] via 204.134.83.9, 00:00:09, Serial0/3
```

An additional step you might want to take in general troubleshooting or verification is to ping each and every network device in the service provider network. By executing the `ping` command, you are only verifying standard connectivity. If anything is misconfigured here, MPLS or tag switching will not function correctly.

CEF Verification

To ensure that CEF is running, there are two options. Personally, I usually use the `show running-configuration` command and look for `ip cef`. An alternative way to verify that CEF is running is to use the `show ip cef` command. If CEF is not enabled on a device that it should be enabled on, you'll need to go back to global configuration and execute the `ip cef` command.

In the network in Figure 2.7, CEF is not enabled on Peer 1 and Peer 2, but it is enabled on the Atlanta POP, Core, and Raleigh POP routers. To verify this, the command `show ip cef` will be executed on each network device.

The following output shows that CEF is not enabled on Peer 1. (In this output, the Next Hop column contains the router ID of a neighboring device from which the prefix was received.)

```
Peer1#show ip cef
%CEF not running
Prefix              Next Hop              Interface
```

On the Atlanta POP router, you can verify that CEF is up and running, as shown in the following output:

```
Atlanta#show ip cef
Prefix              Next Hop             Interface
0.0.0.0/32          receive
192.168.1.1/32      192.168.3.5          Serial0/1
192.168.2.1/32      204.134.83.6         Serial0/0
192.168.3.4/30      attached             Serial0/1
192.168.3.4/32      receive
192.168.3.6/32      receive
192.168.3.7/32      receive
192.168.3.8/30      204.134.83.6         Serial0/0
204.134.83.1/32     receive
204.134.83.2/32     204.134.83.6         Serial0/0
204.134.83.3/32     204.134.83.6         Serial0/0
204.134.83.4/30     attached             Serial0/0
204.134.83.4/32     receive
204.134.83.5/32     receive
204.134.83.7/32     receive
204.134.83.8/30     204.134.83.6         Serial0/0
224.0.0.0/4         drop
224.0.0.0/24        receive
255.255.255.255/32  receive
```

On the Core router, you can verify that CEF is up and running, as shown in the following output:

```
Core#show ip cef
Prefix              Next Hop             Interface
0.0.0.0/32          receive
204.134.83.1/32     204.134.83.5         Serial0/1
204.134.83.2/32     receive
204.134.83.3/32     204.134.83.10        Serial0/0
204.134.83.4/30     attached             Serial0/1
204.134.83.4/32     receive
204.134.83.6/32     receive
204.134.83.7/32     receive
204.134.83.8/30     attached             Serial0/0
204.134.83.8/32     receive
```

```
204.134.83.9/32      receive
204.134.83.11/32     receive
224.0.0.0/4          drop
224.0.0.0/24         receive
255.255.255.255/32   receive
```

On the Raleigh POP router, you can verify that CEF is up and running, as shown in the following output:

```
Raleigh#show ip cef
Prefix               Next Hop             Interface
0.0.0.0/32           receive
192.168.1.1/32       204.134.83.9         Serial0/3
192.168.2.1/32       192.168.3.10         Serial0/1
192.168.3.4/30       204.134.83.9         Serial0/3
192.168.3.8/30       attached             Serial0/1
192.168.3.8/32       receive
192.168.3.9/32       receive
192.168.3.11/32      receive
204.134.83.1/32      204.134.83.9         Serial0/3
204.134.83.2/32      204.134.83.9         Serial0/3
204.134.83.3/32      receive
204.134.83.4/30      204.134.83.9         Serial0/3
204.134.83.8/30      attached             Serial0/3
204.134.83.8/32      receive
204.134.83.10/32     receive
204.134.83.11/32     receive
224.0.0.0/4          drop
224.0.0.0/24         receive
255.255.255.255/32   receive
```

On Peer 2, you can verify that CEF is not configured, as shown in the following output:

```
Peer2#show ip cef
%CEF not running
Prefix               Next Hop             Interface
```

MPLS Verification

To verify that MPLS is enabled, you can either execute a `show running-configuration` command or use the `show mpls interfaces` command. If tag switching is being used in the service provider network, the command `show tag-switching interfaces` should be used. The output of the two commands is virtually identical in Cisco IOS. If MPLS or tag switching is not configured for an interface, you'll need to add it. If MPLS or tag switching is configured on an interface that it does not need to be configured on, use the `no` form of the MPLS or tag switching command to disable it.

In the network in Figure 2.7 that we're using as a troubleshooting example, the Atlanta POP, Core, and Raleigh POP routers have been configured with tag switching.

On the Atlanta POP router, only the Serial 0/0 interface has tag switching enabled. To verify this, execute the `show tag-switching interfaces` command on the Atlanta POP router as follows:

```
Atlanta#show tag-switching interfaces
Interface              IP     Tunnel    Operational
Serial0/0              Yes    No        Yes
```

On the Core router, the Serial 0/0 and Serial 0/1 interfaces have tag switching enabled. To verify this, execute the `show tag-switching interfaces` command on the Core router as follows:

```
Core#show tag-switching interfaces
Interface              IP     Tunnel    Operational
Serial0/0              Yes    No        Yes
Serial0/1              Yes    No        Yes
```

On the Raleigh POP router, only the Serial 0/3 interface has tag switching enabled. To verify this, execute the `show tag-switching interfaces` command on the Raleigh POP router as follows:

```
Raleigh#show tag-switching interfaces
Interface              IP     Tunnel    Operational
Serial0/3              Yes    No        Yes
```

Label Distribution and Bindings

The IOS command you use to verify that labels are being exchanged between neighbors depends on whether you are using MPLS or tag switching. To verify that MPLS labels are being exchanged, use the `show mpls ldp discovery` command. If tag switching is being used in the service provider network, the command `show tag-switching tdp discovery` should be used. In the network in the troubleshooting example, tag switching is being used.

The output of the show tag-switching tdp discovery command as executed on the Atlanta POP router is as follows:

```
Atlanta#show tag-switching tdp discovery
Local TDP Identifier:
    204.134.83.1:0
TDP Discovery Sources:
    Interfaces:
        Serial0/0: xmit/recv
            TDP Id: 204.134.83.2:0
```

NOTE There are many similarities in output between the MPLS and tag switching versions of commands executed on a Cisco IOS router. For example, if the show mpls ldp discovery command is used, the output displays LDP.

The output of the show tag-switching tdp discovery command as executed on the Core router is as follows:

```
Core#show tag-switching tdp discovery
Local TDP Identifier:
    204.134.83.2:0
TDP Discovery Sources:
    Interfaces:
        Serial0/0: xmit/recv
            TDP Id: 204.134.83.3:0
        Serial0/1: xmit/recv
            TDP Id: 204.134.83.1:0
```

The output of the show tag-switching tdp discovery command as executed on the Raleigh POP router is as follows:

```
Raleigh#show tag-switching tdp discovery
Local TDP Identifier:
    204.134.83.3:0
TDP Discovery Sources:
    Interfaces:
        Serial0/3: xmit/recv
            TDP Id: 204.134.83.2:0
```

If you don't see a neighbor, and you are certain that either tag switching or MPLS has been enabled, you'll need to verify the neighbor with the `ping` command. If you can't ping the missing neighbor, you need to do basic troubleshooting such as verifying that the interface is properly attached, is up, or has the proper encapsulation to fix the connectivity problem.

Binding Verification

If you want more information on all the label bindings in the network, there are many IOS commands you can use. You have already learned about the `show mpls forwarding-table` and `show tag-switching forwarding-table` commands. If you really want to get the nitty-gritty on labels (or tags), use the `show mpls ldp bindings` or `show tag-switching tdp bindings` command.

The output of the `show tag-switching tdp bindings` command as executed on the Atlanta POP router is as follows:

```
Atlanta#show tag-switching tdp bindings
  tib entry: 192.168.3.4 255.255.255.252, rev 16
       local binding:  tag: imp-null
  tib entry: 204.134.83.1 255.255.255.255, rev 4
       local binding:  tag: imp-null
       remote binding: tsr: 204.134.83.2:0, tag: 26
  tib entry: 204.134.83.2 255.255.255.255, rev 8
       local binding:  tag: 28
       remote binding: tsr: 204.134.83.2:0, tag: imp-null
  tib entry: 204.134.83.3 255.255.255.255, rev 6
       local binding:  tag: 27
       remote binding: tsr: 204.134.83.2:0, tag: 27
  tib entry: 204.134.83.4 255.255.255.252, rev 10
       local binding:  tag: imp-null
       remote binding: tsr: 204.134.83.2:0, tag: imp-null
  tib entry: 204.134.83.8 255.255.255.252, rev 2
       local binding:  tag: 26
       remote binding: tsr: 204.134.83.2:0, tag: imp-null
```

The output of the `show tag-switching tdp bindings` command as executed on the Core router is as follows:

```
Core#show tag-switching tdp bindings
  tib entry: 192.168.3.4 255.255.255.252, rev 15
       remote binding: tsr: 204.134.83.1:0, tag: imp-null
```

```
tib entry: 192.168.3.8 255.255.255.252, rev 16
     remote binding: tsr: 204.134.83.3:0, tag: imp-null
tib entry: 204.134.83.1 255.255.255.255, rev 4
     local binding:  tag: 26
     remote binding: tsr: 204.134.83.3:0, tag: 26
     remote binding: tsr: 204.134.83.1:0, tag: imp-null
tib entry: 204.134.83.2 255.255.255.255, rev 8
     local binding:  tag: imp-null
     remote binding: tsr: 204.134.83.3:0, tag: 27
     remote binding: tsr: 204.134.83.1:0, tag: 28
tib entry: 204.134.83.3 255.255.255.255, rev 6
     local binding:  tag: 27
     remote binding: tsr: 204.134.83.3:0, tag: imp-null
     remote binding: tsr: 204.134.83.1:0, tag: 27
tib entry: 204.134.83.4 255.255.255.252, rev 10
     local binding:  tag: imp-null
     remote binding: tsr: 204.134.83.3:0, tag: 28
     remote binding: tsr: 204.134.83.1:0, tag: imp-null
tib entry: 204.134.83.8 255.255.255.252, rev 2
     local binding:  tag: imp-null
     remote binding: tsr: 204.134.83.3:0, tag: imp-null
     remote binding: tsr: 204.134.83.1:0, tag: 26
```

The output of the `show tag-switching tdp bindings` command as executed on the Raleigh POP router is as follows:

```
Raleigh#show tag-switching tdp bindings
  tib entry: 192.168.3.8 255.255.255.252, rev 16
       local binding:  tag: imp-null
  tib entry: 204.134.83.1 255.255.255.255, rev 4
       local binding:  tag: 26
       remote binding: tsr: 204.134.83.2:0, tag: 26
  tib entry: 204.134.83.2 255.255.255.255, rev 8
       local binding:  tag: 27
       remote binding: tsr: 204.134.83.2:0, tag: imp-null
  tib entry: 204.134.83.3 255.255.255.255, rev 6
       local binding:  tag: imp-null
       remote binding: tsr: 204.134.83.2:0, tag: 27
```

```
tib entry: 204.134.83.4 255.255.255.252, rev 10
     local binding:  tag: 28
     remote binding: tsr: 204.134.83.2:0, tag: imp-null
tib entry: 204.134.83.8 255.255.255.252, rev 2
     local binding:  tag: imp-null
     remote binding: tsr: 204.134.83.2:0, tag: imp-null
```

Troubleshooting the Network

The easiest way to troubleshoot an MPLS or tag switching network is to do a ping across the service provider network. Let's do a ping from Peer 1 to the loopback address (192.168.2.1) of Peer 2. Here are the results:

```
Peer1#ping 192.168.2.1

Type escape sequence to abort.
Sending 5, 100-byte ICMP Echos to 192.168.2.1, timeout
  is 2 seconds:
!!!!!
Success rate is 100 percent (5/5), round-trip min/avg/max
   = 116/118/120 ms
```

Everything works, right? Right! What if you do the ping from the Atlanta POP router? The answer is as follows, with a ping as executed on the Atlanta POP router:

```
Atlanta#ping 192.168.2.1

Type escape sequence to abort.
Sending 5, 100-byte ICMP Echos to 192.168.2.1, timeout
  is 2 seconds:
.....
Success rate is 0 percent (0/5)
```

As you can see from the ping output from the Atlanta POP to the loopback of Peer 2, the `ping` command does not work. You might be asking yourself, "Why doesn't this command work?" The answer has to do with routing protocols and what routes are known by each network device.

To start with, let's look at Peer 1's routing table:

```
Peer1#show ip route
.
. output omitted
.
Gateway of last resort is not set

     192.168.1.0 255.255.255.255 is subnetted, 1 subnets
C       192.168.1.1 is directly connected, Loopback0
     192.168.2.0 255.255.255.255 is subnetted, 1 subnets
B       192.168.2.1 [20/0] via 192.168.3.6, 00:37:21
     192.168.3.0 255.255.255.252 is subnetted, 2 subnets
B       192.168.3.8 [20/0] via 192.168.3.6, 00:37:21
C       192.168.3.4 is directly connected, Serial0
```

When a ping is done from Peer 1 to the loopback of Peer 2 (192.168.2.1), is there a route to get to the destination network? Yes. There's a BGP route with a next hop address of 192.168.3.6.

The packet is sent to 192.168.3.6, which is the Atlanta POP router. The Atlanta POP router's routing table is as follows:

```
Atlanta#show ip route
.
. output omitted
.
Gateway of last resort is not set

     204.134.83.0 255.255.255.0 is variably subnetted,
  5 subnets, 2 masks
R       204.134.83.8 255.255.255.252
           [120/1] via 204.134.83.6, 00:00:05, Serial0/0
C       204.134.83.1 255.255.255.255 is directly
  connected, Loopback0
R       204.134.83.3 255.255.255.255
           [120/2] via 204.134.83.6, 00:00:05, Serial0/0
R       204.134.83.2 255.255.255.255
           [120/1] via 204.134.83.6, 00:00:05, Serial0/0
```

```
C        204.134.83.4 255.255.255.252 is directly
  connected, Serial0/0
     192.168.1.0 255.255.255.255 is subnetted, 1 subnets
B       192.168.1.1 [20/0] via 192.168.3.5, 14:12:49
     192.168.2.0 255.255.255.255 is subnetted, 1 subnets
B       192.168.2.1 [200/0] via 204.134.83.3, 00:41:22
     192.168.3.0 255.255.255.252 is subnetted, 2 subnets
B       192.168.3.8 [200/0] via 204.134.83.3, 00:41:23
C       192.168.3.4 is directly connected, Serial0/1
```

The packet destined from Peer 1 to Peer 2 arrives at the Atlanta POP router. Does the Atlanta POP router have a path to get to the loopback of Peer 2 (192.168.2.1)? Yes. There's a BGP route to 192.168.2.1 with a next hop address of 204.134.83.3 (Raleigh). How does the Atlanta POP router get the packet to the Raleigh POP router? It sends it as a labeled, or in this case, a tagged packet, as you can see in the following output:

```
Atlanta#show tag-switching forwarding-table
Local Outgoing  Prefix                       Bytes tag Outgoing  Next Hop
tag   tag or VC or Tunnel Id                 switched  interface
26    Pop tag   204.134.83.8 255.255.255.252 0         Se0/0     point2point
27    27        204.134.83.3 255.255.255.255 0         Se0/0     point2point
28    Pop tag   204.134.83.2 255.255.255.255 0         Se0/0     point2point
```

By observing the output of the `show tag-switching forwarding-table` command on the Atlanta POP, you can see that the packet is sent as a labeled, or in this case, a tagged packet. What is the outbound label? 27. What is the outbound interface? Serial 0/0. What is the neighboring device connected via Serial 0/0 (look back at Figure 2.7)? The Core router.

Let's look at the Core router's routing table:

```
Core#show ip route
.
. output omitted
.
Gateway of last resort is not set

     204.134.83.0 255.255.255.0 is variably subnetted,
  5 subnets, 2 masks
```

```
C       204.134.83.8 255.255.255.252 is directly
  connected, Serial0/0
R       204.134.83.1 255.255.255.255
            [120/1] via 204.134.83.5, 00:00:18, Serial0/1
R       204.134.83.3 255.255.255.255
            [120/1] via 204.134.83.10, 00:00:01, Serial0/0
C       204.134.83.2 255.255.255.255 is directly
  connected, Loopback0
C       204.134.83.4 255.255.255.252 is directly
  connected, Serial0/1
```

Does the Core router have a route in its routing table to forward a packet to Peer 2 (192.168.2.1)? No. Without MPLS, or tag switching, the packet would be dropped right here. The Core router only knows about the IGP (RIP in this example) routes. The Core router does not forward the packet, but instead it does tag switching. The output of the `show tag-switching forwarding-table` command as executed on the Core router is as follows:

```
Core#show tag-switching forwarding-table
Local Outgoing Prefix                       Bytes tag Outgoing  Next Hop
tag   tag or VC or Tunnel Id                switched  interface
26    Pop tag  204.134.83.1 255.255.255.255 179542    Se0/1     point2point
27    Pop tag  204.134.83.3 255.255.255.255 139085    Se0/0     point2point
```

What happens to the packet? Well, from the Atlanta POP router, the packet is sent with a tag of 27. By observing the output of the `show tag-switching forwarding-table` command on the Core router, you can see that an inbound tagged packet of 27 arriving at the Core router has its tag popped and is forwarded as untagged IP out interface Serial 0/0. So here at the Core router, there is no routing, only switching of labeled, or in this case, tagged packets.

Now let's move on to the Raleigh POP router. An unlabeled IP packet arrives destined for network 192.168.2.1. The Raleigh POP router's routing table is as follows:

```
Raleigh#show ip route
.
. output omitted
.
```

```
Gateway of last resort is not set

     204.134.83.0 255.255.255.0 is variably subnetted,
  5 subnets, 2 masks
C       204.134.83.8 255.255.255.252 is directly
  connected, Serial0/3
R       204.134.83.1 255.255.255.255
           [120/2] via 204.134.83.9, 00:00:10, Serial0/3
C       204.134.83.3 255.255.255.255 is directly
  connected, Loopback0
R       204.134.83.2 255.255.255.255
           [120/1] via 204.134.83.9, 00:00:10, Serial0/3
R       204.134.83.4 255.255.255.252
           [120/1] via 204.134.83.9, 00:00:10, Serial0/3
     192.168.1.0 255.255.255.255 is subnetted, 1 subnets
B       192.168.1.1 [200/0] via 204.134.83.1, 01:03:10
     192.168.2.0 255.255.255.255 is subnetted, 1 subnets
B       192.168.2.1 [20/0] via 192.168.3.10, 01:03:01
     192.168.3.0 255.255.255.252 is subnetted, 2 subnets
C       192.168.3.8 is directly connected, Serial0/1
B       192.168.3.4 [200/0] via 204.134.83.1, 01:03:12
```

Does the Raleigh POP router have a path to get to the loopback (192.168.2.1) of Peer 1? Yes, there's a BGP route to 192.168.2.1. What is the outbound interface? Serial 0/1.

The packet arrives on Peer 2. Peer 2 needs to send a response to the ping. The routing table of Peer 2 is as follows:

```
Peer2#show ip route
.
. output omitted
.
Gateway of last resort is not set

     192.168.1.0 255.255.255.255 is subnetted, 1 subnets
B       192.168.1.1 [20/0] via 192.168.3.9, 01:06:37
     192.168.2.0 255.255.255.255 is subnetted, 1 subnets
C       192.168.2.1 is directly connected, Loopback0
```

```
     192.168.3.0 255.255.255.252 is subnetted, 2 subnets
C       192.168.3.8 is directly connected, Serial0
B       192.168.3.4 [20/0] via 192.168.3.9, 01:06:37
```

Does the Peer 2 router have a path to get back to Peer 1? Yes. The entire process you just observed will now be repeated in reverse.

What if you are on the Atlanta POP router and you try a ping to Peer 2 (192.168.2.1)? It fails, as you can see in the following output:

```
Atlanta#ping 192.168.2.1

Type escape sequence to abort.
Sending 5, 100-byte ICMP Echos to 192.168.2.1,
  timeout is 2 seconds:
.....
Success rate is 0 percent (0/5)
```

Why does this ping fail? Because the source address (204.134.83.5) is unknown to Peer 2. Observe the `traceroute` command as executed on the Atlanta POP router:

```
Atlanta#traceroute 192.168.2.1

Type escape sequence to abort.
Tracing the route to 192.168.2.1

  1 204.134.83.6 32 msec 32 msec 32 msec
  2 204.134.83.10 32 msec 28 msec 28 msec
  3  *  *  *
  4  *  *  *
```

How far does the `traceroute` command get? Only to the Raleigh POP router. Peer 2 has no way to respond to the source.

Let's illustrate by changing how the `ping` command is used. This time I'm going to source the ping from an interface that Peer 2 knows about:

```
Atlanta#ping
Protocol [ip]:
Target IP address: 192.168.2.1
Repeat count [5]:
Datagram size [100]:
Timeout in seconds [2]:
```

```
Extended commands [n]: y
Source address or interface: 192.168.3.6
Type of service [0]:
Set DF bit in IP header? [no]:
Validate reply data? [no]:
Data pattern [0xABCD]:
Loose, Strict, Record, Timestamp, Verbose[none]:
Sweep range of sizes [n]:
Type escape sequence to abort.
Sending 5, 100-byte ICMP Echos to 192.168.2.1, timeout
  is 2 seconds:
!!!!!
Success rate is 100 percent (5/5), round-trip min/avg/max
  = 88/88/88 ms
```

Peer 2 knows about the 192.168.3.4 network. Take a look at Peer 2's routing table:

```
Peer2#show ip route
.
. output omitted
.
Gateway of last resort is not set

     192.168.1.0 255.255.255.255 is subnetted, 1 subnets
B       192.168.1.1 [20/0] via 192.168.3.9, 01:06:37
     192.168.2.0 255.255.255.255 is subnetted, 1 subnets
C       192.168.2.1 is directly connected, Loopback0
     192.168.3.0 255.255.255.252 is subnetted, 2 subnets
C       192.168.3.8 is directly connected, Serial0
B       192.168.3.4 [20/0] via 192.168.3.9, 01:06:37
```

Confused yet? The best way to test to make sure that everything works is to do a ping from one CE device to another CE device. If it works, then MPLS or tag switching is enabled and working properly. If the ping fails, you don't have a complete LSP through the service provider network.

Let me show you what a failure looks like. I've disabled tag switching on the Core router, which means that there isn't a complete LSP between the Atlanta and Raleigh POP routers.

Let's ping from Peer 1 to the loopback (192.168.2.1) of Peer 2. The `ping` command as executed on Peer 1 is as follows:

```
Peer1#ping 192.168.2.1

Type escape sequence to abort.
Sending 5, 100-byte ICMP Echos to 192.168.2.1, timeout
  is 2 seconds:
.....
Success rate is 0 percent (0/5)
```

It fails, right? Right! There is no LSP between the Atlanta and Raleigh POP routers. Notice the following output from the `traceroute` command:

```
Peer1#traceroute 192.168.2.1

Type escape sequence to abort.
Tracing the route to 192.168.2.1

  1 192.168.3.6 16 msec 16 msec 16 msec
  2  *   *   *
```

How far does the packet get? Only to the Atlanta POP router. Let's enable tag switching on the Core router and try the `ping` command again from Peer 1 to the loopback (192.168.2.1) of Peer 2. The output of the `ping` command is as follows:

```
Peer1#ping 192.168.2.1

Type escape sequence to abort.
Sending 5, 100-byte ICMP Echos to 192.168.2.1, timeout
  is 2 seconds:
!!!!!
Success rate is 100 percent (5/5), round-trip min/avg/max
  = 116/117/120 ms
```

Now that tag switching has been enabled again on the Core router, everything works because there is an end-to-end LSP between the Atlanta and Raleigh POP routers. In the following output from the `traceroute` command, the packet makes it all the way through the service provider network:

```
Peer1#traceroute 192.168.2.1
```

```
Type escape sequence to abort.
Tracing the route to 192.168.2.1

  1 192.168.3.6 16 msec 16 msec 16 msec
  2 204.134.83.6 48 msec 48 msec 48 msec
  3 204.134.83.10 44 msec 44 msec 44 msec
  4 192.168.3.10 [AS 65002] 60 msec *  60 msec
```

Hiding Service Provider Devices

In the previous section, I executed a `traceroute` command where all the service provider devices showed up in the `traceroute` output. To hide service provider devices, you need to execute the `no tag-switching ip propagate-ttl` on every device in the service provider network. Once this command is enabled on each and every service provider router, a client only sees the ingress and egress PE routers, not all the P devices. The required configuration for the troubleshooting network is as follows:

```
Core#conf t
Enter configuration commands, one per line. End with CNTL/Z.
Core(config)#no tag-switching ip propagate-ttl

Raleigh#conf t
Enter configuration commands, one per line. End with CNTL/Z.
Raleigh(config)#no tag-switching ip propagate-ttl

Atlanta#conf t
Enter configuration commands, one per line. End with CNTL/Z.
Atlanta(config)#no tag-switching ip propagate-ttl
```

NOTE: The MPLS version of this command is `no mpls ip propagate-ttl`.

The output of the `traceroute` command on Peer 1 to the loopback of Peer 2 is as follows:

```
Peer1#traceroute 192.168.2.1
```

```
Type escape sequence to abort.
Tracing the route to 192.168.2.1

  1 192.168.3.6 16 msec 16 msec 16 msec
  2 204.134.83.10 44 msec 44 msec 44 msec
  3 192.168.3.10 [AS 65002] 60 msec *  60 msec
```

What's missing from the `traceroute` output without the `no tag-switching propagate-ttl` command? The Core router. To return the network to its original configuration, you need to use the `tag-switching propagate-ttl` command.

Summary

To keep packets from being dropped, a traditional router needs to know about all the destination networks or have a default route. If a packet arrives for a destination network that the router doesn't know how to reach, the packet will be dropped. Not every router in an MPLS network needs full knowledge of every destination network. Typically, PE routers are running BGP and an IGP. P routers only run an IGP, thus freeing up resources on the P routers.

Customer devices do not need MPLS functionality, and packets are sent to a PE router as unlabeled IP. The PE router performs a label imposition and sends the newly labeled packet along its way. Each LSR in the LSP does not examine the Layer 3 portion of the packet, only the label. Actually, if the LSR examines the packet, the packet is dropped if the LSR does not have a corresponding route to the destination network. Before the labeled packet leaves the network, the next-to-last LSR in the path pops the label through a process called penultimate hop popping. The egress PE forwards the packet based on the Layer 3 header.

Frame-mode MPLS is called independent control with unsolicited downstream. Using this technique, LSPs are set up quickly. As soon as an IP prefix appears, a label is bound to it immediately. Neighbors are told of the new binding without having to request it.

Troubleshooting an MPLS or tag switching network is pretty straightforward. The best way to test to make sure that everything works is to do a ping from one CE device to another CE device. If it works, then MPLS or tag switching is enabled and working properly. If the ping fails, it is likely that a core service provider router is not configured with MPLS or tag switching.

If you are sure that MPLS or tag switching is configured properly, you should perform basic troubleshooting such as verifying that the interface is properly attached, is up, or has the proper encapsulation to fix the connectivity problem.

Exam Essentials

Understand routing protocols in an MPLS network. With MPLS deployed in the core of the service provider network, it is not necessary to run BGP on every network device. In the core of the network, an IGP such as OSPF or IS-IS is used. On edge routers, an IGP and BGP is used.

Be able to identify packet flow in an MPLS network. Customer devices do not need MPLS functionality, and they send unlabeled IP packets to the PE router. The PE router, or edge-LSR, imposes a label and sends the packet to the next LSR in the LSP. Each LSR along the LSP does not examine the Layer 3 information of the packet. Packets are label-switched using the MPLS label. The next-to-last router in the LSP pops the label and forwards it as unlabeled IP. The LSR receiving the unlabeled IP packet does a Layer 3 lookup and forwards the packet to its ultimate destination.

Be able to configure tag switching. Tag switching uses TDP to exchange tags with neighboring TSRs using well-known TCP port 711. For tag switching to work, CEF must be enabled. Once CEF has been enabled, tag switching is globally configured. Once tag switching has been globally configured, each appropriate interface needs to be configured as well. The commands to configure tag switching on a router are as follows:

```
P1#config t
P1(config)#ip cef
P1(config)#tag-switching advertise-tags
P1(config-if)#interface serial 0/0
P1(config-if)#tag-switching ip
```

Be able to configure MPLS. Configuring MPLS is very similar to configuring tag switching. Instead of TDP, MPLS uses LDP to exchange labels with neighboring LSRs using well-known TCP port 646. Just like tag switching, MPLS requires that CEF be enabled globally. Once CEF has been enabled, MPLS is configured globally. Each appropriate interface also needs to be configured for MPLS as well. The commands to configure MPLS are as follows:

```
P1#config t
P1(config)#ip cef
P1(config)#mpls ip
P1(config-if)#interface serial 0/0
P1(config-if)#mpls ip
```

Understand frame-mode label distribution. Frame-mode MPLS label distribution is called independent control with unsolicited downstream. When a new FEC appears on an LSR, a label is immediately bound to it. This is called independent control. Once a new label is bound to the FEC, the LSR tells its neighbors about it without them having to ask. This is called unsolicited downstream.

Key Terms

Before you take the exam, be certain you are familiar with the following terms:

downstream

downstream-on-demand

edge-LSR

egress router

independent control

ingress router

label imposition

ordered control

popping

pushing

tag switching router (TSR)

unsolicited downstream

upstream

Review Questions

1. Which IOS command enables CEF in global configuration mode?
   A. `cef ip`
   B. `cef enable`
   C. `ip cef`
   D. `ip cef enable`

2. Which IOS command enables MPLS in global configuration mode?
   A. `ip mpls`
   B. `mpls ip`
   C. `mpls advertise labels`
   D. `tag-switching advertise labels`

3. Which IOS command enables MPLS on an interface?
   A. `ip mpls`
   B. `mpls ip`
   C. `mpls advertise labels`
   D. `tag-switching advertise labels`

4. Which IOS command enables tag switching globally on a router?
   A. `ip mpls`
   B. `mpls ip`
   C. `tag-switching advertise-tags`
   D. `tag-switching advertise labels`

5. Which IOS command enables tag switching on an interface?
   A. `ip mpls`
   B. `mpls ip`
   C. `ip tag-switching`
   D. `tag-switching ip`

6. Which IOS command do you use to verify TDP neighbors?
   A. `show tag-switching neighbor`
   B. `show tag-switching tdp neighbor`
   C. `show tag-switching tdp-neighbor`
   D. `tag-switching ip neighbor`
7. What IOS command do you use to verify LDP neighbors?
   A. `show mpls neighbor`
   B. `show mpls ldp neighbor`
   C. `show mpls ldp-neighbor`
   D. `mpls ip neighbor`
8. Which protocol does Cisco's tag switching use to exchange labels between neighbors?
   A. CDP
   B. LDP
   C. TDP
   D. MDP
9. Which protocol does MPLS use to exchange labels between neighbors?
   A. CDP
   B. LDP
   C. TDP
   D. MDP
10. Frame mode label distribution can be described as __________ with __________?
   A. Independent control; downstream-on-demand
   B. Independent control; unsolicited downstream
   C. Ordered control; downstream-on-demand
   D. Ordered control; unsolicited downstream

11. Which MPLS-enabled device uses ordered control?

   A. ATM-LSR

   B. Edge-LSR

   C. LSR

   D. LSP

12. Which TCP port does TDP use to exchange tags with a peer?

   A. 17

   B. 1017

   C. 117

   D. 711

13. Which TCP port does LDP use to exchange labels with a peer?

   A. 46

   B. 646

   C. 1046

   D. 466

14. Which device in the network typically imposes labels on packets?

   A. C

   B. CE

   C. P

   D. PE

15. Which device does not need MPLS functionality?

   A. CE

   B. PE

   C. P

   D. None of the above

16. Packets enter the network at the __________ and exit at the __________.

    A. Incoming router; exiting router

    B. Ingress router; exiting router

    C. Ingress router; egress router

17. When a labeled packet is received by an LSR, the LSR __________.

    A. Does a Layer 3 lookup

    B. Label-switches the packet

    C. None of the above

18. The LDP/TDP identifier is __________. (Choose the best answer.)

    A. The highest IP address of an active interface

    B. The lowest IP address of the configured loopback interfaces

    C. The lowest IP address of an active interface

    D. The highest IP address of the configured loopback interfaces

19. MPLS in an ATM environment uses __________ with __________.

    A. Independent control; downstream-on-demand

    B. Ordered control; downstream-on-demand

    C. Independent control; unsolicited downstream

    D. Ordered control; unsolicited downstream

20. TDP and LDP are __________.

    A. Compatible

    B. The same

    C. Incompatible

    D. None of the above

Answers to Review Questions

1. C. MPLS and tag switching will not work without CEF. The command to enable CEF in global configuration mode is `ip cef`.
2. B. The command to enable MPLS in global configuration mode is `mpls ip`.
3. B. The command to enable MPLS on an interface is `mpls ip`. The `mpls ip` command is not only used to configure MPLS globally; it's also used to configure MPLS on an interface.
4. C. To enable tag switching globally, use the `tag-switching advertise-tags` command.
5. D. To enable tag switching on an interface, use the `tag-switching ip` command.
6. B. To view TDP neighbors, use the `show tag-switching tdp neighbor` command.
7. B. To view LDP neighbors, use the `show mpls ldp neighbor` command.
8. C. Tag switching uses TDP to exchange labels between neighbors.
9. B. MPLS uses LDP to exchange labels between neighbors.
10. B. Frame-mode MPLS label distribution can be described as independent control with unsolicited downstream. Independent control means immediately bind a label to an FEC. Unsolicited downstream means to advertise the new binding without waiting for the neighbors to send a request.
11. A. ATM-LSRs wait on labels from a downstream LSR. This method is called ordered control.
12. D. TDP uses TCP port 711 to exchange tags with a peer after a neighbor has been discovered.
13. B. LDP uses TCP port 646 to exchange labels with a peer after a neighbor has been discovered.
14. D. Packets enter the network as unlabeled IP. The PE, or edge-LSR, imposes labels on packets.

15. A. Customer devices do not need MPLS functionality to connect to an MPLS-enabled service provider network.

16. C. Packets enter the network at an ingress router and exit the network at the egress router.

17. B. LSRs label-switch packets. If an unlabeled packet is received, the LSR performs a Layer 3 lookup on the packet.

18. D. The LDP/TDP identifier is first based on the highest IP address of the configured loopback interfaces. If there are no loopbacks, the highest IP address of the active interfaces is used.

19. D. MPLS in an ATM environment and cell-mode MPLS use ordered control with downstream-on-demand.

20. C. You can run both protocols on the same LSR, which is useful for migrations from a TDP to an LDP environment, but LDP and TDP are not compatible. For neighbors to exchange labels, the interface they communicate over must run the same protocol.

Chapter 3

MPLS and ATM

CCIP MPLS EXAM TOPICS COVERED IN THIS CHAPTER:

- ✓ Describe frame-mode MPLS and cell-mode MPLS.
- ✓ Describe the loop-detection and prevention mechanisms in MPLS.
- ✓ Identify the IOS commands and their proper syntax used to configure frame-mode MPLS on ATM PVC on IOS platforms.
- ✓ Identify the IOS commands and their proper syntax used to configure cell-mode MPLS on ATM interfaces on IOS platforms.
- ✓ Identify the IOS commands and their proper syntax used to monitor operations and troubleshoot typical cell-mode MPLS failures on IOS platforms.

In Chapter 2, "Frame-Mode MPLS," you learned how frame-mode MPLS operates and how it is configured in Cisco IOS routers. This chapter discusses frame-mode MPLS in an ATM network. In particular, you'll learn how frame-mode MPLS is implemented across non-MPLS-enabled routers and how to configure a PE router for frame-mode MPLS across an ATM link.

In this chapter, you'll also learn about cell-mode MPLS, what is required to turn non-MPLS ATM switches into ATM-LSRs, and how cell-mode devices forward labeled packets across the network.

This is the last chapter in the book that discusses generic MPLS operation. After this chapter, it'll be VPNs from here on out.

Frame-Mode MPLS and ATM

The biggest difference between frame-mode and cell-mode MPLS is in how the MPLS control plane in ATM works. The control plane of the MPLS architecture is responsible for binding a label to network routes and distributing those bindings among other MPLS-enabled routers. Remember the statement, "Labels are bound to routes in the routing table." In frame-mode MPLS, routers are directly connected across frame-mode interfaces such as PPP. Routers, with frame-mode MPLS enabled, use pure IP to exchange information such as label bindings and routing table updates.

NOTE One of the requirements for MPLS is that control-plane information be exchanged using pure unlabeled IP.

ATM switches don't have any direct interfaces to use for the exchange of IP-based control-plane communication, so a virtual circuit (VC) must be configured between LSRs.

Recall that Chapter 2 used the simple router-based service provider network illustrated in Figure 3.1.

FIGURE 3.1 A simple router-based service provider network

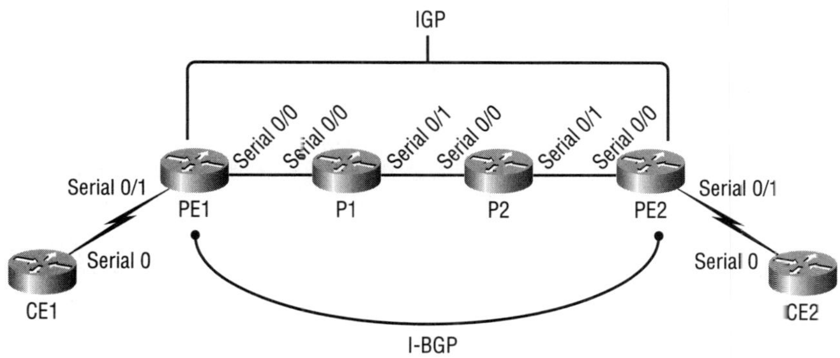

In Figure 3.1, all the network devices are connected together through frame-based interfaces. In the case of Figure 3.1, given that serial interfaces are shown, either Cisco's High-Level Data Link Control (HDLC) or Point-to-Point Protocol (PPP) encapsulation is supported. Either way, these are frame-mode interfaces. With frame-mode interfaces, routers exchange control-plane information such as label bindings and routing updates directly.

In Figure 3.2, the core routers (P1 and P2) have been replaced with non-MPLS ATM switches.

FIGURE 3.2 A simple service provider network with an ATM core

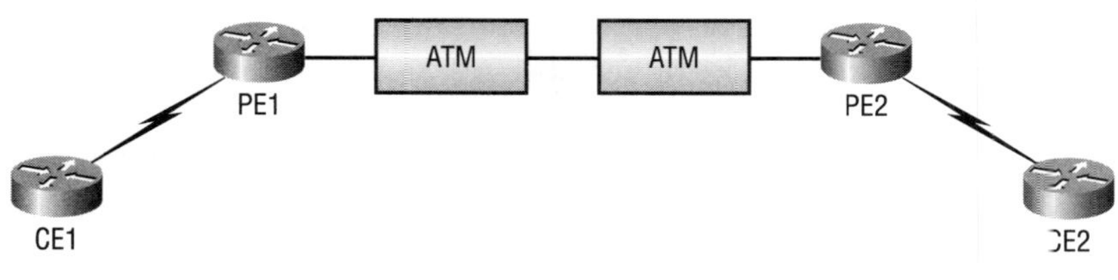

Remember that control-plane traffic must take place with unlabeled IP packets. How can MPLS be implemented in the network shown in Figure 3.2? With a permanent virtual circuit (PVC) between the edge-LSRs. In Figure 3.3, a PVC has been set up between PE1 and PE2.

FIGURE 3.3 Edge-LSRs connected with a PVC

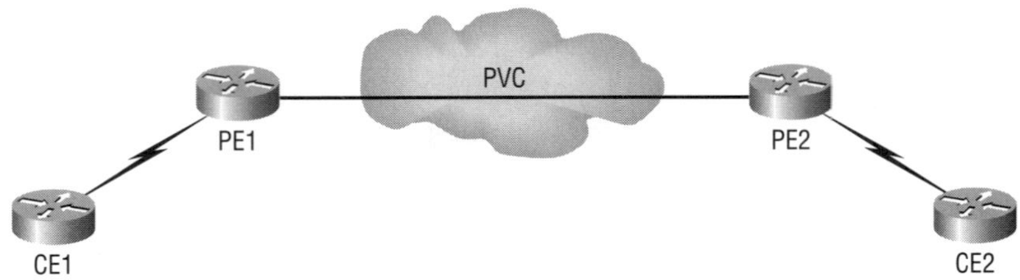

Let's talk about Figure 3.3 without adding MPLS to the network. Suppose a user on CE1 wants to send data to a user on CE2. When a packet arrives from CE1 on PE1, it is an unlabeled IP packet (no MPLS yet). PE1 examines the packet and makes a forwarding decision (no MPLS deployed yet). In Figure 3.3, to get a packet to CE2, it must be forwarded to PE2. The packet is placed in the PVC and traverses the ATM core until it arrives at PE2 (still no MPLS). PE2 examines the packet and forwards it to CE2.

Now that you've seen the network without MPLS, let's talk about the network with MPLS. To start with, PE1 and PE2 are MPLS-capable routers with ATM interfaces. PE1 and PE2 are edge-LSRs. In addition, PE1 and PE2 can be called *ATM edge-LSRs*.

Let me explain ATM edge-LSRs. A *label switch router (LSR)* is a Cisco IOS router/switch that is capable of forwarding packets based on labels. An *edge label switch router (edge-LSR)* is a more specific term for the PE routers that sit at the edge of the service provider network. An ATM edge-LSR is an edge-LSR with at least one ATM interface.

As you can see in Figure 3.3, the ATM network is shown as a cloud with a PVC connecting PE1 and PE2. The ATM switches use *virtual path identifier (VPI)* and *virtual channel identifier (VCI)* mappings to create the PVC. The ATM switches do not examine the packets they are transporting; they only switch them based on the VPI/VCI values.

The routers, being IP devices, simply place packets on the PVC, and the ATM network does the rest. PE1 and PE2, connected by a PVC, exchange MPLS control-plane information with pure IP packets.

So, with MPLS enabled, the network operates similarly to what you saw in Chapter 2. For example, suppose a user on CE1 wants to send data to a user on CE2. CE1 sends an unlabeled IP packet to PE1. PE1 receives the packet and forwards it to PE2. In the network in Figure 3.3, PE1 does not apply a label to the packet (remember penultimate hop popping). Instead, PE1 forwards the packet as unlabeled IP to PE2 as the next hop. If there was an MPLS-capable router in the path from PE1 to PE2, a label would be imposed.

So, what do you need to remember about frame-mode MPLS? Well, part of the MPLS architecture is that control-plane information must be exchanged with plain old IP. ATM does not have interfaces supporting plain old IP. To implement MPLS in conjunction with a non-MPLS ATM core, PVCs must be set up between PE routers.

The problem with this method of MPLS deployment is scalability. To allow for maximum redundancy and optimum routing, a full mesh of VCs must be created between all the ATM edge-LSRs, resulting an full-mesh overlay topology. If you remember back to Chapter 1, "An Introduction to MPLS," one of the reasons for going to MPLS was to avoid the scalability problems inherent in full-mesh overlay topologies.

However, if you don't have MPLS-capable switches, this is how it is done.

Before moving on to frame-mode MPLS and ATM configuration, let's talk about loop detection and prevention. Frame-mode MPLS uses standard IP TTL to detect routing loops. Without MPLS, an IP packet has its TTL decremented by 1 by each router it passes through. For MPLS, the TTL (Time-to-Live) field from the IP TTL is decremented by 1 by the ingress edge-LSR, and then copied into the MPLS label TTL field. Upon exiting the MPLS network, the MPLS label TTL value is copied back into the IP TTL field. If this field is set to 0, the packet is discarded.

To prevent loops, frame-mode MPLS relies on the routing protocol to ensure that the network is loop-free. By relying on the routing protocol to prevent loops, an LSR uses the same loop-prevention mechanisms as non-MPLS routers.

Frame-Mode MPLS and ATM Configuration

The trick in configuring frame-mode MPLS does not have anything to do with which MPLS or tag switching commands are used. The trick is how the ATM sub-interface on the ATM edge-LSR router is set up.

There are two options available when setting up ATM sub-interfaces: `mpls` and `point-to-point`. If a sub-interface is set up as `mpls`, when MPLS is enabled, it will run in cell mode. When a sub-interface is set up as `point-to-point`, when MPLS is enabled, it will run in frame mode.

Let me illustrate. Chapter 2 introduced you to basic MPLS configuration. For example, the IOS commands to configure MPLS on a router are as follows:

```
PE1#config t
PE1(config)#ip cef
PE1(config)#mpls ip
PE1(config-if)#interface serial 0/0
PE1(config-if)#mpls ip
```

The IOS commands to configure tag switching on a router are as follows:

```
PE1#config t
PE1(config)#ip cef
PE1(config)#tag-switching advertise-tags
PE1(config-if)#interface serial 0/0
PE1(config-if)#tag-switching ip
```

In the preceding configuration commands, frame-mode MPLS is enabled because the interface in question is a serial interface. Frame-mode MPLS means that label distribution will be independent control with unsolicited downstream.

So, what does all this have to do with ATM? Let me show you. Earlier in this section, I said that the trick is in how the ATM sub-interface on the ATM edge-LSR router is set up. When an ATM sub-interface is configured with the `point-to-point` option, MPLS operates in frame mode. For example, in Figure 3.4, PE1 and PE2 are connected with an ATM PVC. The ATM sub-interfaces on the PE routers are configured with the `point-to-point` command.

FIGURE 3.4 ATM frame-mode interface configuration network

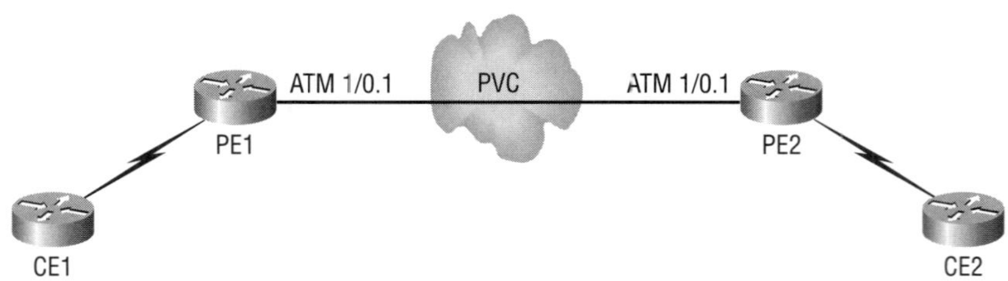

When MPLS is set up on a serial interface, it runs in frame mode. When MPLS is set up on a point-to-point ATM sub-interface, it runs in frame mode. The relevant configuration, assuming that the global configuration

tasks are complete, for MPLS on a router with an ATM interface is as follows:

```
interface ATM1/0
 no ip address
!
interface ATM1/0.1 point-to-point
 ip address 192.168.1.5 255.255.255.0
 pvc 0/100
 encapsulation aal5snap
 mpls ip
```

To verify your configuration, use the `show mpls ldp neighbor` command:

```
ATM_P1# show mpls ldp neighbor
Peer LDP Ident: 192.168.1.1:0; Local TDP Ident 192.168.1.2:0
      TCP connection: 192.168.1.1:11033 - 192.168.1.2.647
   State: Oper; PIEs sent/rcvd: 8/8; ; Downstream
   Up time: 00:02:15
   LDP discovery sources:
     ATM1/0.1
   Addresses bound to peer LDP Ident:
   192.168.1.10       192.168.1.1
```

The configuration to enable tag switching on a router with an ATM interface, assuming that tag switching is globally enabled, is as follows:

```
interface ATM1/0
 no ip address
!
interface ATM1/0.1 point-to-point
 ip address 192.168.1.5 255.255.255.0
 pvc 0/100
 encapsulation aal5snap
 tag-switching ip
```

To verify your configuration, use the `show tag-switching tdp neighbor` command:

```
ATM_P1# show tag-switching tdp neighbor
Peer TDP Ident: 192.168.1.1:0; Local TDP Ident
```

```
192.168.1.2:0
   TCP connection: 192.168.1.1:11004 - 192.168.1.2.678
State: Oper; PIEs sent/rcvd: 1506/1500; ; Downstream
Up time: 12:36:08
TDP discovery sources:
  ATM1/0.1
Addresses bound to peer TDP Ident:
192.168.1.10       192.168.1.1
```

Cell-Mode MPLS

First of all, most ATM switches don't support MPLS without a little modification. For MPLS to work on ATM switches, they must be upgraded to ATM-LSRs.

An *ATM label switch router (ATM-LSR)* is an ATM switch that is capable of forwarding packets based on labels. Cisco ATM switches such as the LightStream 1010 support MPLS without any modification. If MPLS functionality is not native on the switch, a controller card is required to implement MPLS. For example, when an external *label switch controller (LSC)* is added to the switch, the LSC can exchange routes and labels with its neighbors. The LSC communicates with the ATM switch using VC 0/32.

Now that an ATM switch is an ATM-LSR, it supports two different signaling protocols running simultaneously in a ships-passing-in-the-night fashion. For MPLS, LDP is running. For ATM, UNI and PNNI are running. These signaling protocols run side by side, but they don't communicate directly with each other.

If you are not an ATM guru, let me explain what all this means. Let's go back to frame-mode MPLS for a minute. A label was applied by the ingress edge-LSR and then label-switched across the service provider network. The LSRs in the service provider core did not look at the Layer 3 information; instead, they only examined the label.

Well, ATM switches can't examine labels; they must switch traffic based only on VPI/VCI values. Therefore, for ATM, the label is mapped to the VPI/VCI values. In essence, the label replaces the VPI/VCI value. The process of an unlabeled IP packet entering the network, having a label imposed, and then being label-switched has not changed. The only thing that's different is that in ATM, the label is the VPI/VCI value.

Label Binding with ATM

If you aren't already familiar with ATM, label binding can get a little confusing. I'll explain what you need to know for the exam so you don't have to spend the next year learning all about ATM.

To really understand how MPLS works in an ATM environment, let's start with how labels get bound. MPLS in an ATM network uses ordered control with downstream-on-demand.

Ordered control *Ordered control* occurs when an upstream LSR must wait for a label to be received from its downstream LSR. Ordered control takes longer to set up a label-switched path (LSP) and is used by MPLS-enabled ATM switches (ATM-LSRs).

Downstream-on-demand *Downstream-on-demand* occurs when an upstream LSR, using the Label Request message, requests a label from its downstream neighbor.

Figure 3.5 illustrates a service provider network with two POP locations (Melbourne and Ft. Lauderdale) connected together with two ATM-LSRs (Orlando_ATM and Miami_ATM).

FIGURE 3.5 A service provider network with ATM-LSRs

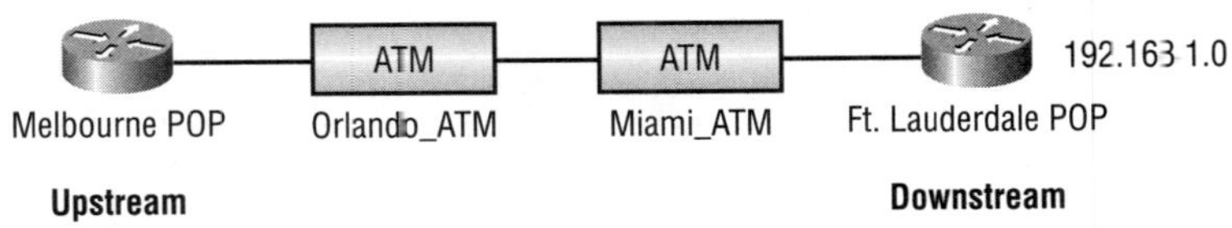

Before discussing about how labels get allocated, let's first identify what is meant by upstream and what is meant by downstream. In Figure 3.5, the network 192.168.1.0 is being advertised from the Ft. Lauderdale POP router. Eventually, through the routing protocol used in the service provider core, the route will be learned by the Melbourne POP router. So traffic coming from the Melbourne POP going to the Ft. Lauderdale POP moves from left to right. The Melbourne POP router is *upstream* and the Ft. Lauderdale POP is *downstream*.

MPLS in an ATM network uses ordered control with downstream-on-demand. It's also true that cell-mode MPLS operates though ordered control and downstream-on-demand.

When exactly does ordered control occur? *Ordered control* occurs when an upstream LSR, in this case the Melbourne POP router, must wait for a label to be received from its downstream LSR (or in the case of Figure 3.5, its downstream ATM-LSR, the Orlando_ATM switch). All this means is that the Melbourne POP router does not create a label, but instead it waits to be told what label to use by the Orlando_ATM switch.

Downstream-on-demand occurs when an upstream LSR, in this case the Melbourne POP router using the Label Request message, requests a label from its downstream neighbor, the Orlando_ATM switch.

So how do labels get bound in the network shown in Figure 3.5? Using the most basic terminology, the Melbourne POP router needs to know the LSP between it and the Ft. Lauderdale POP. So the Melbourne POP router asks its neighbor, the Orlando_ATM switch, which label it should use. The Orlando_ATM switch asks the Miami_ATM switch. The Miami_ATM switch asks the Ft. Lauderdale POP router. The Ft. Lauderdale POP router tells the Miami_ATM switch, who tells the Orlando_ATM switch, who tells the Melbourne POP router which label to use, and in the case of ATM, which VPI/VCI values to use.

Now, let's add a little detail. Figure 3.6 illustrates the label request and VPI/VCI mapping flow.

FIGURE 3.6 A service provider network with label and VPI/VCI mappings

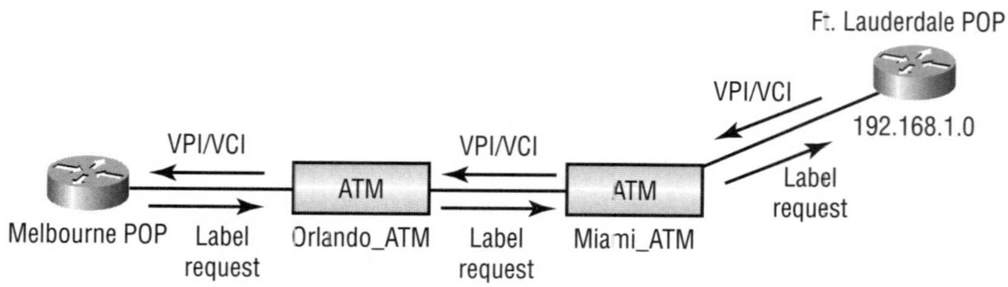

As you read what happens between LSRs in an ATM environment, I want you to focus on the VPI/VCI mappings.

The Melbourne POP router sees a route in its routing table for the network 192.168.1.0. To send traffic to the network 192.168.1.0, the Melbourne POP router sends a request to its downstream ATM-LSR, Orlando_ATM, requesting a label for the network 192.168.1.0.

The Orlando_ATM switch, upon receiving the request, sends a request to its downstream ATM-LSR, Miami_ATM, requesting a label for the network 192.168.1.0. When the request arrives at the Miami_ATM switch, a request is sent to the Ft. Lauderdale POP router requesting a label for the network 192.168.1.0.

At the Ft. Lauderdale POP router, two options exist for the network 192.168.1.0. Either the network 192.168.1.0 is reachable from a downstream ATM-LSR, or it needs to have the label popped (recall penultimate hop popping). A new label is allocated out of the pool of free VCs on the LC-ATM interface. This new label is added to the label forwarding information base (LFIB) with the associated VPI/VCI pair. The new VPI/VCI pair is sent back to the Miami_ATM switch through either TDP or LDP.

NOTE

An *LC-ATM* is a label-switching controlled ATM interface where the VPI/VCI is assigned through MPLS or tag switching (LDP or TDP).

At the Miami_ATM switch, a new label is allocated out of the pool of free VCs on the LC-ATM interface. A mapping between the outgoing VPI/VCI (from the Ft. Lauderdale POP router) and the incoming VPI/VCI (that is going to be sent to the Orlando_ATM switch) is created. The new VPI/VCI pair is sent back to the Orlando_ATM switch.

At the Orlando_ATM switch, a new label is allocated out of the pool of free VCs on the LC-ATM interface. A mapping between the outgoing VPI/VCI (from the Miami_ATM switch) and the incoming VPI/VCI (that is going to be sent to the Melbourne POP router) is created. The new VPI/VCI pair is sent back to the Melbourne POP router.

The important information to get out of all of this is that labels are being assigned and mapped to VPI/VCI pairs.

Cell-Mode Label Switching

This section uses the simple service provider network illustrated in Figure 3.7 to explain how cell-mode label switching works across an ATM-LSR network.

FIGURE 3.7 A cell-mode service provider network

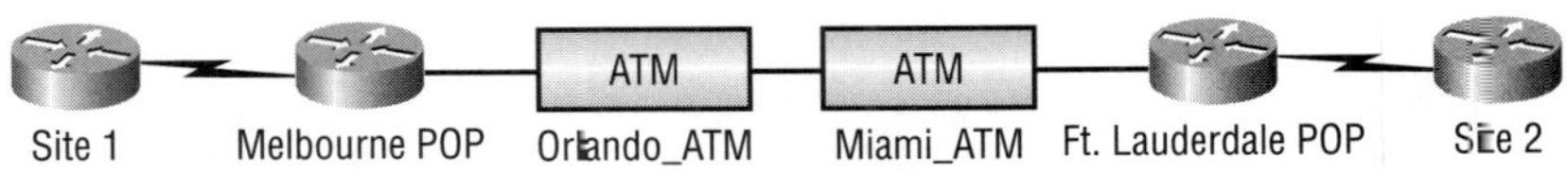

Table 3.1 lists the role of each device in the network in Figure 3.7.

TABLE 3.1 Cell-Mode Service Provider Network Device Roles

Device	Function
Site 1	Non-MPLS router
Site 2	Non-MPLS router
Melbourne POP	Router functioning as an ATM edge-LSR
Ft. Lauderdale POP	Router functioning as an ATM edge-LSR
Orlando_ATM	ATM switch functioning as an ATM-LSR
Miami_ATM	ATM switch functioning as an ATM-LSR

The easiest way to discuss label switching in cell-mode MPLS is to first relate it to frame-mode MPLS. If the network in Figure 3.7 is enabled for frame-mode MPLS, what happens? An unlabeled IP packet enters the network, and the ingress edge-LSR applies a label that is used to label-switch the packet through the service provider network, ultimately delivering it to the egress edge-LSR.

How are things different in cell-mode MPLS? An unlabeled packet enters the network, and the ingress ATM edge-LSR uses the VPI/VCI mappings as the label. Each ATM-LSR in the LSP through the service provider network switches the packet based solely on the VPI/VCI values. That's it! Just remember: in cell-mode MPLS, labels equal VPI/VCI values.

VC Merge

Cisco ATM-LSRs make use of a function called *virtual circuit merge (VC merge)* to solve the cell-interleaving problem and reduce the number of labels used in the ATM-LSR network, or ATM-LSR domain.

NOTE: An *ATM-LSR domain* is a series of ATM-LSRs connected together with LC-ATM interfaces.

Let's start with the problem called cell interleaving.

In Figure 3.8, an IP packet enters the network at the POP 1 router. The POP 1 router performs a lookup, and the mapping of label to the VPI/VCI value is identified. The IP packet is broken up, or segmented, into ATM cells, and the VPI/VCI value is applied to each cell as it is sent to ATM 1. For simplicity's sake, the cells from POP 1 are illustrated in Figure 3.8 with a label; in reality, it's a VPI/VCI value.

FIGURE 3.8 Cell interleaving

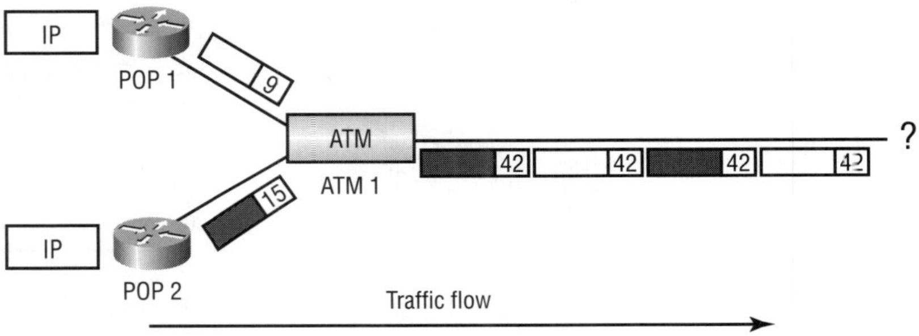

Also in Figure 3.8, an IP packet enters the network at the POP 2 router. The POP 2 router performs a lookup, and the mapping of a label to the VPI/VCI value is identified. The IP packet is broken up, or segmented, into ATM cells, and the VPI/VCI value is applied to each cell as it is sent to ATM 1. Again, for simplicity's sake, the cells from POP 2 are illustrated with a label; in reality, it's a VPI/VCI value.

To view the number of tags used, execute the `show tag-switching atm-tdp summary` command. The local value in the field tells you how many tags have been assigned by the TSR on the interface. The corresponding MPLS command can be found at `www.cisco.com`.

```
R1#show tag-switching atm-tdp summary

Total number of destinations: 691

TC-ATM bindings summary
interface  total  active  bindwait  local  remote  other
ATM0/0/0   490    488     1         300    302     1
```

If the ATM switch (in Figure 3.8, it's called ATM 1) uses the same label for cells traveling to a common destination, the receiving device does not know how to reassemble the cells into packets. How can this problem be fixed? By using multiple labels for each flow. Look at Figure 3.9. On ATM 1, the flow of cells from POP 1 uses label 49, and the flow of cells from POP 2 uses label 61. When these cells are received by an end device that needs to reassemble the cells back into packets, it's easy to tell the cells apart by their labels.

FIGURE 3.9 Cells with multiple labels

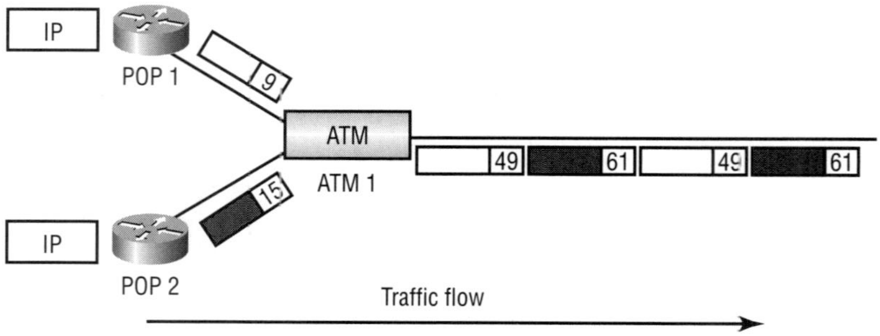

There is one drawback to this solution. ATM 1 uses many labels. For each flow, ATM 1 sends a downstream-on-demand–style request to its downstream ATM-LSR, requesting labels for each flow.

VC merge fixes cell interleaving and reduces the number of labels required by buffering cell flows and forwarding them in a serialized fashion. Consider the example illustrated in Figure 3.10. The cell flow from POP 2 is buffered, while the flow of cells from POP 1 is sent out the outbound interface. When the cell flow from POP 1 is complete, the cell flow from POP 2 is sent out the outbound interface. A downstream device needing to reassemble the cells receives each flow in order.

FIGURE 3.10 An ATM network with VC merge

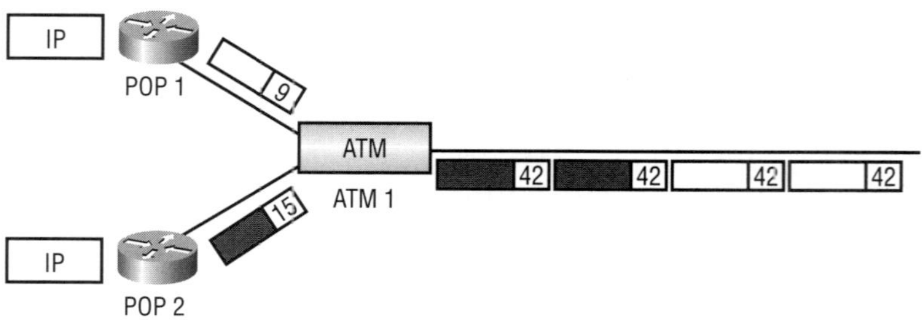

Through VC merge, an ATM-LSR can reuse the same label for multiple cell flows. VC merge solves the cell-interleaving problem and allows the ATM-LSR to preserve label space. VC merge is enabled on ATM-LSRs by default. To verify that the ATM-LSR has the VC merge capability enabled, use the `show mpls atm-ldp capability` command. If VC merge is not enabled, use the `mpls ldp atm vc-merge` command to re-enable it. For troubleshooting cell-mode MPLS, use standard commands such as `show mpls interfaces` for verification.

Loop Prevention

Before moving into cell-mode MPLS configuration, let's talk just a bit about loop detection and prevention. Cell-mode loop detection and prevention is a little different than in frame-mode MPLS because ATM cells do not have a TTL field. Cell-mode MPLS devices rely, just as their frame-mode counterparts do, on the routing protocol to ensure that the network is loop-free and to prevent loops from occurring.

Instead of the TTL value, Cisco uses the LDP hop-count object *Type-Length-Value (TLV)*. When an ATM-LSR receives a Label Request message with the LDP hop-count object TLV, it increments the hop-count value by 1. Frame-mode MPLS decrements the TTL, but cell-mode MPLS increments the TLV. The default Cisco hop count is 254, and that value is configurable. When the maximum TLV value is reached, a loop-detected message is sent back to the device that originated the label request.

Cell-Mode MPLS Configuration

In frame-mode MPLS, a VC is set up between PE (ATM edge-LSR) routers. To configure the PE LC-ATM interface, a sub-interface is configured with the `point-to-point` command option. The IOS commands for frame-mode MPLS configuration on a PE ATM edge-LSR are as follows:

```
interface ATM1/0
 no ip address
!
interface ATM1/0.1 point-to-point
```

To configure the PE LC-ATM interface for cell-mode MPLS, the sub-interface is configured with the `mpls` command option. The IOS commands for cell-mode MPLS configuration on a PE ATM edge-LSR are as follows:

```
interface ATM1/0
 no ip address
```

```
!
interface ATM1/0.1 mpls
```

To configure the PE LC-ATM interface for cell-mode tag switching, the sub-interface is configured with the `tag-switching` command option. The IOS commands for cell-mode tag switching configuration on a PE ATM edge-LSR are as follows:

```
interface ATM1/0
 no ip address
!
interface ATM1/0.1 tag-switching
```

NOTE The configuration in this section is only for cell-mode MPLS on routers with LC-ATM interfaces. IP addresses and MPLS, or tag switching, must still be enabled on the LC-ATM interface.

To configure cell-mode MPLS on an ATM-LSR, the `mpls ip` command is used under the interface. (There are no sub-interfaces on an ATM-LSR.) The IOS commands for cell-mode MPLS configuration on an ATM-LSR are as follows:

```
!
interface ATM1/0/0
 mpls ip
```

The IOS commands for cell-mode tag switching configuration on an ATM-LSR are as follows:

```
!
interface ATM1/0/0
 tag-switching ip
```

It looks just like frame-mode router configuration, doesn't it? (The answer is Yes. If you think No, go back and reread Chapter 2.)

Summary

In this chapter, you learned about frame-mode MPLS in ATM networks and cell-mode MPLS. When ATM switches do not support MPLS, PE routers with ATM interfaces, acting as ATM edge-LSRs, are connected together with a standard ATM PVC. To configure the ATM edge-LSRs, the ATM sub-interface is configured with the `point-to-point` option, which indicates frame-mode MPLS.

For cell-mode MPLS, an ATM switch functions as an ATM-LSR. Cell-mode MPLS is different from frame-mode MPLS in that with cell-mode MPLS, an unlabeled packet enters the network and the ingress ATM edge-LSR and the VPI/VCI mappings are used as the label. Each ATM-LSR in the LSP through the service provider network switches the packet based solely on the VPI/VCI values. In cell-mode MPLS, both the ATM switch, now functioning as an ATM-LSR, and the edge routers with ATM interfaces functioning as ATM edge-LSRs need to be configured for cell-mode MPLS. On the ATM edge-LSR, you need to specify either `mpls` or `tag-switching` as an option when configuring the ATM sub-interface. On the ATM-LSR, an interface is configured for MPLS or tag switching using either the `mpls ip` or the `tag-switching ip` options. To save labels and fix cell interleaving, Cisco uses VC merge, which is enabled on ATM-LSRs by default.

For loop prevention, both cell-mode and frame-mode MPLS make use of the routing protocol to prevent a loop. Frame-mode MPLS decrements the TTL value, and cell-mode increments the TLV.

Exam Essentials

Understand frame-mode MPLS in an ATM environment. In an ATM environment, frame-mode MPLS indicates that the ATM switches do not support MPLS. ATM edge-LSRs are connected together with PVCs through the non-MPLS ATM network.

Understand cell-mode MPLS. ATM switches operate by switching cells based on VPI/VCI values. ATM switches can't examine labels; they must switch traffic based only on VPI/VCI values. MPLS works in an ATM network by mapping the label to the VPI/VCI value. In essence, the label replaces the VPI/VCI value. The process of an unlabeled IP packet entering the network, having a label imposed, and then being label-switched has not changed. The only thing that's different is that in ATM, the label is the VPI/VCI value.

Be able to configure cell-mode MPLS on an ATM-LSR. For cell-mode MPLS, both the ATM-LSR and ATM edge-LSRs need to be configured.

On a PE ATM edge-LSR such as a router, the relevant IOS commands for cell-mode MPLS configuration are as follows:

```
interface ATM1/0
 no ip address
!
interface ATM1/0.1 mpls
```

Remember that on the ATM edge-LSR, it is the `mpls` or `tag-switching` command option on the sub-interface configuration that configures it as cell-mode MPLS.

The relevant IOS commands for cell-mode tag switching configuration on a PE ATM edge-LSR are as follows:

```
interface ATM1/0
 no ip address
!
interface ATM1/0.1 tag-switching
```

To configure cell-mode MPLS on an ATM-LSR, the `mpls ip` command is used under the interface. (There are no sub-interfaces on an ATM-LSR.) The relevant IOS commands for cell-mode MPLS configuration on an ATM-LSR are as follows:

```
!
interface ATM1/0/0
 mpls ip
```

To configure cell-mode tag switching on an ATM-LSR, the `tag-switching ip` command is used under the interface. (There are no sub-interfaces on an ATM-LSR.) The relevant IOS commands for cell-mode tag switching configuration on an ATM-LSR are as follows:

```
!
interface ATM1/0/0
 tag-switching ip
```

Be able to configure frame-mode MPLS on an ATM edge-LSR. For frame-mode MPLS, only the ATM edge-LSRs need to be configured. There are no ATM switches supporting MPLS-only routers with ATM interfaces connected through a standard ATM PVC. On the ATM edge-LSR such as a router, the relevant IOS commands for frame-mode configuration on an ATM edge-LSR are as follows:

```
interface ATM1/0
 no ip address
!
interface ATM1/0.1 point-to-point
```

Remember that on the ATM edge-LSR, it is the `point-to-point` option on the sub-interface configuration that makes it frame-mode MPLS.

Describe the loop detection and prevention mechanisms in MPLS Both frame-mode and cell-mode MPLS use the routing protocol to prevent routing loops. For MPLS, the TTL field from the IP TTL is decremented by 1 by the ingress edge-LSR, and then copied into the MPLS label TTL field. Upon exiting the MPLS network, the MPLS label TTL value is copied back into the IP TTL field. For cell-mode MPLS, instead of the TTL value, Cisco uses the LDP hop-count object TLV. When an ATM-LSR receives a Label Request message with the LDP hop-count object TLV, it increments the hop-count value by 1. The default Cisco hop count is 254, and that value is configurable. Once this value is reached, a loop-detected message is sent to the device that originated the label request.

Key Terms

Before you take the exam, be certain you are familiar with the following terms:

ATM label switch router (ATM-LSR)	LC-ATM
ATM-LSR domain	ordered control
downstream	Type-Length-Value (TLV)
downstream-on-demand	upstream
edge label switch router	virtual channel identifier (VCI)
label switch controller (LSC)	virtual circuit merge (VC merge)
label switch router (LSR)	virtual path identifier (VPI)

Review Questions

1. It is an MPLS requirement that control-plane traffic be exchanged using ___________.

   A. Broadcast

   B. Unlabeled IP

   C. Multicast

   D. Labeled IP over VC 0/32

2. Which of the following needs to be set up on an ATM switch for frame-mode MPLS?

   A. MPLS or tag switching

   B. A sub-interface with the `point-to-point` option configured

   C. VC 0/32

   D. PVC

3. Routers with serial interfaces run ___________ MPLS.

   A. Frame-mode

   B. Cell-mode

4. Which of the following terms best describes a core ATM switch with MPLS enabled?

   A. ATM-LSR

   B. ATM edge-LSR

   C. LSR

   D. None of the above

5. An LSC communicates with an ATM-LSR on which of the following VCs?

   A. 0/1

   B. 0/7

   C. 0/32

   D. 0/4096

6. Which of the following methods is used by cell-mode MPLS to bind labels? (Choose two.)

   A. ordered control

   B. independent control

   C. downstream-on-demand

   D. unsolicited downstream

7. Cell-mode MPLS does not switch traffic based on a label but instead uses the __________ values.

   A. SVC/PVC

   B. DLCI

   C. VCI/VIP

   D. VPI/VCI

8. Based on the following code, what is being configured?

```
interface ATM1/0
 no ip address
!
interface ATM1/0.1 point-to-point
 ip address 192.168.1.5 255.255.255.0
 pvc 0/100
 encapsulation aal5snap
 mpls ip
```

   A. MPLS is being configured for cell mode on an ATM edge-LSR.

   B. Cell-mode MPLS is being configured on an ATM-LSR.

   C. Frame-mode MPLS is being configured on an ATM edge-LSR.

   D. Frame-mode MPLS is being configured on an ATM-LSR.

9. Based on the following code, what is being configured?

```
interface ATM1/0
 no ip address
!
interface ATM1/0.1 mpls
```

A. MPLS is being configured for cell mode on an ATM edge-LSR.

B. Cell-mode MPLS is being configured on an ATM-LSR.

C. Frame-mode MPLS is being configured on an ATM edge-LSR.

D. Frame-mode MPLS is being configured on an ATM-LSR.

10. Based on the following code, what is being configured?

```
interface ATM1/0
 mpls ip
```

A. MPLS is being configured for cell-mode on an ATM edge-LSR.

B. Cell-mode MPLS is being configured on an ATM-LSR.

C. Frame-mode MPLS is being configured on an ATM edge-LSR.

D. Frame-mode MPLS is being configured on an ATM-LSR.

11. ATM-LSRs use which of the following signaling protocols to exchange labels?

A. UNI

B. MNI

C. PNNI

D. LDP

12. Which capability does Cisco use to preserve labels and ensure the proper assembly of cells?

A. Cell interleaving

B. LDP

C. VC merge

D. None of the above

13. Which of the following command options configures an ATM edge-LSR for cell-mode MPLS?

A. `tag-switching`

B. `mpls`

C. `point-to-point`

D. `cell-mode`

14. Which of the following command options configures an ATM edge-LSR for frame-mode MPLS?

    A. `tag-switching`

    B. `mpls`

    C. `point-to-point`

    D. `cell-mode`

15. Which of the following command options configures an ATM edge-LSR for cell-mode tag switching?

    A. `tag-switching`

    B. `mpls`

    C. `point-to-point`

    D. `cell-mode`

16. Which of the following commands enables VC merge on an ATM-LSR?

    A. `mpls ldp atm vc-merge`

    B. `mpls ip atm vc-merge`

    C. `mpls ip atm vcmerge`

    D. `mpls ip atm vc merge`

17. By default, VC merge is ___________.

    A. Enabled

    B. Disabled

18. For cell-mode MPLS, the default hop-count object TLV value is ___________.

    A. 254

    B. 16,534

    C. 256

    D. 16,536

19. Which of the following is used by both frame-mode and cell-mode MPLS to prevent loops?

    A. TLV

    B. TTL

    C. Routing protocol

    D. None of the above

20. Based on the following code, what is being configured?

```
interface ATM1/0
 tag-switching ip
```

    A. Tag switching is being configured for cell-mode on an ATM edge-LSR.

    B. Cell-mode tag switching is being configured on an ATM-LSR.

    C. Frame-mode tag switching is being configured on an ATM edge-LSR.

    D. Frame-mode tag switching is being configured on an ATM-LSR.

Answers to Review Questions

1. B. One of the requirements for MPLS is that control-plane information be exchanged using pure unlabeled IP.

2. D. For frame-mode MPLS, or tag switching, a PVC needs to be set up between LSRs. The ATM switches have no MPLS functionality, and the PVC is set up as normal.

3. A. Routers with interfaces such as Ethernet, PPP (serial), and HDLC (serial) run frame-mode MPLS.

4. A. An ATM switch enabled with MPLS is referred to as an ATM-LSR.

5. C. An LSC communicates with an ATM-LSR over VC 0/32.

6. A, C. Cell-mode MPLS uses ordered control and downstream-on-demand to assign labels.

7. D. ATM switches can't read labels; therefore they must switch traffic based on the VPI/VCI values.

8. C. The configuration is being performed on an ATM edge LSR. The `point-to-point` option indicates frame-mode MPLS.

9. A. The configuration is being performed on an ATM edge LSR. The `mpls` option indicates cell-mode MPLS.

10. B. MPLS is being configured for an ATM interface (not sub-interface), which indicates that MPLS is being enabled on an ATM-LSR. The `mpls` option indicates cell-mode MPLS.

11. D. When MPLS is enabled on an ATM-LSR, LDP is used to exchange labels. Standard ATM signaling such as UNI and PNNI is still being used on the ATM-LSR. Standard ATM and MPLS control-plane signaling run as "ships passing in the night."

12. C. VC merge solves both cell-interleaving (ensuring the proper assembly of cells) problems and preserves labels for future use.

13. B. On an ATM edge-LSR, as the sub-interface is configured, the `mpls` command option is applied for cell-mode MPLS.

14. C. On an ATM edge-LSR, as the sub-interface is configured, the `point-to-point` command option is applied for frame-mode MPLS.

15. A. On an ATM edge-LSR, as the sub-interface is configured, the `tag-switching` command option is applied for cell-mode tag switching.

16. A. To enable VC merge on an ATM-LSR, use the `mpls ldp atm vc-merge` command.

17. A. VC merge is enabled by default on a Cisco IOS ATM-LSR.

18. A. The default hop-count object TLV value is 254. This can be changed based on network requirements.

19. C. The routing protocol is used to prevent loops in both frame-mode and cell-mode MPLS.

20. B. Tag switching is being configured for an ATM interface (not sub-interface), which indicates that tag switching is being enabled on an ATM-LSR.

Chapter 4

VPNs: An Overview

CCIP MPLS EXAM TOPICS COVERED IN THIS CHAPTER:

- ✓ Identify major virtual private network topologies, their characteristics, and usage scenarios.
- ✓ Describe the differences between an overlay VPN and a peer-to-peer VPN.
- ✓ List the major technologies supporting overlay VPNs and peer-to-peer VPNs.

This chapter is primarily a history lesson. There are many technologies that were used to connect sites together well before the concept of MPLS virtual private networks (VPNs) came along. This chapter starts with a review of dedicated point-to-point, or leased line, connections. Then it explains how, as less expensive alternatives to point-to-point connections, VPNs connect sites together with virtual circuits (VCs). VPN topologies are also covered in this chapter.

Just a few years ago, service providers began to offer peer-to-peer VPNs. Peer-to-peer VPNs are very different from traditional VPNs in that customer routers actually peer with service provider routers. This chapter will explain the characteristics of peer-to-peer VPNs in detail.

This chapter lays the foundation for you to really understand the mechanisms used for MPLS VPNs. Although no material in this chapter deals specifically with MPLS, it does cover the necessary exam objectives. For the MPLS exam, you are required to know about overlay and peer-to-peer VPNs, which MPLS VPNs may replace. You also need to know the usage scenarios, topologies, and the differences between them.

VPNs 101

I assume that most of you who have purchased this study guide already know 90% of the material in this chapter. Just to make sure that you're up to speed on VPNs, this section covers the history of VPNs, including point-to-point connections and how they segued into VPNs. In addition, this section describes the basic VPN technologies and topologies. If you are a seasoned veteran, feel free to skim this section. If you're wondering what a VPN is, keep reading.

Point-to-Point Connections

Point-to-point connections, or *leased lines*, are not VPNs; they're dedicated private links through a service provider network. Point-to-point connections offer guaranteed bandwidth and privacy through a service provider network, but they come at a price. Because the service provider is giving the customer guaranteed bandwidth, they're paying for it all the time. It doesn't matter if you're not using any of the connection between 6 P.M. and 8 A.M.; you're still paying for it. In addition, since you're the only person using the connection, you get guaranteed privacy.

Point-to-point connections are expensive because the service provider can't make use of statistical multiplexing. Statistical multiplexing is based on the principle that not everyone needs to use all the bandwidth they are paying for at any given time. Since not everyone will use all the bandwidth all the time, the service provider can sell more bandwidth than is actually present in the network.

Figure 4.1 illustrates connectivity with dedicated point-to-point links connecting customer devices.

FIGURE 4.1 Dedicated point-to-point connectivity

In Figure 4.1, customer routers R1 and R2 are totally unaware of the infrastructure behind their dedicated point-to-point connection. It's important to remember that point-to-point connections are private, secure, and expensive.

Virtual Private Networks

VPNs emerged as an alternative to dedicated point-to-point connections because VPNs deliver the same benefits of dedicated point-to-point links but without the high cost. The earliest VPNs were made available with Frame Relay and X.25. By establishing VCs between the customer devices, the service provider was able to emulate dedicated point-to-point connections while sharing a common service provider infrastructure and therefore reducing costs.

In Figure 4.2, customer routers are shown connected through the service provider network with VCs.

FIGURE 4.2 Customer connectivity with virtual circuits

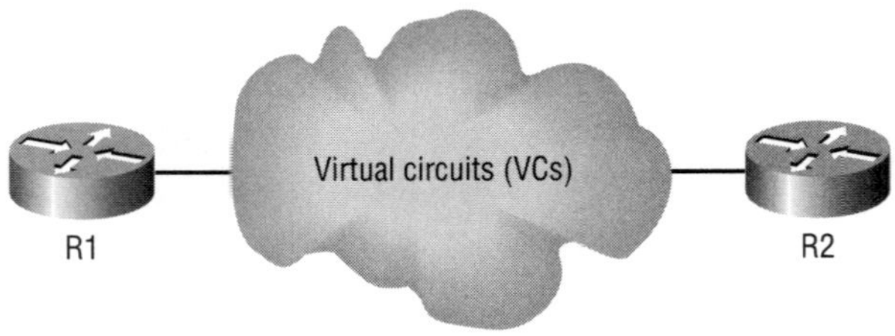

When customers are connected with virtual circuits through a shared service provider infrastructure, it is called an *overlay*. There are three common overlay VPN topologies that you need to know about: full-mesh, partial mesh, and hub-and-spoke.

Full-Mesh Topology

A *full-mesh* topology is where every site in the network is directly connected to every other site in the network. Figure 4.3 illustrates a full-mesh topology. In Figure 4.3, there are four routers connected together with six VCs.

FIGURE 4.3 A full-mesh topology

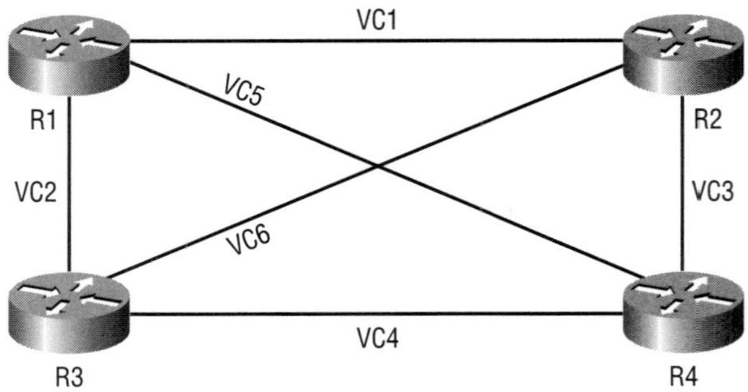

With a full-mesh topology, it's easy to ensure optimal routing and redundancy. For example, in Figure 4.3, traffic from R1 to R2 follows VC1. Traffic from R1 to R4 follows VC5. In a fully meshed environment, traffic takes the most direct route. Figure 4.4 illustrates an example of the redundancy provided with a full-mesh topology, where VC1 and VC2 are unavailable. R1 can still send traffic to R2; since some of the surviving VCs are still up, traffic flows from R1 to R4 to R2, as you can see in Figure 4.5.

FIGURE 4.4 A full-mesh topology with failed VCs

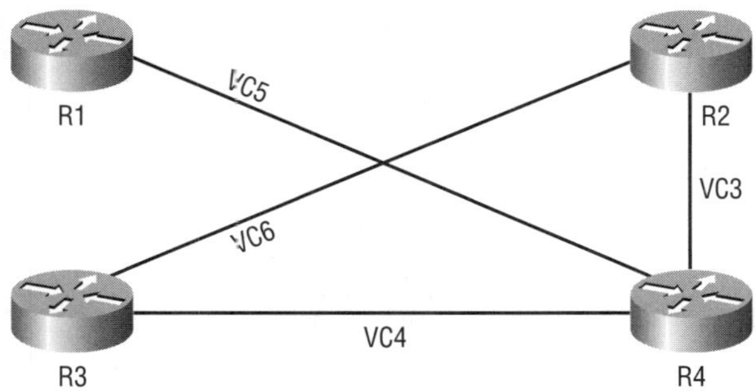

FIGURE 4.5 Traffic flow for a full-mesh topology with failed VCs

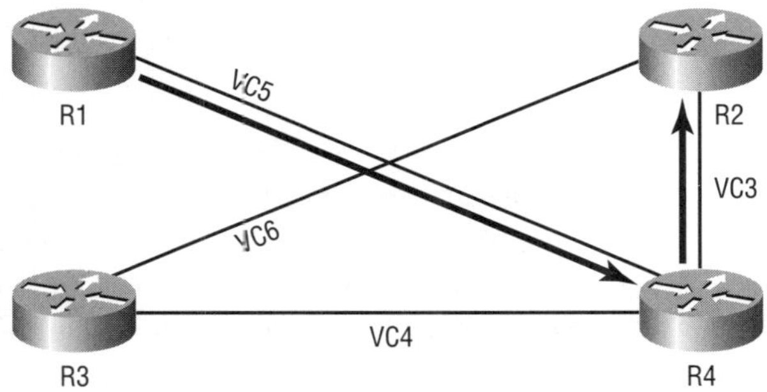

Now that you know about the advantages of a full-mesh topology, let's discuss some of its drawbacks. In the simple network illustrated in Figure 4.3, with four routers connected together in a full-mesh, only six VCs are required. One of the big problems with a full-mesh overlay is that it does not scale well. The best way to illustrate the scalability problem is to take it to the extreme. How many VCs are required to fully mesh 100 routers together? A total of 4950! Another disadvantage of implementing a full-mesh topology is cost. Try telling your finance person that you need 4950 virtual circuits. They aren't as expensive as leased lines, but they aren't cheap.

Partial-Mesh Topology

So, you don't want a full-mesh topology, or you can't afford it. What are your alternatives? One alternative to a full-mesh topology is a *partial-mesh* topology, where each site is directly connected to one or two other sites in the network. Figure 4.6 illustrates a partial-mesh topology.

FIGURE 4.6 A partial-mesh topology

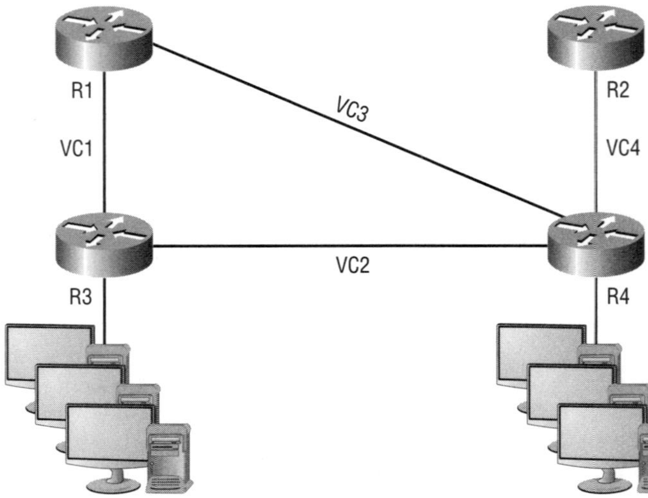

In Figure 4.6, the connectivity requirements are resource driven. For example, all sites (R1, R2, and R3) need to connect to resources located off of R4. Notice in Figure 4.6 that VC2, VC3, and VC4 give the sites R1, R2, and R3 a direct connection to R4. In addition, R1 needs to connect to data located off of R3. To provide for connectivity, VC1 runs between them. A partial-mesh topology has fewer virtual circuits and therefore costs less than a full-mesh topology.

Hub-and-Spoke Topology

A *hub-and-spoke* topology is the least expensive of all VPNs to implement. A hub-and-spoke topology is most often implemented by financial organizations because they usually have centralized resources that need to be accessed by remote branch offices. With a hub-and-spoke topology, the spoke sites don't need to communicate with each other, only with the central, or *hub*, site. Figure 4.7 illustrates a hub-and-spoke topology.

In Figure 4.7, the hub site is R1. Each router (R2, R3, and R4) has a direct connection to R1. From a traffic standpoint, R2, R3, and R4 cannot communicate directly with each other unless R1 provides transit between them.

A hub-and-spoke topology is the least expensive network topology to implement, but it does not offer any redundancy. For example, if VC1 goes down between R1 and R2, then R2 will not be able to access any data at the hub. Figure 4.8 illustrates this situation.

FIGURE 4.7 A hub-and-spoke topology

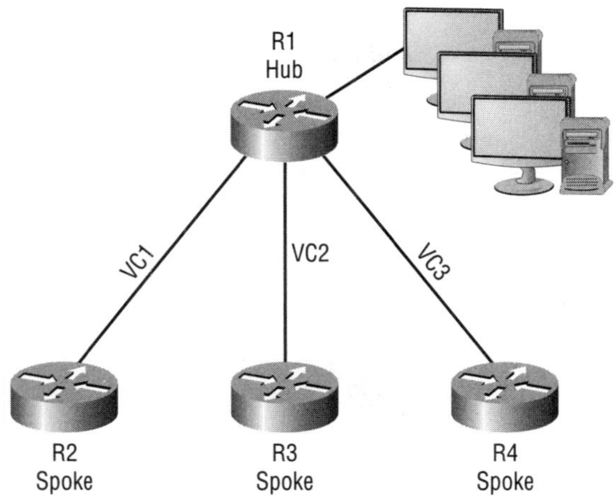

FIGURE 4.8 A hub-and-spoke topology with a VC failure

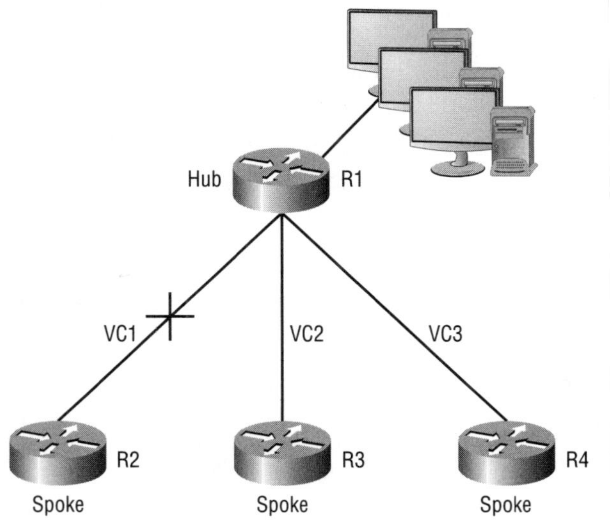

Redundant Hub-and-Spoke Topology

The *redundant hub-and-spoke* topology is an extension of the standard hub-and-spoke topology. A standard hub-and-spoke topology has a single point of failure in the connections that link the spoke sites with the hub site. For example, Figure 4.9 illustrates a standard hub-and-spoke topology.

FIGURE 4.9 A standard hub-and-spoke topology

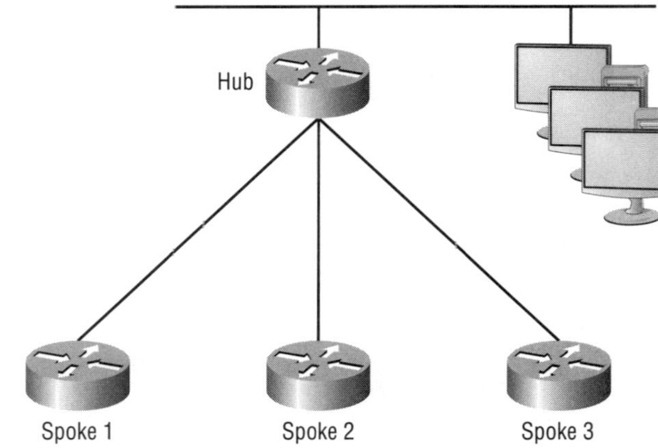

What happens when the connection between Spoke 1 and the hub becomes unavailable? Spoke 1 loses connectivity to the hub. To remedy this problem, you can use a redundant hub-and-spoke topology, illustrated in Figure 4.10. In a redundant hub-and-spoke topology, there are multiple hubs and multiple connections between the hubs and the spokes. That way, if one connection goes down, the connectivity is provided via another connection.

FIGURE 4.10 A redundant hub-and-spoke topology

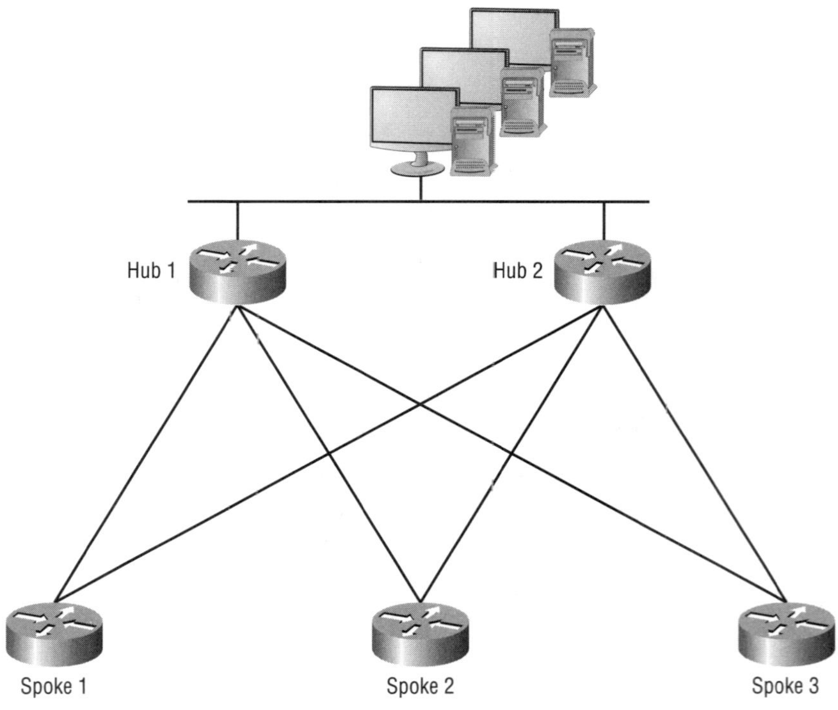

What happens if one of the links goes down between Spoke 1 and one of the hubs in Figure 4.10? Connectivity is still available through the alternate connection. What happens if Hub 2 goes down in its entirety? The hub site is still available through Hub 1.

In addition to designing a network for redundancy as in the redundant hub-and-spoke topology, redundancy can also be implemented by using multiple service providers. Figure 4.11 shows a simple redundant hub-and-spoke topology where all the connections are with a single service provider.

FIGURE 4.11 A redundant hub-and-spoke topology with a single service provider

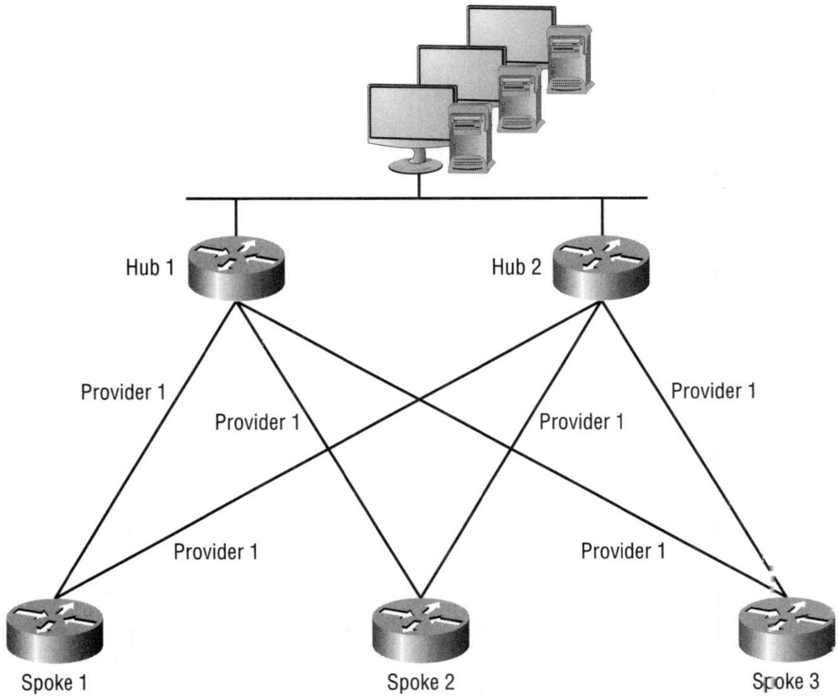

If there is a catastrophic problem with the single service provider, a spoke site, or multiple spoke sites, can lose *all* connectivity. Instead of using a single service provider, multiple service providers can be used to improve upon the redundant hub-and-spoke design and guarantee connectivity.

Figure 4.12 illustrates such a situation. All the spokes have connectivity to Hub 1 through Provider 1 and connectivity to Hub 2 through Provider 2. If Provider 1 has a catastrophic failure, all the Provider 1 links will go down. Assuming that Provider 2 is not experiencing any failures, redundancy is preserved through the alternate connections.

FIGURE 4.12 A redundant hub-and-spoke topology with multiple service providers

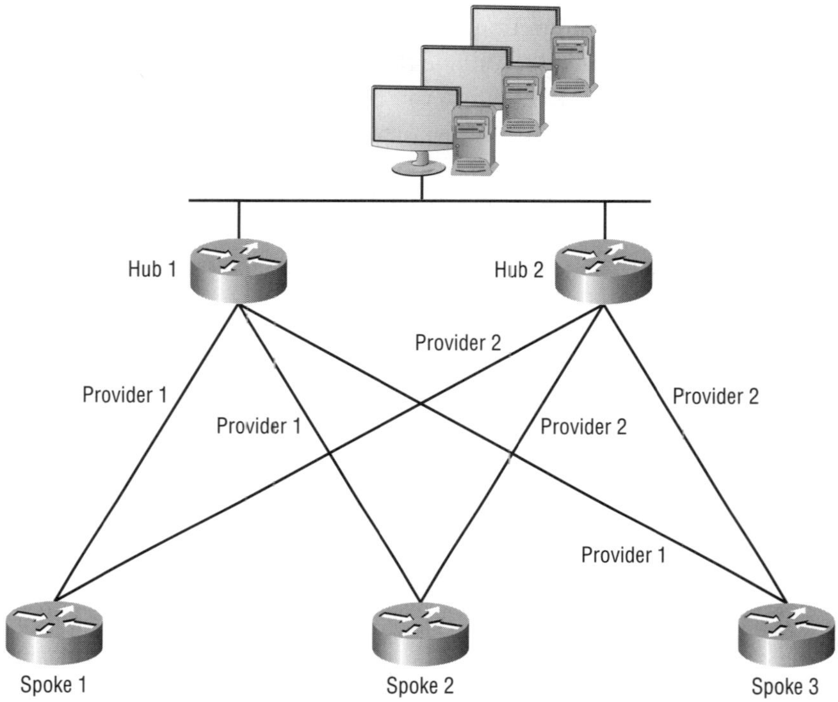

VPN Technologies

This chapter is exposing you to overlay VPN topologies and traditional Layer 2 overlay VPN technologies such Frame Relay, X.25, and ATM. There are, however, other VPN technologies that you should be aware of. I'll start with the bottom of the OSI model and work my way up.

Layer 1: Physical layer VPNs At Layer 1 of the OSI model, technologies such as SONET, E1, T1, and ISDN are used to provide VPNs.

Layer 2: Data Link layer VPNs At Layer 2 of the OSI model, technologies such as Frame Relay, X.25, and ATM are used to provide VPNs.

Layer 3: Network layer VPNs At Layer 3 of the OSI model, technologies such as IPSec and GRE tunnels are used to provide VPNs.

Although there are many possible technologies, they all suffer from the same problem: they do not scale well.

Categories of VPNs

In addition to topological definitions, VPNs can also be categorized by the business need they fill or by the characterization of services they provide. There are three categories of VPNs:

Intranets An *intranet* is a collection of sites that are controlled by the same organization. An example of an intranet is a single company with all its sites connected together in a single network. Figure 4.13 shows multiple sites connected in an intranet.

FIGURE 4.13 A simple intranet

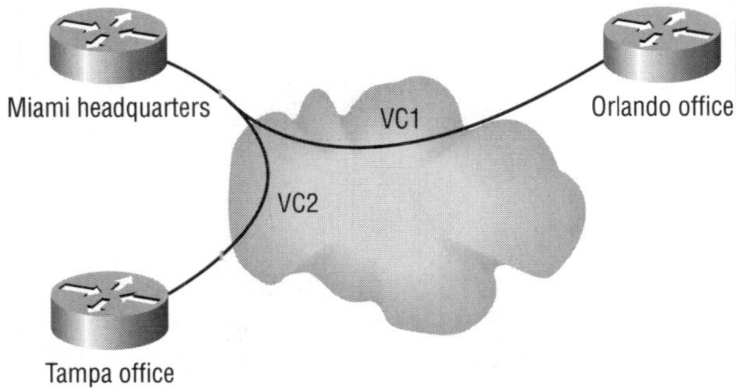

Extranet An *extranet* is a connection between two or more organizations. An example of an extranet might be a company with a connection to a partner company. Figure 4.14 shows two company sites connected together in an extranet.

FIGURE 4.14 A simple extranet

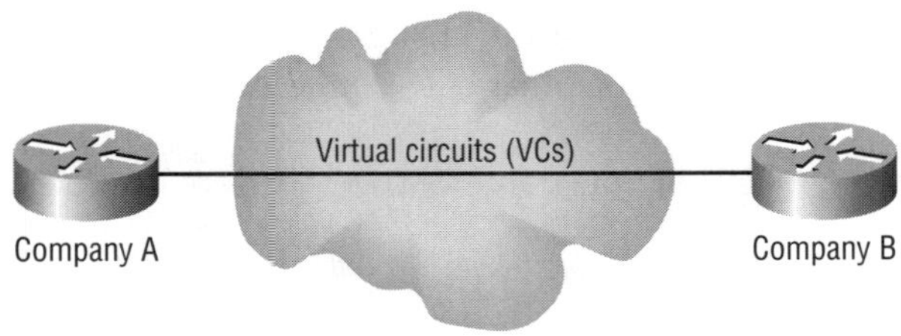

Combination of intranets and extranets Oftentimes, VPNs are a combination of both intranets and extranets. Figure 4.15 shows two companies with both intranets and extranets deployed.

In Figure 4.15, both Company A and Company B have an intranet deployed. A separate connection runs between the headquarters of Company A and Company B, creating the extranet. An extranet poses a security risk not present in intranets because Company A may have unauthorized access to Company B's network (and vice versa). In the combination network, both Company A and Company B must take efforts to secure their sites.

FIGURE 4.15 A two-company network with intranets and extranets

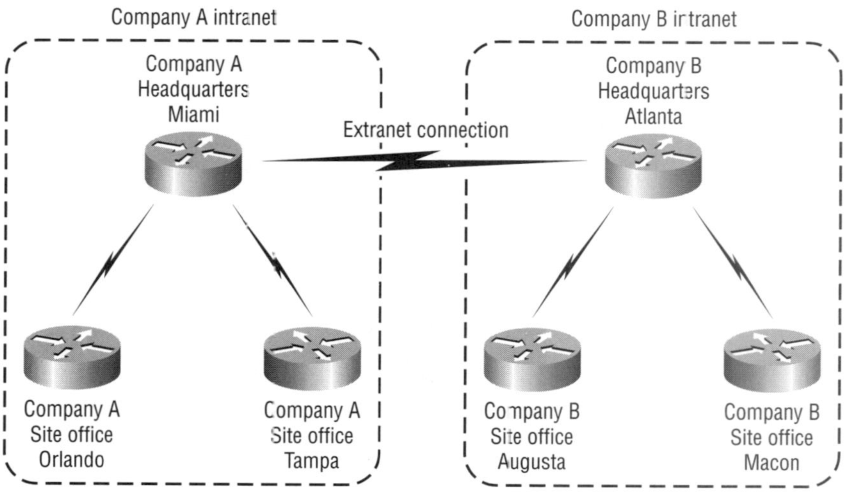

VPN Routing

So now that you know about the various VPN topologies, you need to know about routing inside a VPN. Figure 4.16 illustrates a simple network, with two customer sites connected with point-to-point links.

FIGURE 4.16 A simple point-to-point network

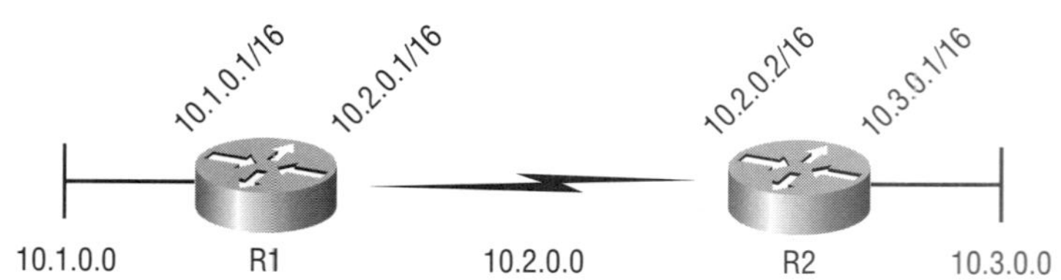

Table 4.1 lists the IP addresses and interfaces of the network devices in Figure 4.16.

TABLE 4.1 Point-to-Point Network Addressing

Device	Interface	IP Address
R1	Serial 0	10.2.0.1
R1	Ethernet0	10.1.0.1
R2	Serial 0	10.2.0.2
R2	Ethernet0	10.3.0.1

Instead of just adding the routing table to this section, let's go through a routing table exercise that I use in my classes. We'll start with R1. What are the connected interfaces? 10.2.0.1 and 10.1.0.1. Suppose the router has a 16-bit mask (/16 or 255.255.0.0). What are the two networks that R1 knows about as being directly connected? 10.2.0.0 and 10.1.0.0.

Now let's move to R2. What are the connected interfaces on R2? 10.2.0.2 and 10.3.0.1. Using a 16-bit mask, the two networks that R2 knows are directly connected are 10.2.0.0 and 10.3.0.0. So based on the information you have so far, you can build two routing tables. Table 4.2 contains the routing table for R1, and Table 4.3 contains the routing table for R2.

TABLE 4.2 R1 Routing Table

Network	Method	Interface
10.1.0.0	Directly connected	Ethernet0
10.2.0.0	Directly connected Serial 0	Serial 0

TABLE 4.3 R2 Routing Table

Network	Method	Interface
10.3.0.0	Directly connected	Ethernet0
10.2.0.0	Directly connected Serial 0	Serial 0

What happens to the routing tables when a routing protocol is enabled such as RIP? The router R1 advertises 10.1.0.0 to R2. The router R2 advertises 10.3.0.0. Table 4.4 contains the new routing table for R1, and Table 4.5 contains the new routing table for R2.

TABLE 4.4 R1 Routing Table with RIP

Network	Method	Interface
10.1.0.0	Directly connected	Ethernet0
10.2.0.0	Directly connected	Serial 0
10.3.0.0	RIP	Serial 0

TABLE 4.5 R2 Routing Table with RIP

Network	Method	Interface
10.1.0.0	RIP	Serial 0
10.2.0.0	Directly connected	Serial 0
10.3.0.0	Directly connected	Ethernet0

There's a reason that I'm going through all this basic material for you. First of all, there is no service provider infrastructure showing up on the customer routers R1 and R2. R1 and R2 are totally oblivious to anything behind their point-to-point connection. In addition, the service provider is totally oblivious to the IP addressing and routing protocols being run on the customer routers. R1 and R2 are on a private and isolated connection. If the customers misconfigure an IP address or a routing protocol, the service provider is unaware of it.

Since point-to-point networks are well isolated and private, it is possible to have customers using the exact same IP addressing scheme. For example, suppose a consultant sets up a network for Customer A using an IP addressing scheme of 10.1.0.0, 10.2.0.0, and 10.3.0.0. And suppose the very same consultant sets up a network for Customer B using 10.1.0.0, 10.2.0.0, and 10.3.0.0. Figure 4.17 illustrates the point-to-point networks for both Customer A and Customer B.

FIGURE 4.17 Point-to-point networks for Customer A and Customer B

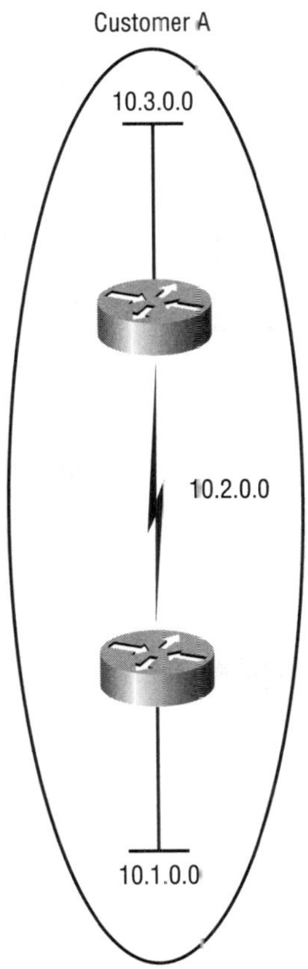

VPNs came about as a less expensive alternative to point-to-point links. Figure 4.18 illustrates a simple VPN with two customer sites connected with a single VC, simulating the original point-to-point connectivity illustrated in Figure 4.17.

FIGURE 4.18 A simple VPN with two customer sites

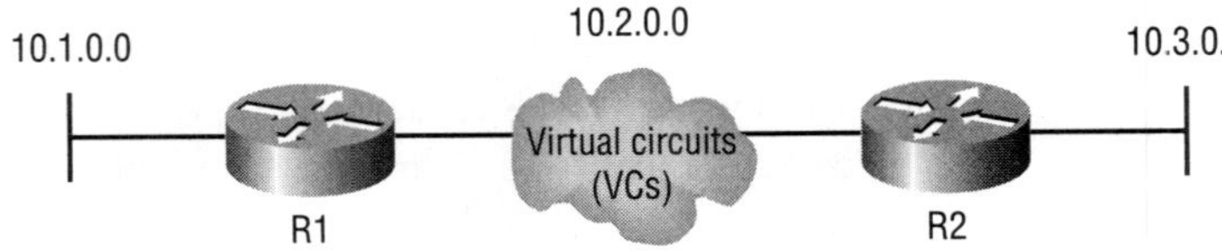

Table 4.6 lists the IP addresses and interfaces of the network devices in Figure 4.18.

TABLE 4.6 VPN Addressing

Device	Interface	IP Address
R1	Serial 0	10.2.0.1
R1	Ethernet0	10.1.0.1
R2	Serial 0	10.2.0.2
R2	Ethernet0	10.3.0.1

Just like the point-to-point example, R1 and R2 build routing tables based on directly connected interfaces. Table 4.7 contains the routing table for R1, and Table 4.8 contains the routing table for R2.

TABLE 4.7 R1 Routing Table

Network	Method	Interface
10.1.0.0	Directly connected	Ethernet0
10.2.0.0	Directly connected S0	Serial 0

TABLE 4.8 R2 Routing Table

Network	Method	Interface
10.3.0.0	Directly connected	Ethernet0
10.2.0.0	Directly connected S0	Serial 0

When a routing protocol such as RIP is enabled, the router R1 advertises 10.1.0.0 to R2 and the router R2 advertises 10.3.0.0. Table 4.9 contains the new routing table for R1, and Table 4.10 contains the new routing table for R2.

Just like point-to-point links, network devices connected together with VCs in a VPN have no knowledge of the service provider infrastructure. With a VPN, R1 and R2 are totally oblivious to anything behind their VC connection. In addition, the service provider is totally oblivious to the IP addressing and routing protocols being run on the customer routers. If the customers misconfigure an IP address or a routing protocol, the service provider is unaware of it.

TABLE 4.9 R1 Routing Table with RIP

Network	Method	Interface
10.1.0.0	Directly connected	Ethernet0
10.2.0.0	Directly connected	Serial 0
10.3.0.0	RIP	Serial 0

TABLE 4.10 R2 Routing Table with RIP

Network	Method	Interface
10.1.0.0	RIP	Serial 0
10.2.0.0	Directly connected	Serial 0
10.3.0.0	Directly connected	Ethernet0

VPNs result in well-isolated networks with the same privacy as point-to-point connections. With VPNs, it's possible to have customers using the exact same IP addressing scheme. For example, suppose a consultant sets up a network for Customer A using an IP addressing scheme of 10.1.0.0, 10.2.0.0, and 10.3.0.0. And suppose the very same consultant sets up a network for Customer B using 10.1.0.0, 10.2.0.0, and 10.3.0.0. Figure 4.19 illustrates the VPNs for both Customer A and Customer B.

FIGURE 4.19 VPNs for Customer A and Customer B

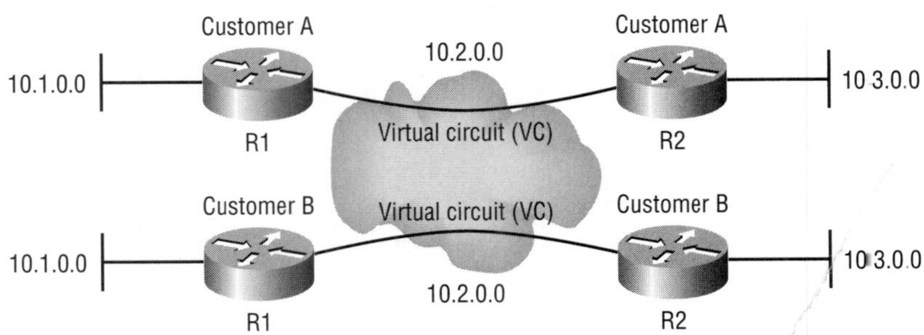

Peer-to-Peer VPNs

Service providers, in an effort to offer improved services to customers, began to implement *peer-to-peer VPNs* a few years ago. Peer-to-peer VPNs are a departure from the traditional overlay VPNs. The biggest difference between peer-to-peer VPNs and traditional VPNs is that a customer router peers with a service provider device instead of with another customer device.

Figure 4.20 illustrates a peer-to-peer VPN.

FIGURE 4.20 A peer-to-peer VPN network

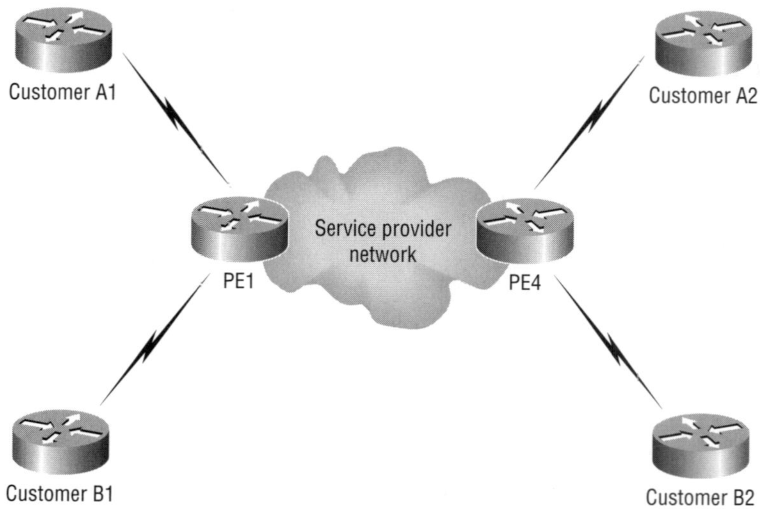

For the more experienced reader, Figure 4.20 is extremely scary. In Figure 4.20, customer routers actually peer with service provider devices. If you remember back to how traditional VPNs operated, the service provider network was transparent to the customer. With a traditional overlay VPN, the customer and service provider networks were well isolated from one another. Now, as you can see in Figure 4.20, the service provider network is visible.

Let's discuss peer-to-peer VPNs in more detail.

Optimal Routing

There are many benefits associated with peer-to-peer VPNs. The first of these benefits is *optimal routing*. To get optimal routing with a traditional

VPN, you need a full-mesh topology. You may recall that a full-mesh topology is expensive (in addition to being complex). To illustrate how peer-to-peer VPNs offer optimal routing, let's look at an example.

First, let's talk about optimal routing with an overlay VPN. In Figure 4.21, four customer sites in New York, Raleigh, Atlanta, and D.C. are connected with VCs in a full-mesh topology.

FIGURE 4.21 A full-mesh VPN with four customer sites

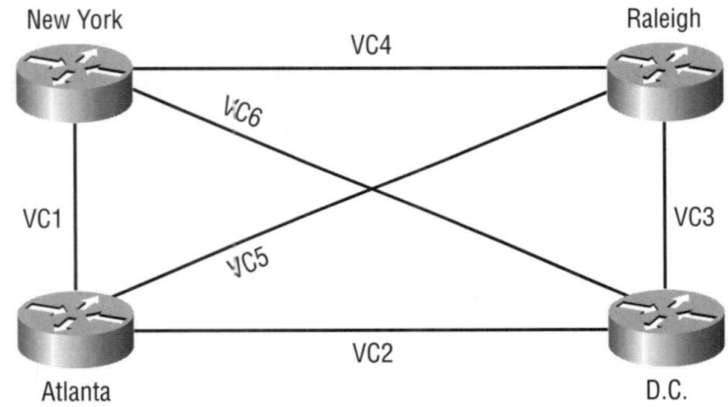

Figure 4.21 illustrates optimal routing. Notice that traffic from New York to Atlanta is directed over VC1. Traffic from New York to Raleigh is directed over VC4. Traffic from New York to D.C. is directed over VC6. Optimal routing is achieved through a full-mesh topology.

In Figure 4.22, the very same sites are connected with a peer-to-peer VPN. Customer sites use public addresses, and their routes are carried by the service provider. When traffic from New York needs to get to Atlanta, the next hop router is PE1. It is up to the service provider to make sure that traffic takes the most optimal path between New York and Atlanta. Traffic from New York to D.C. goes to PE1, and again it is up to the service provider to make sure that traffic follows the optimal path to D.C.

Notice the number of connections in Figure 4.22. The New York router has a single connection to PE1, Atlanta has a single connection to PE2, Raleigh has a single connection to PE3, and D.C. has a single connection to PE4. To add another site into the peer-to-peer VPN, from a connection standpoint, only requires one new connection between the new customer site and a service provider PE router. This is much better than needing to set up, or provision, a whole new set of VCs to create a full mesh in a traditional VPN.

FIGURE 4.22 A peer-to-peer VPN with four customer sites

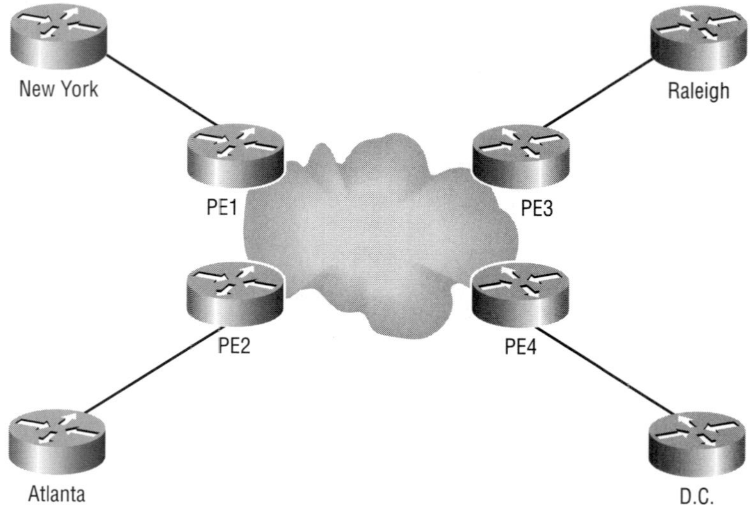

Adding a site to a peer-to-peer VPN is illustrated in Figure 4.23. Notice that the Charlotte site is connected to the service provider router PE3, along with the Raleigh site.

FIGURE 4.23 Peer-to-peer VPN provisioning

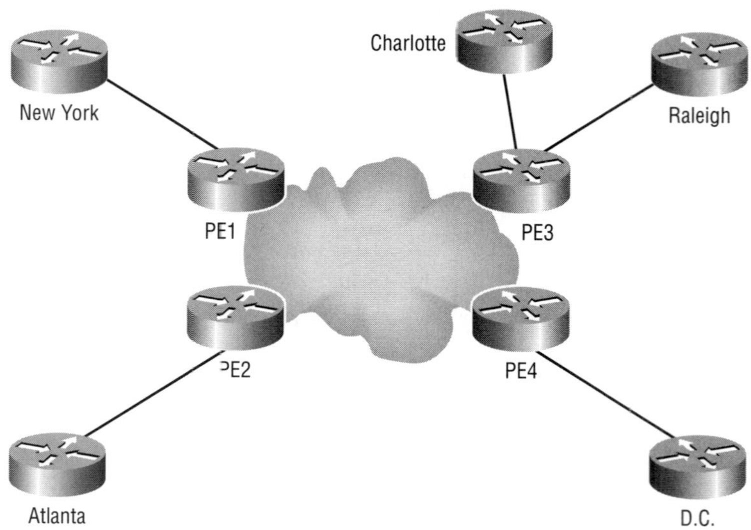

Peer-to-Peer Security

So far, you've learned about peer-to-peer VPNs from the standpoint of optimal routing and ease of provisioning. You may recall that one of the selling features of VPNs is the security and privacy of a dedicated point-to-point connection without the cost. This is a section on peer-to-peer VPNs, so there must be some privacy and security. Well, there is privacy and security, but only after someone configures it.

Let's look at an example. Figure 4.24 illustrates a simple peer-to-peer VPN that I'll use to discuss peer-to-peer VPN security.

FIGURE 4.24 A simple peer-to-peer VPN

How do you provide security to the New York and D.C. sites? Access lists? Too risky. If someone on the service provider side misconfigures an access list, you can lose security. How do you provide some type of privacy? Route filters? Too time-consuming. As you can tell, I'm not a fan of all the management required for peer-to-peer VPNs.

Peer-to-Peer VPN Routing

Before learning more detailed information about peer-to-peer VPNs, you need to understand routing inside peer-to-peer VPNs. The important thing to remember about routing in a peer-to-peer VPN is that the service provider network is responsible for optimal site-to-site routing. Since the service provider is responsible for optimal transport, it needs to know all the network routes. In traditional VPNs, the service provider did not know the details of customer routing; in peer-to-peer VPNs, it must.

NOTE With peer-to-peer VPNs, a service provider now knows the IP networks used by customers. Peer-to-peer VPNs do not support overlapping addresses or private addresses without per-site address translation.

Figure 4.25 is a simple peer-to-peer VPN with both the customer and relevant service provider networks illustrated.

FIGURE 4.25 A simple peer-to-peer VPN

The service provider in this VPN needs to know about both customer networks (204.134.83.0 and 204.134.84.0). What methods can the service provider devices use to learn about the customer networks? A routing protocol could be run between the PE routers and the customer routers, but then it would be necessary to redistribute the learned customer networks into Border Gateway Protocol (BGP) for use in the service provider cloud.

NOTE If the customer uses dynamic routing protocols, the service provider becomes responsible for convergence.

Instead of a routing protocol, static routes could be configured on the PE routers, and then those static routes could be redistributed into BGP. For example, on PE1, a static route of 204.134.83.0 would be configured to point to the New York router. Since the service provider is ensuring optimal paths for traffic between the two sites, the static routes need to be redistributed into BGP.

How about the customer routers? If a routing protocol is being used between the PE routers and the customer routers, routes need to be redistributed from BGP into whatever protocol is being run between the PE routers and the customer routers. If static routes are configured on the PE routers, the default routes could be used, but that would really mess up security.

Peer-to-Peer VPN Security

What is meant by "really mess up security?" First of all, access lists are used to prevent unauthorized access to the customer networks. Access lists slow down PE routers and are prone to error by human hands.

In addition to access lists, a lack of routing information is important for security. Back in Chapter 2, "Frame-Mode MPLS," I reviewed traditional Layer 3 forwarding. If a router does not have a route to a remote network, the packet is dropped. Don't think of peer-to-peer VPNs in the context of site-to-site connectivity plus the Internet. Only think of peer-to-peer VPNs as replacing traditional VPNs.

Customer routers should only know about routes for their VPN. They don't have Internet routes (they could, but that would be another entire book) or routes to other networks used by other VPNs. If customer routers only have routes for their VPN, the routing table is providing some security. If a default route is used anywhere in the network, security is out the door.

For example, suppose Customer A and Customer B both use the same service provider for a peer-to-peer VPN. An evil employee in Customer A's network decides to hack Customer B's network. So the evil employee, somehow knowing an IP address of some server in Customer B's network, tries to telnet to the remote server. The packet is sent to the outbound Customer A router and is dropped because the router does not have a route to get to the Customer B server. (Remember the routing table is providing some security.) If a default route is used by the Customer A router, the evil telnet session is sent through the service provider network and ultimately to the Customer B server.

Remember that communication is a two-way street. The Customer B server tries send a packet back to the evil hacker, but it will be dropped by the outbound Customer B router because it does not have a route to get to the evil hacker's computer. (Remember that the routing protocol is providing some type of security.) If a default route were configured on Customer B's router, communication would be possible.

To make sure that even if the customers use default routes, there is some security, access lists need to be configured on the service provider PE routers. What happens if the service provider misconfigures the access list and Customer B gets hacked? Can you smell the lawsuit?

To keep from worrying about all of this, some service providers might run separate routing protocols for each individual customer VPN. Although this approach is used, it has some serious drawbacks such as increased management, network complexity, and routing table overhead on all associated devices.

As you can see so far, peer-to-peer VPNs require a lot of work. In Chapter 5, "MPLS VPNs," you'll be introduced to MPLS VPNs, and you'll immediately see why they are preferable to the types of peer-to-peer VPNs that are described in this chapter.

Speaking of peer-to-peer VPNs, there are two types: *shared router* and *dedicated router*.

Shared router In Figure 4.26, different customers connect to the same PE. For example, Customer A1 and Customer B1 connect to the New York PE. "Shared router" really means "shared routing table." On the PE, there is only one routing table. Security and route filtering are a pain because of the amount of management overheard required for security and routing table isolation.

FIGURE 4.26 A shared router VPN implementation

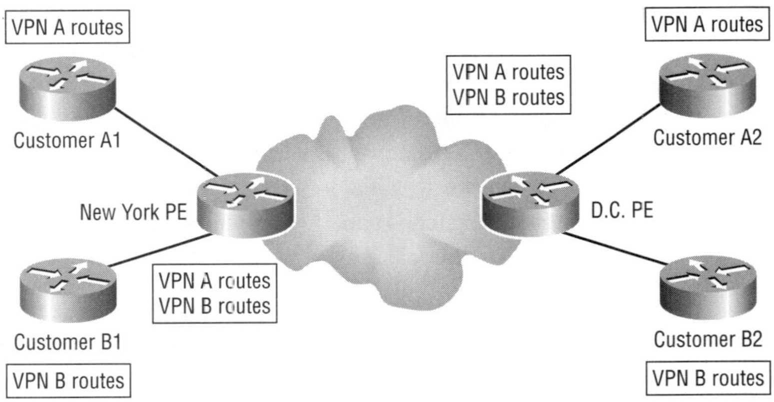

Dedicated router To get away from sharing a single routing table on a PE and all the management that is required, a service provider can provide a dedicated PE router for each VPN customer. Figure 4.27 illustrates a dedicated router implementation.

Dedicated routers offer more security but at a substantial price (a dedicated PE router for each separate VPN customer).

FIGURE 4.27 A dedicated router VPN implementation

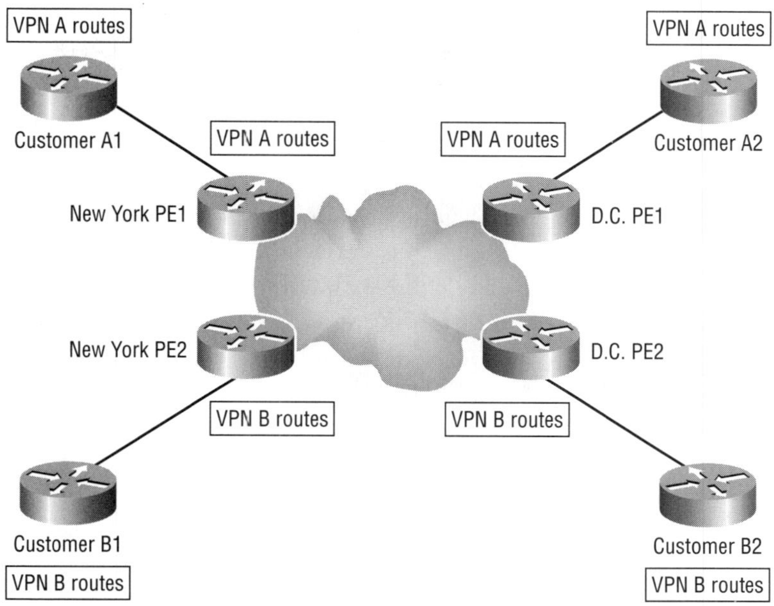

Real World Peer-to-Peer Networks

To give you an example of how peer-to-peer VPN networks look in the real world, let's run through a quick example.

Suppose there's a customer with a simple VPN using Frame Relay. Figure 4.28 illustrates this customer's network.

FIGURE 4.28 A simple VPN using Frame Relay

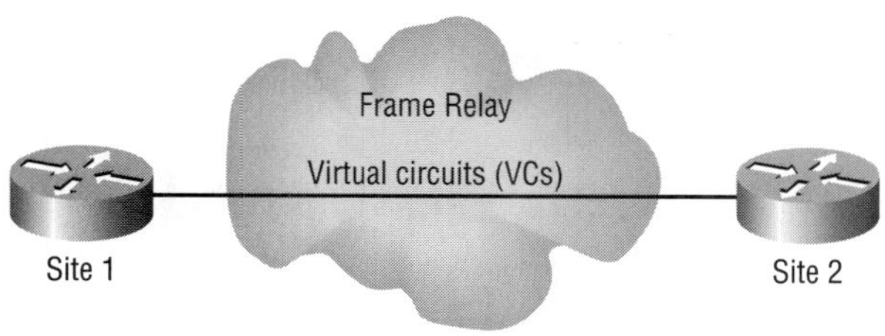

Now the customer wants a peer-to-peer VPN. Figure 4.29 illustrates the new peer-to-peer network.

FIGURE 4.29 A simple peer-to-peer VPN

So far, nothing should be new. What you really need to know is that technologies such as Frame Relay, ISDN, DSL, etc. are still in use by the service provider. Figure 4.30 illustrates a real world example where Site 1 and Site 2 connect to the PE routers through Frame Relay.

FIGURE 4.30 A real world peer-to-peer VPN network

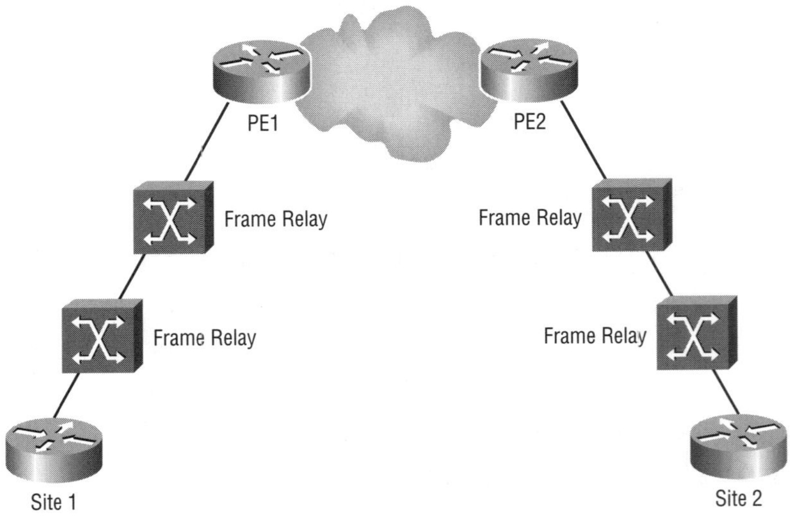

Overlay VPNs Compared to Peer-to-Peer VPNs

Overlay VPN technology has been around for a long while. Since it's been around for so long, everyone knows how it works. In addition, the service provider and customer sites are well isolated from each other. Remember, to ensure optimal routing, a full-mesh topology needs to be implemented between all customer sites. All those VCs don't come for free, and full-mesh VPNs can get quite complex, especially in large environments.

Peer-to-peer VPNs are a solution to the full-mesh problem. With peer-to-peer VPNs, the service provider becomes involved with customer routing and ensures optimal path selection through the service provider network. Every customer site connects and gets, in essence, a full-mesh topology simply as a function of the peer-to-peer VPN. Drawbacks? Security, management, and added network complexity.

Neither overlay nor peer-to-peer VPNs are based on MPLS. In Chapter 5, you'll learn about MPLS VPNs allowing peer-to-peer VPNs to be implemented in a simpler and more secure manner.

Summary

This chapter explained that VPNs provide the same security and privacy of dedicated point-to-point connections without the costs. There are many types of technologies used to implement VPNs. At Layer 1, there is SONET, E1, T1, and ISDN. At Layer 2, there is Frame Relay, X.25, and ATM. At Layer 3, there is GRE and IPSec. When each site in a VPN is from the same company, the network is called an intranet. When sites are from different companies, or organizations, the network is called an extranet.

How VPNs are connected together also falls under topological categories. A full-mesh topology is when every site is connected to every other site. A partial-mesh topology is when some sites are fully meshed and other sites are not. In a hub-and-spoke topology, spoke sites are connected only to a hub site. Financial organizations make extensive use of hub-and-spoke topologies because they usually have centralized resources that need to be accessed by remote branch offices.

In an effort to offer improved services to customers, service providers began to implement peer-to-peer VPNs. The biggest difference between peer-to-peer VPNs and traditional VPNs is that a customer actually peers with a service provider device. The two ways to implement a peer-to-peer VPN is using either a dedicated or a shared PE router. A peer-to-peer VPN using a shared router requires extensive management using access lists and route filters to ensure security. Peer-to-peer VPNs with a dedicated router are easier to implement, but they're expensive.

Overlay VPNs are based on well-known and established technologies that keep customer sites isolated. The problem is that they don't scale. Peer-to-peer VPNs are an improvement, but they're extremely difficult to manage and secure.

Exam Essentials

Be able to describe virtual private networks. VPNs evolved as a cheaper but just-as-good alternative to point-to-point connections. In a VPN, customer sites are connected together with VCs. The customer network does not know the details of the service provider. Conversely, the service provider does not know about customer IP addresses or routing protocols.

Be able to define the major VPN topologies. There are essentially three major VPN topologies: full-mesh, partial-mesh, and hub-and-spoke. A full-mesh topology ensures optimal routing and redundancy. The drawback of a full-mesh topology is the number of VCs required to implement it. A partial-mesh topology has fewer virtual circuits and therefore costs less than a full-mesh topology. A partial-mesh topology does not offer the same optimal routing as a full-mesh topology. A hub-and-spoke topology is the cheapest of all VPNs to implement. A hub-and-spoke topology is most often implemented by financial organizations.

Understand peer-to-peer VPNs. To offer better services to customers, service providers began to implement peer-to-peer VPNs. The biggest difference between peer-to-peer VPNs and traditional VPNs is that a customer router actually peers with a service provider device. With a peer-to-peer VPN, a service provider becomes responsible for routing protocol convergence, knows the details of customer networks, and must work overtime to ensure security. There are two ways that peer-to-peer VPNs are implemented: dedicated router and shared router. A dedicated peer-to-peer VPN uses a single PE, or a set of PE routers, for a single customer. A shared peer-to-peer VPN has many customers connecting to the same PE router. A shared PE has the most security problems.

Be able to compare overlay and peer-to-peer VPNs. Overlay VPN technology has been around for a while and everyone knows how they work. With an overlay VPN, the service provider and customer sites are well isolated from each other. To have optimal routing in an overlay VPN, you need a full-mesh topology.

Peer-to-peer VPNs eliminate the need for a full mesh of VCs. With a peer-to-peer VPN solution, the service provider becomes involved with customer routing and ensures optimal path selection through the service provider network. Every customer site connects and gets, in essence, a full mesh simply as a function of the peer-to-peer VPN.

Key Terms

Before you take the exam, be certain you are familiar with the following terms:

dedicated router

extranet

full-mesh topology

hub-and-spoke topology

intranet

leased lines

optimal routing

overlay

partial-mesh topology

peer-to-peer VPNs

point-to-point connections

redundant hub-and-spoke topology

shared router

Review Questions

1. VPNs emerged as a technology to replace __________.

   A. Point-to-point connections

   B. Overlays

   C. Tag-switched VPNs

   D. Full-mesh topologies

2. Which of the following is not an overlay VPN topology?

   A. Full-mesh

   B. Partial-mesh

   C. Hub-and-spoke

   D. Peer-to-peer

3. Which of the following topologies is usually used by financial organizations?

   A. Full-mesh

   B. Partial-mesh

   C. Hub-and-spoke

   D. Peer-to-peer

4. If optimal routing is desired in a VPN topology, which of the following topologies is the best?

   A. Full-mesh

   B. Partial-mesh

   C. Hub-and-spoke

   D. None of the above

5. In an overlay VPN, a customer router __________ aware of the service provider infrastructure.

   A. Is

   B. Is not

6. In which of the following VPN methods is it the most difficult to implement proper security?

   A. Simple VPN

   B. Overlay

   C. Peer-to-peer

   D. None of the above

7. In a peer-to-peer VPN, a customer router __________ aware of the service provider infrastructure.

   A. Is

   B. Is not

8. Which of the following peer-to-peer VPN methods has the most security problems associated with it?

   A. Dedicated router

   B. Shared router

9. A peer-to-peer VPN offers the same optimal traffic flow as a __________ topology?

   A. Full-mesh

   B. Partial-mesh

   C. Hub-and-spoke

   D. None of the above

10. Which of the following overlay VPN topologies is the least expensive to implement?

    A. Full-mesh

    B. Partial-mesh

    C. Hub-and-spoke

    D. None of the above

11. IPSec and GRE tunnels are Layer __________ VPN technologies?

    A. 1

    B. 2

    C. 3

    D. 7

12. Which of the following is a Layer 1 VPN technology?

    A. IPSec

    B. Frame Relay

    C. GRE

    D. ISDN

13. A(n) __________ is where everyone being connected is part of the same company or organization.

    A. Intranet

    B. Extranet

    C. Combination of intranet and extranet

    D. None of the above

14. A(n) __________ is where sites from different companies or organizations are connected.

    A. Intranet

    B. Extranet

    C. Combination of intranet and extranet

    D. None of the above

15. Frame Relay and ATM are Layer ________ VPN technologies.

    A. 1

    B. 2

    C. 3

    D. 7

16. Which of the following topologies provides the most redundancy?

    A. Full-mesh

    B. Partial-mesh

    C. Hub-and-spoke

    D. None of the above

17. Which of the following peer-to-peer VPN methods is the most expensive to implement?

    A. Dedicated router

    B. Shared router

18. Which of the following overlay VPN topologies is typically used by financial organizations?

    A. Full-mesh

    B. Partial-mesh

    C. Hub-and-spoke

    D. None of the above

19. In a peer-to-peer VPN, the __________ becomes responsible for routing protocol convergence.

    A. Customer

    B. Service provider

    C. Edge-LSR

    D. PE

20. Which of the following are valid peer-to-peer VPN methods? (Choose two.)

    A. Dedicated router

    B. Full-mesh

    C. Partial-mesh

    D. Shared router

Answers to Review Questions

1. A. Point-to-point connections are expensive. VPNs emerged as a cheaper alternative with the same security and privacy.
2. D. The major overlay VPN topologies are full-mesh, partial-mesh, and hub-and-spoke.
3. C. Since most financial organizations have centralized resources that need to be accessed by remote branch offices, a hub-and-spoke topology is usually used for their networks.
4. A. To ensure optimal routing between sites, a full-mesh topology is the best alternative.
5. B. With overlay VPNs, a customer router is not aware of the service provider infrastructure.
6. C. Hands down, peer-to-peer VPNs require the most management to implement proper security.
7. A. With peer-to-peer VPNs, customer routers are aware of the service provider infrastructure because they peer with the service provider routers.
8. B. A shared router peer-to-peer VPN has the most security problems because different customers connect to the same router.
9. A. A peer-to-peer VPN ensures optimal traffic flow. To implement optimal traffic flow between sites with an overlay VPN, a full-mesh topology is required.
10. C. A hub-and-spoke topology, with the least number of VCs, is the least expensive of all overlay VPNs to implement.
11. C. IPSec and GRE are Layer 3 VPN technologies.
12. D. ISDN is a Layer 1 VPN technology. Other technologies at Layer 1 are E1, T1, and SONET.
13. A. In an intranet, sites from the same company or organization are connected in a single network.
14. B. An extranet is when sites from different companies or organizations are connected.

15. B. Frame Relay and ATM are Layer 2 VPN technologies. An additional technology at Layer 2 is X.25.

16. A. If you have the money, nothing beats a full-mesh topology for redundancy.

17. A. A dedicated router peer-to-peer VPN requires that each VPN have its own dedicated router used only for that VPN. Dedicated router peer-to-peer VPNs are the most expensive to implement.

18. C. A hub-and-spoke topology is often used by financial organizations because they usually have centralized resources that need to be accessed by remote branch offices.

19. B. In a peer-to-peer VPN, the service provider becomes responsible for routing protocol convergence.

20. A, D. The two ways to implement peer-to-peer VPNs are dedicated router and shared router.

Chapter 5

MPLS VPNs

CCIP MPLS EXAM TOPICS COVERED IN THIS CHAPTER:

- ✓ Describe the major architectural blocks of MPLS VPN.
- ✓ Describe the MPLS VPN routing model and packet forwarding.
- ✓ Identify the IOS commands and their proper syntax used to configure virtual routing and forwarding tables.
- ✓ Identify the IOS commands and their proper syntax used to configure Multi-Protocol BGP in MPLS VPN backbone.

Here in Chapter 5, I'll begin to pull together all the information you've learned so far. This chapter starts with a walk-through of the configuration tasks required to configure an IGP, BGP between edge routers, and MPLS. MPLS VPNs are discussed from a 35,000-foot view. You'll learn about the virtual routing and forwarding tables and about route distinguishers. You will also learn the ins and outs of their configuration.

There is a great deal of configuration required to make MPLS VPNs work. This chapter describes only the basic configuration required to get the network set up to support MPLS VPNs. What you learn in this chapter will be complemented by a discussion in Chapter 6, "MPLS VPNs and RIP," of routing inside MPLS VPNs and several configuration exercises.

Pay close attention to the configuration commands for MPLS, MP-BGP, and MPLS VPNs discussed in this chapter. Take things slow. This chapter gets you ready for the full-blown end-to-end service provider implementation described in Chapter 6.

Service Provider Configuration

Before talking about MPLS VPNs, let's put all the pieces together. *MPLS VPNs* are an add-on service to an already-up-and-functioning MPLS network.

To start with, you've already been exposed to everything necessary to configure a simple network for MPLS support. You may remember a few things from previous chapters. The service provider network runs an IGP (such as OSPF or IS-IS) on all provider devices. BGP is configured only on the network's edge.

The reason you're doing all the configuration in this chapter is so that you're aware of all the technologies running in the background that make an MPLS network really work. The next section of this chapter talks about configuring MPLS VPNs in a service provider network where MPLS is already set up.

So, let's get to the service provider network configuration. Figure 5.1 illustrates a simple network with just the service provider devices.

FIGURE 5.1 A simple service provider network

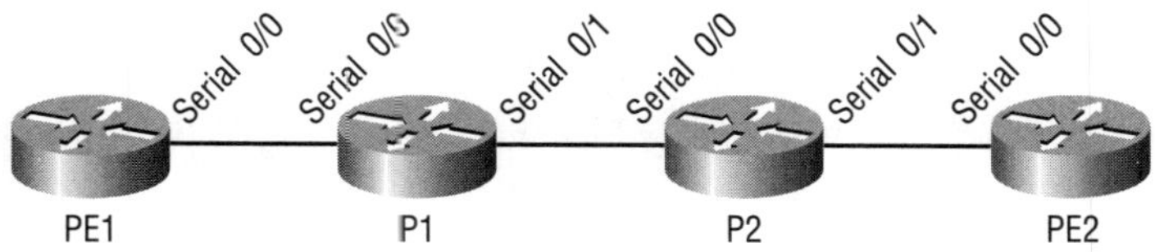

Table 5.1 lists the IP addresses and interfaces of all the service provider devices in Figure 5.1.

TABLE 5.1 Service Provider IP Addressing

Device	Serial 0/0	Serial 0/1	Loopback 0
PE1	192.168.1.10		192.168.1.1
P1	192.168.1.9	192.168.1.14	192.168.1.2
P2	192.168.1.13	192.168.1.18	192.168.1.3
PE2	192.168.1.17		192.168.1.4

Assuming that you already know how to configure hostnames, bring interfaces up, assign IP addresses, and the like, the first task is to configure all the routing protocols. To avoid confusion with basic IGP routing, let's use RIPv2 in this configuration example.

On router PE1, you configure RIPv2 with the following commands:

```
PE1#config t
PE1(config)#router rip
PE1(config-router)#version 2
PE1(config-router)#network 192.168.1.0
```

On router P1, you configure RIPv2 with the following commands:

```
P1#config t
P1(config)#router rip
P1(config-router)#version 2
P1(config-router)#network 192.168.1.0
```

On router P2, you configure RIPv2 with the following commands:

```
P2#config t
P2(config)#router rip
P2(config-router)#version 2
P2(config-router)#network 192.168.1.0
```

On router PE2, you configure RIPv2 with the following commands:

```
PE2#config t
PE2(config)#router rip
PE2(config-router)#version 2
PE2(config-router)#network 192.168.1.0
```

Now that you have an IGP up and running, the next thing you need to do is configure BGP on the PE routers.

On router PE1, you configure BGP with the following commands:

```
PE1#config t
PE1(config)#router bgp 1
PE1(config-router)#no synchronization
PE1(config-router)#network 192.168.1.1 mask 255.255.255.255
PE1(config-router)#neighbor 192.168.1.4 remote-as 1
PE1(config-router)#neighbor 192.168.1.4 update-source Loopback0
PE1(config-router)#no auto summary
PE1(config-router)#redistribute static
```

On router PE2, you configure BGP with the following commands:

```
PE2#config t
PE2(config)#router bgp 1
PE2(config-router)#no synchronization
PE2(config-router)#network 192.168.1.4 mask 255.255.255.255
PE2(config-router)#neighbor 192.168.1.1 remote-as 1
PE2(config-router)#neighbor 192.168.1.1 update-source Loopback0
PE2(config-router)#no auto summary
PE2(config-router)#redistribute static
```

Now that all the routing protocols are in place, the final task is to enable MPLS on PE1, P1, P2, and PE2.

On PE1, you configure MPLS for Serial 0/0 only with the following commands:

```
PE1#config t
PE1(config)#ip cef
PE1(config)#mpls ip
PE1(config-if)#interface serial 0/0
PE1(config-if)#mpls ip
```

On P1, you configure MPLS for both Serial 0/0 and Serial 0/1 with the following commands:

```
P1#config t
P1(config)#ip cef
P1(config)#mpls ip
P1(config-if)#interface serial 0/0
P1(config-if)#mpls ip
P1(config-if)#exit
P1(config)#interface serial 0/1
P1(config-if)#mpls ip
```

On P2, you configure MPLS for both Serial 0/0 and Serial 0/1 with the following commands:

```
P2#config t
P2(config)#ip cef
P2(config)#mpls ip
P2(config-if)#interface serial 0/0
P2(config-if)#mpls ip
P2(config-if)#exit
P2(config)#interface serial 0/1
P2(config-if)#mpls ip
```

On PE2, you configure MPLS for Serial 0/0 only with the following commands:

```
PE2#config t
PE2(config)#ip cef
PE2(config)#mpls ip
PE2(config-if)#interface serial 0/0
PE2(config-if)#mpls ip
```

So you can see from these sets of commands that setting up MPLS is pretty easy: an IGP on all routers, BGP on the edge routers, and MPLS configured globally and then specified for an interface. Piece of cake, eh?

If you want to configure tag switching, you configure an IGP, BGP, and then tag switching on the same device. The commands to configure tag switching are described in the next few paragraphs.

On PE1, you configure tag switching for Serial 0/0 only with the following commands:

```
PE1#config t
PE1(config)#ip cef
PE1(config)#tag-switching advertise tags
PE1(config-if)#interface serial 0/0
PE1(config-if)#tag-switching ip
```

On P1, you configure tag switching for both Serial 0/0 and Serial 0/1 with the following commands:

```
P1#config t
P1(config)#ip cef
P1(config)#tag-switching advertise tags
P1(config-if)#interface serial 0/0
P1(config-if)#tag-switching ip
P1(config-if)#exit
P1(config)#interface serial 0/1
P1(config-if)#tag-switching ip
```

On P2, you configure tag switching for both Serial 0/0 and Serial 0/1 with the following commands:

```
P2#config t
P2(config)#ip cef
P2(config)#tag-switching advertise tags
P2(config-if)#interface serial 0/0
P2(config-if)#tag-switching ip
P2(config-if)#exit
P2(config)#interface serial 0/1
P2(config-if)#tag-switching ip
```

On PE2, you configure tag switching for Serial 0/0 only with the following commands:

```
PE1#config t
PE1(config)#ip cef
```

```
PE1(config)#tag-switching advertise tags
PE1(config-if)#interface serial 0/0
PE1(config-if)#tag-switching ip
```

MPLS VPNs

As you learned in Chapter 4, "VPNs: An Overview," there are many ways to connect customer sites together. Point-to-point links provide guaranteed security and privacy, but they're expensive. Virtual private networks (VPNs) are an alternative to point-to-point links.

As a new service offering, providers introduced *peer-to-peer VPNs* several years ago. A peer-to-peer VPN was radically different from other VPNs in that the customer router actually peered with a service provider device. Now that the customer and service provider were communicating with each other, a whole new set of problems arose. How do you manage security? An overlapping address space? The answer was simply more network management, including access lists and route filters.

MPLS VPNs offer the same privacy and security as a traditional VPN without the worries. Overlapping address spaces, intranets, extranets, and even hub-and-spoke topologies are supported in an MPLS VPN. The next few sections describe the characteristics of MPLS VPNs.

Virtual Router

The most basic concept of an MPLS VPN is that of a *virtual router*. If you remember back to Chapter 4, there were two ways to implement a peer-to-peer VPN: dedicated router and shared router. An MPLS VPN combines these two functions into what is called a virtual router.

So far in this book I haven't yet bored you with any RFCs. Hey, you're studying MPLS so you can pass a test, right? Well, I want to use a little snippet from RFC 2917, "A Core MPLS IP VPN Architecture," to explain the basic principles of a virtual router.

RFC 2917 states the following:

> "A virtual router is a collection of threads, either static or dynamic, in a routing device, that provides routing and forwarding services much like physical routers. A virtual router need not be a separate operating system process (although it could be); it simply has to provide the illusion that a dedicated router is available to satisfy the

> needs of the network(s) to which it is connected. A virtual router, like its physical counterpart, is an element in a routing domain. The other routers in this domain could be physical or virtual routers themselves. Given that the virtual router connects to a specific (logically discrete) routing domain and that a physical router can support multiple virtual routers, it follows that a physical router supports multiple (logically discrete) routing domains. From the user (VPN customer) standpoint, it is imperative that the virtual router be as equivalent to a physical router as possible. In other words, with very minor and very few exceptions, the virtual router should appear for all purposes (configuration, management, monitoring, and troubleshooting) like a dedicated physical router."

Remember that an MPLS VPN is different from a peer-to-peer VPN. An MPLS VPN works by acting like a dedicated router (with separate routing tables) but is on a single router (just like a shared peer-to-peer VPN).

In plain language, a virtual router is a single router that appears to be many routers. Customer routing tables are kept separated from one another, even though they all connect to the same router. In essence, from the customer's perspective, they have a dedicated router just for them. From the service provider's perspective, a single router simulates all the necessary mechanisms to provide this perspective to the customer.

Virtual Routing and Forwarding Tables

To implement the concept of virtual routers, Cisco uses an IOS mechanism called a *virtual routing and forwarding (VRF) table*. A VRF is made up of the following components:

- A VRF-specific IP routing table
- A CEF (Cisco Express Forwarding) table
- Interfaces in the VRF
- Routing protocol rules and filters

A VRF is essentially a dedicated routing table, with routing table mechanisms, for a particular customer. Remember that we're talking about a *virtual* router here.

NOTE Any commands executed on the router in global configuration mode apply to the router as a whole or globally.

MPLS Operational Overview

Before getting started on the particulars of the operation of an MPLS VPN, I'd first like to give you the 35,000-foot view. Figure 5.2 illustrates a simple service provider network that we'll use for this discussion.

FIGURE 5.2 A simple service provider network

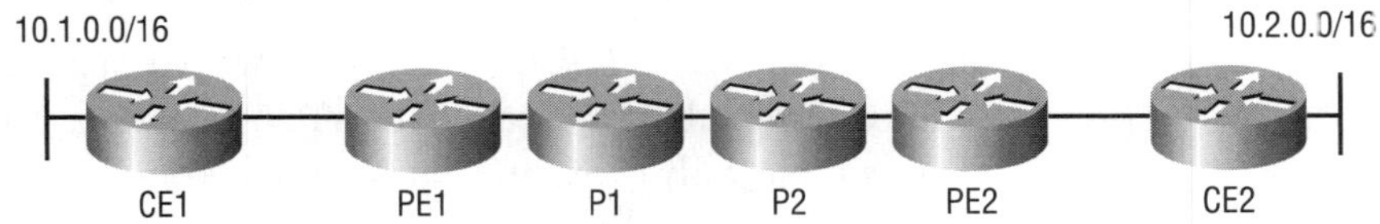

Notice in Figure 5.2 that CE1 and CE2 have private addresses. The service provider network uses public addresses. In Figure 5.2, only two customer sites are connected together in the VPN. Although there are no problems with overlapping addresses in Figure 5.2, most service providers do not like to carry private customer network addresses through their backbone. Therefore, Network Address Translation (NAT) is used to convert the private customer networks to a public address space determined by the service provider. In addition, as more customers are added, there will certainly be a problem with overlapping private addresses. Therefore, NAT is used to prevent the overlapping addresses.

With the advent of a VRF, a single router can "pretend" to be many routers by maintaining separate routing tables for each VRF, thereby eliminating the need for NAT to support customer VPNs. Figure 5.3 shows the routing tables as they would exist on devices in the service provider network.

FIGURE 5.3 Routing tables with VRFs

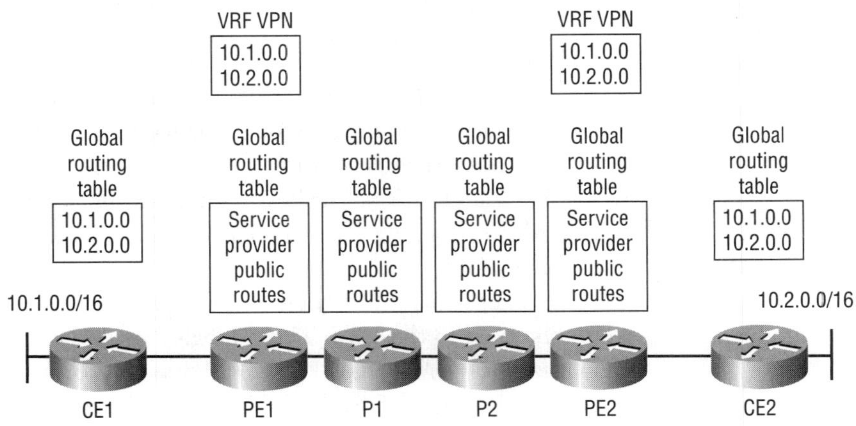

NOTE For Internet access, NAT would still be required for private-IP-address-to-public-IP-address translation.

Notice in Figure 5.3 that there are two types of routing tables: one for the router as a whole (global) and another representing the VRF (vrf vpn). Router CE1 has a global routing table. The routing table on CE1 contains only routes for the VPN. On PE1, there are two separate routing tables. One of the routing tables is used for the VPN. The other routing table, the global routing table, only contains routes for the service provider network. Routers P1 and P2 have no knowledge whatsoever of the customer routes coming from CE1 and CE2. Finally, router PE2 has both a global routing table and a separate routing table just for the customer's VPN.

You may be wondering how all of this is going to work. Recall the discussions in the first two chapters of this book. In an MPLS-enabled network, it is not necessary for every device in the network to know about every possible network route. In addition, labels can be stacked. In the case of MPLS VPNs, IP packets enter the network as unlabeled IP. The edge-LSR not only applies a label for the packet to move through the network, but it also provides a VPN label. This process is called *label stacking*. Figure 5.4 illustrates this operation.

FIGURE 5.4 MPLS VPN label stacking

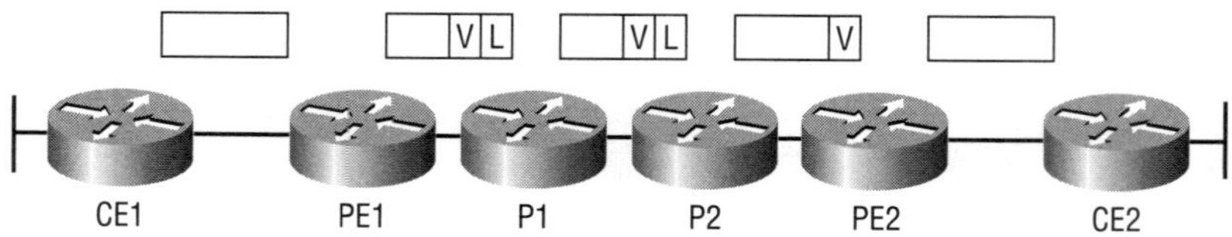

Why is the VPN label important? Well, how else does an egress LSR know which VPN a packet is destined for? Figure 5.5 illustrates a subset of the service provider network. Notice in this figure that there are two customers (Customer X and Customer Y) with IP addressing that overlaps. If a packet arrives at PE2 with a destination address on the 10.1.0.0 network, router PE2 has no idea which 10.1.0.0 network the packet should go to.

To remedy this situation, the PE2 router assigns labels to customer routes that show up in the VRF. Those labels are then propagated through *Multi-Protocol BGP (MP-BGP)*. MP-BGP *must* be configured for an MPLS VPN to work. In Figure 5.6, the PE2 router has assigned a label of 32 to the

10.1.0.0 network for Customer X and propagated that to P2. When a packet arrives at PE2, the router sees the VPN label first. Since PE2 assigned the label, it knows exactly where the packet goes.

FIGURE 5.5 Forwarding packets without labels on VPNs with overlapping network addresses

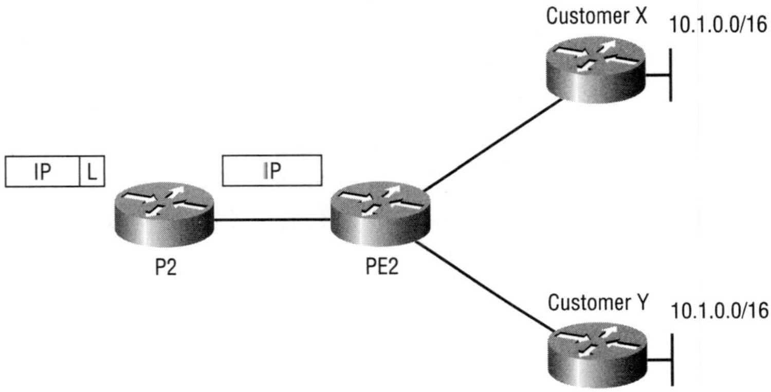

FIGURE 5.6 Forwarding packets with labels on VPNs with overlapping network addresses

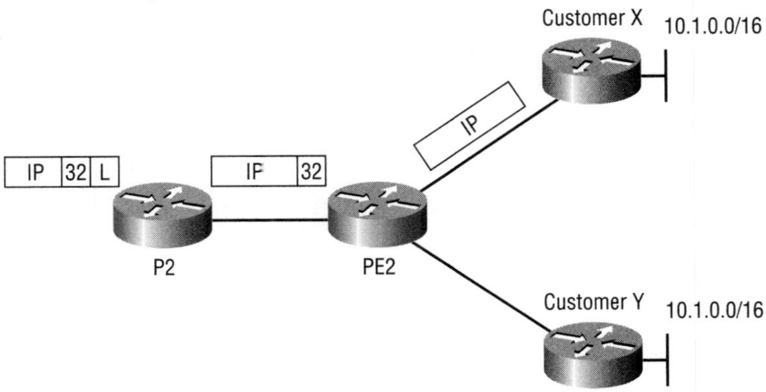

MP-BGP Configuration

MP-BGP must be configured between all routers that need to propagate or exchange VPN routes.

> **NOTE** VPN routes are referred to as *VPN version 4 (VPNv4) routes*.

To configure MP-BGP, the `address-family vpnv4` command is used from within the traditional BGP configuration. An *address family* is sometimes referred to as a *routing context*. In this case, the `address family vpnv4` command is used within global BGP configuration. Therefore, this special context does not need a new BGP process. (Only one BGP is supported on a Cisco IOS router.) Neighbors, if already configured in global BGP, simply need to be activated.

Communities must be configured as well. There are two types of communities: extended and standard. Standard communities have not been replaced by extended communities. It is necessary to specify extended communities between MP-BGP neighbors for proper VPN operation. The default operation of BGP is to send no community values. Therefore, you must manually configure MP-BGP to send both standard and extended communities.

Based on the configuration illustrated in Figure 5.1 earlier in this chapter, the final task is to configure MP-BGP between PE1 and PE2. Just to refresh your memory, Figure 5.7 illustrates the example service provider network.

FIGURE 5.7 A service provider network

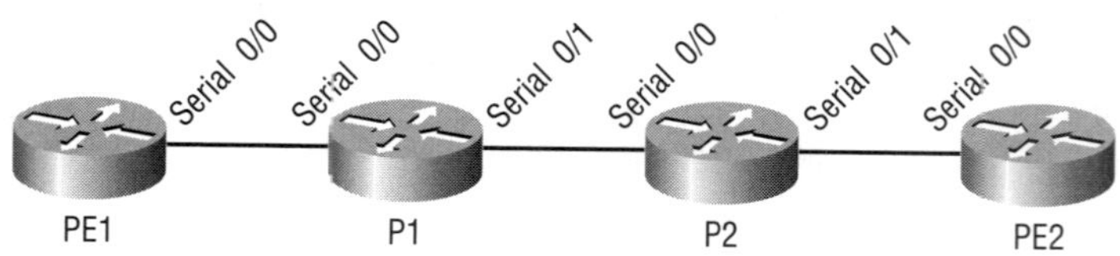

Table 5.2 lists the IP addresses and interfaces for all the devices in the service provider network in Figure 5.7.

TABLE 5.2 Service Provider IP Addressing

Device	Serial 0/0	Serial 0/1	Loopback 0
PE1	192.168.1.10		192.168.1.1
P1	192.168.1.9	192.168.1.14	192.168.1.2
P2	192.168.1.13	192.168.1.18	192.168.1.3
PE2	192.168.1.17		192.168.1.4

On the PE1 router, you configure MP-BGP with the following commands:

```
PE1#config t
PE1(config)#router bgp 1
PE1(config-router)#address-family vpnv4
PE1(config-router)#neighbor 192.168.1.4 activate
PE1(config-router)#neighbor 192.168.1.4 next-hop self
PE1(config-router)#neighbor 192.168.1.4 send-community both
```

On the PE2 router, you configure MP-BGP with the following commands:

```
PE2#config t
PE2(config)#router bgp 1
PE2(config-router)#address-family vpnv4
PE2(config-router)#neighbor 192.168.1.1 activate
PE2(config-router)#neighbor 192.168.1.1 next-hop self
PE1(config-router)#neighbor 192.168.1.1 send-community both
```

A sample output from the `show running-config` command is as follows. In this output, locate the global BGP commands and then the MP-BGP commands under the `address-family vpnv4` section:

```
router bgp 1
 no synchronization
 network 192.168.1.1 mask 255.255.255.255
 neighbor 192.168.1.4 remote-as 1
 neighbor 192.168.1.4 update-source Loopback0
 redistribute static
!
address-family vpnv4
 neighbor 192.168.1.4 activate
 neighbor 192.168.1.4 next-hop self
 neighbor 192.168.1.4 send-community both
```

NOTE: Neighbors are first specified in global BGP, and then for MP-BGP, neighbors are activated.

An MPLS VPN Example

As with everything in MPLS, the best way to understand MPLS VPNs is with an example. Let's begin with a business scenario. Customer A has one location in Atlanta and a second location in Raleigh. Customer B also has one location in Atlanta and a second location in Raleigh. Currently, both Customer A and Customer B have their sites connected with an overlay VPN, as illustrated in Figure 5.8. Note on this figure that Customer A1 refers to Customer A's site in Atlanta, Customer B1 refers to Customer B's site in Atlanta, Customer A2 refers to Customer A's site in Raleigh, and Customer B2 represents Customer B's site in Raleigh.

Customer A has requested an MPLS VPN to connect its two sites. Customer B has also requested an MPLS VPN. Figure 5.9 illustrates the new topology for both Customer A and Customer B.

FIGURE 5.8 Customer A and Customer B sites connected with an overlay VPN

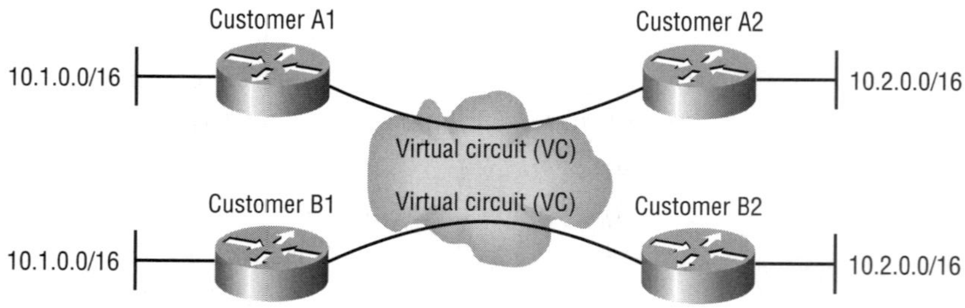

FIGURE 5.9 New topology for an MPLS VPN for Customer A and Customer B

Notice in Figure 5.9 how this new topology looks like a shared router peer-to-peer VPN.

VRF

On the Atlanta and Raleigh PE routers in Figure 5.9, the first requirement in configuring an MPLS VPN is to create a VRF for each customer. VRF names are case-sensitive and are somewhat complex to manage in large environments. For simplicity, we'll create a VRF for Customer A and call it VPN_A. For Customer B, we'll use the name VPN_B. From global configuration mode, the `ip vrf` *`vpn_name`* command will be used. Notice after the execution of the `ip vrf` *`vpn_name`* command how the prompt changes:

```
Atlanta#config t
Atlanta(config)#ip vrf VPN_A
Atlanta(config-vrf)#
```

Route Distinguisher

The next thing you must configure for VRF VPN_A is a mandatory parameter called the *route distinguisher (RD)*. A route distinguisher is a 64-bit value that is used to keep possibly overlapping addresses from actually doing so in MP-IBGP. Whenever a route is redistributed from the VRF into MP-IBGP, the route distinguisher is pre-pended to the 32-bit *Network Layer Reachability Information (NLRI)*, producing a new 96-bit VPNv4 address.

WARNING

If the route distinguisher has not been configured, the newly created VRF will not be saved in the running configuration.

When configuring the route distinguisher, it's important to note that the first 16 bits (called the *high-order bits*) are reserved to specify the extended BGP community type. Therefore, there are 48 bits that you use to specify the route distinguisher. The route distinguisher can be entered in two ways: 16-bit:32-bit or 32-bit:16-bit.

Although both formats are valid, the official recommendation is to use the 16-bit:32-bit method. The first 16 bits should be the service provider autonomous system (AS) number, and the second 32 bits should be a significant number of the service provider's choosing. If the 32-bit:16-bit method is used, the first 32 bits should be an IP address, and the remaining 16 bits should be a significant number of the service provider's choosing.

To configure the route distinguisher, use the `rd` command as follows:

```
Atlanta(config-vrf)#rd #:#
```

To illustrate the importance of the route distinguisher, suppose the networks for Customer A and Customer B were set up by the same consultant, and the consultant used the 10.0.0.0 private address space for each customer. Both Customer A and Customer B use the same 10.1.0.0 /16 addresses in Atlanta. In Raleigh, both customers use the address 10.2.0.0 /16. With an overlay VPN, overlapping customer addresses were not an issue for the service provider. However, with the advent of peer-to-peer routing and MPLS VPNs, overlapping customer addresses are carried by the service provider and can cause routing problems. The route distinguisher fixes this problem.

As you can see in Table 5.3, without a route distinguisher, these routes would overlap in MP-BGP.

TABLE 5.3 Overlapping Addresses

Atlanta	Customer A	10.1.0.0 /16
Atlanta	Customer B	10.1.0.0 /16
Raleigh	Customer A	10.2.0.0 /16
Raleigh	Customer B	10.2.0.0 /16

Let's resume the configuration of the VRF using the following commands:

```
Atlanta#config t
Atlanta(config)#ip vrf VPN_A
Atlanta(config-vrf)#rd 1:1
Atlanta(config-vrf)#exit
Atlanta(config)#ip vrf VPN_B
Atlanta(config-vrf)rd 1:2

Raleigh#config t
Raleigh(config)#ip vrf VPN_A
Raleigh(config-vrf)#rd 1:1
Raleigh(config-vrf)#exit
Raleigh(config)#ip vrf VPN_B
Raleigh(config-vrf)rd 1:2
```

With the route distinguishers configured, the addresses will not overlap in MP-BGP. When customer routes are redistributed into MP-BGP to transit the service provider backbone, the route distinguisher value is prepended to the NLRI, as you can see in Table 5.4.

TABLE 5.4 Overlapping Addresses with Route Distinguisher

Atlanta	Customer A	1:1:10.1.0.0 /16
Atlanta	Customer B	1:2:10.1.0.0 /16
Raleigh	Customer A	1:1:10.2.0.0 /16
Raleigh	Customer B	1:2:10.2.0.0 /16

Now let's add a little more detail. As mentioned earlier, VRF names are case-sensitive. The following configuration is possible but not recommended:

```
Atlanta#config t
Atlanta(config)#ip vrf VPN_A
Atlanta(config-vrf)#rd 1:1
Atlanta(config-vrf)#exit
Atlanta(config)#ip vrf VPN_B
Atlanta(config-vrf)rd 1:2

Raleigh#config t
Raleigh(config)#ip vrf vpn_a
Raleigh(config-vrf)#rd 1:1
Raleigh(config-vrf)#exit
Raleigh(config)#ip vrf vpn_b
Raleigh(config-vrf)rd 1:2
```

As you see in the preceding example, the VRF names in Raleigh and Atlanta are different (VRF names are case-sensitive), but everything works just fine. This is because VRF names are only locally significant (the VRF names are only applicable on the router they're configured on). It is important not to give the VRF name too much weight because it is just a name. For example, the following configuration works as well:

```
Atlanta#config t
Atlanta(config)#ip vrf VPN_A
Atlanta(config-vrf)#rd 1:1
Atlanta(config-vrf)#exit
```

```
Atlanta(config)#ip vrf VPN_B
Atlanta(config-vrf)rd 1:2

Raleigh#config t
Raleigh(config)#ip vrf VPN_1
Raleigh(config-vrf)#rd 1:1
Raleigh(config-vrf)#exit
Raleigh(config)#ip vrf VPN_2
Raleigh(config-vrf)rd 1:2
```

Since this is such an important concept, let's look at one more example just to make sure you understand the use of the VRF name:

```
Atlanta#config t
Atlanta(config)#ip vrf VPN_A
Atlanta(config-vrf)#rd 1:1
Atlanta(config-vrf)#exit
Atlanta(config)#ip vrf VPN_B
Atlanta(config-vrf)rd 1:2

Raleigh#config t
Raleigh(config)#ip vrf JAMES
Raleigh(config-vrf)#rd 1:1
Raleigh(config-vrf)#exit
Raleigh(config)#ip vrf KEVIN
Raleigh(config-vrf)rd 1:2
```

All that the `ip vrf` *`vpn_name`* command does is create a VRF for the customer. It's important to have a naming convention (that takes into account case-sensitivity) to make management easier as more VRFs are added to support more VPNs.

NOTE VRF names are case-sensitive and locally significant. Don't read too much into them; it's only a name.

Now that you understand VRF naming, you need to learn more about the route distinguisher. The purpose of a route distinguisher is to keep possibly overlapping addresses from doing so in global MP-IBGP.

Will the following configuration work?

```
Atlanta#config t
Atlanta(config)#ip vrf VPN_A
Atlanta(config-vrf)#rd 1:1
Atlanta(config-vrf)#exit
Atlanta(config)#ip vrf VPN_B
Atlanta(config-vrf)rd 1:2

Raleigh#config t
Raleigh(config)#ip vrf vpn_a
Raleigh(config-vrf)#rd 1:3
Raleigh(config-vrf)#exit
Raleigh(config)#ip vrf vpn_b
Raleigh(config-vrf)rd 1:4
```

Before you answer the question, let's discuss it further. The only thing a route distinguisher does is keep customer routes unique in MP-IBGP. Look at Table 5.5. Do the routes overlap in global MP-BGP? The answer is No. (Remember, No is good; you don't want overlapping addresses in MP-BGP.) This configuration is valid.

TABLE 5.5 Addresses with Route Distinguisher

Atlanta	Customer A	1:1:10.1.0.0 /16
Atlanta	Customer B	1:2:10.1.0.0 /16
Raleigh	Customer A	1:3:10.2.0.0 /16
Raleigh	Customer B	1:4:10.2.0.0 /16

A route distinguisher is the closest thing to a VPN identifier that exists. When configuring a VRF, it does not become active nor does it stay in configuration until a route distinguisher is configured.

Let's look at one more example. Does the following configuration work?

```
Atlanta#config t
Atlanta(config)#ip vrf VPN_A
Atlanta(config-vrf)#rd 1:1
Atlanta(config-vrf)#exit
```

```
Atlanta(config)#ip vrf VPN_B
Atlanta(config-vrf)rd 1:2

Raleigh#config t
Raleigh(config)#ip vrf vpn_a
Raleigh(config-vrf)#rd 1:2
Raleigh(config-vrf)#exit
Raleigh(config)#ip vrf vpn_b
Raleigh(config-vrf)rd 1:1
```

Although your first reaction might be that it does not work, consider this question in further detail: What is the purpose of a route distinguisher? To keep possible overlapping IP address from doing so in MP-IBGP. Look at Table 5.6. Do the addresses overlap in MP-IBGP? The answer is No. (Remember, No is good.) The preceding configuration is valid.

TABLE 5.6 Addresses with Route Distinguisher

Atlanta	Customer A	1:1:10.1.0.0 /16
Atlanta	Customer B	1:2:10.1.0.0 /16
Raleigh	Customer A	1:3:10.2.0.0 /16
Raleigh	Customer B	1:4:10.2.0.0 /16

For simple VPNs such as this example, each *customer* requires a unique route distinguisher. To support complex topologies, each VRF may require a unique route distinguisher. Only one route distinguisher can be configured per VRF; you can't have two VRFs on the same router using the same route distinguisher. For this reason, a route distinguisher is generally regarded as a locally significant VPN identifier.

After all of this configuration, the VPN is still not yet completely configured. In the next chapter, we'll complete this configuration and discuss routing protocols in MPLS. Make sure that you're familiar with the configuration and concepts presented in this chapter. Once you get to Chapter 6, you'll be hammered on routing protocols and MPLS VPNs. Be sure you're ready.

Route Distinguisher in MP-BGP

The route distinguisher value is prepended to customer routes carried in MP-BGP. To get more information about what routes have what route distinguisher values, use the `show ip bgp vpnv4 all` command. A sample output is as follows:

```
Atlanta#show ip bgp vpnv4 all
BGP table version is 21, local router ID is 204.134.83.1
.
.output omitted
.
   Network          Next Hop     Metric LocPrf Weight Path
Route Distinguisher: 65000:1 (default for vrf vpn_1)
*> 192.168.1.1/32   192.168.3.5     782         32768 ?
*>i192.168.2.1/32   204.134.83.3    782    100      0 ?
*> 192.168.3.4/30   0.0.0.0           0         32768 ?
*>i192.168.3.8/30   204.134.83.3      0    100      0 ?
```

Notice in the output that a route distinguisher of 65000:1 is being used. In the real world, you probably won't want to see all the route distinguishers, only a particular one for a single VRF. To view only the routes prepended with a single route target, use the `show ip bgp vpnv4 rd` *`route-target-value`* command. You can find more information about these commands and their uses at `www.cisco.com`.

MP-IBGP Configuration Example

This section revisits the simple network you saw in Chapter 2, "Frame-Mode MPLS." In this example, you'll be configuring and verifying MP-BGP in preparation for configuring VPNs in Chapter 6.

Figure 5.10 contains a simple service provider network.

FIGURE 5.10 A simple service provider network

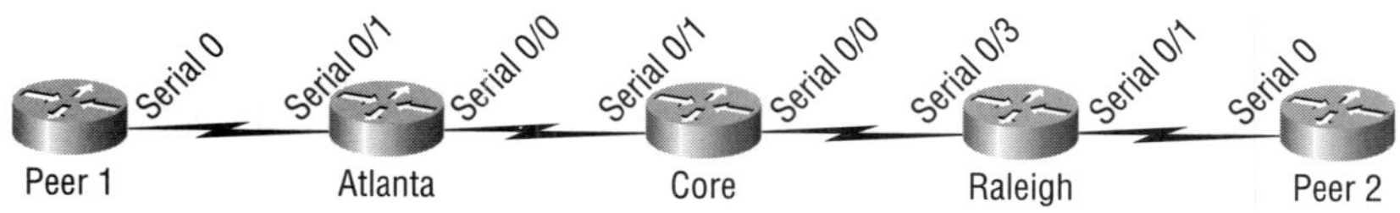

Table 5.7 lists the IP addresses and interfaces of all the service provider devices in Figure 5.10.

TABLE 5.7 Service Provider IP Addressing

Device	Loopback 0	Serial 0/0	Serial 0/1	Serial 0/3
Atlanta	204.134.83.1/32	204.134.83.5/30	192.168.3.6/30	N/A
Core	204.134.83.2/32	204.134.83.9/30	204.134.83.6/30	N/A
Raleigh	204.134.83.3/32	N/A	192.168.3.9/30	204.134.83.10/30

Table 5.8 lists the IP addresses of the peer devices in Figure 5.10.

TABLE 5.8 PE Customer Link Addressing

Device	Loopback 0	Serial 0
Peer 1	192.168.1.1/32	192.168.3.5/30
Peer 2	192.168.2.1/32	192.168.3.10/30

Initial Network Configuration

In the example in Figure 5.10, the network is already configured with an IGP, BGP, and tag switching. The IGP runs on the Atlanta, Core, and Raleigh routers. Tag switching has been enabled on the internal links for the Atlanta, Core, and Raleigh routers. BGP has been configured between the Atlanta and Raleigh routers.

Device Configuration

The configuration of the Atlanta POP router is as follows:

```
Atlanta#show running-config
Building configuration...

Current configuration : 1492 bytes
!
```

```
version 12.1
service timestamps debug uptime
service timestamps log uptime
no service password-encryption
!
hostname Atlanta
!
enable password cisco
!
!
!
!
!
memory-size iomem 25
ip subnet-zero
ip tcp synwait-time 5
no ip domain-lookup
!
ip cef
cns event-service server
!
!
!
!
!
interface Loopback0
 ip address 204.134.83.1 255.255.255.255
!
interface Serial0/0
 description *** Link to Core Router ***
 ip address 204.134.83.5 255.255.255.252
 tag-switching ip
 no fair-queue
 clockrate 64000
!
interface Serial0/1
 description *** Link to Peer1 ***
```

```
 no ip address
 shutdown
 clockrate 64000
!
interface Serial0/2
 no ip address
 shutdown
 clockrate 64000
!
interface Serial0/3
 no ip address
 shutdown
 clockrate 64000
!
interface Ethernet1/0
 no ip address
 shutdown
!
interface Ethernet1/1
 no ip address
 shutdown
!
interface Ethernet1/2
 no ip address
 shutdown
!
interface Ethernet1/3
 no ip address
 shutdown
!
router rip
 version 2
 network 204.134.83.0
!
router bgp 65000
 no synchronization
```

```
 bgp log-neighbor-changes
 neighbor 204.134.83.3 remote-as 65000
 neighbor 204.134.83.3 update-source Loopback0
 neighbor 204.134.83.3 next-hop-self
 no auto-summary
!
ip classless
no ip http server
!
!
!
line con 0
 exec-timeout 0 0
 privilege level 15
 logging synchronous
 transport input none
 ip netmask-format decimal
line aux 0
line vty 0 4
 privilege level 15
 password cisco
 logging synchronous
 login
 ip netmask-format decimal
!
end
```

The configuration of the Core router is as follows:

```
Core#show running-config
Building configuration...

Current configuration : 1249 bytes
!
version 12.1
service timestamps debug uptime
service timestamps log uptime
no service password-encryption
```

```
!
hostname Core
!
enable password cisco
!
!
!
!
!
memory-size iomem 25
ip subnet-zero
ip tcp synwait-time 5
no ip domain-lookup
!
ip cef
cns event-service server
!
!
!
!
!
interface Loopback0
 ip address 204.134.83.2 255.255.255.255
!
interface Serial0/0
 description *** Connection to Raleigh POP ***
 ip address 204.134.83.9 255.255.255.252
 tag-switching ip
 no fair-queue
!
interface Serial0/1
 description *** Connection to Atlanta POP ***
 ip address 204.134.83.6 255.255.255.252
 tag-switching ip
!
interface Serial0/2
```

```
 no ip address
 shutdown
!
interface Serial0/3
 no ip address
 shutdown
!
interface Ethernet1/0
 no ip address
 shutdown
!
interface Ethernet1/1
 no ip address
 shutdown
!
interface Ethernet1/2
 no ip address
 shutdown
!
interface Ethernet1/3
 no ip address
 shutdown
!
router rip
 version 2
 network 204.134.83.0
!
ip classless
no ip http server
!
!
!
line con 0
 exec-timeout 0 0
 privilege level 15
 logging synchronous
```

```
 transport input none
 ip netmask-format decimal
line aux 0
line vty 0 4
 privilege level 15
 password cisco
 logging synchronous
 login
 ip netmask-format decimal
!
end
```

The configuration of the Raleigh POP router is as follows:

```
Raleigh#show running-config
Building configuration...

Current configuration : 1531 bytes
!
version 12.1
service timestamps debug uptime
service timestamps log uptime
no service password-encryption
!
hostname Raleigh
!
enable password cisco
!
!
!
!
!
memory-size iomem 25
ip subnet-zero
ip tcp synwait-time 5
no ip domain-lookup
!
ip cef
```

```
cns event-service server
!
!
!
!
!
interface Loopback0
 ip address 204.134.83.3 255.255.255.255
!
interface Serial0/0
 no ip address
 shutdown
 no fair-queue
 clockrate 64000
!
interface Serial0/1
 description *** Link to Peer2 ***
 no ip address
 shutdown
 clockrate 64000
!
interface Serial0/2
 no ip address
 shutdown
 clockrate 64000
!
interface Serial0/3
 description *** Link to Core Router ***
 ip address 204.134.83.10 255.255.255.252
 tag-switching ip
 clockrate 64000
!
interface Ethernet1/0
 no ip address
 shutdown
!
```

```
interface Ethernet1/1
 no ip address
 shutdown
!
interface Ethernet1/2
 no ip address
 shutdown
!
interface Ethernet1/3
 no ip address
 shutdown
!
router rip
 version 2
 network 204.134.83.0
!
router bgp 65000
 no synchronization
 bgp log-neighbor-changes
 neighbor 204.134.83.1 remote-as 65000
 neighbor 204.134.83.1 update-source Loopback0
 neighbor 204.134.83.1 next-hop-self
 no auto-summary
!
ip classless
no ip http server
!
!
!
line con 0
 exec-timeout 0 0
 privilege level 15
 logging synchronous
 transport input none
 ip netmask-format decimal
line aux 0
line vty 0 4
 privilege level 15
```

```
 password cisco
 logging synchronous
 login
 ip netmask-format decimal
!
end
```

MP-IBGP Configuration

There are two routers that need MP-IBGP configured between them: Atlanta and Raleigh. Under global BGP, the Atlanta and Raleigh routers are neighbors. The `activate` command is used to enable MP-BGP. The configuration for MP-IBGP on the Atlanta router is as follows:

```
Atlanta(config)#router bgp 65000
Atlanta(config-router)#address-family vpnv4
Atlanta(config-router-af)#neighbor 204.134.83.3 activate
Atlanta(config-router-af)#neighbor 204.134.83.3 send-
  community both

00:44:48: %BGP-5-ADJCHANGE: neighbor 204.134.83.3 Down
  Address family activated
```

The configuration for MP-IBGP on the Raleigh router is as follows:

```
Raleigh#conf t
Enter configuration commands, one per line. End with CNTL/Z.
Raleigh(config)#router bgp 65000
Raleigh(config-router)#address-family vpnv4
Raleigh(config-router-af)#neighbor 204.134.83.1 activate
00:46:08: %BGP-5-ADJCHANGE: neighbor 204.134.83.1 Down
  Address family activated
Raleigh(config-router-af)#neighbor 204.134.83.1 send-
  community both
```

Raleigh Running-Config

By viewing the running-config of the Raleigh POP router, you can see that I-BGP is configured:

```
Raleigh#show running-config
Building configuration...
```

```
Current configuration : 1997 bytes
!
version 12.1
service timestamps debug uptime
service timestamps log uptime
no service password-encryption
!
hostname Raleigh
!
enable password cisco
!
!
!
!
!
memory-size iomem 25
ip subnet-zero
ip tcp synwait-time 5
no ip domain-lookup
!
!
ip vrf vpn_1
 rd 65000:1
 route-target export 65000:1
 route-target import 65000:1
ip cef
cns event-service server
!
!
!
!
!
interface Loopback0
 ip address 204.134.83.3 255.255.255.255
!
interface Serial0/0
 no ip address
```

```
 shutdown
 no fair-queue
 clockrate 64000
!
interface Serial0/1
 description *** Link to Peer2 ***
 no ip address
 shutdown
 clockrate 64000
!
interface Serial0/2
 no ip address
 shutdown
 clockrate 64000
!
interface Serial0/3
 description *** Link to Core Router ***
 ip address 204.134.83.10 255.255.255.252
 tag-switching ip
 clockrate 64000
!
interface Ethernet1/0
 no ip address
 shutdown
!
interface Ethernet1/1
 no ip address
 shutdown
!
interface Ethernet1/2
 no ip address
 shutdown
!
interface Ethernet1/3
 no ip address
 shutdown
!
```

```
router rip
 version 2
 network 204.134.83.0
 !
 address-family ipv4 vrf vpn_1
 version 2
 redistribute bgp 65000 metric transparent
 network 192.168.3.0
 no auto-summary
 exit-address-family
!
router bgp 65000
 no synchronization
 bgp log-neighbor-changes
 neighbor 204.134.83.1 remote-as 65000
 neighbor 204.134.83.1 update-source Loopback0
 neighbor 204.134.83.1 next-hop-self
 no auto-summary
 !
 address-family ipv4 vrf vpn_1
 redistribute rip
 no auto-summary
 no synchronization
 exit-address-family
 !
 address-family vpnv4
 neighbor 204.134.83.1 activate
 neighbor 204.134.83.1 send-community both
 no auto-summary
 exit-address-family
!
ip classless
no ip http server
!
!
!
```

```
line con 0
 exec-timeout 0 0
 privilege level 15
 logging synchronous
 transport input none
 ip netmask-format decimal
line aux 0
line vty 0 4
 privilege level 15
 password cisco
 logging synchronous
 login
 ip netmask-format decimal
!
end
```

Atlanta Running-Config

By viewing the running-config of the Atlanta POP router, you can see that I-BGP is configured:

```
Atlanta#show running-config
Building configuration...

Current configuration : 1972 bytes
!
version 12.1
service timestamps debug uptime
service timestamps log uptime
no service password-encryption
!
hostname Atlanta
!
enable password cisco
!
!
!
!
!
```

```
memory-size iomem 25
ip subnet-zero
ip tcp synwait-time 5
no ip domain-lookup
!
!
ip vrf vpn_1
 rd 65000:1
 route-target export 65000:1
 route-target import 65000:1
ip cef
cns event-service server
!
!
!
!
!
interface Loopback0
 ip address 204.134.83.1 255.255.255.255
!
interface Serial0/0
 description *** Link to Core Router ***
 ip address 204.134.83.5 255.255.255.252
 tag-switching ip
 no fair-queue
 clockrate 64000
!
interface Serial0/1
 description *** Link to Peer1 ***
 no ip address
 shutdown
 clockrate 64000
!
interface Serial0/2
 no ip address
 shutdown
 clockrate 64000
!
```

```
interface Serial0/3
 no ip address
 shutdown
 clockrate 64000
!
interface Ethernet1/0
 no ip address
 shutdown
!
interface Ethernet1/1
 no ip address
 shutdown
!
interface Ethernet1/2
 no ip address
 shutdown
!
interface Ethernet1/3
 no ip address
 shutdown
!
router rip
 version 2
 network 204.134.83.0
 !
 address-family ipv4 vrf vpn_1
 version 2
 redistribute bgp 65000 metric transparent
 network 192.168.3.0
 no auto-summary
 exit-address-family
!
router bgp 65000
 no synchronization
 bgp log-neighbor-changes
 neighbor 204.134.83.3 remote-as 65000
```

```
 neighbor 204.134.83.3 update-source Loopback0
 neighbor 204.134.83.3 next-hop-self
 no auto-summary
 !
 address-family ipv4 vrf vpn_1
 redistribute rip
 no auto-summary
 no synchronization
 exit-address-family
 !
 address-family vpnv4
 neighbor 204.134.83.3 activate
 neighbor 204.134.83.3 send-community both
 no auto-summary
 exit-address-family
!
ip classless
no ip http server
!
!
!
line con 0
 exec-timeout 0 0
 privilege level 15
 logging synchronous
 transport input none
 ip netmask-format decimal
line aux 0
line vty 0 4
 privilege level 15
 password cisco
 logging synchronous
 login
 ip netmask-format decimal
!
end
```

Verification

At this stage in the network, there's really not much troubleshooting that you can do. In Chapter 6, you'll be able to verify MP-IBGP configuration by watching the routes from one site being populated through MP-IBGP to another site.

For right now, you can verify MP-IBGP using the `show ip bgp neighbors` command. The output from this command as executed on the Raleigh POP router is as follows:

```
Raleigh#show ip bgp neighbors
BGP neighbor is 204.134.83.1, remote AS 65000, internal link
  BGP version 4, remote router ID 204.134.83.1
  BGP state = Established, up for 00:00:29
  Last read 00:00:28, hold time is 180, keepalive interval
    is 60 seconds
  Neighbor capabilities:
    Route refresh: advertised and received
    Address family IPv4 Unicast: advertised and received
    Address family VPNv4 Unicast: advertised and received
  Received 14 messages, 0 notifications, 0 in queue
  Sent 14 messages, 0 notifications, 0 in queue
  Route refresh request: received 0, sent 0
  Default minimum time between advertisement runs is
    5 seconds

 For address family: IPv4 Unicast
  BGP table version 13, neighbor version 13
  Index 2, Offset 0, Mask 0x4
  NEXT_HOP is always this router
  2 accepted prefixes consume 72 bytes
  Prefix advertised 6, suppressed 0, withdrawn 0

 For address family: VPNv4 Unicast
  BGP table version 1, neighbor version 1
  Index 1, Offset 0, Mask 0x2
  Community attribute sent to this neighbor
  0 accepted prefixes consume 0 bytes
  Prefix advertised 0, suppressed 0, withdrawn 0
```

```
    Connections established 3; dropped 2
    Last reset 00:01:05, due to Address family activated
  Connection state is ESTAB, I/O status: 1, unread input
    bytes: 0
  Local host: 204.134.83.3, Local port: 179
  Foreign host: 204.134.83.1, Foreign port: 11003

  Enqueued packets for retransmit: 0, input: 0  mis-
    ordered: 0 (0 bytes)

  Event Timers (current time is 0x2B458C):
  Timer          Starts    Wakeups            Next
  Retrans             5          0             0x0
  TimeWait            0          0             0x0
  AckHold             4          2             0x0
  SendWnd             0          0             0x0
  KeepAlive           0          0             0x0
  GiveUp              0          0             0x0
  PmtuAger            0          0             0x0
  DeadWait            0          0             0x0

  iss: 3802456742  snduna: 3802456895  sndnxt: 3802456895
    sndwnd:  16232
  irs: 3801264201  rcvnxt: 3801264354  rcvwnd:      16232
    delrcvwnd:    152

  SRTT: 146 ms, RTTO: 1283 ms, RTV: 1137 ms, KRTT: 0 ms
  minRTT: 28 ms, maxRTT: 300 ms, ACK hold: 200 ms
  Flags: passive open, nagle, gen tcbs

  Datagrams (max data segment is 536 bytes):
  Rcvd: 7 (out of order: 0), with data: 4, total data
    bytes: 152
  Sent: 7 (retransmit: 0), with data: 4, total data
    bytes: 152
```

If the BGP session is not established, you need to verify that you have configured the neighbor correctly. If everything is configured correctly, make sure you can reach the remote neighbor by pinging the remote neighbor's IP address.

Summary

After an IGP has been set up in the core and MPLS or tag switching has been enabled, MP-BGP needs to be configured to support MPLS VPNs. First, enter global BGP and specify the neighbor. After the neighbor is specified, it is later activated. After you've fully set up MP-BGP, you're ready to implement MPLS VPNs.

Cisco makes use of an IOS mechanism called a virtual routing and forwarding (VRF) table to implement a virtual router. VRFs allow for separate and isolated routing tables on a single Cisco router. VRF names are locally significant and case-sensitive. To create a VRF, you use the `ip vrf` *`vpn_name`* command.

Before the VRF becomes active, you must configure a route distinguisher. A route distinguisher is 64 bits in total. You can only configure 48 bits of the 64. The two supported formats for identifying route distinguishers are 16-bit:32-bit and 32-bit:16-bit. The recommended way to configure a route distinguisher is AS number:32-bit number. Remember, the route distinguisher is prepended to the NLRI and creates the VPNv4 address, for a total of 96 bits. The major responsibility of the route distinguisher is to keep possibly overlapping IP addresses from doing so in MP-BGP. To configure the route distinguisher, use the `rd #:#` command.

Exam Essentials

Understand MPLS VPN packet forwarding. An MPLS VPN builds on the principles of standard MPLS. Packets enter an IP network and receive a VPN label and a standard label to traverse the service provider network. LSRs along the LSP between edge devices do not know about customer networks, and they use the standard label to label-switch packets. Once the packet arrives at the egress PE, the VPN label is used to direct the packet to the correct VPN. Customer routers require no MPLS functionality.

Understand and be able to configure Multi-Protocol BGP (MP-BGP). Multi-Protocol BGP (MP-BGP) is a requirement for the proper operation of MPLS VPNs. From a network design standpoint, an IGP runs in the service provider core, and BGP runs between edge routers. To enable the edge routers to support MPLS VPNs, MP-BGP must be configured.

A special context is used called address families. MP-BGP must be activated between BGP neighbors and extended communities sent. To configure MP-BGP, you must first enter the `address-family vpnv4` command from inside BGP configuration. Neighbors must be activated with the `activate` command. Extended communities must be configured with the `send-community extended` command. Both standard and extended communities can be configured with the `send-community both` command.

Understand and be able to configure a virtual routing and forwarding (VRF) table. A VRF is used by Cisco to implement the concept of virtual routers. A VRF is composed of an IP routing table, a CEF table, interfaces, and routing protocol rules and filters. Global routes are not in the VRF. Likewise, VRF routes are not in the global routing table. To configure a VRF, enter global configuration mode and use the `ip vrf` *`vpn_name`* command. VRF names are locally significant and case-sensitive.

Understand and be able to configure a route distinguisher (RD). To keep possibly overlapping IP address from doing so as they traverse the service provider backbone, a route distinguisher (RD) is used. An RD is 48 bits long. The recommended RD format is 16-bit:32-bit. The first 16 bits should be the service provider AS number. The last 32 bits are some number that is significant to the service provider. To configure an RD, use the `rd #:#` command.

Key Terms

Before you take the exam, be certain you are familiar with the following terms:

address family

label stacking

MPLS VPNs

Multi-Protocol BGP (MP-BGP)

Network Layer Reachability Information (NLRI)

peer-to-peer VPNs

route distinguisher (RD)

routing context

virtual router

virtual routing and forwarding (VRF) table

VPN version 4 (VPNv4) routes

Review Questions

1. How many bits long is a route distinguisher?

   A. 16

   B. 32

   C. 48

   D. 64

2. VPN names __________ case-sensitive.

   A. Are

   B. Are not

3. Which of the following protocols is used to propagate VPN labels between edge routers?

   A. TDP

   B. LDP

   C. Standard BGP with extended communities

   D. MP-BGP

4. In Multi-Protocol BGP (MP-BGP), neighbors need to be __________.

   A. Configured

   B. Activated

   C. Sent standard communities

   D. Configured with VDP

5. Which of the following commands is used to configure a VRF?

   A. `rd #.#`

   B. `ip vrf` *`vpn_name`*

   C. `address-family vpnv4`

   D. `send-community both`

6. Which of the following commands is used to configure a route distinguisher?

   A. `rd #.#`

   B. `ip vrf` *`vpn_name`*

   C. `address-family vpnv4`

   D. `send-community both`

7. Which of the following commands configures MP-BGP to send extended communities? (Choose all that apply.)

   A. `send-community standard`

   B. `send community extended`

   C. `send-community both`

   D. `send-community extended`

8. Which of the following commands is used to enter MP-BGP configuration from BGP?

   A. `rd #.#`

   B. `ip vrf` *`vpn_name`*

   C. `address-family vpnv4`

   D. `send-community both`

9. How long in bits is the VPNv4 address?

   A. 32

   B. 48

   C. 64

   D. 96

10. Which of the following is the preferred route distinguisher identification scheme?

A. 16:32

B. 16:16:32

C. 32:16

D. 32:64

11. To have a single route appear as many routers, which of the following mechanisms is used?

A. RD

B. VPNv4

C. VPN

D. VRF

12. Which of the following mechanisms keeps overlapping addresses from doing so in MP-BGP?

A. RD

B. VPNv4

C. VPN

D. VRF

13. Which of the following is not a component of a VRF?

A. VRF-specific routes

B. CEF

C. Global routing table

D. None of the above

14. MPLS VPNs offer __________ security as traditional overlay VPNs.

A. The same

B. Worse

C. Better

D. None of the above

15. P routers __________ knowledge of a customer's VPN routes.

    A. Do have

    B. Do not have

16. A(n) __________ imposes the VPN label.

    A. LSR

    B. LSP

    C. Edge-LSR

    D. None of the above

17. By default, BGP sends __________.

    A. Standard communities

    B. Extended communities

    C. No communities

18. What types of routes are in the PE router's global routing table?

    A. Customer routes

    B. Service provider routes

    C. Customer and service provider routes

    D. None of the above

19. What types of routes are in the PE router's VRF for a particular customer?

    A. Customer routes

    B. Service provider routes

    C. Customer and service provider routes

    D. None of the above

20. MP-BGP within an AS is called __________.

    A. MP-BGP

    B. MP-IBGP

    C. MP-EBGP

    D. MP-MBGP

Answers to Review Questions

1. D. A route distinguisher is 64 bits long.
2. A. VPN names are case-sensitive. It is best to have a well-defined naming convention so things don't get too confusing.
3. D. MP-BGP must be configured to allow the exchange of VPN routing information, VPN labels, etc.
4. B. MP-BGP neighbors need to be activated.
5. B. The command to configure a VRF is `ip vrf` *`vpn_name`*. Don't forget, the VRF name is case-sensitive.
6. A. The command to configure a route distinguisher is `rd #.#`.
7. C, D. For MP-BGP to work right, you must specify an extended community with the `send-community extended` command. Alternatively, you can send both extended and standard communities with the `send-community both` command.
8. C. The command to enter MP-BGP configuration from BGP is `address-family vpnv4`.
9. D. The VPNv4 address consists of the standard NLRI (32 bits) plus the route distinguisher (64 bits) for a grand total of 96 bits.
10. A. The recommended route distinguisher format is the service provider autonomous system (AS) number (16 bits), followed by a colon, and then followed by a number that's significant to the service provider (32 bits). Therefore, 16:32 is the correct answer.
11. D. The VRF is like a mini routing table within a router. A VRF makes it seem like there are multiple logical routers.
12. A. The 64-bit route distinguisher is prepended to the NLRI, keeping addresses from overlapping in MP-BGP.
13. C. A VRF is its own separate entity. The VRF does not have any routes from the global routing table.
14. A. An MPLS VPN is just as good as an overlay VPN.
15. B. P routers run only an IGP. P routers don't need to know any of the customer's VPN routers to do their job of label-switching packets.

16. C. Packets enter the network at the edge as unlabeled IP. The edge-LSR imposes the VPN label.

17. C. BGP sends no communities by default.

18. B. The global, or regular routing table, on a PE router contains the service provider routes only.

19. A. Only customer routes show up in the VRF.

20. B. With BGP, when a connection is between routers in the same AS, it is called Internal BGP (IBGP). For MP-BGP routers in the same AS, the connection is MP-IBGP.

Chapter 6

MPLS VPNs and RIP

CCIP MPLS EXAM OBJECTIVES COVERED IN THIS CHAPTER:

- ✓ List the major technologies supporting overlay VPNs and peer-to-peer VPNs.
- ✓ Identify the pros and cons of MPLS VPN implementations in comparison with other peer-to-peer VPN implementations.
- ✓ Describe the major architectural blocks of MPLS VPN.
- ✓ Identify the IOS commands and their proper syntax used to configure virtual routing and forwarding tables.
- ✓ Identify the IOS commands and their proper syntax used to configure Multi-Protocol BGP in the MPLS VPN backbone.
- ✓ Identify the IOS commands and their proper syntax used to configure PE-CE routing protocols.
- ✓ Identify the IOS commands and their proper syntax used to monitor MPLS VPN operations.
- ✓ Identify the IOS commands and their proper syntax used to troubleshoot typical failures in MPLS VPN implementation.

Chapter 5, "MPLS VPNs," introduced you to most, but not all, of the required configuration commands and technology necessary to implement a simple MPLS-based VPN. This chapter will introduce you to route targets and virtual routing and forwarding (VRF) table route redistribution.

In this chapter, all of the pieces that you've seen so far will be unified into an end-to-end network solution. You'll learn how to configure a simple MPLS VPN using RIP as the CE routing protocol. In addition, in an actual network, you'll learn the configuration, verification, and troubleshooting of a simple MPLS VPN.

A Review of VPNs

Before I start talking about routing inside MPLS VPNs, let's first review what you've already learned. Point-to-point connections, or leased lines, are dedicated private links through a service provider network. Point-to-point links offer guaranteed bandwidth and privacy through a service provider network, but they're expensive.

VPNs emerged as an alternative to dedicated point-to-point links. VPNs deliver the same benefits of dedicated point-to-point links but without the high cost. There are many technologies that are used to support overlay VPNs. From a Layer 1 perspective, VPNs can be implemented with SONET, T1, E1, ISDN, etc. From a Layer 2 perspective, VPNs can be implemented with Frame Relay, ATM, X.25, etc. From a Layer 3 perspective, IP tunneling technologies such as IPSec and GRE can be used to implement a VPN.

A few years ago, peer-to-peer VPNs were introduced. The biggest difference between peer-to-peer VPNs and traditional VPNs is that in a peer-to-peer VPN, a customer and a service provider exchange routing information. The two ways to implement peer-to-peer VPNs are dedicated router and shared router.

MPLS-based VPNs offer the same privacy and security as traditional VPNs, but without the worries. Overlapping address spaces, intranets, extranets, and even hub-and-spoke topologies are supported in an MPLS VPN.

Configuring a Simple MPLS VPN

Chapter 5 explained most, but not all, of what is required to set up an MPLS VPN. In this chapter, I'll expand on what you learned in Chapter 5 about MPLS VPN configuration. To start with, let's revisit the simple service provider network illustrated in Figure 6.1.

FIGURE 6.1 A simple service provider network

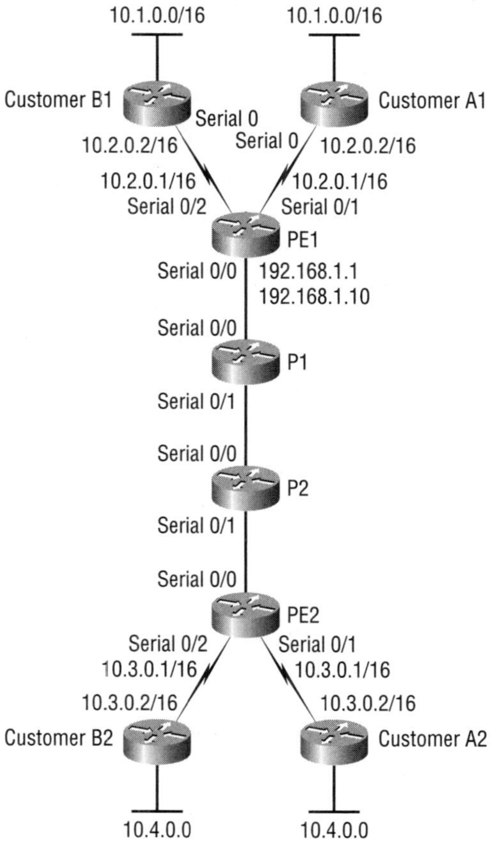

Table 6.1 lists the IP addresses and interfaces of all the service provider network devices in Figure 6.1.

TABLE 6.1 Service Provider IP Addressing

Device	Serial 0/0	Serial 0/1	Loopback 0
PE1	192.168.1.10		192.168.1.1
P1	192.168.1.9	192.168.1.14	192.168.1.2
P2	192.168.1.13	192.168.1.18	192.168.1.3
PE2	192.168.1.17		192.168.1.4

As you can see in Figure 6.1, the network has grown a bit. Table 6.2 lists the IP addresses and interfaces of the new PE devices in Figure 6.1.

TABLE 6.2 PE Customer Link Addressing

Device	Serial 0/1	Serial 0/2	Mask
PE1	10.2.0.1	10.2.0.1	/16
PE2	10.3.0.1	10.3.0.1	/16

Table 6.3 lists the IP addresses and interfaces of all the customer devices in Figure 6.1.

TABLE 6.3 PE Customer Link Addressing

Device	Serial 0	Ethernet0	Mask
Customer A1	10.2.0.2	10.1.0.1	/16
Customer A2	10.3.0.2	10.4.0.1	/16
Customer B1	10.2.0.2	10.1.0.1	/16
Customer B2	10.3.0.2	10.4.0.1	/16

For the sake of this discussion, let's say that MPLS and MP-IBGP are configured already. Since the MP-BGP backbone is already in place, you only need to concentrate on configuring the VPNs.

From a business standpoint, you need to configure a simple VPN for Customer A and Customer B. Customer A has two sites (Customer A1 and Customer A2), and Customer B has two sites (Customer B1 and Customer B2).

Chapter 5 introduced the concepts of VRFs and route distinguishers, so let's set up a VRF and configure the route distinguishers on PE1 for Customer A and Customer B using the following commands:

```
PE1#config t
PE1(config)#ip vrf vpn_a
PE1(config-vrf)#rd 1:1
PE1(config-vrf)#exit
PE1(config)#ip vrf vpn_b
PE1(config-vrf)rd 1:2
```

Use the following commands to set up the VRFs and configure the route distinguishers on PE2 for both customers:

```
PE2#config t
PE2(config)#ip vrf vpn_a
PE2(config-vrf)#rd 1:1
PE2(config-vrf)#exit
PE2(config)#ip vrf vpn_b
PE2(config-vrf)rd 1:2
```

NOTE: If the preceding syntax doesn't ring any bells, go back and re-read Chapter 5.

That's pretty much where we left things in Chapter 5. The next section explains how to configure interfaces to be part of a VRF.

Configuring VRF Interfaces

After you've created the VRF and configured the route distinguisher, interfaces must be added to the VRF. You're probably thinking to yourself, "Add the interface to the VRF?" If you remember back to Chapter 5, a VRF is like a virtual router.

When you execute the `show ip route` command, you always see the connected interfaces in the global routing table. Since a VRF is a virtual routing table, the interfaces need to be in it. In Figure 6.1, Serial 0/1 connects to Customer A1 and Serial 0/2 connects to Customer B1. These interfaces need to be added to their particular VRF.

So on PE1, to put Serial 0/1 in Customer A's VRF (vpn_a), you use the `ip vrf forwarding` command. The configuration for Customer A is as follows:

```
PE1#config t
PE1(config)#interface serial 0/1
PE1(config-if)#ip vrf forwarding vpn_a
```

NOTE After the interface is placed in a VRF, it loses its IP address configuration. The IP address will need to be reconfigured.

```
PE1(config-if)#ip address 10.2.0.1 mask 255.255.0.0
```

The interface that used to be present in the global routing table is now associated with a VRF. To verify that the Serial 0/1 interface is now associated with the VRF, use the `show ip route vrf vpn_a connected` command. The output from this command is as follows:

```
PE1#show ip route vrf vpn_a connected
C       10.2.0.1 is directly connected, Serial0/1
```

WARNING MPLS VPN security can be negated with misconfiguration. Make sure the right interface is in the right VRF.

The same process needs to be repeated on PE1 for Customer B (vpn_b) using the following commands:

```
PE1#config t
PE1(config)#interface serial 0/2
PE1(config-if)#ip vrf forwarding vpn_b
PE1(config-if)#ip address 10.2.0.1 mask 255.255.0.0
```

Verify that the Serial 0/2 interface is now associated with the VRF using the `show ip route vrf vpn_b connected` command as follows:

```
PE1#show ip route vrf vpn_b connected
C       10.2.0.1 is directly connected, Serial0/2
```

To complete the configuration on PE2, interfaces need to be added to the appropriate VRFs using the following commands:

```
PE2#config t
PE2(config)#interface serial 0/1
PE2(config-if)#ip vrf forwarding vpn_a
PE2(config-if)#ip address 10.3.0.1 mask 255.255.0.0
PE2(config)#interface serial 0/2
PE2(config-if)#ip vrf forwarding vpn_b
PE2(config-if)#ip address 10.3.0.1 mask 255.255.0.0
```

Don't forget, when you do this for real, always make sure that the correct interface is in the correct VRF or the two customers might get access to each other's networks.

Believe it or not, you're still not done configuring everything necessary to set up a VPN. You still have route targets and routing protocols to configure. Make sure that you're comfortable with the steps required to configure the VRF interfaces described in this section. Routing protocols and route targets are coming next.

Running RIP in an MPLS VPN

Learning how to configure route targets and VPN routing protocol is usually best illustrated with an example. This section uses RIPv2 to introduce the route targets and address families for routing protocols.

Figure 6.2 illustrates the routing protocols in use in the example service provider network.

FIGURE 6.2 Network routing protocol usage

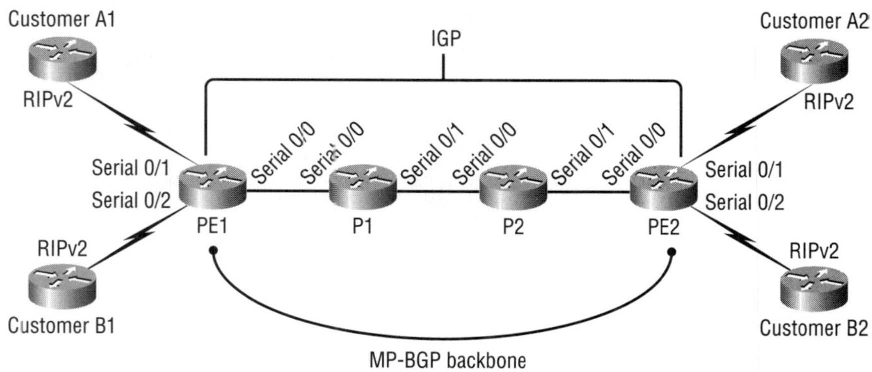

Take a look at Figure 6.2. Notice that the MP-IBGP connections between PE1 and PE2 are referred to as an *MP-BGP backbone*. The MP-BGP backbone is used to carry customer routes across the service provider backbone.

Forget about MPLS-based VPNs for a moment and look at Figure 6.3.

FIGURE 6.3 Routing protocols: an alternate view

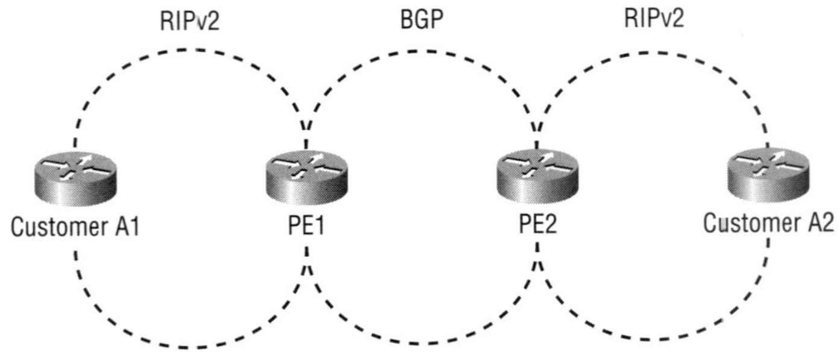

Figure 6.3 illustrates the network routing protocols without the MP-BGP backbone. In Figure 6.3, the network is presented as RIP-BGP-RIP. How do you get routes from one RIP network to the other if they are traversing a BGP network? *Redistribution*. Redistribution is the process by which routes from one routing protocol are imported or exported into another routing protocol.

Figure 6.4 illustrates redistribution between the RIP and BGP networks.

FIGURE 6.4 Redistribution for Customer A

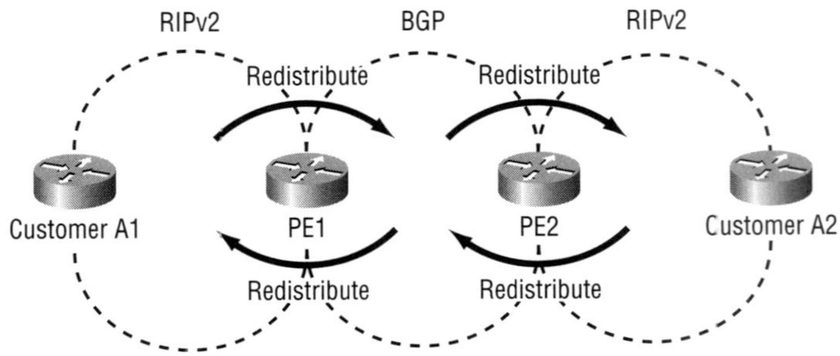

Figure 6.5 illustrates the same principle of redistribution for Customer B.

FIGURE 6.5 Redistribution for Customer B

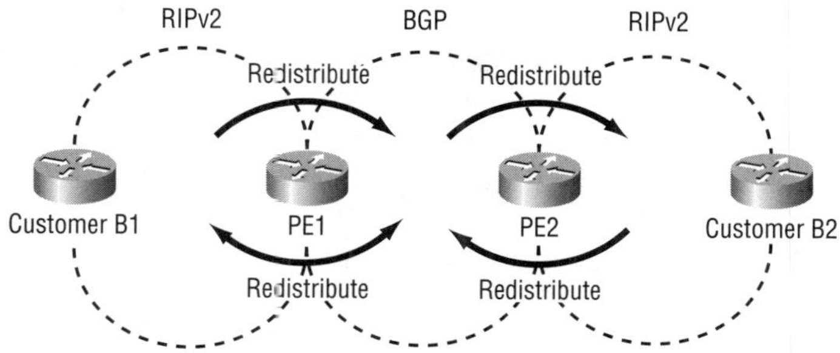

Configuring RIPv2 with *Address-Family ipv4*

Now you need to configure RIPv2 to exchange routes with the customer routers. Without MPLS VPN functionality, only one global version of RIP is available on a Cisco router. What I mean by this is you only get one *routing context* for RIP that is configured with the `router rip` command. With MPLS functionality, you still get one routing process for RIP (`router rip`) but with separate routing contexts.

Cisco IOS implements routing contexts to provide for separate isolated instances of a single routing protocol. For example, a single router may support many separate customers with a single instance of a routing protocol through the use of routing contexts.

The best way to understand routing contexts is to show you how it works for Customer A and Customer B.

What happens if you use the `router rip` command on PE1? You enter RIP configuration that is global to the router. Remember that VRFs allow for separate virtual routers to run on a single Cisco router. On PE1, Customer A is running RIPv2 and Customer B is running RIPv2. There are two separate VRFs already configured: vpn_a and vpn_b. Interfaces are in the correct VRFs. Let's configure RIPv2 first on the Customer A1 router.

One of the benefits of MPLS VPNs is that customers do not require any MPLS VPN functionality. So from the customer perspective, standard RIPv2 configuration applies. Let's configure simple RIP on Customer A1 with the following commands:

```
CustomerA1#config t
CustomerA1(config)#router rip
```

```
CustomerA1 (config-router)#version 2
CustomerA1 (config-router)#network 10.0.0.0
```

That's it; a simple procedure on the customer router. What about on PE1? Well, don't even think about MPLS VPNs, VRFs, or anything else for right now. Take a look at Figure 6.6 and just think about regular route configuration.

FIGURE 6.6 Customer A1 and PE1 only

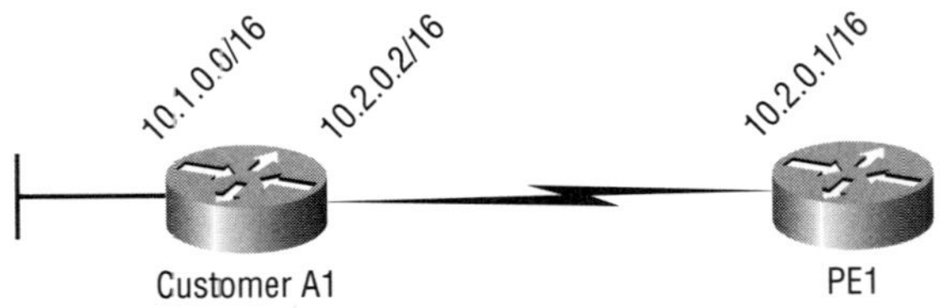

What do you do on PE1 to configure RIP to run between it and the customer router (forgetting about MPLS VPNs for a minute)? You need to execute the following commands to implement the configuration:

```
PE1#config t
PE1(config)#router rip
PE1(config-router)#version 2
PE1(config-router)#network 10.0.0.0
```

Normal stuff, right? I hope so! How do you configure RIP only for the Customer A VRF? By using the `address-family ipv4 vrf` *`vpn_name`* command. The proper configuration of PE1 for Customer A (vpn_a) is as follows:

```
PE1#config t
PE1(config)#router rip
PE1(config-router)#version 2
PE1(config-router)#address-family ipv4 vrf vpn_a
PE1(config-router-af)#network 10.0.0.0
```

To configure RIPv2 to run in the VRF for Customer B (vpn_b), the process needs to be repeated. The commands to configure Customer B are as follows:

```
PE1#config t
PE1(config)#router rip
PE1(config-router)#version 2
```

```
PE1(config-router)#address-family ipv4 vrf vpn_b
PE1(config-router-af)#network 10.0.0.0
```

Now RIPv2 is running, in separate contexts, for both Customer A and Customer B. To verify that everything works right, run the `show ip router vrf` *vpn_name* command and look for routes being learned from the customer routers.

Configuring Redistribution

As mentioned earlier in this chapter, to get routes from one side of the network to the other, you need to do redistribution. RIP is running in the VRF. How do you get routes from context RIP into MP-BGP? With the `redistribute` command.

Redistribution is a little different with MP-BGP than with regular BGP. When you make a VRF, an MP-BGP routing context is created and accessed under the `address-family ipv4 vrf` *vpn_name* section in MP-BGP. So MP-BGP has a routing context for a particular VRF, just like RIP.

A good way to think about it is that there is a conduit for each VPN running inside MP-BGP. Figure 6.7 illustrates this principle.

FIGURE 6.7 MP-BGP conduits

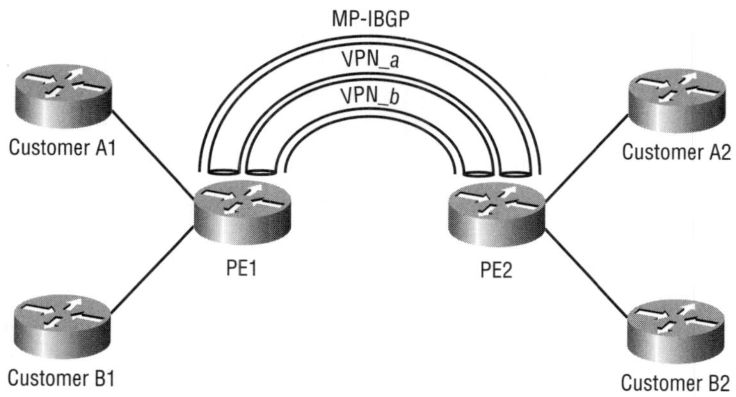

Redistribution is a two-way process—from RIP into BGP and from BGP into RIP. On PE1, for Customer A, the following configuration is required for redistribution:

```
PE1#config t
PE1(config)#router rip
```

```
PE1(config-router)#address-family ipv4 vrf vpn_a
PE1(config-router-af)#redistribute bpg 1 metric transparent
PE1(config-router-af)#exit
PE1(config-router)#exit
PE1(config)#router bgp 1
PE1(config-router)#address-family ipv4 vrf vpn_a
PE1(config-router-af)#redistribute rip
```

NOTE If you are experienced with BGP, you may be interested in the metric transparent. With the metric transparent in the `redistribute` command, the service provider MP-IBGP backbone preserves the RIP hop count. The RIP hop count is carried in the MED. From RIP, the hop count goes in the MED. Redistribution from MP-IBGP back into RIP copies the MED (hop count) back into the RIP hop count.

For Customer B, the configuration for redistribution needs to be repeated as follows:

```
PE1#config t
PE1(config)#router rip
PE1(config-router)#address-family ipv4 vrf vpn_b
PE1(config-router-af)#redistribute bpg 1 metric transparent
PE1(config-router-af)#exit
PE1(config-router)#exit
PE1(config)#router bgp 1
PE1(config-router)#address-family ipv4 vrf vpn_b
PE1(config-router-af)#redistribute rip
```

Route Targets

Thought you were done? Wrong! There's one last item to configure: route targets. Route targets are carried in extended BGP communities. They are 64 bits in length (only 48 bits of which can be configured), and they're used to support complex VPN topologies. A route target is the closest thing to a VPN identifier that exists. A route target is similar to a route distinguisher. The two ways to configure a route target are 16-bit:32-bit or 32-bit:16-bit.

There are two types of route targets:

Export Route Target When routes are redistributed from a routing protocol context (that's the `address-family ipv4` part), they get tagged with an *export route target* when they are redistributed into MP-BGP. The route target is carried with the route from one PE device to another.

Import Route Target When routes are redistributed from MP-BGP into a routing protocol context for a VRF, the PE uses the configured *import route target* value to match routes for redistribution.

Let's go through an example to see how route targets work. In Figure 6.8, vpn_a and vpn_b routes on PE1 are redistributed into MP-BGP.

FIGURE 6.8 Routes from PE1 into MP-BGP

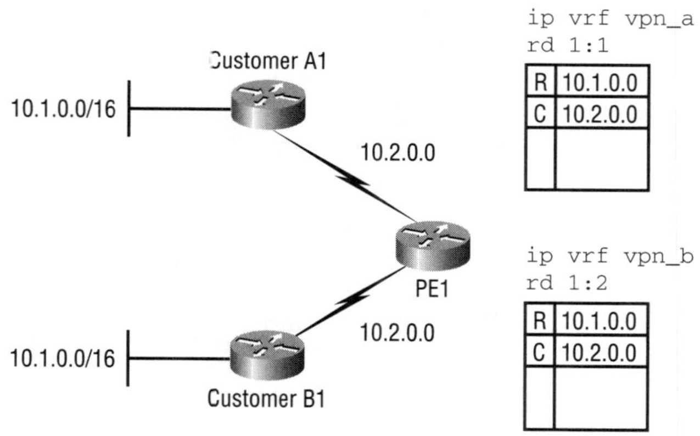

Figure 6.9 illustrates routes from PE1 as they arrive at PE2.

FIGURE 6.9 Routes from PE1 arriving at PE2

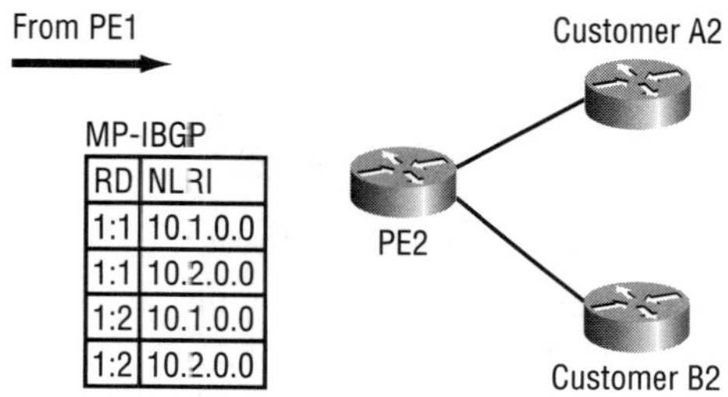

How does PE2 know which routes need to be redistributed into its VPNs? The route distinguisher could be used, but it's too simple to support more complex topologies because there is only one route distinguisher value specified.

Figure 6.10 shows routes from PE2 as they are redistributed into MP-BGP.

FIGURE 6.10 Routes from PE2 into MP-BGP

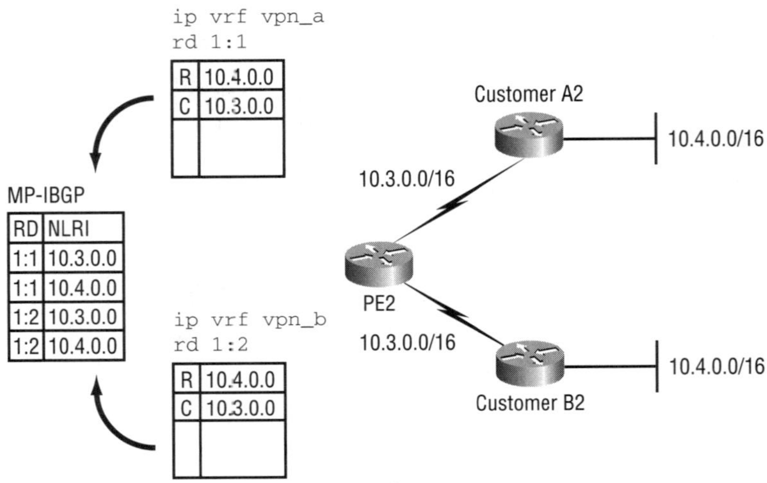

Figure 6.11 illustrates routes from PE2 as they are received at PE1.

FIGURE 6.11 Routes from PE2 arriving at PE1

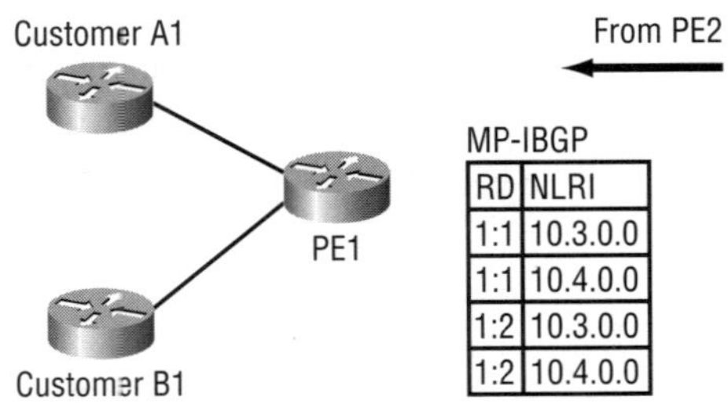

How does PE1 know which routes need to be redistributed into its VPNs? Again, the route distinguisher could be used, but it is not an effective solution for complex topologies. The route target feature was developed because route distinguishers don't work for complex topologies.

Configuring Route Targets

Route targets are configured from inside VRF configuration. To configure an export route target, use the `route-target export` *`number`* command. To configure an import route target, use the `route-target import` *`number`* command.

> **NOTE** It's possible to have multiple import and export route targets. Chapter 8, "Advanced MPLS Topics," explains how this works.

Remember, route targets are attached to VPN routes when they are redistributed into MP-BGP (export route targets). Route targets are also used (or read) when routes are redistributed from MP-BGP back into the VRF routing protocol (import route targets).

Let me show you how all of this works. Since route distinguishers can't be used to differentiate between routes in MP-BGP, route targets must be used.

On PE1, from VRF configuration, you need to configure route targets for vpn_a and vpn_b as follows:

```
PE1#config t
PE1(config)#ip vrf vpn_a
PE1(config-vrf)#route-target export 100:1
PE1(config-vrf)#exit
PE1(config)#ip vrf vpn_b
PE1(config-vrf)route-target export 500:7
```

Route Target Value Selection

For a simple VPN like the one I'm using to explain the configuration commands with, the route target value is usually the same as the route distinguisher value. You might be inclined to link the route distinguisher and route targets together because they can have the same values, but they serve very different purposes. The route distinguisher keeps IP prefixes from overlapping in MP-BGP. The route target is used to help differentiate VPN routes. Don't confuse the two. The values in the example network of 100:1 and 500:7 are an attempt to keep you from linking the route distinguisher and route target values.

Figure 6.12 illustrates VPN routes from PE1 with the configured route targets.

FIGURE 6.12 VPN routes from PE1 with route targets

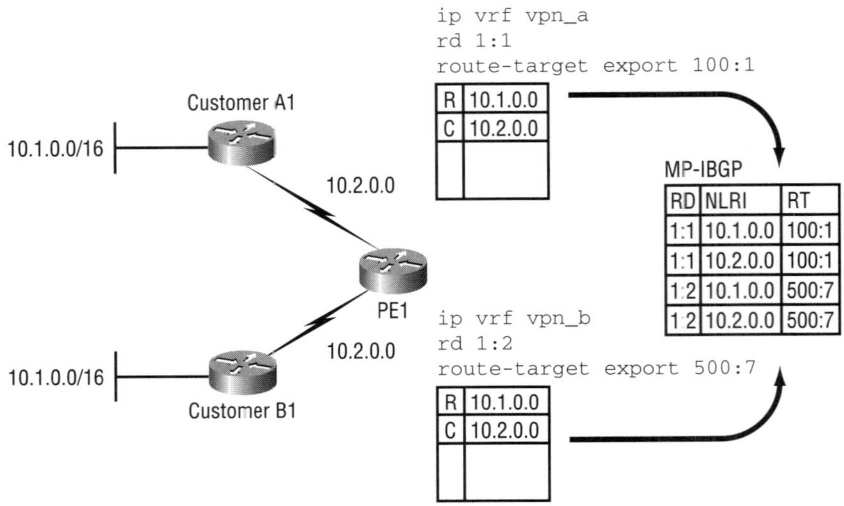

Figure 6.13 illustrates VPN routes from PE1 as they arrive at PE2.

FIGURE 6.13 VPN routes from PE1 arriving at PE2

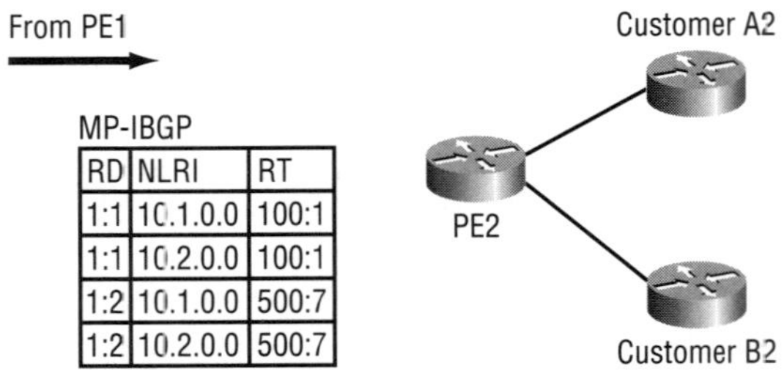

When PE2 does a redistribute from MP-BGP into the routing protocol for a particular VRF, it needs to have an import route target configured. The configuration for PE2 is as follows:

```
PE2#config t
PE2(config)#ip vrf vpn_a
PE2(config-vrf)#route-target import 100:1
PE2(config-vrf)#exit
PE2(config)#ip vrf vpn_b
PE2(config-vrf)route-target import 500:7
```

What about export route targets on PE2? Let's choose an arbitrary value of 5:1 for vpn_a and 70:3 for vpn_b. The export route target configuration is as follows:

```
PE2#config t
PE2(config)#ip vrf vpn_a
PE2(config-vrf)#route-target export 5:1
PE2(config-vrf)#exit
PE2(config)#ip vrf vpn_b
PE2(config-vrf)route-target export 70:3
```

Figure 6.14 illustrates routes from PE2 as they arrive at PE1.

FIGURE 6.14 VPN routes from PE2 arriving at PE1

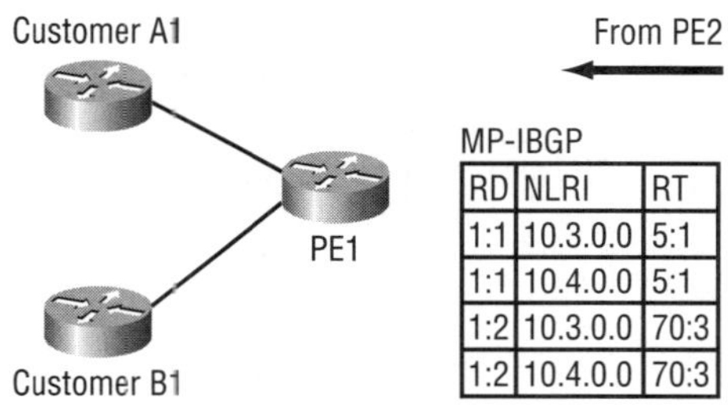

RD	NLRI	RT
1:1	10.3.0.0	5:1
1:1	10.4.0.0	5:1
1:2	10.3.0.0	70:3
1:2	10.4.0.0	70:3

What import route targets must be configured on PE1? For vpn_a, an import route target must be configured for 5:1. For vpn_b, an import route target must be configured for 70:3. The import route target configuration for PE1 is as follows:

```
PE1#config t
PE1(config)#ip vrf vpn_a
PE1(config-vrf)#route-target import 5:1
PE1(config-vrf)#exit
PE1(config)#ip vrf vpn_b
PE1(config-vrf)route-target import 70:3
```

A Review of Simple VPN Configuration

I'd like to take this section of the chapter to review the major configuration steps again for you. Figure 6.15 illustrates the same simple network used throughout this book.

FIGURE 6.15 A simple service provider network

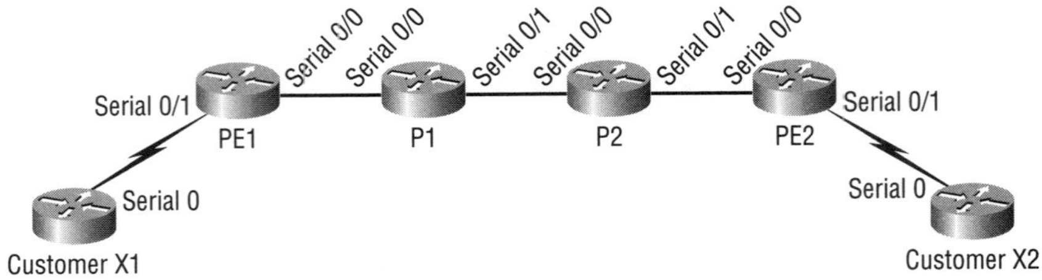

Table 6.4 lists the IP addresses and interfaces of all the service provider devices in Figure 6.15.

TABLE 6.4 Service Provider IP Addressing

Device	Serial 0/0	Serial 0/1	Loopback 0
PE1	192.168.1.10		192.168.1.1
P1	192.168.1.9	192.168.1.14	192.168.1.2
P2	192.168.1.13	192.168.1.18	192.168.1.3
PE2	192.168.1.17		192.168.1.4

Table 6.5 lists the IP addresses and interfaces of the Customer X devices.

TABLE 6.5 PE Customer Link Addressing

Device	Serial 0	Ethernet0	Mask
Customer X1	10.2.0.2	10.1.0.1	/16
Customer X2	10.3.0.2	10.4.0.1	/16

Configuring MPLS in the Service Provider Network

Currently, all the devices in the service provider network already have IP addresses. The first thing you need to do is configure an IGP. For this simple network, the IGP will be RIPv2.

On the PE1 router, you configure RIPv2 with the following commands:

```
PE1#config t
PE1(config)#router rip
PE1(config-rotuer)#version 2
PE1(config-router)#network 192.168.1.0
```

On the P1 router, you configure RIPv2 with the following commands:

```
P1#config t
P1(config)#router rip
P1(config-rotuer)#version 2
P1(config-router)#network 192.168.1.0
```

On the P2 router, you configure RIPv2 with the following commands:

```
P2#config t
P2(config)#router rip
P2(config-rotuer)#version 2
P2(config-router)#network 192.168.1.0
```

On the PE2 router, you configure RIPv2 with the following commands:

```
PE2#config t
PE2(config)#router rip
PE2(config-rotuer)#version 2
PE2(config-router)#network 192.168.1.0
```

Now that an IGP is up and running, you need to configure BGP on the PE routers.

On the PE1 router, you configure BGP with the following commands:

```
PE1#config t
PE1(config)#router bgp 1
PE1(config-router)#no synchronization
PE1(config-router)#network 192.168.1.1 mask 255.255.255.255
PE1(config-router)#neighbor 192.168.1.4 remote-as 1
PE1(config-router)#neighbor 192.168.1.4 update-source Loopback0
PE1(config-router)#no auto summary
PE1(config-router)#redistribute static
```

On the PE2 router, you configure BGP with the following commands:

```
PE2#config t
PE2(config)#router bgp 1
PE2(config-router)#no synchronization
```

```
PE2(config-router)#network 192.168.1.4 mask 255.255.255.255
PE2(config-router)#neighbor 192.168.1.1 remote-as 1
PE2(config-router)#neighbor 192.168.1.1 update-source Loopback0
PE2(config-router)#no auto summary
PE2(config-router)#redistribute static
```

Now that all the routing protocols are in place, you need to enable MPLS on the routers.

On the PE1 router, you configure MPLS for Serial 0/0 only with the following commands:

```
PE1#config t
PE1(config)#ip cef
PE1(config)#mpls ip
PE1(config-if)#interface serial 0/0
PE1(config-if)#mpls ip
```

On the P1 router, you configure MPLS for both Serial 0/0 and Serial 0/1 with the following commands:

```
P1#config t
P1(config)#ip cef
P1(config)#mpls ip
P1(config-if)#interface serial 0/0
P1(config-if)#mpls ip
P1(config-if)#exit
P1(config)#interface serial 0/1
P1(config-if)#mpls ip
```

On the P2 router, you configure MPLS for both Serial 0/0 and Serial 0/1 with the following commands:

```
P2#config t
P2(config)#ip cef
P2(config)#mpls ip
P2(config-if)#interface serial 0/0
P2(config-if)#mpls ip
P2(config-if)#exit
P2(config)#interface serial 0/1
P2(config-if)#mpls ip
```

On the PE2 router, you configure MPLS for Serial 0/0 only with the following commands:

```
PE1#config t
PE1(config)#ip cef
PE1(config)#mpls ip
PE1(config-if)#interface serial 0/0
PE1(config-if)#mpls ip
```

Since you will be implementing MPLS VPNs, go ahead and set up MP-BGP between PE1 and PE2.

On the PE1 router PE1, you configure MP-BGP with the following commands:

```
PE1#config t
PE1(config)#router bgp 1
PE1(config-router)#address-family vpnv4
PE1(config-router)#neighbor 192.168.1.4 activate
PE1(config-router)#neighbor 192.168.1.4 next-hop-self
PE1(config-router)#neighbor 192.168.1.4 send-community both
```

On the PE2 router, you configure MP-BGP with the following commands:

```
PE2#config t
PE2(config)#router bgp 1
PE2(config-router)#address-family vpnv4
PE2(config-router)#neighbor 192.168.1.1 activate
PE2(config-router)#neighbor 192.168.1.1 next-hop-self
PE1(config-router)#neighbor 192.168.1.1 send-community both
```

Simple VPN Configuration

To set up a simple VPN for Customer X, VRFs need to be configured on PE1 and PE2. You'll need to create a VRF; let's call it customer_x. You'll use a route distinguisher of 1:1 and a route target of 1:1. Here are the commands to accomplish this:

```
PE1#config t
PE1(config)#ip vrf customer_x
PE1(config-vrf)#rd 1:1
PE1(config-vrf)#route-target both 1:1
```

The `route-target both` command is the equivalent of entering the two commands `route-target import` and `route-target export`. When you view the configuration with the `show running-configuration` command, you'll see the configuration as `route-target import` and `route-target export`. The `route-target both` command is a shortcut.

To place the Serial 0/1 interface on PE1 into the VRF for Customer X, use the following commands:

```
PE1#config t
PE1(config)#interface serial 0/1
PE1(config-if)#ip vrf forwarding customer_x
```

Remember that the IP address on the interface goes away after it is associated with a VRF. You'll need to configure it with the IP address again, as follows:

```
PE1(config-if)#ip address 10.2.0.1 mask 255.255.0.0
```

The configuration of PE2 is pretty much a repeat of the configuration of PE1:

```
PE2#config t
PE2(config)#ip vrf customer_x
PE2(config-vrf)#rd 1:1
PE2(config-vrf)#route-target both 1:1
PE2(config-vrf)#exit
PE1(config)#interface serial 0/1
PE1(config-if)#ip vrf forwarding customer_x
PE1(config-if)#ip address 10.3.0.1 mask 255.255.0.0
```

Configuring the PE-CE Routing Protocol

The last thing you need to do is configure a routing protocol between the PE routers and the Customer X routers. Let's configure RIPv2. The first step is to get the customer routers running RIPv2. Here are the commands for Customer X1:

```
CustomerX1#config t
CustomerX1(config)#router rip
CustomerX1(config-router)#version 2
CustomerX1(config-router)#network 10.0.0.0
```

You need to execute the same commands on Customer X2:

```
CustomerX2#config t
```

```
CustomerX2(config)#router rip
CustomerX2(config-router)#version 2
CustomerX2(config-router)#network 10.0.0.0
```

Now on to the service provider devices. On PE1 and PE2, you need to configure RIPv2 for the VRF and redistribution of BGP routes into RIP. In addition, you need to configure RIP routes to be redistributed into BGP. The following commands accomplish this configuration:

```
PE1#config t
PE1(config)#router rip
PE1(config)#version 2
PE1(config-router)#address-family ipv4 vrf customer_x
PE1(config-router-af)#redistribute bpg 1 metric transparent
PE1(config-router-af)#exit
PE1(config-router)#exit
PE1(config)#router bgp 1
PE1(config-router)#address-family ipv4 vrf customer_x
PE1(config-router-af)#redistribute rip
```

The same commands can be used to accomplish the configuration on PE2:

```
PE2#config t
PE2(config)#router rip
PE2(config)#version 2
PE2(config-router)#address-family ipv4 vrf customer_x
PE2(config-router-af)#redistribute bpg 1 metric transparent
PE2(config-router-af)#exit
PE2(config-router)#exit
PE2(config)#router bgp 1
PE2(config-router)#address-family ipv4 vrf customer_x
PE2(config-router-af)#redistribute rip
```

Lab: Configuring an MPLS VPN

To really hammer home all of the configuration steps that you've been exposed to, I'd like to go through the configuration one more time. This section uses the same simple network you first saw in Chapter 2, "Frame-Mode

MPLS." For this section, you'll be using the simple service provider network illustrated in Figure 6.16.

FIGURE 6.16 A simple service provider network

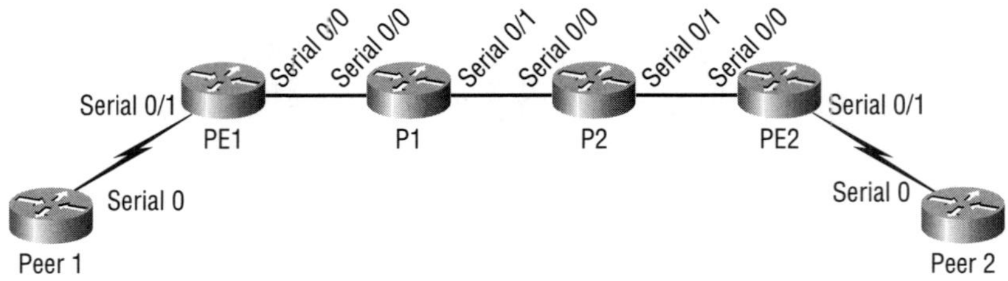

Figure 6.17 illustrates the routing protocol utilization for this network.

FIGURE 6.17 Routing protocol utilization

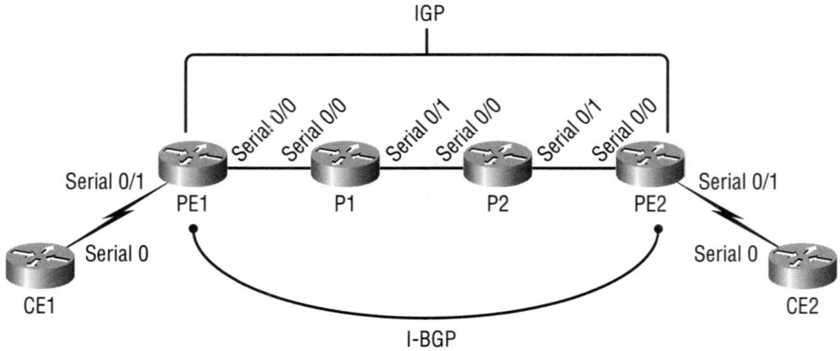

Table 6.6 lists the IP addresses and interfaces for the CE devices in Figure 6.16.

TABLE 6.6 Customer Addressing

Device	Loopback 0	Serial 0
Peer 1	192.168.1.1/32	192.168.3.5/30
Peer 2	192.168.2.1/32	192.168.3.10/30

Table 6.7 lists the IP addresses and interfaces of all the service provider devices in Figure 6.16.

TABLE 6.7 Service Provider Addressing

Device	Loopback 0	Serial 0/0	Serial 0/1	Serial 0/3
Atlanta	204.134.83.1/32	204.134.83.5/30	192.168.3.6/30	N/A
Core	204.134.83.2/32	204.134.83.9/30	204.134.83.6/30	N/A
Raleigh	204.134.83.3/32	N/A	192.168.3.9/30	204.134.83.10/30

Configuring POP Routers

Presently, the network is set up with an IGP (RIPv2), tag switching, and MP-BGP between the Atlanta and Raleigh POP routers.

The configuration of the Raleigh POP router is as follows:

```
Raleigh#show running-config
Building configuration...

Current configuration : 1997 bytes
!
version 12.1
service timestamps debug uptime
service timestamps log uptime
no service password-encryption
!
hostname Raleigh
!
enable password cisco
!
!
!
!
!
memory-size iomem 25
```

```
ip subnet-zero
ip tcp synwait-time 5
no ip domain-lookup
!
!
ip vrf vpn_1
 rd 65000:1
 route-target export 65000:1
 route-target import 65000:1
ip cef
cns event-service server
!
!
!
!
!
interface Loopback0
 ip address 204.134.83.3 255.255.255.255
!
interface Serial0/0
 no ip address
 shutdown
 no fair-queue
 clockrate 64000
!
interface Serial0/1
 description *** Link to Peer2 ***
 ip address 192.168.3.9 255.255.255.252
 clockrate 64000
!
interface Serial0/2
 no ip address
 shutdown
 clockrate 64000
!
interface Serial0/3
```

```
 description *** Link to Core Router ***
 ip address 204.134.83.10 255.255.255.252
 tag-switching ip
 clockrate 64000
!
interface Ethernet1/0
 no ip address
 shutdown
!
interface Ethernet1/1
 no ip address
 shutdown
!
interface Ethernet1/2
 no ip address
 shutdown
!
interface Ethernet1/3
 no ip address
 shutdown
!
router rip
 version 2
 network 204.134.83.0
 !
router bgp 65000
 no synchronization
 bgp log-neighbor-changes
 neighbor 204.134.83.1 remote-as 65000
 neighbor 204.134.83.1 update-source Loopback0
 neighbor 204.134.83.1 next-hop-self
 no auto-summary
 !
 !
 address-family vpnv4
 neighbor 204.134.83.1 activate
```

```
 neighbor 204.134.83.1 send-community both
 no auto-summary
 exit-address-family
!
ip classless
no ip http server
!
!
!
line con 0
 exec-timeout 0 0
 privilege level 15
 logging synchronous
 transport input none
 ip netmask-format decimal
line aux 0
line vty 0 4
 privilege level 15
 password cisco
 logging synchronous
 login
 ip netmask-format decimal
!
end
```

The configuration of the Atlanta POP router is as follows:

```
Atlanta#show running-config
Building configuration...

Current configuration : 1972 bytes
!
version 12.1
service timestamps debug uptime
service timestamps log uptime
no service password-encryption
!
```

```
hostname Atlanta
!
enable password cisco
!
!
!
!
!
memory-size iomem 25
ip subnet-zero
ip tcp synwait-time 5
no ip domain-lookup
!
!
ip cef
cns event-service server
!
!
!
!
!
interface Loopback0
 ip address 204.134.83.1 255.255.255.255
!
interface Serial0/0
 description *** Lirk to Core Router ***
 ip address 204.134.83.5 255.255.255.252
 tag-switching ip
 no fair-queue
 clockrate 64000
!
interface Serial0/1
 description *** Lirk to Peer1 ***
 ip address 192.168.3.6 255.255.255.252
 clockrate 64000
!
interface Serial0/2
```

```
 no ip address
 shutdown
 clockrate 64000
!
interface Serial0/3
 no ip address
 shutdown
 clockrate 64000
!
interface Ethernet1/0
 no ip address
 shutdown
!
interface Ethernet1/1
 no ip address
 shutdown
!
interface Ethernet1/2
 no ip address
 shutdown
!
interface Ethernet1/3
 no ip address
 shutdown
!
router rip
 version 2
 network 204.134.83.0
 !
router bgp 65000
 no synchronization
 bgp log-neighbor-changes
 neighbor 204.134.83.3 remote-as 65000
 neighbor 204.134.83.3 update-source Loopback0
 neighbor 204.134.83.3 next-hop-self
 no auto-summary
 !
```

```
 address-family vpnv4
 neighbor 204.134.83.3 activate
 neighbor 204.134.83.3 send-community both
 no auto-summary
 exit-address-family
!
ip classless
no ip http server
!
!
!
line con 0
 exec-timeout 0 0
 privilege level 15
 logging synchronous
 transport input none
 ip netmask-format decimal
line aux 0
line vty 0 4
 privilege level 15
 password cisco
 logging synchronous
 login
 ip netmask-format decimal
!
```

VPN Configuration

So now the network is all set up, and you need to configure an MPLS VPN. From a business case standpoint, Peer 1 and Peer 2 require a simple MPLS-based VPN. Peer 1 and Peer 2 will run RIPv2 to exchange network routes.

The first thing to configure on the Atlanta POP router is a VRF with a route distinguisher and a route target. The configuration for the Atlanta POP is implemented using the following commands:

```
Atlanta#conf t
Enter configuration commands, one per line. End with CNTL/Z.
```

```
Atlanta(config)#ip vrf vpn_1
Atlanta(config-vrf)#rd 65000:1

Atlanta(config-vrf)#route-target both 65000:1
```

The next step is to associate the interface that connects to Peer 1 to the VRF using the following commands:

```
Atlanta(config)#int s 0/1
Atlanta(config-if)#ip vrf forwarding vpn_1
% Interface Serial0/1 IP address 192.168.3.6 removed due
  to enabling VRF vpn_1
Atlanta(config-if)#ip address 192.168.3.6 255.255.255.252
```

The third step is to configure a routing context for the VRF in RIPv2 with the following commands:

```
Atlanta(config)#router rip
Atlanta(config-router)#address-family ipv4 vrf vpn_1
Atlanta(config-router-af)#network 192.168.3.0
```

The fourth step is to configure redistribution using the following commands:

```
Atlanta(config-router-af)#redistribute bgp 65000 metric
  transparent
```

Now on to BGP. You need to configure the redistribution for the VPN into BGP for the VRF by executing the following commands:

```
Atlanta(config-router-af)#exit
Atlanta(config-router)#exit
Atlanta(config)#router bgp 65000
Atlanta(config-router)#address-family ipv4 vrf vpn_1
Atlanta(config-router-af)#redistribute rip
```

You need to repeat these configuration steps on the Raleigh POP router. The first thing to configure on the Raleigh POP is a VRF with a route distinguisher and a route target by executing the following commands:

```
Raleigh#conf t
Enter configuration commands, one per line.  End with
  CNTL/Z.
```

```
Raleigh(config)#ip vrf vpn_1

Raleigh(config-vrf)#rd 65000:1

Raleigh(config-vrf)#route-target both 65000:1
```

Next, you need to associate the interface that connects to Peer 1 to the VRF using the following commands:

```
Raleigh(config-vrf)#exit
Raleigh(config)#int s 0/1
Raleigh(config-if)#ip vrf forwarding vpn_1
% Interface Serial0/1 IP address 192.168.3.9 removed due
  to enabling VRF vpn_1
Raleigh(config-if)#ip address 192.168.3.9 255.255.255.252
```

To configure a routing context for the VRF in RIPv2, use the following commands:

```
Raleigh(config)#router rip
Raleigh(config-router)#address-family ipv4 vrf vpn_1
Raleigh(config-router-af)#network 192.168.3.0
```

To configure redistribution on the Raleigh POP router, use the following command:

```
Raleigh(config-router-af)#redistribute bgp 65000 metric
  transparent
```

Now on to BGP. You configure the redistribution for the VPN into BGP for the VRF with the following commands:

```
Raleigh(config-router-af)#exit
Raleigh(config-router)#exit
Raleigh(config)#router bgp 65000
Raleigh(config-router)#address-family ipv4 vrf vpn_1
Raleigh(config-router-af)#redistribute rip
```

Raleigh Running-Config

This section contains the running-config of the Raleigh POP router. Try to get in the habit of reading and verifying the configurations of the routers.

```
Raleigh#show running-config
Building configuration...

Current configuration : 1997 bytes
!
version 12.1
service timestamps debug uptime
service timestamps log uptime
no service password-encryption
!
hostname Raleigh
!
enable password cisco
!
!
!
!
!
memory-size iomem 25
ip subnet-zero
ip tcp synwait-time 5
no ip domain-lookup
!
!
ip vrf vpn_1
 rd 65000:1
 route-target export 65000:1
 route-target import 65000:1
ip cef
cns event-service server
!
!
!
!
!
interface Loopback0
```

```
 ip address 204.134.83.3 255.255.255.255
!
interface Serial0/0
 no ip address
 shutdown
 no fair-queue
 clockrate 64000
!
interface Serial0/1
 description *** Link to Peer2 ***
 ip vrf forwarding vpn_1
 ip address 192.168.3.9 255.255.255.252
 clockrate 64000
!
interface Serial0/2
 no ip address
 shutdown
 clockrate 64000
!
interface Serial0/3
 description *** Link to Core Router ***
 ip address 204.134.83.10 255.255.255.252
 tag-switching ip
 clockrate 64000
!
interface Ethernet1/0
 no ip address
 shutdown
!
interface Ethernet1/1
 no ip address
 shutdown
!
interface Ethernet1/2
 no ip address
 shutdown
!
```

```
interface Ethernet1/3
 no ip address
 shutdown
!
router rip
 version 2
 network 204.134.83.0
 !
 address-family ipv4 vrf vpn_1
 version 2
 redistribute bgp 65000 metric transparent
 network 192.168.3.0
 no auto-summary
 exit-address-family
!
router bgp 65000
 no synchronization
 bgp log-neighbor-changes
 neighbor 204.134.83.1 remote-as 65000
 neighbor 204.134.83.1 update-source Loopback0
 neighbor 204.134.83.1 next-hop-self
 no auto-summary
 !
 address-family ipv4 vrf vpn_1
 redistribute rip
 no auto-summary
 no synchronization
 exit-address-family
 !
 address-family vpnv4
 neighbor 204.134.83.1 activate
 neighbor 204.134.83.1 send-community both
 no auto-summary
 exit-address-family
!
ip classless
```

```
no ip http server
!
!
!
line con 0
 exec-timeout 0 0
 privilege level 15
 logging synchronous
 transport input none
 ip netmask-format decimal
line aux 0
line vty 0 4
 privilege level 15
 password cisco
 logging synchronous
 login
 ip netmask-format decimal
!
end
```

Atlanta Running-Config

This section contains the running-config of the Atlanta POP router. Try to get in the habit of reading and verifying the configurations of the routers.

```
Atlanta#show running-config
Building configuration...

Current configuraticn : 1972 bytes
!
version 12.1
service timestamps cebug uptime
service timestamps log uptime
no service password-encryption
!
hostname Atlanta
!
```

```
enable password cisco
!
!
!
!
!
memory-size iomem 25
ip subnet-zero
ip tcp synwait-time 5
no ip domain-lookup
!
!
ip vrf vpn_1
 rd 65000:1
 route-target export 65000:1
 route-target import 65000:1
ip cef
cns event-service server
!
!
!
!
!
interface Loopback0
 ip address 204.134.83.1 255.255.255.255
!
interface Serial0/0
 description *** Link to Core Router ***
 ip address 204.134.83.5 255.255.255.252
 tag-switching ip
 no fair-queue
 clockrate 64000
!
interface Serial0/1
 description *** Link to Peer1 ***
 ip vrf forwarding vpn_1
```

```
 ip address 192.168.3.6 255.255.255.252
 clockrate 64000
!
interface Serial0/2
 no ip address
 shutdown
 clockrate 64000
!
interface Serial0/3
 no ip address
 shutdown
 clockrate 64000
!
interface Ethernet1/0
 no ip address
 shutdown
!
interface Ethernet1/1
 no ip address
 shutdown
!
interface Ethernet1/2
 no ip address
 shutdown
!
interface Ethernet1/3
 no ip address
 shutdown
!
router rip
 version 2
 network 204.134.83.0
 !
 address-family ipv4 vrf vpn_1
 version 2
 redistribute bgp 65000 metric transparent
```

```
 network 192.168.3.0
 no auto-summary
 exit-address-family
!
router bgp 65000
 no synchronization
 bgp log-neighbor-changes
 neighbor 204.134.83.3 remote-as 65000
 neighbor 204.134.83.3 update-source Loopback0
 neighbor 204.134.83.3 next-hop-self
 no auto-summary
 !
 address-family ipv4 vrf vpn_1
 redistribute rip
 no auto-summary
 no synchronization
 exit-address-family
 !
 address-family vpnv4
 neighbor 204.134.83.3 activate
 neighbor 204.134.83.3 send-community both
 no auto-summary
 exit-address-family
!
ip classless
no ip http server
!
!
!
line con 0
 exec-timeout 0 0
 privilege level 15
 logging synchronous
 transport input none
 ip netmask-format decimal
line aux 0
```

```
line vty 0 4
 privilege level 15
 password cisco
 logging synchronous
 login
 ip netmask-format decimal
!
end
```

Peer 1 Running-Config

The Peer 1 router is configured with standard RIPv2; it is configured to advertise its WAN segment and its loopback addresses. This section contains the running-config of the Peer 1 router. Try to get in the habit of reading and verifying the configurations of the routers.

```
Peer1#show running-config
Building configuration...

Current configuration : 836 bytes
!
version 12.1
service timestamps debug uptime
service timestamps log uptime
no service password-encryption
!
hostname Peer1
!
enable password cisco
!
!
!
!
!
ip subnet-zero
ip tcp synwait-time 5
no ip domain-lookup
```

```
!
!
!
!
interface Loopback0
 ip address 192.168.1.1 255.255.255.255
!
interface Ethernet0
 no ip address
 shutdown
!
interface Serial0
 description *** Link to Atlanta POP ***
 ip address 192.168.3.5 255.255.255.252
 no fair-queue
!
interface Serial1
 no ip address
 shutdown
!
router rip
 version 2
 network 192.168.1.0
 network 192.168.3.0
!
ip classless
no ip http server
!
!
line con 0
 exec-timeout 0 0
 privilege level 15
 logging synchronous
 transport input none
 ip netmask-format decimal
line aux 0
```

```
line vty 0 4
 privilege level 15
 password cisco
 logging synchronous
 login
 ip netmask-format decimal
!
end
```

Peer 2 Running-Config

The Peer 2 router is configured with standard RIPv2; it is configured to advertise its WAN segment and its loopback addresses. This section contains the running-config of the Peer 2 router. Try to get in the habit of reading and verifying the configurations of the routers.

```
Peer2#show running-config
Building configuration...

Current configuration : 1063 bytes
!
version 12.1
service timestamps debug uptime
service timestamps log uptime
no service password-encryption
!
hostname Peer2
!
enable password lab
!
!
!
!
!
ip subnet-zero
ip tcp synwait-time 5
```

```
no ip domain-lookup
!
!
!
!
interface Loopback0
 ip address 192.168.2.1 255.255.255.255
!
interface Ethernet0
 no ip address
 shutdown
!
interface Serial0
 description *** Link to PE2 ***
 ip address 192.168.3.10 255.255.255.252
 no fair-queue
!
interface Serial1
 no ip address
 shutdown
!
router rip
 version 2
 network 192.168.2.0
 network 192.168.3.0
!
ip classless
no ip http server
!
!
line con 0
 exec-timeout 0 0
 privilege level 15
 logging synchronous
 transport input none
 ip netmask-format decimal
```

```
line aux 0
line vty 0 4
 privilege level 15
 password lab
 logging synchronous
 login
 ip netmask-format decimal
!
end
```

Verification with Ping

To verify that the VPN works, all you need to do is a ping from one peer to the other. The following output is the result of a ping from Peer 2 to Peer 1:

```
Peer2#ping 192.168.1.1

Type escape sequence to abort.
Sending 5, 100-byte ICMP Echos to 192.168.1.1, timeout
  is 2 seconds:
!!!!!
Success rate is 100 percent (5/5), round-trip min/avg/max
  = 116/119/120 ms
```

Routing Table Isolation

First of all, let's talk about routing table isolation and its implications. On the Raleigh and Atlanta POP routers, no customer (Peer 1 and Peer 2) routes show up in the global routing table. The routing tables of the Atlanta and Raleigh POP routers are as follows:

```
Raleigh#show ip route
.
. Output Omitted
.
Gateway of last resort is not set

     204.134.83.0 255.255.255.0 is variably subnetted,
       5 subnets, 2 masks
```

```
C       204.134.83.8 255.255.255.252 is directly
  connected, Serial0/3
R       204.134.83.1 255.255.255.255
           [120/2] via 204.134.83.9, 00:00:00, Serial0/3
C       204.134.83.3 255.255.255.255 is directly
  connected, Loopback0
R       204.134.83.2 255.255.255.255
           [120/1] via 204.134.83.9, 00:00:00, Serial0/3
R       204.134.83.4 255.255.255.252
           [120/1] via 204.134.83.9, 00:00:00, Serial0/3

Atlanta#show ip route
.
. Output Omitted
.
Gateway of last resort is not set

     204.134.83.0 255.255.255.0 is variably subnetted,
       5 subnets, 2 masks
R       204.134.83.8 255.255.255.252
           [120/1] via 204.134.83.6, 00:00:07, Serial0/0
C       204.134.83.1 255.255.255.255 is directly
  connected, Loopback0
R       204.134.83.3 255.255.255.255
           [120/2] via 204.134.83.6, 00:00:07, Serial0/0
R       204.134.83.2 255.255.255.255
           [120/1] via 204.134.83.6, 00:00:07, Serial0/0
C       204.134.83.4 255.255.255.252 is directly
  connected,
```

In addition, none of the customer routes (Peer 1 and Peer 2) show up on the Core router. The Core router is only running the IGP (RIPv2) and knows nothing about any of the customer subnets, as you can see in the global routing table of the Core router:

```
Core#show ip route
.
. Output Omitted
.
```

```
Gateway of last resort is not set

     204.134.83.0 255.255.255.0 is variably subnetted,
       5 subnets, 2 masks
C       204.134.83.8 255.255.255.252 is directly
  connected, Serial0/0
R       204.134.83.1 255.255.255.255
           [120/1] via 204.134.83.5, 00:00:19, Serial0/1
R       204.134.83.3 255.255.255.255
           [120/1] via 204.134.83.10, 00:00:26, Serial0/0
C       204.134.83.2 255.255.255.255 is directly
  connected, Loopback0
C       204.134.83.4 255.255.255.252 is directly
  connected, Serial0/1
```

If you see any customer routes in the global routing table, then more than likely, redistribution has been misconfigured. You need to check the redistribution syntax on your PE routers to make sure that they have the proper configuration.

What about on the client routers? They are isolated as well. The client routers do not know any of the details of the service provider network. If you recall, RIPv2 is running as the IGP for the service provider network. RIPv2 is also running on the clients (Peer 1 and Peer 2). The routing tables of the Peer 1 and Peer 2 routers are shown in the following device output. Notice that no service provider routes are in the global routing tables for Peer 1 and Peer 2:

```
Peer1#show ip route
.
. Output Omitted
.
Gateway of last resort is not set

     192.168.1.0 255.255.255.255 is subnetted, 1 subnets
C       192.168.1.1 is directly connected, Loopback0
     192.168.3.0 255.255.255.252 is subnetted, 2 subnets
R       192.168.3.8 [120/1] via 192.168.3.6, 00:00:12,
  Serial0
```

```
C       192.168.3.4 is directly connected, Serial0

Peer2#show ip route
.
. Output Omitted
.
Gateway of last resort is not set

R    192.168.1.0 255.255.255.0 [120/2] via 192.168.3.9,
  00:00:04, Serial0
     192.168.2.0 255.255.255.255 is subnetted, 1 subnets
C       192.168.2.1 is directly connected, Loopback0
     192.168.3.0 255.255.255.252 is subnetted, 2 subnets
C       192.168.3.8 is directly connected, Serial0
R       192.168.3.4 [120/1] via 192.168.3.9, 00:00:05,
  Serial0
```

Verifying VRF Routes

In learning about MPLS VPNs, it's important that you understand the flow of routing information. Let's begin this discussion by looking at the routing table of vpn_1 as it exists on the Atlanta POP router:

```
Atlanta#show ip route vrf vpn_1
.
. Output Omitted
.
Gateway of last resort is not set

R    192.168.1.0 255.255.255.0 [120/1] via 192.168.3.5,
  00:00:08, Serial0/1
B    192.168.2.0 255.255.255.0 [200/1] via 204.134.83.3,
  00:01:22
     192.168.3.0 255.255.255.252 is subnetted, 2 subnets
B       192.168.3.8 [200/0] via 204.134.83.3, 00:06:07
C       192.168.3.4 is directly connected, Serial0/1
```

In the routing table for vpn_1 on the Atlanta POP router, there are BGP routes (indicated by B in the routing table output) and RIPv2 routes (indicated by R in the routing table output). The RIPv2 route in the output that precedes this paragraph was learned from Peer 1. The B routes are from the Raleigh POP; they are Peer 2 RIPv2 routes redistributed into MP-BGP and carried across the service provider backbone.

On the Raleigh POP router, there are also BGP (B) routes and a RIPv2 route (R). The RIPv2 route is learned from Peer 2. The B routes come from the Atlanta POP router. The routing table for vpn_1 is as follows:

```
Raleigh#show ip route vrf vpn_1
.
. Output Omitted
.
Gateway of last resort is not set

B    192.168.1.0 255.255.255.0 [200/1] via 204.134.83.1,
  00:02:57
R    192.168.2.0 255.255.255.0 [120/1] via 192.168.3.10,
  00:00:12,  Serial0/1
     192.168.3.0 255.255.255.252 is subnetted, 2 subnets
C       192.168.3.8 is directly connected, Serial0/1
B       192.168.3.4 [200/0] via 204.134.83.1, 00:09:12
```

Summary

In this chapter, you were able to put all the pieces together to implement a simple MPLS VPN. First of all, from a service provider network standpoint, you need to configure an IGP in the core of the network and configure BGP between the PE routers. In preparation for MPLS VPNs, MP-BGP is configured under `address-family vpnv4` in BGP.

To configure a VRF, the `ip vrf` *`vpn_name`* command is used. Route distinguishers are assigned using the `rd #:#` command. For a simple VPN, the import and export route targets are the same, and they should match the route distinguisher value. The shortcut to configuring the import and export route target in one line is the `route-target both` *`number`* command.

To configure RIPv2 for use in an MPLS VPN, the clients use standard Cisco IOS. PE routers have VRF routing contexts for RIP. To configure the

VRF routing contexts in RIP, you need to use the `address-family ipv4 vrf` *`vpn_name`* command. Inside the routing context, standard IOS syntax is used to configure the routing protocol.

Routes from RIP need to be redistributed into MP-BGP. Under the `address-family ipv4 vrf` *`vpn_name`* section in BGP, the `redistribute rip` command is used to redistribute RIP routes into MP-BGP. MP-BGP routes need to be redistributed into RIP. To ensure that the RIP hop count is preserved, you use the `redistribute bgp AS# metric transparent` command to redistribute BGP routes into RIP under the VRF routing context in RIP.

Troubleshooting an MPLS VPN is usually done by viewing the routing tables on various devices in the network. Routes learned from the CE should be visible in the VRF routing table on the neighboring PE. To view the VRF routing table, use the `show ip route vrf` *`vpn_name`* command. Routes redistributed into MP-BGP are learned by other MP-BGP neighbor PE routes and displayed as BGP (`B`) routes in the VRF routing table. The simplest way to troubleshoot a VPN is to make sure that the clients can ping one another. If the CE routers can ping one another, the VPN should be set up correctly.

Exam Essentials

Understand routing contexts. Cisco uses an IOS mechanism called a routing context to provide for separate instances of routing protocols. To configure RIP for a particular VPN, you use the `address-family ipv4 vrf` *`vpn_name`* command.

Understand and be able to configure MPLS VPNs and redistribution. The PE routers run routing contexts that allow for isolated routing protocol instances for separate customers. Routes learned from customers must be redistributed into the MP-BGP backbone for transit across the service provider network. Routes from other VPNs must be redistributed from MP-BGP back into the appropriate routing context.

Understand and be able to configure route targets. Route targets are used to support complex VPN topologies. A route target is 64 bits in size, but only 48 bits are configurable. Just like a route distinguisher, a route target is either 16-bit:32-bit or 32-bit:16-bit. For simple VPN implementations, the route target value is usually the same as the route distinguisher value. Remember, there is no correlation between the route distinguisher and the route target; they perform different functions. It is possible to have multiple import and export route targets.

Understand and be able to configure import and export route targets. When routes are redistributed from a routing context into MP-BGP, the export route target value is applied. To configure the export route target, you use the `route-target export` *`number`* command. To redistribute routes from MP-BGP back into the right VPN, the route target value is read. To import routes into a VRF, you use the `route-target import` *`number`* command. For simple VPNs, the import and export route target values are the same. To save time, you can use the `route-target both` *`number`* command, which is the same as executing the `route-target import` *`number`* and `route-target export` *`number`* commands.

Key Terms

Before you take the exam, be certain you are familiar with the following terms:

export route target	redistribution
import route target	routing context
MP-BGP backbone	virtual routing and forwarding (VRF) table

Review Questions

1. How many bits long is a route target?

   A. 16

   B. 32

   C. 48

   D. 64

2. For simple VPNs, the route distinguisher and route target values should be ___________.

   A. The same

   B. Different

3. Which of the following commands configures an import route target?

   A. `route-target both` *`number`*

   B. `route-target import` *`number`*

   C. `route-target export` *`number`*

   D. `route target both` *`number`*

4. Which of the following commands is *not* used when configuring RIP for a particular VPN?

   A. `router rip`

   B. `address-family ipv4 vrf` *`vpn_name`*

   C. `address-family vpnv4`

5. ISDN is a ___________ VPN technology.

   A. Layer 1

   B. Layer 2

   C. Layer 3

   D. Layer 4

6. IPSec is a __________ VPN technology.

   A. Layer 1

   B. Layer 2

   C. Layer 3

   D. Layer 4

7. Frame Relay is a __________ VPN technology.

   A. Layer 1

   B. Layer 2

   C. Layer 3

   D. Layer 4

8. Which command do you use to view the VRF routing table?

   A. `show ip route` *vpn_name*

   B. `show ip route vrf` *vpn_name*

   C. `show ip route ipv4 vrf` *vpn_name*

   D. `show ip vrf route` *vpn_name*

9. Which of the following are valid route target formats? (Choose all that apply.)

   A. 8:32

   B. 16:32

   C. 32:16

   D. 16:48

10. To configure MP-BGP, a neighbor must be configured globally and then __________.

    A. Configured

    B. Activated

    C. Sent standard communities

    D. Configured with VDP

11. Which of the following sets of commands is the right way to configure RIP redistribution in BGP for an VRF?

    A. `router bgp` *`AS#`*
       `redistribute rip`

    B. `router bgp 65000`
       `address-family vpnv4`
       `redistribute rip`

    C. `router bgp` *`AS#`*
       `address-family ipv4 vrf` *`vpn_name`*
       `redistribute rip`

12. Which of the following sets of commands is the right way to configure BGP redistribution in RIP for a VRF?

    A. `router rip`
       `redistribute bgp` *`AS#`* `metric transparent`

    B. `router rip`
       `address-family ipv4 vrf` *`vpn_name`*
       `redistribute` *`AS#`* `metric transparent`

    C. `router rip`
       `address-family vpnv4`
       `redistribute bgp` *`AS#`* `metric transparent`

13. Which of the following commands is used on the PE to verify that a route is being received from a CE router?

    A. `show ip route`

    B. `show ip route vrf` *`vpn_name`*

    C. `show ip route vpnv4` *`vpn_name`*

    D. `show ip route` *`vpn_name`*

14. Which of the following are Layer 3 VPN technologies? (Choose all that apply.)

    A. IPSec

    B. Frame Relay

    C. GRE

    D. ISDN

15. Which of the following commands is used to view the global IP routing table on a PE router?

    A. `show ip route`

    B. `show ip route vrf` *`vpn_name`*

    C. `show ip route vpnv4` *`vpn_name`*

    D. `show ip route` *`vpn_name`*

16. Which of the following commands is used to associate an interface with a VRF?

    A. `vrf forwarding` *`vpn_name`*

    B. `mpls vrf forwarding` *`vpn_name`*

    C. `tag-switching forwarding` *`vpn_name`*

    D. `ip vrf forwarding` *`vpn_name`*

17. After you associate an interface with a VRF, the ___________.

    A. Interface needs to be activated with the `no shutdown` command

    B. Router must be rebooted

    C. IP address is removed and must be reconfigured

    D. VRF needs to be reinitialized

18. CE routers participating in a VPN ___________ learn service provider backbone routes.

    A. Do

    B. Do not

    C. Must

    D. None of the above

19. What is the easiest way to verify whether a VPN is working properly?

    A. Ping from one CE device to another.

    B. Ping from one CE to a core service provider router.

    C. Ping from the CE to the adjacent PE.

    D. None of the above.

20. RIP routes learned from a customer show up as (R) in the PE routing table for the VRF. When a RIP route is redistributed and sent to another PE through MP-BGP, how is that route displayed in the VRF?

A. R

B. M

C. B

D. None of the above

Answers to Review Questions

1. D. A route target is 64 bits long, but only 48 bits of it are configurable.
2. A. For simple VPNs, the route distinguisher and route target values are usually the same.
3. B. To configure only an import route target, you use the `route-target import` *`number`* command.
4. C. The `address-family vpnv4` command is used to configure MP-BGP, not a routing context.
5. A. ISDN is a Layer 1 VPN technology. Additional technologies at this layer are T1, E1, and SONET.
6. C. IPSec is a Layer 3 VPN technology. An additional technology at this layer is a GRE tunnel.
7. B. Frame Relay is a Layer 2 VPN technology. Additional technologies at this layer are ATM and X.25.
8. B. The command to view the VRF routing table is `show ip route vrf` *`vpn_name`*.
9. B, C. Just like the route distinguisher, the two acceptable ways of configuring a route target is 16-bit:32-bit or 32-bit:16 bit.
10. B. MP-BGP neighbors need to be activated.
11. C. Redistribution for a VRF is configured under `address-family ipv4 vrf` *`vpn_name`*.
12. B. Redistribution for a VRF is configured under `address-family ipv4 vrf` *`vpn_name`*.
13. B. If you use the `show ip route` command, you see the global routing table. To verify that a route is being learned from a CE router, you want to look at the routing table for the VRF. The command to view the VRF routing table is `show ip route vrf` *`vpn_name`*.
14. A, C. IPSec and GRE are Layer 3 VPN technologies. Frame Relay is a Layer 2 VPN technology, and ISDN is a Layer 1 VPN technology.

15. A. To view the global routing table on a PE, use the `show ip route` command.

16. D. To associate an interface with a VRF, use the command `ip vrf forwarding` *`vpn_name`*.

17. C. Once an interface is associated with a VRF, it loses its IP address and must be reconfigured.

18. B. Routing tables are well isolated with MPLS VPNs. The CE routers participating in the VPN do not learn any service provider backbone routes.

19. A. The easiest way to verify that a VPN works is to ping from one CE device to another. If the ping works, you know that VRFs, redistribution, etc. are configured properly.

20. C. In this example, RIP routes are being redistributed into MP-BGP. The original RIP route is received by another MP-BGP router and added to the VRF as a (`B`) route because it was learned through MP-BGP.

Chapter 7

MPLS VPNs and OSPF

CCIP MPLS EXAM OBJECTIVES COVERED IN THIS CHAPTER:

- ✓ Describe how OSPF operates inside a VPN.
- ✓ Describe the enhanced OSPF hierarchical model.
- ✓ Explain the interactions between OSPF and MP-BGP.

In Chapter 6, "MPLS VPNs and RIP," you learned how to implement a simple VPN using RIPv2 as the customer routing protocol. This chapter discusses OSPF as the dynamic routing protocol used between CE and PE routers.

OSPF is a well-established protocol that is used by both service providers and enterprises. Given the unique challenges of facilitating proper path selection, many extensions have been added to OSPF. This chapter explains the enhancements made to the OSPF hierarchy, OSPF routing loop prevention, and how OSPF operates and in an MPLS VPN network.

This chapter covers everything that you've seen so far. There's a lab at the end of this chapter that demonstrates all the necessary configuration steps for setting up a simple MPLS VPN using OSPF as the dynamic routing protocol between the CE and PE routers.

MP-BGP and OSPF

Open Shortest Path First (OSPF) is a popular routing protocol that is used by both enterprises and service providers. Officially, RIPv2, OSPF, and E-BGP are dynamic routing protocols supported by Cisco between PE and CE routers. In addition, static routes can be configured instead of using a dynamic routing protocol.

NOTE Static routes are discussed in Chapter 8, "Advanced MPLS Topics."

This chapter is devoted to OSPF. Before discussing OSPF and its operation for MPLS VPNs, let's start with a review of OSPF.

A Review of OSPF

OSPF is a hierarchical routing protocol that breaks a network into *areas*. All OSPF areas must be connected to the *backbone area* (Area 0). The entire OSPF network is called the *OSPF domain*. Figure 7.1 illustrates a simple OSPF network.

FIGURE 7.1 A simple OSPF network

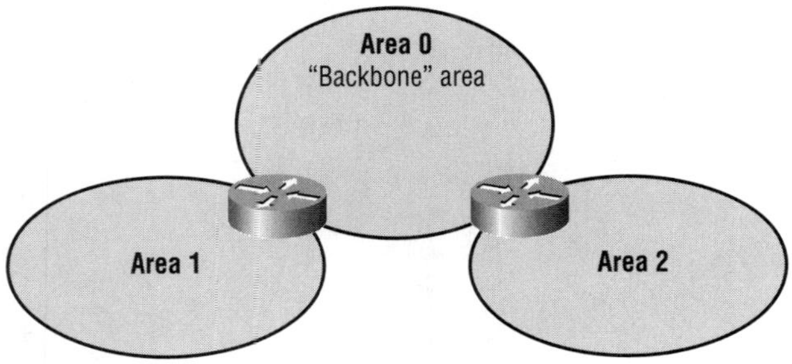

Notice in Figure 7.1 that the network is divided into three areas: Area 0, Area 1, and Area 2. Area 1 and Area 2 are connected to Area 0, which is the OSPF backbone. For now, just remember that in standard OSPF, all the areas must be connected to Area 0.

OSPF Router Types

There are several OSPF router types that you need to be familiar with. Refer to Figure 7.2 as I explain each of these OSPF router types.

Backbone router In OSPF, Area 0 is the backbone area. Any router that has an interface configured for Area 0 is called a *backbone router*.

Internal router Any router that has all its interfaces configured for a single area is said to be an *internal router*.

Area border router (ABR) An *area border router (ABR)* is a router that has interfaces configured for two or more areas. For example, a router with Serial 0/0 in Area 0 and Serial 0/1 in Area 1 is an ABR.

Autonomous system boundary router (ASBR) An *autonomous system boundary router (ASBR)* is a router that has at least one interface in the OSPF domain and one interface connecting to an external network. An example of an external network might be a connection to another AS running RIP.

FIGURE 7.2 An OSPF network with router types

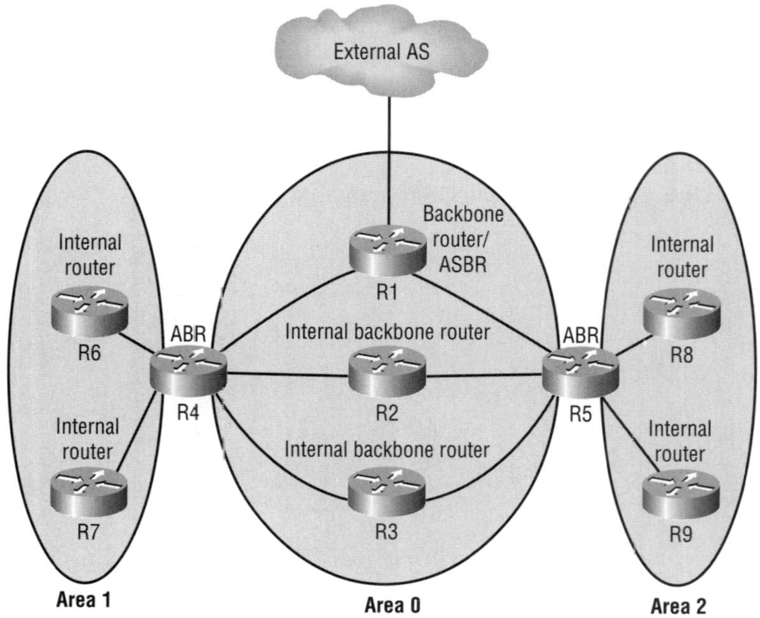

As you may have already noticed in Figure 7.2, some routers can be more than one router type. To eliminate any confusion with these terms, I'll describe each router illustrated in Figure 7.2 and discuss its type(s).

R1: Backbone router/ASBR R1 has a total of three interfaces. Two interfaces are in Area 0, making R1 a backbone router. R1 has a third interface that's connected to an external AS, making it also an ASBR. Since all of R1's interfaces are not in a single area, R1 is not an internal router.

R2: Internal router/backbone router R2 has two interfaces. Both of R2's interfaces are in Area 0, making it a backbone router. Since both interfaces are in the same area, R2 is also an internal router.

R3: Internal router/backbone router R3 has two interfaces. Both of R3's interfaces are in Area 0, making it a backbone router. Since both interfaces are in the same area, R3 is also an internal router.

R4: Backbone router/ABR R4 has two interfaces. One interface connects to Area 0, making R4 a backbone router. The second interface connects to a different area, making R4 an ABR.

R5: Backbone router/ABR R5 has two interfaces. One interface connects to Area 0, making R5 a backbone router. The second interface connects to a different area, making R5 also an ABR.

R6: Internal router R6 has two interfaces. Both of R6's interfaces are in Area 1, making R6 an internal router.

R7: Internal router R7 has two interfaces. Both of R7's interfaces are in Area 1, making it an internal router.

R8: Internal router R8 has two interfaces. Both of R8's interfaces are in Area 2, making R8 an internal router.

R9: Internal router R9 has two interfaces. Both of R9's interfaces are in Area 2, making R9 an internal router.

Link State Advertisements

OSPF uses *link state advertisements (LSAs)* to exchange routing information between other OSPF-enabled routers. Table 7.1 lists the five main types of LSAs that will be discussed in this chapter.

TABLE 7.1 OSPF LSA Types

LSA Type	Advertisement	Description
1	Router LSA	Router LSAs are only flooded in the area that they originate in. They contain information about the router and its directly connected links.
2	Network LSA	Network LSAs are generated by a designated router (DR) and are flooded only in the area that they originate in. They contain information about the routers that are connected to a multi-access network.
3	Summary LSA	Summary LSAs are generated by ABRs, and they contain information about networks from outside the area. For example, a Type 1 or Type 2 LSA will be advertised as a Type 3 LSA by an ABR and is flooded throughout the OSPF domain.

TABLE 7.1 OSPF LSA Types *(continued)*

LSA Type	Advertisement	Description
4	ASBR summary LSA	ASBR summary LSAs are generated by ABRs, and they contain information about ASBRs from outside the area.
5	External LSA	External LSAs are generated by ASBRs, and they contain information about networks from outside the OSPF domain. External LSAs are flooded throughout the OSPF domain.

To help you understand the important LSA types, let's lock at two examples. In Figure 7.3, the router R5 generates an LSA Type 1 or Type 2. Once the update is received on R3, the ABR/ASBR, it is forwarded across the backbone area as a Type 3 LSA. When this Type 3 LSA is received by R2, an ABR, it is forwarded into Area 1 as a Type 3 LSA. The moral of the story is that Type 1 or Type 2 LSAs are only used inside a single area. They are forwarded to other areas as Type 3 LSAs.

FIGURE 7.3 Type 1 or Type 2 updates

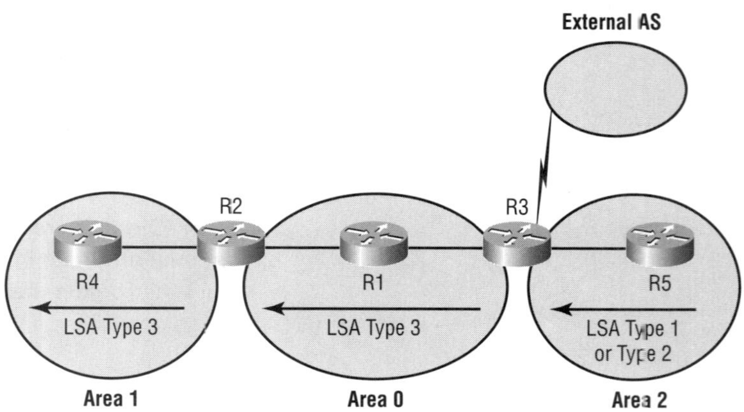

In Figure 7.4, an external route is learned by R3, an ABR/ASBR, and an LSA Type 5 is generated. Notice that the update is flooded throughout the OSPF network as a Type 5, or external LSA.

FIGURE 7.4 Flooding of LSA Type 5

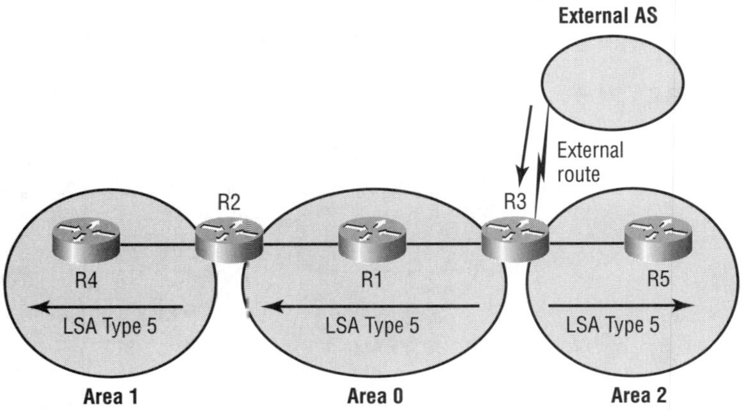

NOTE There are two types of external routes (Type 5): E1 and E2. The default for Cisco devices is E2.

OSPF for MPLS VPNs

Whenever an MPLS VPN is established, the service provider is inserted between the customer sites. For example, Figure 7.5 illustrates a simple two-site OSPF network connected together with Frame Relay.

FIGURE 7.5 A two-site OSPF network

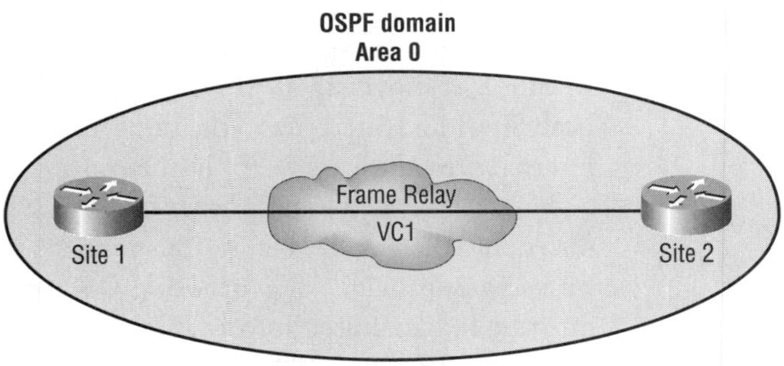

When the service provider is inserted between the two customer sites, OSPF routes must be redistributed from OSPF into BGP, and then back into

OSPF. As you can see in Figure 7.6, an OSPF from Site 1 traverses the service provider network as a BGP route. For the route to be sent to Site 2, the BGP route must be redistributed back into OSPF.

FIGURE 7.6 OSPF-to-BGP redistribution

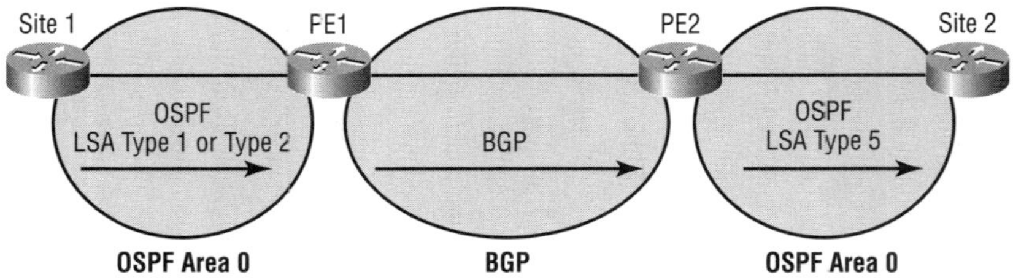

There's a "gotcha" here that needs a little explaining. Figure 7.7 illustrates a simple two-site OSPF network connected with Frame Relay.

FIGURE 7.7 A two-site OSPF network with addresses

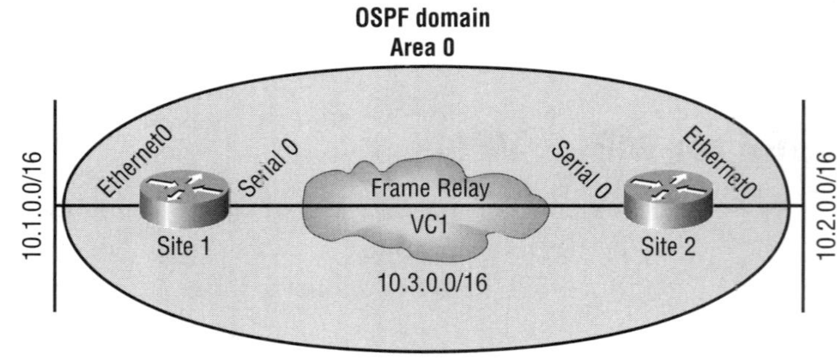

In Figure 7.7, the network 10.1.0.0/16 shows up as connected (C) in the routing table on the Site 1 router. When network 10.1.0.0/16 is learned by Site 2, it shows up as (O) in the routing table. The reason for this is that both Site 1 and Site 2 are in the same area (Area 0). Routes that are from the internal area show up as (O) in the routing table.

Now let's take a look at what happens when the service provider is introduced into the picture. Figure 7.8 shows a customer OSPF network separated by a service provider BGP network. OSPF routes from both Site 1 and Site 2 must be redistributed into BGP to traverse the service provider network. Since both PE1 and PE2 are connected to an OSPF area and to an external autonomous system (the service provider BGP backbone), they can be called ASBRs. Remember that routes from external autonomous systems are advertised into OSPF as Type 5 LSAs.

The Cisco IOS default is to mark the external route as (O E2) or as an OSPF external Type 2 route. So, what does this mean? Well, the 10.1.0.0/16 network advertisement from Site 1 shows up as an external route (O E2) instead of as an internal route (O) at Site 2. Conversely, the 10.2.0.0/16 network advertisement from Site 2 shows up as an external route (O E2) instead of as an internal route (O) at Site 1.

FIGURE 7.8 OSPF-to-BGP redistribution with addresses

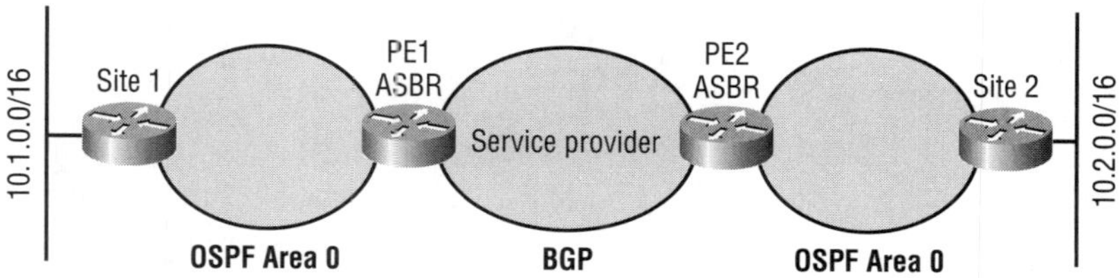

No big deal, right? Wrong! In Figure 7.8, everything works fine. The problem that you'll encounter is when an alternate connection exists between the two sites. In Figure 7.9, Site 1 and Site 2 are connected to the service provider. In addition, they have an alternate connection through Frame Relay just in case the service provider network is unavailable.

FIGURE 7.9 OSPF network with an alternate connection

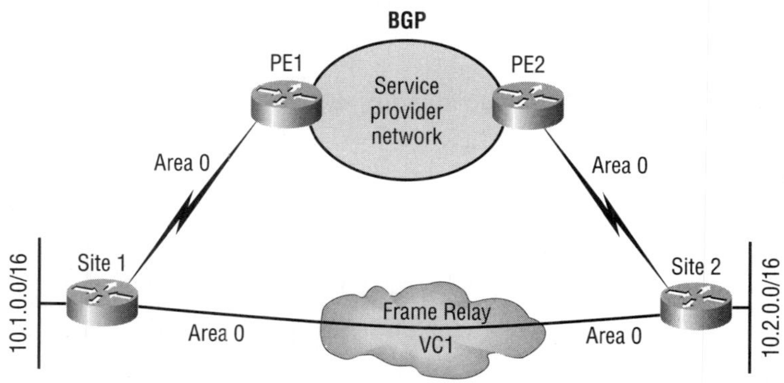

The gotcha is that internal (O) routes are always preferred over external (O E2) routes. Let me explain. Site 1 generates an OSPF route for the network 10.1.0.0/16. The OSPF route is redistributed into BGP and arrives at Site 2 as an external route (O E2). In addition, Site 2 learns of the route through OSPF across the alternate Frame Relay connection, resulting in an internal route (O) in the routing table. Since the primary connection is through the service provider and the alternate connection is there just in case, it's safe to assume that the service provider connection is the fastest. Which way do you want the traffic to travel? Through the fastest connection, which is the service provider network. Here's the gotcha: Since internal routes (O) are preferred over external routes (O E2), the connection through the alternate connection is preferred, and traffic will always flow from Site 1 to Site 2 across the alternate Frame Relay connection as long as it is available.

To get around this problem in MPLS VPNs, a solution called the *OSPF super-backbone* was introduced.

OSPF Super-Backbone

In the OSPF hierarchy, all areas had to connect directly to the backbone area (Area 0). The MP-IBGP backbone, functioning as the super-backbone, replaces the Area 0 requirement, meaning that all areas connect to the super-backbone instead of to the Area 0 backbone. Without the super-backbone, PE routers appear as ASBRs. Now, with the super-backbone, PE routers appear as ABRs. Remember that ASBRs advertise LSA Type 5 routes and ABRs advertise LSA Type 3 routes.

Nothing is better than illustrations when explaining all of this. In Figure 7.10, an OSPF network is separated by the service provider's standard BGP backbone. LSA Type 1 or Type 2 routes from Site 1 are redistributed into BGP by a service provider router (PE1) that appears as an ASBR. PE2, an ASBR, redistributes the route from Site 1 back into OSPF and advertises it to Site 2 as an LSA Type 5.

FIGURE 7.10 OSPF and standard BGP interaction

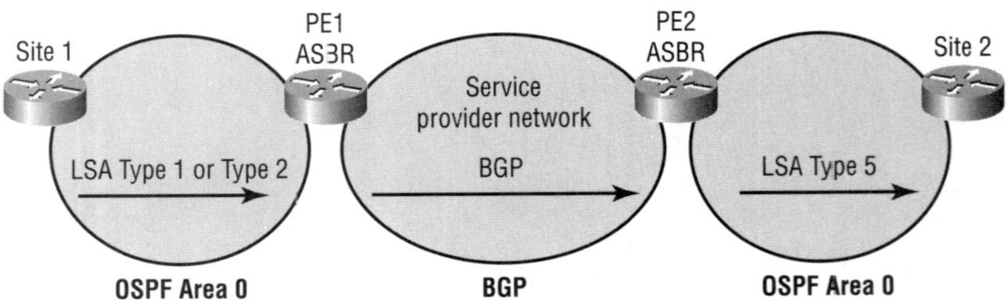

Figure 7.11 illustrates the interaction between standard OSPF and the OSPF super-backbone.

Notice in Figure 7.11 that both PE1 and PE2 appear as ABRs. LSA Type 1 or Type 2 routes from Site 1 are redistributed into BGP by a service provider router (PE1) that appears as an ABR. PE2, an ABR, redistributes the route from Site 1 back into OSPF and advertises it to Site 2 as an LSA Type 3.

LSA Type 3 routes are inter-area routes and are displayed as Type O IA in the routing table.

FIGURE 7.11 OSPF and OSPF super-backbone interaction

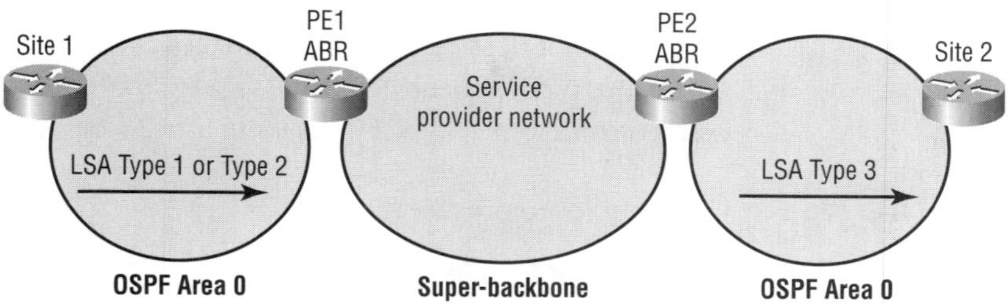

Where the OSPF super-backbone becomes really important is when there are alternate connections between customer sites. In Figure 7.12, two sites are connected through the OSPF super-backbone and an alternate internal OSPF connection. From Site 1, network 10.1.0.0/16 is advertised to PE1 and Site 2 through the alternate connection. The route, received by PE1, will be received by Site 2 as an inter-area route (O IA). The route received from Site 1 across the alternate connection is an internal route (O).

FIGURE 7.12 An alternate connection with super-backbone

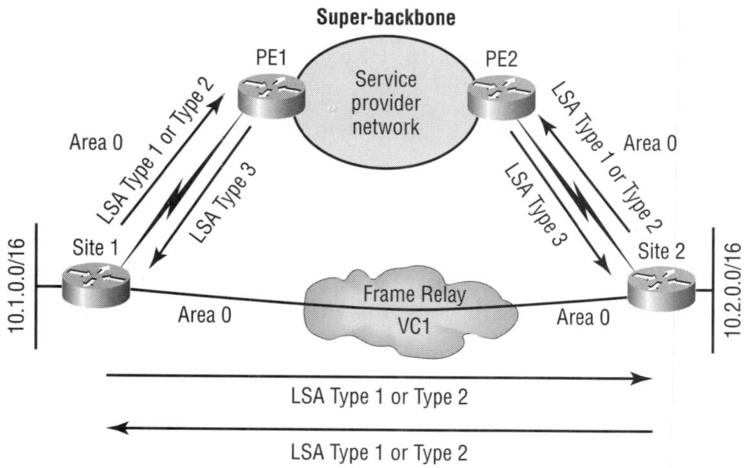

NOTE When a route is redistributed into BGP, the OSPF cost is carried in the MED.

The OSPF super-backbone is made possible by a new BGP extended community that carries the route type and area across the service provider's BGP backbone. Since the route type is being carried in the extended community, an LSA Type 3 stays an LSA Type 3 and an LSA Type 5 stays a Type 5. In Figure 7.13, an external route is learned by Site 1 and is sent to PE1 as an external route (Type 5). PE1 redistributes the route into BGP and preserves the route type. When the route is redistributed into OSPF by PE2, the preserved route type (Type 5) results in Site 2 learning an external route (O E2).

FIGURE 7.13 External route preservation

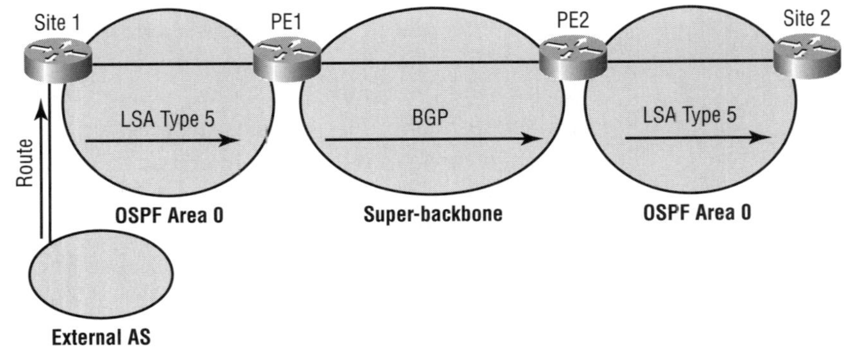

In Figure 7.14, the external AS is connected to PE1. When routes from outside the OSPF domain are sent to Site 1 and Site 2, they are correctly sent as Type 5 routes (O E2).

FIGURE 7.14 An external AS connected to a PE

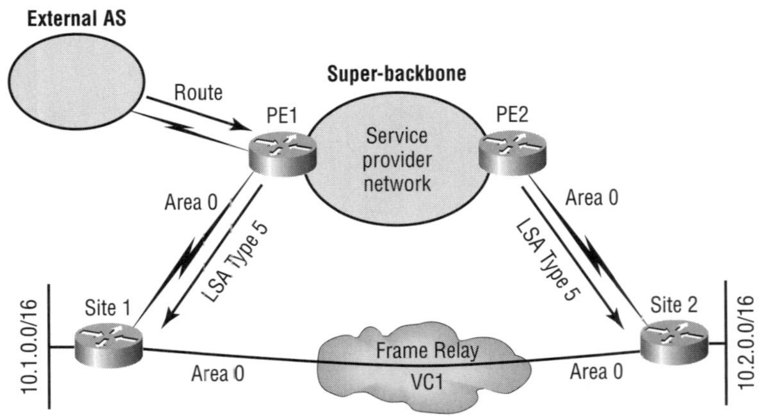

Preventing Routing Loops

OSPF does a good job of preventing routing loops by preferring certain types of routes to others. However, with an OSPF super-backbone, these loop prevention mechanisms don't work anymore. To illustrate, look at Figure 7.15; two sites are redundantly connected through a service provider's OSPF super-backbone.

FIGURE 7.15 Two sites redundantly connected through an OSPF super-backbone

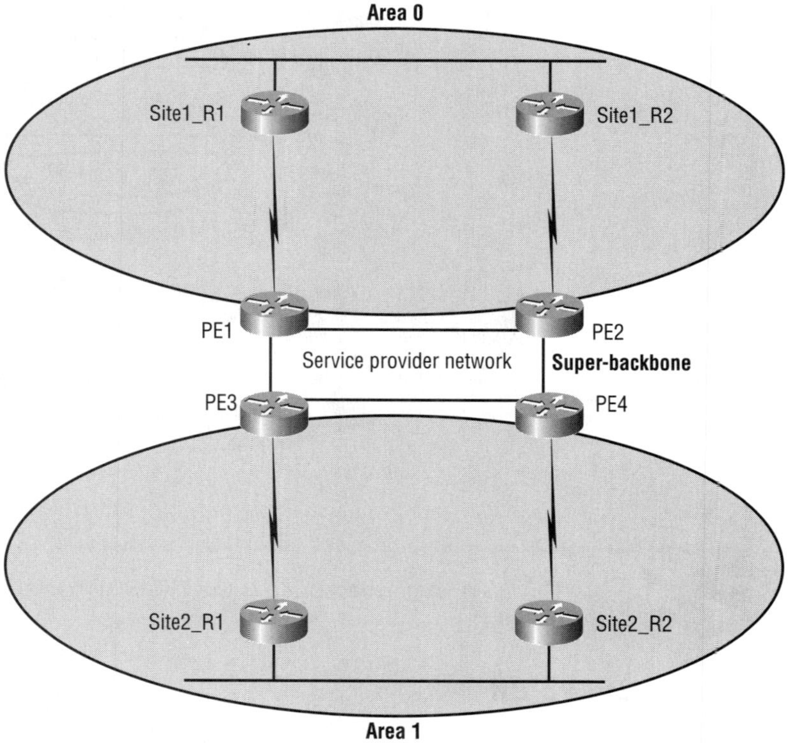

When routes are received from the two sites by the service provider's PE routers, their attributes are preserved in the new BGP extended community and carried through the service provider's OSPF super-backbone. When the routes are redistributed back into OSPF and advertised to each site, they will be LSA Type 3 (`O IA`). These routes will be propagated through each site and may result in a routing loop when redistributed back into the service provider's OSPF super-backbone. Figure 7.16 illustrates this situation.

FIGURE 7.16 A possible routing loop

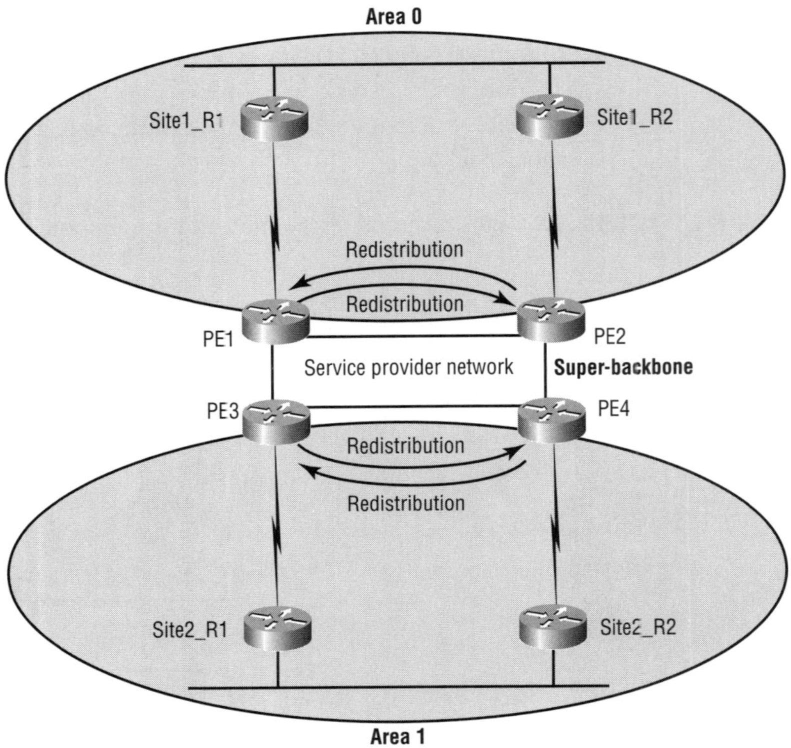

NOTE The OSPF super-backbone is the MP-IBGP backbone.

Down Bit

A new mechanism called the *down bit* is used to prevent routing loops between customer routes and the service provider OSPF super-backbone. When a route is redistributed from MP-IBGP into OSPF, the down bit is set in the Options field of the OSPF LSA header. Another PE router, receiving an LSA with the down bit set, does not redistribute the route into MP-IBGP. Simply put, routes redistributed from MP-IBGP get set with a down bit. Another PE router does not redistribute the same route back into MP-IBGP.

In Figure 7.17, each PE router sets the down bit when a route is redistributed from the OSPF super-backbone (MP-IBGP) into OSPF. When another PE router connected to the same OSPF area receives the route, it is not redistributed.

FIGURE 7.17 A down bit network example

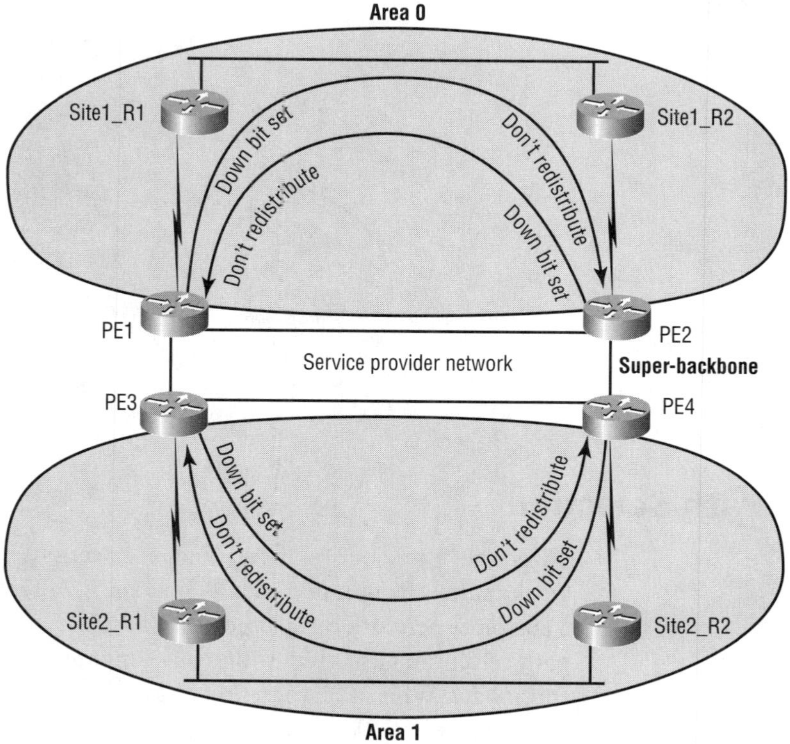

OSPF Tag Field

The down bit does not prevent every possible routing loop. When a route crosses from one OSPF domain to another, it may lose its down bit setting. By default, routes redistributed from BGP into OSPF (standard LSA Type 5 external routes) map the BGP AS number to the *tag field* of the external route. Another PE, seeing its own AS number in the tag field, does not redistribute the route into MP-IBGP, as illustrated in Figure 7.18.

It's important to note that you only get the tag field for external OSPF routes (Type 5) and not intra-area (O) and inter-area (O IA) routes. To get around this, you could simply configure the PE to only redistribute into

MP-IBGP internal OSPF routes. An alternate method of setting the tag field is to have the router between the two OSPF domains set the tag field manually using the `redistribute ospf` *`process-id`* `tag #` command.

FIGURE 7.18 A tag field network example

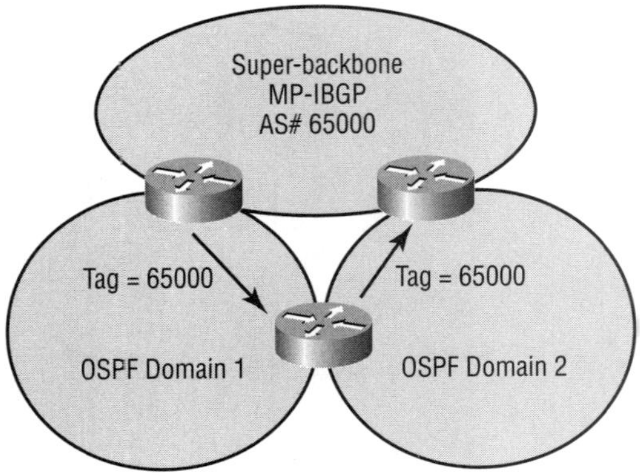

Path Selection

Given the complexities of customer connections to a service provider network, path selection becomes a concern. More than likely, you don't want a customer network being used as a transit for VPN traffic. To ensure proper path selection, Cisco IOS routers use an internal IOS mechanism called the *routing bit*. When a PE router receives a route with the down bit set, the routing bit is cleared. With the routing bit cleared, a route never shows up in the routing table of the PE, even if it is the best route as determined by OSPF. Again, the routing bit is an internal IOS mechanism on the router and is not sent to any neighboring OSPF routers in the customer network.

Real World Scenario

CE-to-PE Protocol Selection

Just because OSPF is discussed in this chapter does not mean that OSPF is the recommended routing protocol for use between CE and PE routers. OSPF has a lot of overhead associated with it due to its operation. As more and more OSPF routing processes are configured on a router, the router has more overhead, and its operation may be slowed.

In addition, PE routers are limited to 32 routing processes. One process is used for connected interfaces, and another process is used for RIPv2. (Remember the command `address-family ipv4 vrf` *vpn_name* to allow for routing contexts under a single RIPv2 process.) Still another process is used for BGP. (Remember the command `address-family ipv4 vrf` *vpn_name* to allow for routing contexts under a single BGP process; MP-BGP and standard BGP all run in the same process.) Therefore, 32 – 1 (Connected) – 1(RIP) – 1 (BGP) = 29. So it's possible to have only 29 OSPF processes running on a PE router.

Why is this important? Well, 100 customers can be supported with a single RIPv2 process. 1000 customers can be supported with a single BGP process. A maximum of 29 OSPF processes can be configured on a single PE router.

In summary, OSPF produces a lot of overhead on the PE router in addition to using up available routing processes. PE routers should already be "big iron" routers, and adding OSPF to the mix does not help much. However, many customers use OSPF and it is supported, with all the bells and whistles, for operation in an MPLS VPN. You may want to migrate your customers from OSPF or convince them to use E-BGP as an alternative routing protocol for communication between their CE and the service provider PE router.

MPLS VPN OSPF Lab

Chapter 6 exposed you to the configuration steps required to set up a simple VPN using RIPv2 as the CE-to-PE routing protocol. In this lab, we'll set up a simple VPN using OSPF as the CE-to-PE routing protocol. To really hammer home all of the configuration steps you've been exposed to, I'll be using the same simple network you first saw in Chapter 2, "Frame-Mode MPLS," illustrated in Figure 7.19.

FIGURE 7.19 A simple service provider network

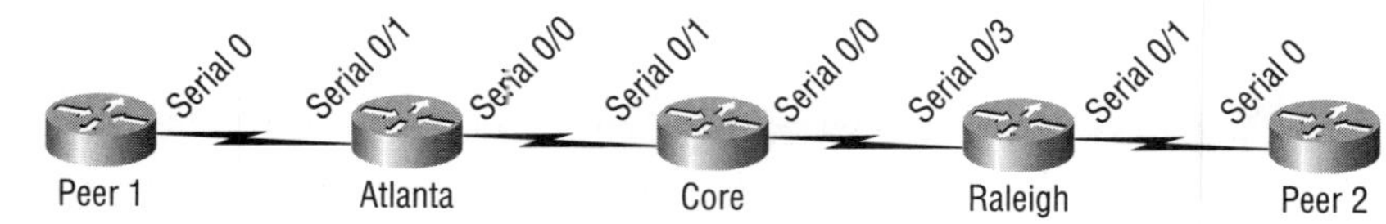

Figure 7.20 illustrates the routing protocol utilization for the network in Figure 7.19.

FIGURE 7.20 Routing protocol utilization

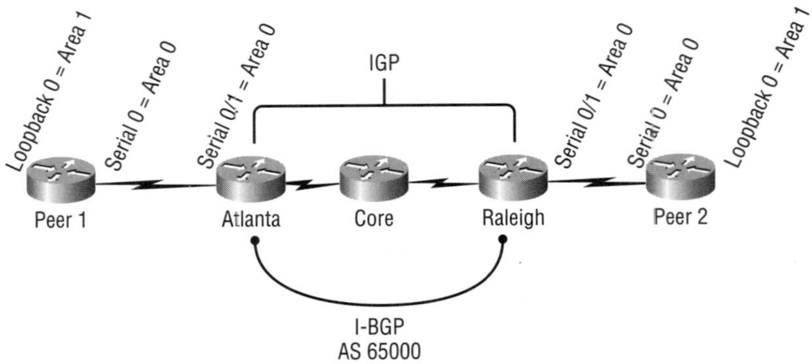

Table 7.2 lists the IP addresses and interfaces of all the CE devices in Figure 7.19.

TABLE 7.2 Customer Addressing

Device	Loopback 0	Serial 0
Peer 1	192.168.1.1/32	192.168.3.5/30
Peer 2	192.168.2.1/32	192.168.3.10/30

Table 7.3 lists the IP addresses and interfaces of the service provider devices in Figure 7.19.

TABLE 7.3 Service Provider Addressing

Device	Loopback 0	Serial 0/0	Serial 0/1	Serial 0/3
Atlanta	204.134.83.1/32	204.134.83.5/ 30	192.168.3.6/30	N/A
Core	204.134.83.2/32	204.134.83.9/30	204.134.83.6/30	N/A
Raleigh	204.134.83.3/32	N/A	192.168.3.9/30	204.134.83.10/30

Device Configuration

Presently, the network is set up with an IGP (RIPv2), tag switching, and MP-BGP between the Atlanta and Raleigh POP routers. The configuration of the Raleigh POP router is as follows:

```
Raleigh#show running-config
Building configuration...

Current configuration : 1997 bytes
!
version 12.1
service timestamps debug uptime
service timestamps log uptime
no service password-encryption
!
hostname Raleigh
!
enable password cisco
!
!
!
!
!
memory-size iomem 25
ip subnet-zero
ip tcp synwait-time 5
no ip domain-lookup
!
!

ip cef
cns event-service server
!
!
!
!
!
```

```
interface Loopback0
 ip address 204.134.83.3 255.255.255.255
!
interface Serial0/0
 no ip address
 shutdown
 no fair-queue
 clockrate 64000
!
interface Serial0/1
 description *** Link to Peer2 ***
 ip address 192.168.3.9 255.255.255.252
 clockrate 64000
!
interface Serial0/2
 no ip address
 shutdown
 clockrate 64000
!
interface Serial0/3
 description *** Link to Core Router ***
 ip address 204.134.83.10 255.255.255.252
 tag-switching ip
 clockrate 64000
!
interface Ethernet1/0
 no ip address
 shutdown
!
interface Ethernet1/1
 no ip address
 shutdown
!
interface Ethernet1/2
 no ip address
 shutdown
!
```

```
interface Ethernet1/3
 no ip address
 shutdown
!
router rip
 version 2
 network 204.134.83.0
 !
router bgp 65000
 no synchronization
 bgp log-neighbor-changes
 neighbor 204.134.83.1 remote-as 65000
 neighbor 204.134.83.1 update-source Loopback0
 neighbor 204.134.83.1 next-hop-self
 no auto-summary
 !
 !
 address-family vpnv4
 neighbor 204.134.83.1 activate
 neighbor 204.134.83.1 send-community both
 no auto-summary
 exit-address-family
!
ip classless
no ip http server
!
!
!
line con 0
 exec-timeout 0 0
 privilege level 15
 logging synchronous
 transport input none
 ip netmask-format decimal
line aux 0
line vty 0 4
 privilege level 15
```

```
 password cisco
 logging synchronous
 login
 ip netmask-format decimal
!
end
```

The configuration of the Atlanta POP router is as follows:

```
Atlanta#show running-config
Building configuration...

Current configuration : 1972 bytes
!
version 12.1
service timestamps debug uptime
service timestamps log uptime
no service password-encryption
!
hostname Atlanta
!
enable password cisco
!
!
!
!
!
memory-size iomem 25
ip subnet-zero
ip tcp synwait-time 5
no ip domain-lookup
!
!
ip cef
cns event-service server
!
!
!
!
!
```

```
interface Loopback0
 ip address 204.134.83.1 255.255.255.255
!
interface Serial0/0
 description *** Link to Core Router ***
 ip address 204.134.83.5 255.255.255.252
 tag-switching ip
 no fair-queue
 clockrate 64000
!
interface Serial0/1
 description *** Link to Peer1 ***
 ip address 192.168.3.6 255.255.255.252
 clockrate 64000
!
interface Serial0/2
 no ip address
 shutdown
 clockrate 64000
!
interface Serial0/3
 no ip address
 shutdown
 clockrate 64000
!
interface Ethernet1/0
 no ip address
 shutdown
!
interface Ethernet1/1
 no ip address
 shutdown
!
interface Ethernet1/2
 no ip address
 shutdown
!
```

```
interface Ethernet1/3
 no ip address
 shutdown
!
router rip
 version 2
 network 204.134.83.0
 !
router bgp 65000
 no synchronization
 bgp log-neighbor-changes
 neighbor 204.134.83.3 remote-as 65000
 neighbor 204.134.83.3 update-source Loopback0
 neighbor 204.134.83.3 next-hop-self
 no auto-summary
 !
 address-family vpnv4
 neighbor 204.134.83.3 activate
 neighbor 204.134.83.3 send-community both
 no auto-summary
 exit-address-family
!
ip classless
no ip http server
!
!
!
line con 0
 exec-timeout 0 0
 privilege level 15
 logging synchronous
 transport input none
 ip netmask-format decimal
line aux 0
line vty 0 4
 privilege level 15
```

```
 password cisco
 logging synchronous
 login
 ip netmask-format decimal
!
```

VPN Configuration

So the service provider network is all set up; now you need to configure an MPLS VPN. From a business case standpoint, Peer 1 and Peer 2 require a simple MPLS-based VPN. Peer 1 and Peer 2 will run OSPF to exchange network routes.

The first thing to configure on the Atlanta POP router is a VRF with a route distinguisher and a route target. The configuration commands for the Atlanta POP router are as follows:

```
Atlanta#conf t
Enter configuration commands, one per line. End with CNTL/Z.

Atlanta(config)#ip vrf vpn_1
Atlanta(config-vrf)#rd 65000:1

Atlanta(config-vrf)#route-target both 65000:1
```

Next, you need to associate the interface that connects to Peer 1 to the VRF using the following commands:

```
Atlanta(config)#int s 0/1
Atlanta(config-if)#ip vrf forwarding vpn_1
% Interface Serial0/1 IP address 192.168.3.6 removed due
  to enabling VRF vpn_1
Atlanta(config-if)#ip address 192.168.3.6 255.255.255.252
```

Now you need to configure a routing context for the VRF in OSPF. To configure global OSPF, use the `router ospf` *`process_id`* command. To configure an OSPF routing context, use the `ospf` *`process_id`* `vrf` *vpn_name* command. The commands to configure an OSPF routing context for vpn_1 are as follows:

```
Atlanta(config)#router ospf 101 vrf vpn_1
Atlanta(config-router)#network 192.168.3.6 0.0.0.0 area 0
```

The following command configures redistribution on the Atlanta POP router:

```
Atlanta(config-router)#redistribute bgp 65000 subnets
```

Now on to BGP. Use the following commands to configure the redistribution for the VPN into BGP for the VRF:

```
Atlanta(config-router)#exit
Atlanta(config)#router bgp 65000
Atlanta(config-router)#address-family ipv4 vrf vpn_1
Atlanta(config-router-af)#redistribute ospf 101 vrf vpn_1
```

You need to repeat these configuration steps on the Raleigh POP router. The first step is to configure a VRF with a route distinguisher and a route target on the Raleigh POP router. The configuration commands are as follows:

```
Raleigh#conf t
Enter configuration commands, one per line. End with CNTL/Z.
Raleigh(config)#ip vrf vpn_1

Raleigh(config-vrf)#rd 65000:1

Raleigh(config-vrf)#route-target both 65000:1
```

Next, you need to associate the interface that connects to Peer 2 to the VRF using the following commands:

```
Raleigh(config-vrf)#exit
Raleigh(config)#int s 0/1
Raleigh(config-if)#ip vrf forwarding vpn_1
% Interface Serial0/1 IP address 192.168.3.9 removed due
  to enabling VRF vpn_1
Raleigh(config-if)#ip address 192.168.3.9 255.255.255.252
```

Now you need to configure OSPF for the VRF:

```
Raleigh(config)#router ospf 101 vrf vpn_1
Raleigh(config-router)#network 192.168.3.9 0.0.0.0 area 0
```

To configure redistribution on the Raleigh POP router, use the following command:

```
Raleigh(config-router)#redistribute bgp 65000 metric
  transparent
```

The next step is to configure the redistribution for the VPN into BGP for the VRF using the following commands:

```
Raleigh(config-router)#exit
Raleigh(config)#router bgp 65000
Raleigh(config-router)#address-family ipv4 vrf vpn_1
Raleigh(config-router-af)#redistribute ospf 101 vrf vpn_1
```

The next section contains the running-configs of the Atlanta and Raleigh POP routers. Try to get in the habit of reading and verifying the configuration.

Raleigh Running-Config

In the following running-config for the Raleigh POP router, notice that the VRF is configured for OSPF. Routes from OSPF are redistributed into BGP and vice versa.

```
Raleigh#show running-config
Building configuration...

Current configuration : 1974 bytes
!
version 12.1
service timestamps debug uptime
service timestamps log uptime
no service password-encryption
!
hostname Raleigh
!
enable password cisco
!
!
!
!
!
memory-size iomem 25
ip subnet-zero
ip tcp synwait-time 5
no ip domain-lookup
!
!
```

```
ip vrf vpn_1
 rd 65000:1
 route-target export 65000:1
 route-target import 65000:1
ip cef
cns event-service server
!
!
!
!
!
interface Loopback0
 ip address 204.134.83.3 255.255.255.255
!
interface Serial0/0
 no ip address
 shutdown
 no fair-queue
 clockrate 64000
!
interface Serial0/1
 description *** Link to Peer2 ***
 ip vrf forwarding vpn_1
 ip address 192.168.3.9 255.255.255.252
 clockrate 64000
!
interface Serial0/2
 no ip address
 shutdown
 clockrate 64000
!
interface Serial0/3
 description *** Link to Core Router ***
 ip address 204.134.83.10 255.255.255.252
 tag-switching ip
 clockrate 64000
!
```

```
interface Ethernet1/0
 no ip address
 shutdown
!
interface Ethernet1/1
 no ip address
 shutdown
!
interface Ethernet1/2
 no ip address
 shutdown
!
interface Ethernet1/3
 no ip address
 shutdown
!
router ospf 101 vrf vpn_1
 log-adjacency-changes
 redistribute bgp 65000 subnets
 network 192.168.3.9 0.0.0.0 area 0
!
router rip
 version 2
 network 204.134.83.0
!
router bgp 65000
 no synchronization
 bgp log-neighbor-changes
 neighbor 204.134.83.1 remote-as 65000
 neighbor 204.134.83.1 update-source Loopback0
 neighbor 204.134.83.1 next-hop-self
 no auto-summary
 !
 address-family ipv4 vrf vpn_1
 redistribute ospf 101
 no auto-summary
```

```
  no synchronization
  exit-address-family
  !
  address-family vpnv4
  neighbor 204.134.83.1 activate
  neighbor 204.134.83.1 send-community both
  no auto-summary
  exit-address-family
 !
 ip classless
 no ip http server
 !
 !
 !
 line con 0
  exec-timeout 0 0
  privilege level 15
  logging synchronous
  transport input none
  ip netmask-format decimal
 line aux 0
 line vty 0 4
  privilege level 15
  password cisco
  logging synchronous
  login
  ip netmask-format decimal
 !
 end
```

Atlanta Running-Config

In the following running-config for the Atlanta POP router, notice that the VRF is configured for OSPF. Routes from OSPF are redistributed into BGP and vice versa.

```
Atlanta#show running-config
Building configuration...
```

```
Current configuration : 1949 bytes
!
version 12.1
service timestamps debug uptime
service timestamps log uptime
no service password-encryption
!
hostname Atlanta
!
enable password cisco
!
!
!
!
!
memory-size iomem 25
ip subnet-zero
ip tcp synwait-time 5
no ip domain-lookup
!
!
ip vrf vpn_1
 rd 65000:1
 route-target export 65000:1
 route-target import 65000:1
ip cef
cns event-service server
!
!
!
!
!
interface Loopback0
 ip address 204.134.83.1 255.255.255.255
!
interface Serial0/0
```

```
 description *** Link to Core Router ***
 ip address 204.134.83.5 255.255.255.252
 tag-switching ip
 no fair-queue
 clockrate 64000
!
interface Serial0/1
 description *** Link to Peer1 ***
 ip vrf forwarding vpn_1
 ip address 192.168.3.6 255.255.255.252
 clockrate 64000
!
interface Serial0/2
 no ip address
 shutdown
 clockrate 64000
!
interface Serial0/3
 no ip address
 shutdown
 clockrate 64000
!
interface Ethernet1/0
 no ip address
 shutdown
!
interface Ethernet1/1
 no ip address
 shutdown
!
interface Ethernet1/2
 no ip address
 shutdown
!
interface Ethernet1/3
 no ip address
```

```
 shutdown
!
router ospf 101 vrf vpn_1
 log-adjacency-changes
 redistribute bgp 65000 subnets
 network 192.168.3.6 0.0.0.0 area 0
!
router rip
 version 2
 network 204.134.83.0
!
router bgp 65000
 no synchronization
 bgp log-neighbor-changes
 neighbor 204.134.83.3 remote-as 65000
 neighbor 204.134.83.3 update-source Loopback0
 neighbor 204.134.83.3 next-hop-self
 no auto-summary
 !
 address-family ipv4 vrf vpn_1
 redistribute ospf 101
 no auto-summary
 no synchronization
 exit-address-family
 !
 address-family vpnv4
 neighbor 204.134.83.3 activate
 neighbor 204.134.83.3 send-community both
 no auto-summary
 exit-address-family
!
ip classless
no ip http server
!
!
!
```

```
line con 0
 exec-timeout 0 0
 privilege level 15
 logging synchronous
 transport input none
 ip netmask-format decimal
line aux 0
line vty 0 4
 privilege level 15
 password cisco
 logging synchronous
 login
 ip netmask-format decimal
!
end
```

Peer Router Configuration

Routers Peer 1 and Peer 2 need to be configured for standard OSPF. The interfaces on Peer 1 and Peer 2 that connect to the PE routers will be configured for OSPF Area 0. The loopback interfaces on both Peer 1 and Peer 2 will be configured for OSPF Area 1.

The commands to configure Peer 1 for OSPF are as follows:

```
Peer1#conf t
Enter configuration commands, one per line. End with CNTL/Z.
Peer1(config)#router ospf 1
Peer1(config-router)#network 192.168.3.5 0.0.0.0 area 0
Peer1(config-router)#network 192.168.1.1 0.0.0.0 area 1
Peer1(config-router)#^Z
Peer1#
```

The commands to configure Peer 2 for OSPF are as follows

```
Peer2#conf t
Enter configuration commands, one per line. End with CNTL/Z.
Peer2(config)#router ospf 1
Peer2(config-router)#network 192.168.3.10 0.0.0.0 area 0
Peer2(config-router)#network 192.168.2.1 0.0.0.0 area 1
Peer2(config-router)#^Z
Peer2#
```

Peer 1 Running-Config

Notice in the following running-config that the Peer 1 router is running only standard OSPF:

```
Peer1#show running-config
Building configuration...

Current configuration : 881 bytes
!
version 12.1
service timestamps debug uptime
service timestamps log uptime
no service password-encryption
!
hostname Peer1
!
enable password cisco
!
!
!
!
!
ip subnet-zero
ip tcp synwait-time 5
no ip domain-lookup
!
!
!
!
interface Loopback0
 ip address 192.168.1.1 255.255.255.255
!
interface Ethernet0
 no ip address
 shutdown
!
interface Serial0
 description *** Link to Atlanta POP ***
```

```
 ip address 192.168.3.5 255.255.255.252
 no fair-queue
!
interface Serial1
 no ip address
 shutdown
!
router ospf 1
 log-adjacency-changes
 network 192.168.1.1 0.0.0.0 area 1
 network 192.168.3.5 0.0.0.0 area 0
!
ip classless
no ip http server
!
!
line con 0
 exec-timeout 0 0
 privilege level 15
 logging synchronous
 transport input none
 ip netmask-format decimal
line aux 0
line vty 0 4
 privilege level 15
 password cisco
 logging synchronous
 login
 ip netmask-format decimal
!
end
```

Peer 2 Running-Config

Notice in the following running-config that the Peer 2 router is running only standard OSPF:

```
Peer2#show running-config
Building configuration...
```

```
Current configuration : 1109 bytes
!
version 12.1
service timestamps debug uptime
service timestamps log uptime
no service password-encryption
!
hostname Peer2
!
enable password lab
!
!
!
!
!
ip subnet-zero
ip tcp synwait-time 5
no ip domain-lookup
!
!
!
!
interface Loopback0
 ip address 192.168.2.1 255.255.255.255
!
interface Ethernet0
 no ip address
 shutdown
!
interface Serial0
 description *** Link to PE2 ***
 ip address 192.168.3.10 255.255.255.252
 no fair-queue
!
interface Serial1
 no ip address
 shutdown
!
```

```
router ospf 1
 log-adjacency-changes
 network 192.168.2.1 0.0.0.0 area 1
 network 192.168.3.10 0.0.0.0 area 0
!
ip classless

no ip http server
!
!
line con 0
 exec-timeout 0 0
 privilege level 15
 logging synchronous
 transport input none
 ip netmask-format decimal
line aux 0
line vty 0 4
 privilege level 15
 password lab
 logging synchronous
 login
 ip netmask-format decimal
!
end
```

Verification with Ping

To verify that the VPN works, all you need to do is a ping from one peer router to the other. The following output is the result of a ping from Peer 2 to Peer 1:

```
Peer2#ping 192.168.1.1

Type escape sequence to abort.
Sending 5, 100-byte ICMP Echos to 192.168.1.1, timeout
  is 2 seconds:
!!!!!
Success rate is 100 percent (5/5), round-trip min/avg/max
  = 116/119/120 ms
```

Routing Table Isolation

As discussed in Chapter 6, the VRF routing table is well isolated from the global routing table on a PE router. Therefore, on the Raleigh and Atlanta POP routers, no customer (Peer 1 and Peer 2) routes show up in the global routing table. The global routing table of the Raleigh POP router is as follows:

```
Raleigh#show ip route
.
. Output Omitted
.
Gateway of last resort is not set

     204.134.83.0 255.255.255.0 is variably subnetted,
  5 subnets, 2 masks
C       204.134.83.8 255.255.255.252 is directly
  connected, Serial0/3
R       204.134.83.1 255.255.255.255
           [120/2] via 204.134.83.9, 00:00:00, Serial0/3
C       204.134.83.3 255.255.255.255 is directly
  connected, Loopback0
R       204.134.83.2 255.255.255.255
           [120/1] via 204.134.83.9, 00:00:00, Serial0/3
R       204.134.83.4 255.255.255.252
           [120/1] via 204.134.83.9, 00:00:00, Serial0/3
```

The global routing table of the Atlanta POP router is as follows:

```
Atlanta#show ip route
.
. Output Omitted
.
Gateway of last resort is not set

     204.134.83.0 255.255.255.0 is variably subnetted,
  5 subnets, 2 masks
R       204.134.83.8 255.255.255.252
           [120/1] via 204.134.83.6, 00:00:07, Serial0/0
```

```
C       204.134.83.1 255.255.255.255 is directly
  connected, Loopback0
R       204.134.83.3 255.255.255.255
           [120/2] via 204.134.83.6, 00:00:07, Serial0/0
R       204.134.83.2 255.255.255.255
           [120/1] via 204.134.83.6, 00:00:07, Serial0/0
C       204.134.83.4 255.255.255.252 is directly
  connected,
```

In addition, none of the customer (Peer 1 and Peer 2) routes show up on the Core router. The Core router is only running the IGP (RIPv2) and knows nothing about any of the customer subnets. The global routing table of the Core router is as follows:

```
Core#show ip route
.
. Output Omitted
.
Gateway of last resort is not set

     204.134.83.0 255.255.255.0 is variably subnetted,
  5 subnets, 2 masks
C       204.134.83.8 255.255.255.252 is directly
  connected, Serial0/0
R       204.134.83.1 255.255.255.255
           [120/1] via 204.134.83.5, 00:00:19, Serial0/1
R       204.134.83.3 255.255.255.255
           [120/1] via 204.134.83.10, 00:00:26, Serial0/0
C       204.134.83.2 255.255.255.255 is directly
  connected, Loopback0
C       204.134.83.4 255.255.255.252 is directly
  connected, Serial0/1
```

If you see any customer routes in the global routing table, then more than likely, redistribution has been misconfigured. You'll need to check the redistribution syntax on your PE routers to make sure that they have the proper configuration.

What about on the client routers? They are isolated from the service provider as well. The client routers do not know any of the details of the service provider network. Notice in the following device output that no service provider routes are in the global routing tables for Peer 1 and Peer 2.

The global routing table for Peer 1 is as follows:

```
Peer1#show ip route
.
. Output Omitted
.

Gateway of last resort is not set

     192.168.1.0 255.255.255.255 is subnetted, 1 subnets
C       192.168.1.1 is directly connected, Loopback0
     192.168.2.0 255.255.255.255 is subnetted, 1 subnets
O IA    192.168.2.1 [110/846] via 192.168.3.6, 00:01:08,
  Serial0
     192.168.3.0 255.255.255.252 is subnetted, 2 subnets
O IA    192.168.3.8 [110/65] via 192.168.3.6, 00:01:08,
  Serial0
C       192.168.3.4 is directly connected, Serial0
```

The global routing table for Peer 2 is as follows:

```
Peer2#show ip route
.
. Output Omitted
.
Gateway of last resort is not set

     192.168.1.0 255.255.255.255 is subnetted, 1 subnets
O IA    192.168.1.1 [110/846] via 192.168.3.9, 00:00:29,
  Serial0
     192.168.2.0 255.255.255.255 is subnetted, 1 subnets
C       192.168.2.1 is directly connected, Loopback0
     192.168.3.0 255.255.255.252 is subnetted, 2 subnets
C       192.168.3.8 is directly connected, Serial0
O IA    192.168.3.4 [110/65] via 192.168.3.9, 00:00:29,
  Serial0
```

Verifying OSPF VRF Routes

Now, let's talk about the flow of routing information through the network. Let's begin this discussion by looking at the VRF routing table of vpn_1 as it exists on the Atlanta POP router:

```
Atlanta#show ip route vrf vpn_1
.
. Output Omitted
.

Gateway of last resort is not set

     192.168.1.0 255.255.255.255 is subnetted, 1 subnets
O IA    192.168.1.1 [110/782] via 192.168.3.5, 00:04:30,
  Serial0/1
     192.168.2.0 255.255.255.255 is subnetted, 1 subnets
B       192.168.2.1 [200/782] via 204.134.83.3, 00:02:22
     192.168.3.0 255.255.255.252 is subnetted, 2 subnets
B       192.168.3.8 [200/0] via 204.134.83.3, 00:02:22
C       192.168.3.4 is directly connected, Serial0/1
```

In the routing table for vpn_1 on the Atlanta POP router, there are two BGP routes (B) and one OSPF inter-area route (O IA). The OSPF inter-area route in the preceding output was learned from Peer 1 and is the loopback of Peer 1. Remember that the loopback was configured for Area 1. The Atlanta POP router is configured for Area 0. The B routes are from the Raleigh POP router (Peer 2 OSPF routes redistributed into MP-BGP and carried across the service provider backbone).

On the Raleigh POP router, there are also BGP routes (B) and one OSPF inter-area route (O IA). The OSPF inter-area is learned from Peer 2. The B routes come from the Atlanta POP. The VRF routing table for vpn_1 is as follows:

```
Raleigh#show ip route vrf vpn_1
.
. Output Omitted
.
Gateway of last resort is not set

     192.168.1.0 255.255.255.255 is subnetted, 1 subnets
```

```
B        192.168.1.1 [200/782] via 204.134.83.1, 00:03:34
     192.168.2.0 255.255.255.255 is subnetted, 1 subnets
O IA     192.168.2.1 [110/782] via 192.168.3.10, 00:05:28,
  Serial0/1
     192.168.3.0 255.255.255.252 is subnetted, 2 subnets
C        192.168.3.8 is directly connected, Serial0/1
B        192.168.3.4 [200/0] via 204.134.83.1, 00:03:34
```

Now let's look at the routing tables as they appear on both Peer 1 and Peer 2. When OSPF routes are redistributed into MP-IBGP (the OSPF super-backbone), their area attributes are preserved in the new extended BGP community. If an inter-area (O IA) or intra-area (O) route is redistributed back into OSPF, it is displayed as an inter-area (O IA) route. Notice that routes, both from Area 0 and Area 1, are displayed as inter-area (O IA) routes in the routing tables of Peer 1 and Peer 2.

The global routing table of Peer 1 is as follows:

```
Peer1#show ip route
.
. Output Omitted
.

Gateway of last resort is not set

     192.168.1.0 255.255.255.255 is subnetted, 1 subnets
C        192.168.1.1 is directly connected, Loopback0
     192.168.2.0 255.255.255.255 is subnetted, 1 subnets
O IA     192.168.2.1 [110/846] via 192.168.3.6, 00:01:08,
  Serial0
     192.168.3.0 255.255.255.252 is subnetted, 2 subnets
O IA     192.168.3.8 [110/65] via 192.168.3.6, 00:01:08,
  Serial0
C        192.168.3.4 is directly connected, Serial0
```

The global routing table of Peer 2 is as follows:

```
Peer2#show ip route
.
. Output Omitted
.
```

```
Gateway of last resort is not set

     192.168.1.0 255.255.255.255 is subnetted, 1 subnets
O IA    192.168.1.1 [110/846] via 192.168.3.9, 00:00:29,
  Serial0
     192.168.2.0 255.255.255.255 is subnetted, 1 subnets
C       192.168.2.1 is directly connected, Loopback0
     192.168.3.0 255.255.255.252 is subnetted, 2 subnets
C       192.168.3.8 is directly connected, Serial0
O IA    192.168.3.4 [110/65] via 192.168.3.9, 00:00:29,
  Serial0
```

Using Ping and Telnet from a PE Router

As discussed previously in this lab, the quickest way to verify that the VRF is up and working is to do a ping from one customer router to another. It is not practical to assume that the service provider will always have access to customer routers. Therefore, extensions have been made to the standard `ping` and `telnet` commands.

When you use the `telnet` command to connect to another device, the global routing table is used to resolve the host. If you want to telnet to a customer router in a VRF, you need to specify the VRF. To telnet to an MPLS VPN customer, use the `telnet host /vrf` *`vpn_name`* command. Here's an example of this; from the Atlanta POP router, a telnet connection is initiated to host 192.168.1.1 in VRF vpn_1:

```
Atlanta#telnet 192.168.1.1 /vrf vpn_1
Trying 192.168.1.1 ... Open


User Access Verification

Password:
Peer1#
```

The `ping` command also has VRF extensions. When you use the `ping` command without any VRF extensions, the global routing table is used to resolve the host. For example, a ping from the Atlanta POP router to the loopback address of Peer 1 produces the following results:

```
Atlanta#ping 192.168.3.5

Type escape sequence to abort.
Sending 5, 100-byte ICMP Echos to 192.168.3.5, timeout
  is 2 seconds:
.....
Success rate is 0 percent (0/5)
```

Notice that the ping fails. A network for 192.168.3.5 is not in the Atlanta POP router's global routing table; instead it's in a VRF. To ping a device in a VPN, use the `ping vrf` *`vpn_name`* `ip` *`host`* command. A ping from the Atlanta POP router to the loopback of Peer 1 produces the following results:

```
Atlanta#ping vrf vpn_1 ip 192.168.3.5

Type escape sequence to abort.
Sending 5, 100-byte ICMP Echos to 192.168.3.5, timeout
  is 2 seconds:
!!!!!
Success rate is 100 percent (5/5), round-trip min/avg/max
  = 28/30/32 ms
```

Let's do one more ping, this time to the loopback address of Peer 2. The output is as follows:

```
Atlanta#ping vrf vpn_1 ip 192.168.3.6

Type escape sequence to abort.
Sending 5, 100-byte ICMP Echos to 192.168.3.6, timeout
  is 2 seconds:
!!!!!
Success rate is 100 percent (5/5), round-trip min/avg/max
  = 56/63/76 ms
```

NOTE

For the `trace` command, VRF extensions are also available. Use ? to learn more about the VRF command options from a Cisco IOS device. Many of the commands you already use to troubleshoot a network have VRF extensions.

Summary

In this chapter you learned about OSPF and how it works when implemented in an MPLS VPN. First of all, OSPF is not the best dynamic routing protocol to use between the PE and CE routers. OSPF is an intensive protocol, and having many instances of it running on a single router can slow the router down. In addition, OSPF can quickly use up the maximum number of routing processes (32) on a PE router.

However, many customers run OSPF, and the service provider needs to support it. To this end, there have been many extensions added to how OSPF works to ensure its proper operation in an MPLS VPN.

To start with, the hierarchy has changed with the introduction of the super-backbone. The super-backbone, or the service provider MP-BGP backbone, replaces the requirement for all OSPF areas to be connected to the OSPF backbone (Area 0). A new extended BGP community is used to preserve OSPF information such as the LSA type. In addition, standard BGP rules still work, such as preserving the OSPF cost in the MED attribute. When a PE router receives an LSA Type 1 or Type 2 from a CE and redistributes it into MP-BGP, a downstream OSPF customer learns this route as an inter-area (`O IA`) router. When an LSA Type 3 route is learned by the PE, the route is propagated through MP-BGP and learned by a downstream OSPF customer router as an inter-area (`O IA`) router. OSPF LSA Type 5 external routes keep their external attributes and are listed as external routes on a downstream OSPF customer router's global routing table.

To make sure that routing loops do not occur, the down bit is used. One PE redistributes a route from MP-BGP into OSPF, and the down bit is set. When the same route is learned by another PE, upon observing the down bit, the route is not redistributed back into MP-BGP. The down bit can be lost, and therefore the tag field (set to the originating BGP AS number) is used. When a PE receives a route, with the tag field set to its own AS number, the route will not be redistributed.

To ensure proper path selection, any route learned with the down bit set results in the routing bit being set on the PE router. Any route with the routing bit set does not show up in the VRF routing table on the PE, even if it is the best path according to OSPF.

To configure global OSPF, you use the `router ospf` *`process_id`* command. To configure an OSPF routing context, you use the `router ospf` *`process_id`* `vrf` *`vpn_name`* command.

Exam Essentials

Be able to describe how OSPF operates in a VPN. OSPF operates normally in an MPLS VPN. Customer routers do not need an IOS upgrade to have an MPLS VPN that uses OSPF as the CE-to-PE routing protocol. What is new is how the service provider handles these routes. To prevent routing loops, the down bit is set when routes are redistributed from MP-BGP into OSPF. The down bit prevents routing loops because when a PE router sees the down bit set, it does not redistribute the route back into MP-BGP. If the down bit is removed as it travels through the customer's network, the tag field, containing the originating BGP AS number, is used to prevent loops. To ensure proper routing, a learned route with the down bit results in the routing bit (only on the PE router) being set. With the routing bit set, the PE router does not use the route, even if it is the best path as dictated by OSPF.

Be able to describe the enhanced OSPF hierarchical model. The standard OSPF rule is that all areas must connect to the backbone area (Area 0). Now, with MPLS, a new super-backbone is available. The super-backbone replaces the old OSPF backbone (an Area 0 requirement). Service provider routers appear as ABRs to customers.

Understand the interaction between OSPF and MP-BGP. When routes are learned by a PE router, from a CE router, the OSPF type is preserved in the new extended BGP community when redistributed into MP-BGP. When an OSPF LSA Type 1 or Type 2 is redistributed into MP-BGP, its attribute is preserved. When an OSPF LSA Type 3 is redistributed into MP-BGP, its attribute is preserved. When an OSPF LSA Type 5 is redistributed into MP-BGP, its attribute is preserved. When these routes are redistributed back into OSPF, an OSPF LSA Type 1 or Type 2 becomes an OSPF LSA Type 3, an OSPF LSA Type 3 remains an OSPF LSA Type 3, and an OSPF Type 5 remains an OSPF Type 5.

Key Terms

Before you take the exam, be certain you are familiar with the following terms:

- area border router (ABR)
- autonomous system boundary router (ASBR)
- backbone area
- backbone router
- down bit
- internal router
- link state advertisements (LSAs)
- OSPF domain
- OSPF super-backbone
- routing bit
- tag field

Review Questions

1. How many routing processes are supported on a PE router?

   A. 16

   B. 32

   C. 48

   D. 64

2. With standard OSPF, all areas must connect to Area __________.

   A. 0

   B. 1

   C. Super-backbone

   D. None of the above

3. Without the OSPF super-backbone, PE routers are viewed as __________ routers.

   A. ABR

   B. ASBR

   C. Internal

   D. External

4. Which of the following commands is used to configure OSPF for a VPN?

   A. `router ospf` *process*

   B. `router ospf` *process*
      `address-family ipv4 vrf` *vpn_name*

   C. `router ospf` *process_id* `vrf` *vpn_name*

   D. None of the above

5. Intra-area routes within a customer network are displayed as __________ in a customer router's global routing table.

   A. `O`

   B. `O IA`

   C. `O E2`

   D. None of the above

6. The OSPF cost is carried in which of the following?

   A. New extended BGP community

   B. MED

   C. Cost field

   D. None of the above

7. Intra-area routes are redistributed into MP-BGP by a PE router. When the route is ultimately learned by a downstream OSPF customer router, the route is displayed as __________ in a customer router's global routing table.

   A. `O`

   B. `O IA`

   C. `O E2`

   D. None of the above

8. Inter-area routes are redistributed into MP-BGP by a PE router. When the route is ultimately learned by a downstream OSPF customer router, the route is displayed as __________ in a customer router's global routing table.

   A. `O`

   B. `O IA`

   C. `O E2`

   D. None of the above

9. External routes are redistributed into MP-BGP by a PE router. When the route is ultimately learned by a downstream OSPF customer router, the route is displayed as ________ in a customer router's global routing table.

   A. `O`

   B. `O IA`

   C. `O E2`

   D. None of the above

10. With the OSPF super-backbone, PE routers are viewed as ________ routers.

   A. ABR

   B. ASBR

   C. Internal

   D. External

11. The BGP AS number is mapped to which of the following?

   A. Down bit

   B. Tag field

   C. Routing bit

   D. None of the above

12. Which of the following is not sent to customer OSPF routers?

   A. Down bit

   B. Tag field

   C. Routing bit

   D. None of the above

13. An inter-area OSPF route is an LSA Type ___________.

    A. 1 or 2

    B. 3

    C. 4

    D. 5

14. An external OSPF route is an LSA Type ___________.

    A. 1 or 2

    B. 3

    C. 4

    D. 5

15. An intra-area OSPF route is an LSA Type ___________.

    A. 1 or 2

    B. 3

    C. 4

    D. 5

16. Which of the following OSPF LSA types is flooded throughout the OSPF domain?

    A. 1 or 2

    B. 3

    C. 4

    D. 5

17. Which of the following OSPF router types generate LSA Type 5 routes?

    A. ABR

    B. ASBR

    C. Internal

    D. Backbone

18. Which of the following OSPF router types generate LSA Type 3 routes?

    A. ABR

    B. ASBR

    C. Internal

    D. Backbone

19. Which of the following are used to prevent routing loops? (Choose all that apply.)

    A. Down bit

    B. Tag field

    C. Routing bit

    D. MED

20. To ensure optimal path selection, the __________ is used.

    A. Down bit

    B. Tag field

    C. Routing bit

    D. None of the above

Answers to Review Questions

1. B. 32 total processes are available. Connected, RIPv2, and BGP all use only one process each. OSPF uses a process for each individual VPN.

2. A. For standard OSPF, all areas must have a connection to Area 0, which is known as the backbone area.

3. B. Without the OSPF super-backbone, the service provider network looks like a standard BGP network. Therefore, PE routers are viewed as ASBRs.

4. C. The `router ospf` *`process_id`* `vrf` *`vpn_name`* command is used to configure OSPF for a VPN.

5. A. Intra-area routes from with the customer's OSPF network are displayed as `O` in a customer router's routing table.

6. B. Standard BGP rules still apply when redistributing OSPF routes into MP-BGP. The OSPF cost is carried in the BGP MED attribute.

7. B. Internal routes, when redistributed back into OSPF from MP-BGP, are LSA Type 3 routes and are displayed as `O IA` in a customer router's global routing table.

8. B. Inter-area routes, when redistributed back into OSPF from MP-BGP, are LSA Type 3 routes and are displayed as `O IA` in a customer router's global routing table.

9. C. External routes, when redistributed back into OSPF from MP-BGP, are LSA Type 5 routes and are displayed as `O E2` in a customer router's global routing table. The Cisco default is `O E2` for external routes.

10. A. With the OSPF super-backbone, PE routers are not viewed as ASBRs but as ABRs.

11. B. The BGP AS number is mapped to the tag field. A PE router does not redistribute a route it learns if the tag field value is equal to its own AS number.

12. C. Routes with the routing bit set will not be displayed in the routing table and will not be sent to customer OSPF routers. The routing bit is used internally by a PE router to mark routes learned where the down bit is set. A route with the routing bit cleared is not displayed in the VRF routing table, even if it is the best OSPF route.

13. B. OSPF routes from one area to another are OSPF LSA Type 3.

14. D. OSPF routes from an external AS are OSPF LSA Type 5.

15. A. OSPF routes from the same area are OSPF LSA Type 1 or Type 2.

16. D. External routes, OSPF LSA Type 5, are flooded throughout the OSPF domain.

17. B. ASBR routers connect to an external AS and generate external, LSA Type 5, routes.

18. A. ABR routers connect to more than one OSPF area generate inter-area, LSA Type 3, routes.

19. A, B. Both the down bit and the tag field are used to prevent routing loops.

20. C. When the routing bit is cleared, a route is not displayed in the global routing table, even if it is the best OSPF route.

Chapter 8

Advanced MPLS Topics

CCIP MPLS EXAM OBJECTIVES COVERED IN THIS CHAPTER:

- ✓ Identify the IOS commands and their proper syntax used to configure advanced MPLS VPN features.

When reviewing Cisco's exam objectives in preparation for the exam, the "and any other relevant topics" line might get you worrying. This chapter tries to address those topics. Although there are no specific exam objectives covered in this chapter, the topics discussed here may show up on the MPLS exam.

So far, you've learned a lot about MPLS and MPLS VPNs. This chapter explains the steps required to set up MPLS VPNs using static routes and E-BGP to communicate with CE routers.

In addition, you've learned all about simple MPLS VPN topologies. This chapter introduces you to more complex MPLS VPN topologies.

Static Routing

Although the exam objectives do not require you to know about *static routes*, I'd like you to see a working example of how static routes can be used in a simple MPLS VPN.

Figure 8.1 illustrates the simple network we'll use in this example.

FIGURE 8.1 A simple service provider network

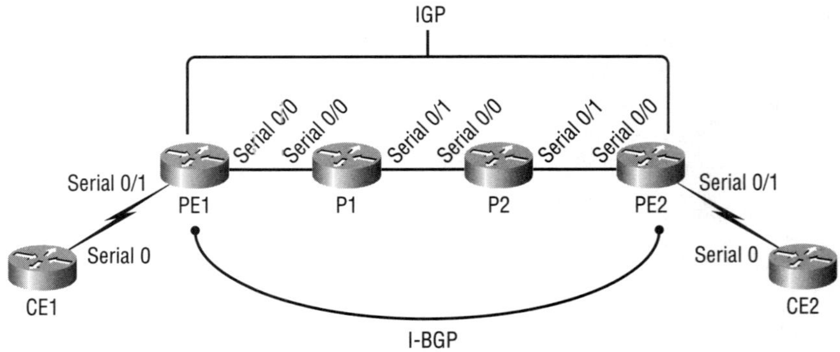

Figure 8.2 illustrates the routing protocol utilization of the network in Figure 8.1.

FIGURE 8.2 Routing protocol utilization

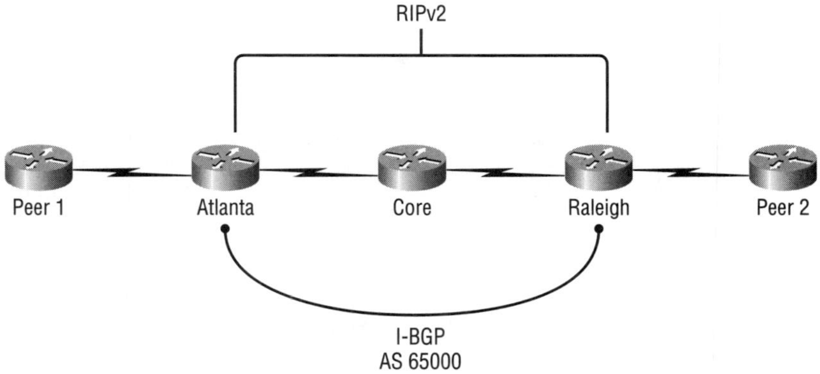

Table 8.1 lists the IP addresses and interfaces of the CE devices in Figure 8.1.

TABLE 8.1 Customer Addressing

Device	Loopback 0	Serial 0
Peer 1	192.168.1.1/32	192.168.3.5/30
Peer 2	192.168.2.1/32	192.168.3.10/30

Table 8.2 lists the IP addresses and interfaces of the service provider devices in Figure 8.1.

TABLE 8.2 Service Provider Addressing

Device	Loopback 0	Serial 0/0	Serial 0/1	Serial 0/3
Atlanta	204.134.83.1/32	204.134.83.5/30	192.168.3.6/30	N/A
Core	204.134.83.2/32	204.134.83.9/30	204.134.83.6/30	N/A
Raleigh	204.134.83.3/32	N/A	192.168.3.9/30	204.134.83.10/30

Device Configuration

Presently, the network is set up with an IGP (RIPv2), tag switching, and MP-BGP between the Atlanta and Raleigh POP routers, as you can see in the running-config of the Raleigh POP router:

```
Raleigh#show running-config
Building configuration...

Current configuration : 1997 bytes
!
version 12.1
service timestamps debug uptime
service timestamps log uptime
no service password-encryption
!
hostname Raleigh
!
enable password cisco
!
!
!
!
!
memory-size iomem 25
ip subnet-zero
ip tcp synwait-time 5
no ip domain-lookup
!
!

ip cef
cns event-service server
!
!
!
!
!
```

```
interface Loopback0
 ip address 204.134.83.3 255.255.255.255
!
interface Serial0/0
 no ip address
 shutdown
 no fair-queue
 clockrate 64000
!
interface Serial0/1
 description *** Link to Peer2 ***
 ip address 192.168.3.9 255.255.255.252
 clockrate 64000
!
interface Serial0/2
 no ip address
 shutdown
 clockrate 64000
!
interface Serial0/3
 description *** Link to Core Router ***
 ip address 204.134.83.10 255.255.255.252
 tag-switching ip
 clockrate 64000
!
interface Ethernet1/0
 no ip address
 shutdown
!
interface Ethernet1/1
 no ip address
 shutdown
!
interface Ethernet1/2
 no ip address
 shutdown
!
```

```
interface Ethernet1/3
 no ip address
 shutdown
!
router rip
 version 2
 network 204.134.83.0
 !
router bgp 65000
 no synchronization
 bgp log-neighbor-changes
 neighbor 204.134.83.1 remote-as 65000
 neighbor 204.134.83.1 update-source Loopback0
 neighbor 204.134.83.1 next-hop-self
 no auto-summary
 !
 !
 address-family vpnv4
 neighbor 204.134.83.1 activate
 neighbor 204.134.83.1 send-community both
 no auto-summary
 exit-address-family
!
ip classless
no ip http server
!
!
!
line con 0
 exec-timeout 0 0
 privilege level 15
 logging synchronous
 transport input none
 ip netmask-format decimal
line aux 0
line vty 0 4
```

```
 privilege level 15
 password cisco
 logging synchronous
 login
 ip netmask-format decimal
!
end
```

Notice in the running-config of the Atlanta POP router that RIPv2, tag switching, and MP-BGP are configured:

```
Atlanta#show running-config
Building configuration...

Current configuration : 1972 bytes
!
version 12.1
service timestamps debug uptime
service timestamps log uptime
no service password-encryption
!
hostname Atlanta
!
enable password cisco
!
!
!
!
!
memory-size iomem 25
ip subnet-zero
ip tcp synwait-time 5
no ip domain-lookup
!
!
ip cef
cns event-service server
!
!
```

```
!
!
!
interface Loopback0
 ip address 204.134.83.1 255.255.255.255
!
interface Serial0/0
 description *** Link to Core Router ***
 ip address 204.134.83.5 255.255.255.252
 tag-switching ip
 no fair-queue
 clockrate 64000
!
interface Serial0/1
 description *** Link to Peer1 ***
 ip address 192.168.3.6 255.255.255.252
 clockrate 64000
!
interface Serial0/2
 no ip address
 shutdown
 clockrate 64000
!
interface Serial0/3
 no ip address
 shutdown
 clockrate 64000
!
interface Ethernet1/0
 no ip address
 shutdown
!
interface Ethernet1/1
 no ip address
 shutdown
!
```

```
interface Ethernet1/2
 no ip address
 shutdown
!
interface Ethernet1/3
 no ip address
 shutdown
!
router rip
 version 2
 network 204.134.83.0
 !
router bgp 65000
 no synchronization
 bgp log-neighbor-changes
 neighbor 204.134.83.3 remote-as 65000
 neighbor 204.134.83.3 update-source Loopback0
 neighbor 204.134.83.3 next-hop-self
 no auto-summary
 !
 address-family vpnv4
 neighbor 204.134.83.3 activate
 neighbor 204.134.83.3 send-community both
 no auto-summary
 exit-address-family
!
ip classless
no ip http server
!
!
!
line con 0
 exec-timeout 0 0
 privilege level 15
 logging synchronous
 transport input none
```

```
 ip netmask-format decimal
line aux 0
line vty 0 4
 privilege level 15
 password cisco
 logging synchronous
 login
 ip netmask-format decimal
!
```

VPN Configuration

Once the service provider network is set up, you need to configure an MPLS VPN. From a business case standpoint, the Peer 1 and Peer 2 routers require a simple MPLS-based VPN. The Peer 1 and Peer 2 routers will use the default routes, and the Atlanta and Raleigh POP routers will use the static routes.

The first thing to configure on the Atlanta POP router is a VRF with a route distinguisher and a route target:

```
Atlanta#conf t
Enter configuration commands, one per line. End with CNTL/Z.
Atlanta(config)#ip vrf vpn_1
Atlanta(config-vrf)#rd 65000:1
Atlanta(config-vrf)#route-target both 65000:1
```

Next, you need to associate the interface that connects to Peer 1 with the VRF:

```
Atlanta(config)#int s 0/1
Atlanta(config-if)#ip vrf forwarding vpn_1
% Interface Serial0/1 IP address 192.168.3.6 removed due
  to enabling VRF vpn_1
Atlanta(config-if)#ip address 192.168.3.6 255.255.255.252
```

Now you need to configure a static route on the Atlanta POP router to point to the loopback of Peer 1. To configure a global static route, use the `ip route` command. To configure a static route for a particular VRF, use the `ip route vrf` *vpn_name* command. The configuration on the Atlanta POP router to configure a static route associated with vpn_1 is as follows. Note that if more routes were made available from the Peer 1 router, you would need to add more static routes.

```
Atlanta(config)#ip route vrf vpn_1 192.168.1.1
  255.255.255.255 Serial0/1 192.168.3.5
```

NOTE For VRF static routes, the outgoing interface must be specified even if the next hop address is given.

Now on to BGP. You need to configure the redistribution of the static route and VRF connected interfaces into BGP:

```
Atlanta(config)#router bgp 65000
Atlanta(config-router)#address-family ipv4 vrf vpn_1
Atlanta(config-router-af)#redistribute connected
Atlanta(config-router-af)#redistribute static
Atlanta(config-router-af)#^Z
Atlanta#
```

You need to repeat the same configuration steps on the Raleigh POP router. First, you need to configure a VRF with a route distinguisher and a route target:

```
Raleigh#conf t
Enter configuration commands, one per line. End with CNTL/Z.
Raleigh(config)#ip vrf vpn_1
Raleigh(config-vrf)#rd
Raleigh(config-vrf)#rd 65000:1
Raleigh(config-vrf)#route
Raleigh(config-vrf)#route-target both 65000:1
```

Next, you need to associate the interface that connects to Peer 1 with the VRF:

```
Raleigh(config-vrf)#exit
Raleigh(config)#int s 0/1
Raleigh(config-if)#ip vrf forwarding vpn_1
% Interface Serial0/1 IP address 192.168.3.9 removed due
  to enabling VRF vpn_1
Raleigh(config-if)#ip address 192.168.3.9 255.255.255.252
```

Now you need to configure a static route on the Atlanta POP router to point to the loopback of Peer 2. To configure a global static route, use the ip route command. To configure a static route for a particular VRF, use the ip route vrf *vpn_name* command. The configuration on the Raleigh POP router to configure a static route associated with vpn_1 is as follows:

```
Raleigh(config)#ip route vrf vpn_1 192.168.2.1
  255.255.255.255 Serial0/1 192.168.3.10
```

Now on to BGP. You need to configure the redistribution of the static route and VRF connected interfaces into BGP:

```
Raleigh(config)#router bgp 65000
Raleigh(config-router)#address-family ipv4 vrf vpn_1
Raleigh(config-router-af)#redistribute connected
Raleigh(config-router-af)#redistribute static
Raleigh(config-router-af)#^Z
Raleigh#
```

The following sections contain the running-configs of the Atlanta and Raleigh POP routers. Try to get in the habit of reading and verifying the configuration.

Raleigh Running-Config

As you review the Raleigh POP router running-config, locate the configuration showing the static route associated with the VRF:

```
Raleigh#show running-config
Building configuration...

Current configuration : 1947 bytes
!
version 12.1
service timestamps debug uptime
service timestamps log uptime
no service password-encryption
!
hostname Raleigh
!
enable password cisco
!
!
```

```
!
!
!
memory-size iomem 25
ip subnet-zero
ip tcp synwait-time 5
no ip domain-lookup
!
!
ip vrf vpn_1
 rd 65000:1
 route-target export 65000:1
 route-target import 65000:1
ip cef
cns event-service server
!
!
!
!
!
interface Loopback0
 ip address 204.134.83.3 255.255.255.255
!
interface Serial0/0
 no ip address
 shutdown
 no fair-queue
 clockrate 64000
!
interface Serial0/1
 description *** Link to Peer2 ***
 ip vrf forwarding vpn_1
 ip address 192.168.3.9 255.255.255.252
 clockrate 64000
!
interface Serial0/2
```

```
 no ip address
 shutdown
 clockrate 64000
!
interface Serial0/3
 description *** Link to Core Router ***
 ip address 204.134.83.10 255.255.255.252
 tag-switching ip
 clockrate 64000
!
interface Ethernet1/0
 no ip address
 shutdown
!
interface Ethernet1/1
 no ip address
 shutdown
!
interface Ethernet1/2
 no ip address
 shutdown
!
interface Ethernet1/3
 no ip address
 shutdown
!
router rip
 version 2
 network 204.134.83.0
!
router bgp 65000
 no synchronization
 bgp log-neighbor-changes
 neighbor 204.134.83.1 remote-as 65000
 neighbor 204.134.83.1 update-source Loopback0
 neighbor 204.134.83.1 next-hop-self
```

```
 no auto-summary
 !
 address-family ipv4 vrf vpn_1
 redistribute connected
 redistribute static
 no auto-summary
 no synchronization
 exit-address-family
 !
 address-family vpnv4
 neighbor 204.134.83.1 activate
 neighbor 204.134.83.1 send-community both
 no auto-summary
 exit-address-family
!
ip classless
ip route vrf vpn_1 192.168.2.1 255.255.255.255
  Serial0/1 192.168.3.10
no ip http server
!
!
!
line con 0
 exec-timeout 0 0
 privilege level 15
 logging synchronous
 transport input none
 ip netmask-format decimal
line aux 0
line vty 0 4
 privilege level 15
 password cisco
 logging synchronous
 login
 ip netmask-format decimal
!
end
```

Atlanta Running-Config

As you review the Atlanta POP router running-config, locate the configuration showing the static route associated with the VRF:

```
Atlanta#show running-config
Building configuration...

Current configuration : 1921 bytes
!
version 12.1
service timestamps debug uptime
service timestamps log uptime
no service password-encryption
!
hostname Atlanta
!
enable password cisco
!
!
!
!
!
memory-size iomem 25
ip subnet-zero
ip tcp synwait-time 5
no ip domain-lookup
!
!
ip vrf vpn_1
 rd 65000:1
 route-target export 65000:1
 route-target import 65000:1
ip cef
cns event-service server
!
!
!
```

```
!
!
interface Loopback0
 ip address 204.134.83.1 255.255.255.255
!
interface Serial0/0
 description *** Link to Core Router ***
 ip address 204.134.83.5 255.255.255.252
 tag-switching ip
 no fair-queue
 clockrate 64000
!
interface Serial0/1
 description *** Link to Peer1 ***
 ip vrf forwarding vpn_1
 ip address 192.168.3.6 255.255.255.252
 clockrate 64000
!
interface Serial0/2
 no ip address
 shutdown
 clockrate 64000
!
interface Serial0/3
 no ip address
 shutdown
 clockrate 64000
!
interface Ethernet1/0
 no ip address
 shutdown
!
interface Ethernet1/1
 no ip address
 shutdown
!
```

```
interface Ethernet1/2
 no ip address
 shutdown
!
interface Ethernet1/3
 no ip address
 shutdown
!
router rip
 version 2
 network 204.134.83.0
!
router bgp 65000
 no synchronization
 bgp log-neighbor-changes
 neighbor 204.134.83.3 remote-as 65000
 neighbor 204.134.83.3 update-source Loopback0
 neighbor 204.134.83.3 next-hop-self
 no auto-summary
 !
 address-family ipv4 vrf vpn_1
 redistribute connected
 redistribute static
 no auto-summary
 no synchronization
 exit-address-family
 !
 address-family vpnv4
 neighbor 204.134.83.3 activate
 neighbor 204.134.83.3 send-community both
 no auto-summary
 exit-address-family
!
ip classless
ip route vrf vpn_1 192.168.1.1 255.255.255.255
  Serial0/1 192.168.3.5
```

```
no ip http server
!
!
!
line con 0
 exec-timeout 0 0
 privilege level 15
 logging synchronous
 transport input none
 ip netmask-format decimal
line aux 0
line vty 0 4
 privilege level 15
 password cisco
 logging synchronous
 login
 ip netmask-format decimal
!
end
```

Peer Router Configuration

The Peer 1 and Peer 2 routers need to be configured with standard default routes. The configuration of the Peer 1 router is as follows:

```
Peer1#conf t
Enter configuration commands, one per line. End with CNTL/Z.
Peer1(config)#ip route 0.0.0.0 0.0.0.0 serial 0
```

The configuration of the Peer 2 router is as follows:

```
Peer2#conf t
Enter configuration commands, one per line. End with CNTL/Z.
Peer2(config)#ip route 0.0.0.0 0.0.0.0 serial 0
```

To verify static routes on the Peer 1 router, use the `show ip route` command:

```
Peer1#show ip route
.
. Output Omitted
.
```

```
Gateway of last resort is 0.0.0.0 to network 0.0.0.0

     192.168.1.0 255.255.255.255 is subnetted, 1 subnets
C       192.168.1.1 is directly connected, Loopback0
     192.168.3.0 255.255.255.252 is subnetted, 1 subnets
C       192.168.3.4 is directly connected, Serial0
S*   0.0.0.0 0.0.0.0 is directly connected, Serial0
```

To verify static routes on the Peer 2 router, use the `show ip route` command:

```
Peer2#show ip route
.
. Output Omitted
.
Gateway of last resort is 0.0.0.0 to network 0.0.0.0

     192.168.2.0 255.255.255.255 is subnetted, 1 subnets
C       192.168.2.1 is directly connected, Loopback0
     192.168.3.0 255.255.255.252 is subnetted, 1 subnets
C       192.168.3.8 is directly connected, Serial0
S*   0.0.0.0 0.0.0.0 is directly connected, Serial0
```

Peer 1 Running-Config

Notice in the running-config for the Peer 1 router that only a standard static route is configured:

```
Peer1#show running-config
Building configuration...

Current configuration : 803 bytes
!
version 12.1
service timestamps debug uptime
service timestamps log uptime
no service password-encryption
!
hostname Peer1
!
```

```
enable password cisco
!
!
!
!
!
ip subnet-zero
ip tcp synwait-time 5
no ip domain-lookup
!
!
!
!
interface Loopback0
 ip address 192.168.1.1 255.255.255.255
!
interface Ethernet0
 no ip address
 shutdown
!
interface Serial0
 description *** Link to Atlanta POP ***
 ip address 192.168.3.5 255.255.255.252
 no fair-queue
!
interface Serial1
 no ip address
 shutdown
!
ip classless
ip route 0.0.0.0 0.0.0.0 Serial0
no ip http server
!
!
line con 0
 exec-timeout 0 0
```

```
 privilege level 15
 logging synchronous
 transport input none
 ip netmask-format decimal
line aux 0
line vty 0 4
 privilege level 15
 password cisco
 logging synchronous
 login
 ip netmask-format decimal
!
end
```

Peer 2 Running-Config

Notice in the running-config for the Peer 2 router that only a standard static route is configured:

```
Peer2#show running-config
Building configuration...

Current configuration : 1030 bytes
!
version 12.1
service timestamps debug uptime
service timestamps log uptime
no service password-encryption
!
hostname Peer2
!
enable password lab
!
!
!
!
!
ip subnet-zero
```

```
ip tcp synwait-time 5
no ip domain-lookup
!
!
!
!
interface Loopback0
 ip address 192.168.2.1 255.255.255.255
!
interface Ethernet0
 no ip address
 shutdown
!
interface Serial0
 description *** Link to PE2 ***
 ip address 192.168.3.10 255.255.255.252
 no fair-queue
!
interface Serial1
 no ip address
 shutdown
!
ip classless
ip route 0.0.0.0 0.0.0.0 Serial0
no ip http server
!
!
line con 0
 exec-timeout 0 0
 privilege level 15
 logging synchronous
 transport input none
 ip netmask-format decimal
line aux 0
line vty 0 4
 privilege level 15
```

```
 password lab
 logging synchronous
 login
 ip netmask-format decimal
!
end
```

Verification with Ping

To verify that the VPN works, all you need to do is a ping from one peer router to the other. The following output appears as the result of a ping from Peer 2 to Peer 1. Notice that the ping works.

```
Peer2#ping 192.168.1.1

Type escape sequence to abort.
Sending 5, 100-byte ICMP Echos to 192.168.1.1, timeout
  is 2 seconds:
!!!!!
Success rate is 100 percent (5/5), round-trip in/avg/max
  = 116/119/120 ms
```

Verifying Static VRF Routes

Now you need to know about the flow of routing information through the network. Let's begin this discussion by looking at the routing table of vpn_1 as it exists on the Atlanta POP router:

```
Atlanta#show ip route vrf vpn_1
.
. Output Omitted
.
Gateway of last resort is not set

     192.168.1.0 255.255.255.255 is subnetted, 1 subnets
S       192.168.1.1 [1/0] via 192.168.3.5, Serial0/1
     192.168.2.0 255.255.255.255 is subnetted, 1 subnets
B       192.168.2.1 [200/0] via 204.134.83.3, 00:03:06
     192.168.3.0 255.255.255.252 is subnetted, 2 subnets
```

```
B       192.168.3.8 [200/0] via 204.134.83.3, 00:03:06
C       192.168.3.4 is directly connected, Serial0/1
```

In the routing table for vpn_1 on the Atlanta POP router, there are two BGP routes (B) and one static route (S). The BGP routes (B) are learned from the Raleigh POP router and are the result of the `redistribute connected` and `redistribute static` commands on the Raleigh POP router. The Atlanta POP router is configured with a static route for 192.168.1.1 that is displayed in the routing table as (S).

On the Raleigh POP router, there are also two BGP routes (B) and one static route (S). The BGP routes (B) are learned from the Atlanta POP router and are the result of the `redistribute connected` and `redistribute static` commands on the Atlanta POP router. The Raleigh POP router is configured with a static route for 192.168.2.1 that is displayed in the routing table as (S).

The routing table for vpn_1 on the Raleigh POP router is as follows:

```
Raleigh#show ip route vrf vpn_1
.
. Output Omitted
.
Gateway of last resort is not set

     192.168.1.0 255.255.255.255 is subnetted, 1 subnets
B       192.168.1.1 [200/0] via 204.134.83.1, 00:02:05
     192.168.2.0 255.255.255.255 is subnetted, 1 subnets
S       192.168.2.1 [1/0] via 192.168.3.10, Serial0/1
     192.168.3.0 255.255.255.252 is subnetted, 2 subnets
C       192.168.3.8 is directly connected, Serial0/1
B       192.168.3.4 [200/0] via 204.134.83.1, 00:02:05
Raleigh#
```

E-BGP and MPLS VPNs

Again, although the exam objectives do not call for you to know about E-BGP as a PE-CE routing protocol, I'd like to describe a working example of how E-BGP can be used in a simple MPLS VPN. Figure 8.3 contains the simple service provider network we'll use in this section.

FIGURE 8.3 A simple service provider network

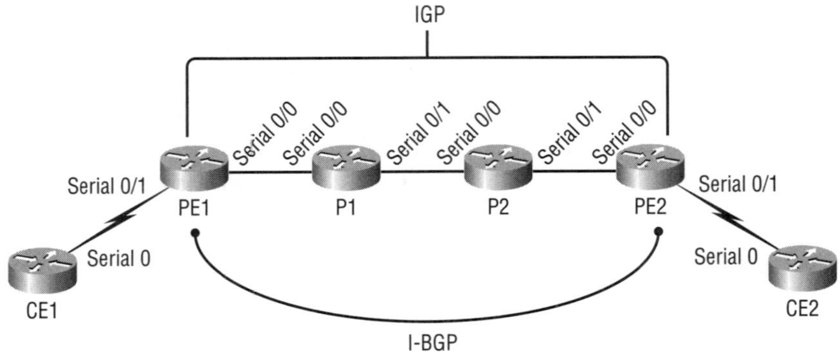

Figure 8.4 illustrates the routing protocol utilization for the network in Figure 8.3.

FIGURE 8.4 Routing protocol utilization

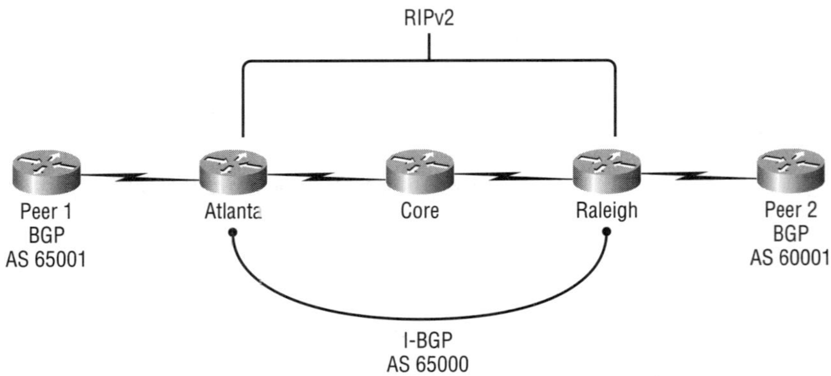

Table 8.3 lists the IP addresses and interfaces of the CE devices in Figure 8.3.

TABLE 8.3 Customer Addressing

Device	Loopback 0	Serial 0
Peer 1	192.168.1.1/32	192.168.3.5/30
Peer 2	192.168.2.1/32	192.168.3.10/30

Table 8.4 lists the IP addresses and interfaces of the service provider devices in Figure 8.3.

TABLE 8.4 Service Provider Addressing

Device	Loopback 0	Serial 0/0	Serial 0/1	Serial 0/3
Atlanta	204.134.83.1/32	204.134.83.5/30	192.168.3.6/30	N/A
Core	204.134.83.2/32	204.134.83.9/30	204.134.83.6/30	N/A
Raleigh	204.134.83.3/32	N/A	192.168.3.9/30	204.134.83.10/30

Device Configuration

Presently, the network is set up with an IGP (RIPv2), tag switching, and MP-BGP between the Atlanta and Raleigh POP routers.

The configuration of the Raleigh POP router is as follows:

```
Raleigh#show running-config
Building configuration...

Current configuration : 1997 bytes
!
version 12.1
service timestamps debug uptime
service timestamps log uptime
no service password-encryption
!
hostname Raleigh
!
enable password cisco
!
!
!
!
!
memory-size iomem 25
```

```
ip subnet-zero
ip tcp synwait-time 5
no ip domain-lookup
!
!

ip cef
cns event-service server
!
!
!
!
!
interface Loopback0
 ip address 204.134.83.3 255.255.255.255
!
interface Serial0/0
 no ip address
 shutdown
 no fair-queue
 clockrate 64000
!
interface Serial0/1
 description *** Link to Peer2 ***
 ip address 192.168.3.9 255.255.255.252
 clockrate 64000
!
interface Serial0/2
 no ip address
 shutdown
 clockrate 64000
!
interface Serial0/3
 description *** Link to Core Router ***
 ip address 204.134.83.10 255.255.255.252
 tag-switching ip
```

```
 clockrate 64000
!
interface Ethernet1/0
 no ip address
 shutdown
!
interface Ethernet1/1
 no ip address
 shutdown
!
interface Ethernet1/2
 no ip address
 shutdown
!
interface Ethernet1/3
 no ip address
 shutdown
!
router rip
 version 2
 network 204.134.83.0
 !
router bgp 65000
 no synchronization
 bgp log-neighbor-changes
 neighbor 204.134.83.1 remote-as 65000
 neighbor 204.134.83.1 update-source Loopback0
 neighbor 204.134.83.1 next-hop-self
 no auto-summary
 !
 !
 address-family vpnv4
 neighbor 204.134.83.1 activate
 neighbor 204.134.83.1 send-community both
 no auto-summary
 exit-address-family
!
```

```
ip classless
no ip http server
!
!
!
line con 0
 exec-timeout 0 0
 privilege level 15
 logging synchronous
 transport input none
 ip netmask-format decimal
line aux 0
line vty 0 4
 privilege level 15
 password cisco
 logging synchronous
 login
 ip netmask-format decimal
!
end
```

The configuration of the Atlanta POP router is as follows:

```
Atlanta#show running-config
Building configuration...

Current configuration : 1972 bytes
!
version 12.1
service timestamps debug uptime
service timestamps log uptime
no service password-encryption
!
hostname Atlanta
!
enable password cisco
!
!
```

```
!
!
!
memory-size iomem 25
ip subnet-zero
ip tcp synwait-time 5
no ip domain-lookup
!
!
ip cef
cns event-service server
!
!
!
!
!
interface Loopback0
 ip address 204.134.83.1 255.255.255.255
!
interface Serial0/0
 description *** Link to Core Router ***
 ip address 204.134.83.5 255.255.255.252
 tag-switching ip
 no fair-queue
 clockrate 64000
!
interface Serial0/1
 description *** Link to Peer1 ***
 ip address 192.168.3.6 255.255.255.252
 clockrate 64000
!
interface Serial0/2
 no ip address
 shutdown
 clockrate 64000
!
```

```
interface Serial0/3
 no ip address
 shutdown
 clockrate 64000
!
interface Ethernet1/0
 no ip address
 shutdown
!
interface Ethernet1/1
 no ip address
 shutdown
!
interface Ethernet1/2
 no ip address
 shutdown
!
interface Ethernet1/3
 no ip address
 shutdown
!
router rip
 version 2
 network 204.134.83.0
 !
router bgp 65000
 no synchronization
 bgp log-neighbor-changes
 neighbor 204.134.83.3 remote-as 65000
 neighbor 204.134.83.3 update-source Loopback0
 neighbor 204.134.83.3 next-hop-self
 no auto-summary
 !
 address-family vpnv4
 neighbor 204.134.83.3 activate
 neighbor 204.134.83.3 send-community both
```

```
 no auto-summary
 exit-address-family
!
ip classless
no ip http server
!
!
!
line con 0
 exec-timeout 0 0
 privilege level 15
 logging synchronous
 transport input none
 ip netmask-format decimal
line aux 0
line vty 0 4
 privilege level 15
 password cisco
 logging synchronous
 login
 ip netmask-format decimal
!
```

E-BGP Operation

Before getting started with any configuration, let's talk about E-BGP operation. E-BGP is supported between PE and CE routers. E-BGP will be configured under the `address-family ipv4` section for a particular VPN. All the standard BGP rules, filters, and assorted bells and whistles still work. Remember to use the ? and CCO (`www.cisco.com`) to get more information on how to configure advanced BGP features in an MPLS VPN E-BGP environment. The new BGP feature that you should know about is *AS-override*.

AS-Override

In Figure 8.5, a customer has a simple MPLS VPN and is using the same AS number at each site.

FIGURE 8.5 A customer VPN using a single AS number

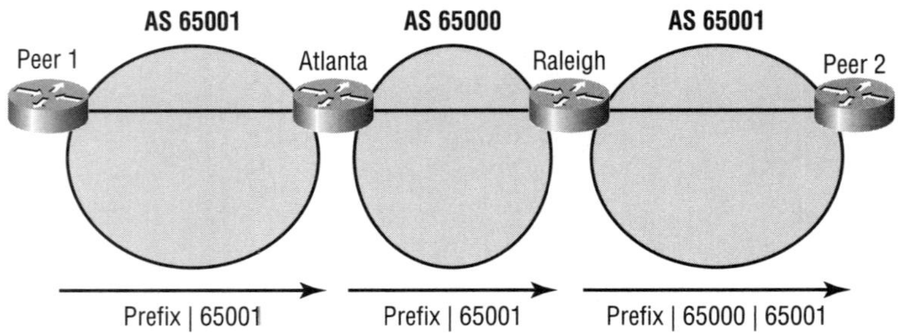

In the VPN in Figure 8.5, a prefix from the Peer 1 router is sent to the Atlanta POP router through an E-BGP connection. The originating AS number (65001) is in the AS path. The prefix is propagated across the service provider network and arrives at the Raleigh POP router. The Raleigh POP router forwards the update to the Peer 2 router and attaches its AS number (65000) to the update. When the Peer 2 router receives the prefix, it is discarded. When the Peer 2 router sees its AS number (65001) in the AS path (65000|65001), it discards the packet. In reality, there is no loop, but the default operation of BGP is to drop the route.

Since customers don't need an IOS upgrade to fix MPLS VPN problems, the service provider PE routers need some way to remedy this situation. The `neighbor ip_address as-override` command is used to replace all copies of the originating AS in an update.

In Figure 8.6, a route originates from the Peer 1 router in AS 65001. The update is propagated through the service provider network with the original AS number. When the update is sent to the Peer 2 router through an E-BGP connection, assuming AS-override has been configured, all instances of the originating AS (65001) are replaced with the service provider's AS number (65000).

FIGURE 8.6 A network with AS-override in operation

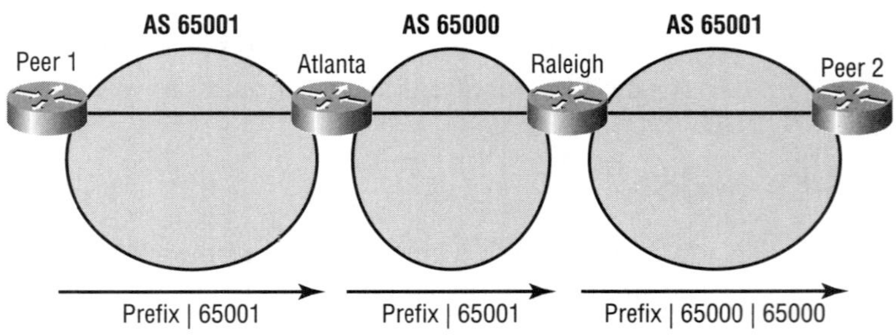

Enough of that, back to configuration.

VPN Configuration

So the service provider network is all set up, and you need to configure an MPLS VPN. From a business case standpoint, the Peer 1 and Peer 2 routers require a simple MPLS-based VPN. E-BGP will be used between the POP routers and the peer routers.

The first thing to configure on the Atlanta POP router is a VRF with a route distinguisher and a route target:

```
Atlanta#conf t
Enter configuration commands, one per line. End with CNTL/Z.
Atlanta(config)#ip vrf
Atlanta(config)#ip vrf vpn_1
Atlanta(config-vrf)#rd 65000:1
Atlanta(config-vrf)#route
Atlanta(config-vrf)#route-target both 65000:1
```

Next, you need to associate the interface that connects to Peer 1 with the VRF:

```
Atlanta(config)#int s 0/1
Atlanta(config-if)#ip vrf forwarding vpn_1
% Interface Serial0/1 IP address 192.168.3.6 removed due
  to enabling VRF vpn_1
Atlanta(config-if)#ip address 192.168.3.6 255.255.255.252
```

Now you need to configure an E-BGP session between the Atlanta POP router and the Peer 1 router:

```
Atlanta(config)#router bgp 65000
Atlanta(config-router)#address-family ipv4 vrf vpn_1
Atlanta(config-router-af)#neighbor 192.168.3.5 remote-as 65001
Atlanta(config-router-af)#neighbor 192.168.3.5 activate
Atlanta(config-router-af)#neighbor 192.168.3.5 as-override
Atlanta(config-router-af)#redistribute connected
Atlanta(config-router-af)#^Z
Atlanta#
```

Now on to the Raleigh POP router. You need to configure an E-BGP session between the Raleigh POP router and the Peer 2 router:

```
Raleigh(config)#router bgp 65000
Raleigh(config-router)#address-family ipv4 vrf vpn_1
Raleigh(config-router-af)#neighbor 192.168.3.10 remote-as 65001
Raleigh(config-router-af)#neighbor 192.168.3.10 activate
```

```
Raleigh(config-router-af)#neighbor 192.168.3.10 as-override
Raleigh(config-router-af)#redistribute connected
Raleigh(config-router-af)#^Z
Raleigh#
```

The following sections contain the running-configs for the Atlanta and Raleigh POP routers. Try to get in the habit of reading and verifying the configuration.

Limiting Routes

There are many BGP features that allow service providers to filter or limit the number of routes that they may learn from an E-BGP peer. If you do not want to use well-known BGP features, it's possible to limit the number of routes in a VRF.

For example, suppose a customer is only paying for simple site-to-site connectivity. The service provider, as a function of MPLS VPN operation, is responsible for convergence and carrying customer routes though the service provider backbone. If the customer is paying for only a simple connection, they may get a price break because of the limited overhead (such as the number of routes the service provider must propagate).

To limit the customer to a set number of routes, the `maximum-routes` command can be used.

Consider another example. Let's say the customer has two sites and has only a total of six routes that will be in the VRF on the PE router. On the PE router, where the VRF is configured, three of the routes are learned from the other site and three routes are generated by the local CE router.

The `maximum-routes` command uses two values, which are based on the maximum number of routes and at what percentage a SYSLOG message should be sent. In the configuration example that follows, after the `maximum-routes` command, the `6` indicates the maximum number of routes and the `75` is a percentage that is used to specify when SYSLOG messages will be sent. Once the six routes are exceeded, new routes are dropped by the PE.

```
ip vrf vpn_z
 rd 100:100
 route-target both 100:100
 maximum-routes 6 75
```

Raleigh Running-Config

Notice in the Raleigh running-config that there is an E-BGP connection to the Peer 2 router:

```
Raleigh#show running-config
Building configuration...

Current configuration : 1962 bytes
!
version 12.1
service timestamps debug uptime
service timestamps log uptime
no service password-encryption
!
hostname Raleigh
!
enable password cisco
!
!
!
!
!
memory-size iomem 25
ip subnet-zero
ip tcp synwait-time 5
no ip domain-lookup
!
!
ip vrf vpn_1
 rd 65000:1
 route-target export 65000:1
 route-target import 65000:1
ip cef
cns event-service server
!
!
!
```

```
!
!
interface Loopback0
 ip address 204.134.83.3 255.255.255.255
!
interface Serial0/0
 no ip address
 shutdown
 no fair-queue
 clockrate 64000
!
interface Serial0/1
 description *** Link to Peer2 ***
 ip vrf forwarding vpn_1
 ip address 192.168.3.9 255.255.255.252
 clockrate 64000
!
interface Serial0/2
 no ip address
 shutdown
 clockrate 64000
!
interface Serial0/3
 description *** Link to Core Router ***
 ip address 204.134.83.10 255.255.255.252
 tag-switching ip
 clockrate 64000
!
interface Ethernet1/0
no ip address
 shutdown
!
interface Ethernet1/1
 no ip address
 shutdown
!
```

```
interface Ethernet1/2
 no ip address
 shutdown
!
interface Ethernet1/3
 no ip address
 shutdown
!
router rip
 version 2
 network 204.134.83.0
!
router bgp 65000
 no synchronization
 bgp log-neighbor-changes
 neighbor 204.134.83.1 remote-as 65000
 neighbor 204.134.83.1 update-source Loopback0
 neighbor 204.134.83.1 next-hop-self
 no auto-summary
 !
 address-family ipv4 vrf vpn_1
 redistribute connected
 neighbor 192.168.3.10 remote-as 65001
 neighbor 192.168.3.10 activate
 neighbor 192.168.3.10 as-override
 no auto-summary
 no synchronization
 exit-address-family
 !
 address-family vpnv4
 neighbor 204.134.83.1 activate
 neighbor 204.134.83.1 send-community both
 no auto-summary
 exit-address-family
!
ip classless
```

```
no ip http server
!
!
!
line con 0
 exec-timeout 0 0
 privilege level 15
 logging synchronous
 transport input none
 ip netmask-format decimal
line aux 0
line vty 0 4
 privilege level 15
 password cisco
 logging synchronous
 login
 ip netmask-format decimal
!
end
```

Atlanta Running-Config

Notice in the Atlanta running-configuration that there is an E-BGP connection to the Peer 1 router:

```
Atlanta#show running-config
Building configuration...

Current configuration : 1934 bytes
!
version 12.1
service timestamps debug uptime
service timestamps log uptime
no service password-encryption
!
hostname Atlanta
!
```

```
enable password cisco
!
!
!
!
!
memory-size iomem 25
ip subnet-zero
ip tcp synwait-time 5
no ip domain-lookup
!
!
ip vrf vpn_1
 rd 65000:1
 route-target export 65000:1
 route-target import 65000:1
ip cef
cns event-service server
!
!
!
!
!
interface Loopback0
 ip address 204.134.83.1 255.255.255.255
!
interface Serial0/0
 description *** Link to Core Router ***
 ip address 204.134.83.5 255.255.255.252
 tag-switching ip
 no fair-queue
 clockrate 64000
!
interface Serial0/1
 description *** Link to Peer1 ***
 ip vrf forwarding vpn_1
```

```
 ip address 192.168.3.6 255.255.255.252
 clockrate 64000
!
interface Serial0/2
 no ip address
 shutdown
 clockrate 64000
!
interface Serial0/3
 no ip address
 shutdown
 clockrate 64000
!
interface Ethernet1/0
 no ip address
 shutdown
!
interface Ethernet1/1
 no ip address
 shutdown
!
interface Ethernet1/2
 no ip address
 shutdown
!
interface Ethernet1/3
 no ip address
 shutdown
!
router rip
 version 2
 network 204.134.83.0
!
router bgp 65000
 no synchronization
 bgp log-neighbor-changes
```

```
 neighbor 204.134.83.3 remote-as 65000
 neighbor 204.134.83.3 update-source Loopback0
 neighbor 204.134.83.3 next-hop-self
 no auto-summary
 !
 address-family ipv4 vrf vpn_1
 redistribute connected
 neighbor 192.168.3.5 remote-as 65001
 neighbor 192.168.3.5 activate
 neighbor 192.168.3.5 as-override
 no auto-summary
 no synchronization
 exit-address-family
 !
 address-family vpnv4
 neighbor 204.134.83.3 activate
 neighbor 204.134.83.3 send-community both
 no auto-summary
 exit-address-family
!
ip classless
no ip http server
!
!
!
line con 0
 exec-timeout 0 0
 privilege level 15
 logging synchronous
 transport input none
 ip netmask-format decimal
line aux 0
line vty 0 4
 privilege level 15
 password cisco
 logging synchronous
```

```
 login
 ip netmask-format decimal
!
end
```

Peer Router Configuration

The Peer 1 and Peer 2 routers need to be configured for standard E-BGP.

The configuration of the Peer 1 router is as follows:

```
Peer1#conf t
Enter configuration commands, one per line. End with CNTL/Z.
Peer1(config)#router bgp 65001
Peer1(config-router)#neighbor 192.168.3.6 remote-as 65000
Peer1(config-router)#redistribute connected
Peer1(config-router)#^Z
Peer1#
```

The configuration of the Peer 2 router is as follows:

```
Peer2#conf t
Enter configuration commands, one per line. End with CNTL/Z.
Peer2(config)#router bgp 65001
Peer2(config-router)#neighbor 192.168.3.9 remote-as 65000
Peer2(config-router)#redistribute connected
Peer2(config-router)#^Z
Peer2#
```

To verify static routes on the Peer 1 router, use the `show ip route` command:

```
Peer1#show ip route
.
. Output Omitted
.

Gateway of last resort is not set

     192.168.1.0 255.255.255.255 is subnetted, 1 subnets
C       192.168.1.1 is directly connected, Loopback0
     192.168.2.0 255.255.255.255 is subnetted, 1 subnets
```

```
B        192.168.2.1 [20/0] via 192.168.3.6, 00:05:08
     192.168.3.0 255.255.255.252 is subnetted, 2 subnets
B        192.168.3.8 [20/0] via 192.168.3.6, 00:06:35
C        192.168.3.4 is directly connected, Serial0
```

To verify static routes on the Peer 2 router, use the `show ip route` command:

```
Peer2#show ip route
.
. Output Omitted
.
Gateway of last resort is not set

     192.168.1.0 255.255.255.255 is subnetted, 1 subnets
B        192.168.1.1 [20/0] via 192.168.3.9, 00:04:02
     192.168.2.0 255.255.255.255 is subnetted, 1 subnets
C        192.168.2.1 is directly connected, Loopback0
     192.168.3.0 255.255.255.252 is subnetted, 2 subnets
C        192.168.3.8 is directly connected, Serial0
B        192.168.3.4 [20/0] via 192.168.3.9, 00:04:31
```

Peer 1 Running-Config

Notice in the Peer 1 running-config that there is an E-BGP connection to the Atlanta POP router:

```
Peer1#show running-config
Building configuration...

Current configuration : 914 bytes
!
version 12.1
service timestamps debug uptime
service timestamps log uptime
no service password-encryption
!
hostname Peer1
!
```

```
enable password cisco
!
!
!
!
!
ip subnet-zero
ip tcp synwait-time 5
no ip domain-lookup
!
!
!
!
interface Loopback0
 ip address 192.168.1.1 255.255.255.255
!
interface Ethernet0
 no ip address
 shutdown
!
interface Serial0
 description *** Link to Atlanta POP ***
 ip address 192.168.3.5 255.255.255.252
 no fair-queue
!
interface Serial1
 no ip address
 shutdown
!
router bgp 65001
 no synchronization
 bgp log-neighbor-changes
 redistribute connected
 neighbor 192.168.3.6 remote-as 65000
 no auto-summary
!
```

```
ip classless
no ip http server
!
!
line con 0
 exec-timeout 0 0
 privilege level 15
 logging synchronous
 transport input none
 ip netmask-format decimal
line aux 0
line vty 0 4
 privilege level 15
 password cisco
 logging synchronous
 login
 ip netmask-format decimal
!
end
```

Peer 2 Running-Config

Notice in the Peer 2 running-config that there is an E-BGP connection to the Atlanta POP router:

```
Peer2#show running-config
Building configuration...

Current configuration : 1141 bytes
!
version 12.1
service timestamps debug uptime
service timestamps log uptime
no service password-encryption
!
hostname Peer2
!
```

```
enable password lab
!
!
!
!
!
ip subnet-zero
ip tcp synwait-time 5
no ip domain-lookup
!
!
!
!
interface Loopback0
 ip address 192.168.2.1 255.255.255.255
!
interface Ethernet0
 no ip address
 shutdown
!
interface Serial0
 description *** Link to PE2 ***
 ip address 192.168.3.10 255.255.255.252
 no fair-queue
!
interface Serial1
 no ip address
 shutdown
!
router bgp 65001
 no synchronization
 bgp log-neighbor-changes
 redistribute connected
 neighbor 192.168.3.9 remote-as 65000
 no auto-summary
```

```
!
ip classless

no ip http server
!
!
line con 0
 exec-timeout 0 0
 privilege level 15
 logging synchronous
 transport input none
 ip netmask-format decimal
line aux 0
line vty 0 4
 privilege level 15
 password lab
 logging synchronous
 login
 ip netmask-format decimal
!
end
```

Verification with Ping

To verify that the VPN works, all you need to do is a ping from one peer router to the other. The following output appears as the result of a ping from Peer 2 to Peer 1:

```
Peer2#ping 192.168.1.1

Type escape sequence to abort.
Sending 5, 100-byte ICMP Echos to 192.168.1.1, timeout
  is 2 seconds:
!!!!!
Success rate is 100 percent (5/5), round-trip in/avg/max
  = 116/119/120 ms
```

Advanced MPLS VPN Topologies

When discussing MPLS VPNs throughout this book, you have seen only simple VPNs. There are many additional topologies that you should know about even though they are not specified in the exam objectives.

Simple VPNs

Throughout this book you have seen only *simple MPLS VPN topologies*. For example, Figure 8.7 illustrates a customer with two sites connected to a service provider.

FIGURE 8.7 A simple VPN topology

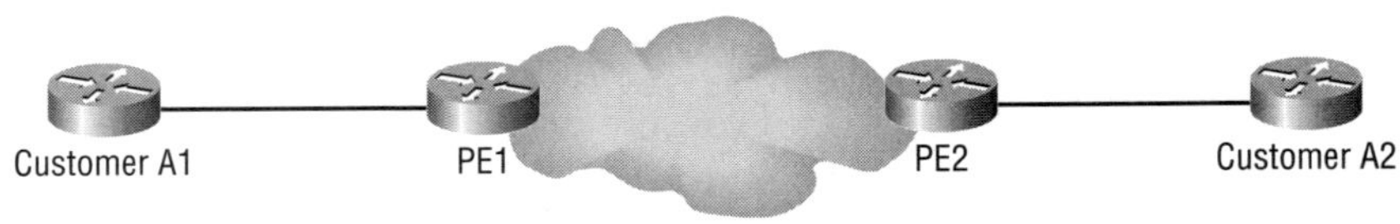

For the sites Customer A1 and Customer A2 to be connected together with an MPLS VPN, a VRF, route distinguisher, routing protocol, and route target must be configured. For the purpose of this discussion of MPLS VPN topologies, I'm interested only in the route targets.

When a route from Customer A1 arrives at PE1, it is redistributed into MP-BGP. Remember that the export route target value is carried in the extended community. When the route arrives at PE2, the import route target value is used to pull the route from MP-BGP into the VRF. For example, the relevant configuration of PE1 is as follows:

```
ip vrf vpn_1
 route-target export 1289:172
 route-target import 1289:172
```

By analyzing the configuration of PE1 and PE2, you can see that routes from PE1, when exported into MP-BGP, carry the export route target value of 1289:172 in the extended community. In addition, routes from PE2, when exported into MP-BGP, carry the export route target value of 1289:172 in the extended community. Both PE1 and PE2 import routes that have an extended community route target value of 1289:172.

Central Services MPLS VPN Topology

Although many of your customers may require only a simple MPLS VPN to meet their connectivity requirements, route targets can be used to support a host of other topologies.

A *Central Services MPLS VPN topology* is where there is some central service, such as data storage facilities or media content, that is being accessed by different sites. Figure 8.8 illustrates a Central Services network.

FIGURE 8.8 A Central Services network

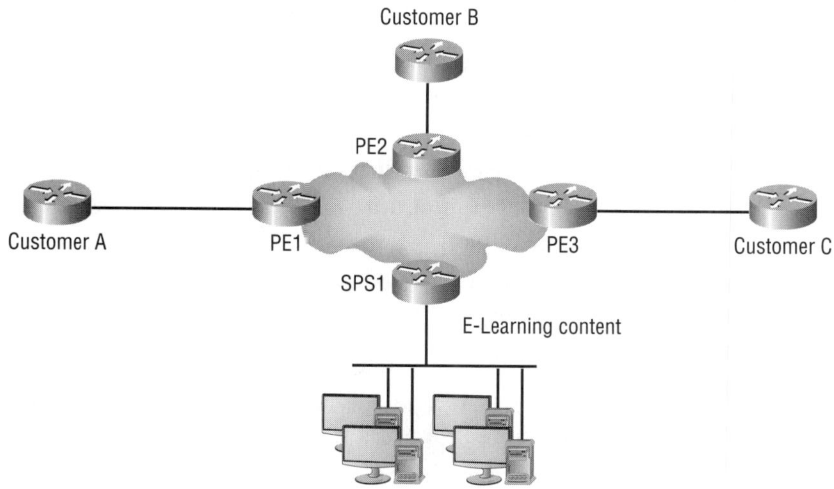

In Figure 8.8, there are three customers: Customer A, Customer B, and Customer C. Each of these three customers is paying the service provider for access to the e-learning content hosted by the service provider.

Customer A, Customer B, and Customer C need to know how to send packets to the e-learning content site. The e-learning content site needs to know how to send packets back to Customer A, Customer B, and Customer C. Customer A, Customer B, and Customer C do not need to send packets to each other.

On PE1, Customer A's routes will be exported with a route target of 100:1. The relevant configuration of PE1 is as follows:

```
ip vrf vpn_a
 route-target export 100:1
```

On PE2, Customer B's routes will be exported with a route target of 100:2. The relevant configuration of PE2 is as follows:

```
ip vrf vpn_b
 route-target export 100:2
```

On PE3, Customer C's routes will be exported with a route target of 100:3. The relevant configuration of PE2 is as follows:

```
ip vrf vpn_c
 route-target export 100:3
```

On SPS1, the e-learning content routes will be exported with a route target of 1289:1027. The relevant configuration of SPS1 is as follows:

```
ip vrf elearning_svc
 route-target export 1289:107
```

On PE1, Customer A needs to know about the e-learning content routes. PE1 is configured to import the routes from the e-learning content. The relevant configuration of PE1 is as follows:

```
ip vrf vpn_a
 route-target export 100:1
 route-target import 1289:1027
```

On PE2, Customer B needs to know about the e-learning content routes. PE2 is configured to import the routes from the e-learning content. The relevant configuration of PE2 is as follows:

```
ip vrf vpn_b
 route-target export 100:2
 route-target import 1289:1027
```

On PE3, Customer C needs to know about the e-learning content routes. PE3 is configured to import the routes from the e-learning content. The relevant configuration of PE3 is as follows:

```
ip vrf vpn_c
 route-target export 100:3
 route-target import 1289:1027
```

On SPS1, the e-learning content needs to know about the Customer A, Customer B, and Customer C routes. SPS1 is configured to import the routes from Customer A, Customer B, and Customer C. The relevant configuration of SPS1 is as follows:

```
ip vrf elearning_svc
 route-target export 1289:1073
```

```
route-target import 100:1
route-target import 100:2
route-target import 100:3
```

Overlay MPLS VPN Topology

One other topology you should know about is an *overlay MPLS VPN topology*. An overlay is essentially a situation where a site participates in more than one VPN. In Figure 8.9, there are two customers: Customer A and Customer B. Customer A has two sites: CustomerA_HQ and CustomerA_Site1. Customer B has two sites: Customer B_HQ and CustomerB_Site1.

FIGURE 8.9 An overlay MPLS VPN topology

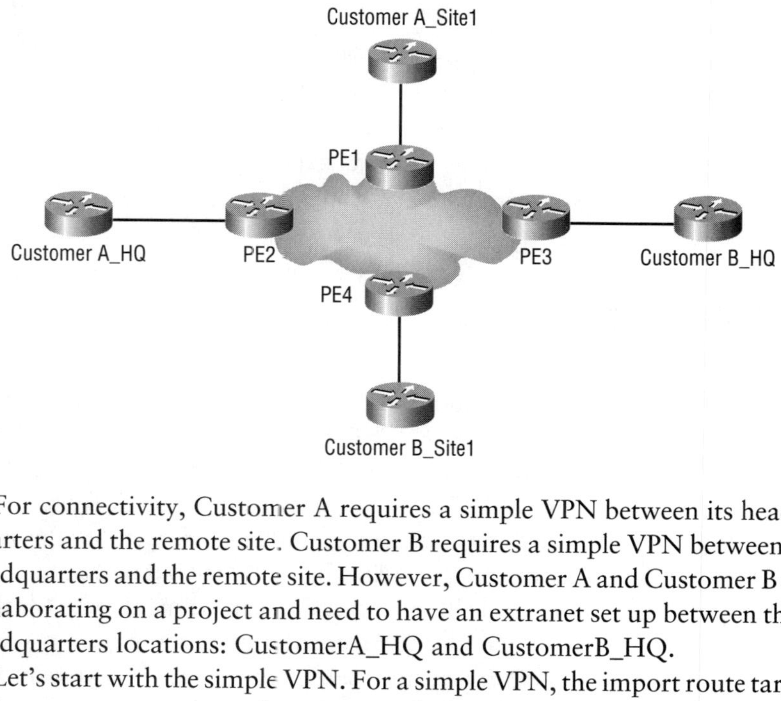

For connectivity, Customer A requires a simple VPN between its headquarters and the remote site. Customer B requires a simple VPN between its headquarters and the remote site. However, Customer A and Customer B are collaborating on a project and need to have an extranet set up between their headquarters locations: CustomerA_HQ and CustomerB_HQ.

Let's start with the simple VPN. For a simple VPN, the import route target and export route target values can match. For CustomerA_VPN, a route distinguisher of 517:1 will be used. For CustomerB_VPN, a route target of 517:38 will be used. On PE1 and PE2, the following configuration exists for CustomerA_VPN:

```
ip vrf customera_vpn
 route-target export 517:1
 route-target import 517:1
```

On PE3 and PE4, the following configuration exists for CustomerB_VPN:

```
ip vrf customerb_vpn
 route-target export 517:38
 route-target import 517:38
```

For an overlay VPN topology, CustomerA_HQ and CustomerB_HQ need to know each other's routes. They both will import and export a route target of 517:2067. The configuration, for CustomerA_HQ, on PE2 is as follows:

```
ip vrf customera_vpn
 route-target export 517:1
 route-target import 517:1
 route-target export 517:2067
 route-target import 517:2067
```

The configuration, for CustomerB_HQ, on PE3 is as follows:

```
ip vrf customerb_vpn
 route-target export 517:38
 route-target import 517:38
 route-target export 517:2067
 route-target import 517:2067
```

Summary

In addition to using RIPv2 as a PE-CE routing protocol as discussed in Chapter 6, "MPLS VPNs and RIP," or OSPF as discussed in Chapter 7, "MPLS VPNs and OSPF," static routes and E-BGP are supported for use in MPLS VPNs. For static routes, a static route is specified with the `ip route vrf` *`vpn_name`* command. Don't forget that this route must be redistributed into MP-BGP with the `redistribute static` command.

An E-BGP connection can be made between a PE and CE router. BGP is a wonderful protocol in that you have advanced filtering and control mechanisms that can be configured. To prevent a network from accepting a malicious number of routes, the `maximum routes` command can be used to limit the number of routes in a VRF. When configuring an E-BGP connection, the neighbor needs to be activated. For topologies where the same AS number is reused, the AS-override allows the service provider to override the AS path.

In addition to simple MPLS VPN topologies, the route distinguisher allows for the support of many more complex topologies. This chapter introduced you to overlay and Central Services MPLS VPN topologies. An overlay VPN is where a site participates in more than one VPN at a time. A Central Services VPN is where some central point must be accessed by several sites, but those sites do not have routing knowledge of each other.

Exam Essentials

Understand static routing for use in MPLS VPNs. If you don't want the associated overhead of running a routing protocol between a PE and CE router, static routes are supported for MPLS VPNs. To configure a static route, use the `ip route vrf` *`vpn_name`* command. Don't forget to redistribute the static route into MP-BGP.

Understand E-BGP for use in MPLS VPNs. E-BGP is supported as a PE-CE routing protocol. When configuring an E-BGP connection to a CE device, the neighbor must be activated. For cases where the same AS number is being reused, the `as-override` command can be used to override the AS path.

Understand complex VPN topologies. An overlay VPN is a topology where a site participates in more than one MPLS VPN. A Central Services VPN topology is the name of a topology where sites connect to some centralized server or service. The sites don't have routing information about each other, only about the Central Services site. The Central Services site has routing knowledge of all sites.

Key Terms

Before you take the exam, be certain you are familiar with the following terms:

- AS-override
- Central Services MPLS VPN topology
- overlay MPLS VPN topology
- simple MPLS VPN topology
- static routes

Review Questions

1. Which command do you use to place a static route into MP-BGP?

   A. `redistribute connected`

   B. `redistribute static`

   C. `redistribute vrf static`

   D. None of the above

2. For static VRF routes, the outgoing interface is ___________.

   A. Mandatory

   B. Optional

   C. None of the above

3. For static VRF routes, the next hop IP address is ___________.

   A. Mandatory

   B. Optional

   C. None of the above

4. What command is used to configure a static VRF route?

   A. `ip route`

   B. `ip route vrf` *vpn_name*

   C. `ip vrf` *vpn_name* `route`

   D. `ip vrf route` *vpn_name*

5. What command is used to configure a standard static route?

   A. `ip route`

   B. `ip route vrf` *vpn_name*

   C. `ip vrf` *vpn_name* `route`

   D. `ip vrf route` *vpn_name*

6. What command is used to advertise the subnets of interfaces in a VRF?

   A. `redistribute static`

   B. `redistribute connected vrf` *`vpn_name`*

   C. `redistribute connected`

   D. `redistribute vrf` *`vpn_name`* `connected`

7. Which of the following routing protocols is *not* supported as a PE-CE routing protocol?

   A. RIPv2

   B. E-BGP

   C. EIGRP

   D. OSPF

8. E-BGP neighbors must be __________.

   A. Redistributed

   B. Activated

   C. Upgraded

   D. None of the above

9. Customers connecting to a PE using E-BGP __________ need to be upgraded to the latest MPLS IOS.

   A. Do

   B. Do not

   C. None of the above

10. Which one of the following features is used to address problems associated with reusing the same AS number between customer sites?

    A. AS path prepending

    B. AS-override

    C. Maximum routes

    D. VC merge

11. Without AS-override, where customer sites reuse the same AS number, routers think there is a ___________.

    A. Down interface

    B. Multihoming

    C. Routing loop

    D. None of the above

12. Which of the following commands is used to configure AS-override?

    A. `neighbor` *`ip_address`* `as-override`

    B. `neighbor` *`ip_address`* `as override`

    C. `neighbor` *`ip_address`* `as-override activate`

    D. `neighbor` *`ip_address`* `as-override vrf` *`vpn_name`*

13. E-BGP routes ___________ need to be redistributed into MP-BGP.

    A. Do

    B. Do not

    C. May

14. Which of the following features is used to limit the number of routes in a VRF?

    A. AS path prepending

    B. AS-override

    C. Maximum routes

    D. VC merge

15. In the following code snippet, what is the maximum number of routes allowed in the VRF?

```
ip vrf vpn-X
 rd 1000:1
 route-target both 1000:1
 maximum-routes 10 75
```

A. 1000:1

B. 10

C. 75

D. None of the above

16. Once the maximum number of routes has entered a VRF when configured with the `maximum-routes` command, additional routes will be __________.

A. Dropped

B. Permitted

C. Permitted with a message being sent to a SYSLOG server

D. None of the above

17. Two sites connected in a VPN topology where the `route-target both` command was used is most likely a __________.

A. Simple MPLS VPN

B. Overlay MPLS VPN

C. Central Services MPLS VPN

18. Which topology best represents the situation where a site participates in more than one VPN?

A. Simple MPLS VPN

B. Overlay MPLS VPN

C. Central Services MPLS VPN

19. Which of the following topologies represents a site that can see all other sites, but the other sites can see it and not each other?

A. Simple MPLS VPN

B. Overlay MPLS VPN

C. Central Services MPLS VPN

20. Which of the following features is used to prevent a malicious flooding of routes into the service provider backbone?

A. AS path prepending

B. AS-override

C. Maximum routes

D. VC merge

Answers to Review Questions

1. B. To place a static route into MP-BGP, you redistribute it with the `redistribute static` command.

2. A. The outgoing interface is mandatory when configuring a static VRF route.

3. B. The outgoing interface is mandatory when configuring a static VRF route, but the next hop IP address is optional.

4. B. To configure a static VRF route, use the `ip route vrf` *vpn_name* command.

5. A. To configure a standard static route, use the `ip route` command.

6. C. To redistribute interface subnets into MP-BGP, use the `redistribute connected` command.

7. C. RIPv2, E-BGP, and OSPF are supported PE-CE routing protocols. EIGRP is not.

8. B. E-BGP neighbors must be activated.

9. B. Customers run standard E-BGP with a PE router and therefore do not need an IOS upgrade.

10. B. AS-override is used to allow a client to reuse the same AS number across multiple sites.

11. C. Without AS-override and where the same AS number is being reused across multiple customer sites, the AS path appears to be a routing loop.

12. A. To configure AS-override, use the `neighbor` *ip_address* `as-override` command.

13. B. E-BGP routes do not need to be redistributed into MP-BGP.

14. C. The maximum routes feature limits the number of routes allowed into a VRF.

15. B. The first option after the `maximum-routes` command is the maximum number of routes allowed in the VRF.

16. A. The default action of the `maximum-routes` command is to drop new routes after the maximum number of routes has been exceeded.

17. A. Two sites connected only to each other is usually a simple MPLS VPN.

18. B. A site that is part of more than one VPN is an overlay MPLS VPN.

19. C. A Central Services MPLS VPN topology is characterized by a central site seeing all subscribing sites, and the subscribing sites seeing the central site but not each other.

20. C. The maximum routes feature limits the number of routes allowed into a VRF and therefore limits the number of routes ending up in the service provider backbone.

Appendix A

Challenge Labs

This appendix contains six challenge labs. The challenge labs will test your ability to configure all of the topics covered in this study guide.

Challenge Lab 1

The following challenge lab tests your ability to configure MPLS, BGP, and MP-IBGP.

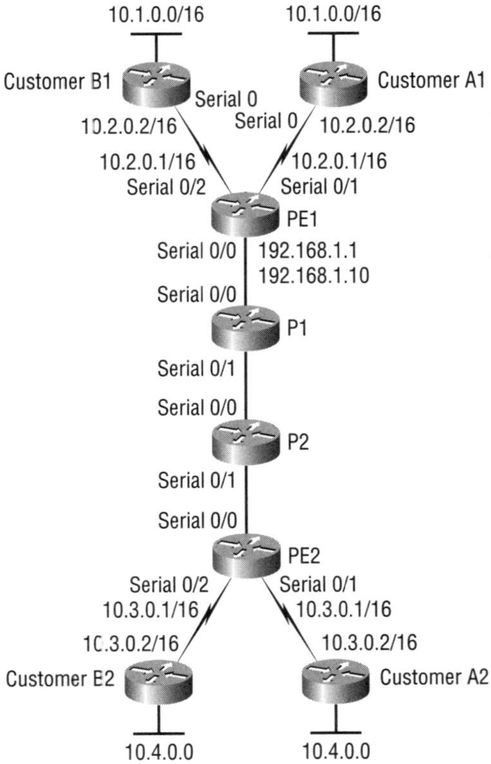

You need to know all the interfaces and IP addressing contained in the following table:

Device	Serial 0/0	Serial 0/1	Loopback 0
PE1	192.168.1.10		192.168.1.1
P1	192.168.1.9	192.168.1.14	192.168.1.2
P2	192.168.1.13	192.168.1.18	192.168.1.3
PE2	192.168.1.17		192.168.1.4

MPLS

This section includes the following lab exercise:

- Lab 1.1: Configure MPLS

LAB 1.1

Configure MPLS

1. Configure MPLS on PE1.
2. Configure MPLS on P1.
3. Configure MPLS on P2.
4. Configure MPLS on PE2.

BGP

This section includes the following lab exercise:

- Lab 1.2: Configure BGP

LAB 1.2

Configure BGP

1. Configure BGP AS 65000 on PE1.
2. Add an I-BGP neighbor statement for PE2 (use the Loopback 0 address).

LAB 1.2 *(continued)*

3. Configure BGP AS 65000 on PE2.
4. Add an I-BGP neighbor statement for PE1 (use the Loopback 0 address).

MP-IBGP

This section includes the following lab exercise:

- Lab 1.3: Configure MP-IBGP

LAB 1.3

Configure MP-IBGP

1. On PE1, activate neighbor PE2.
2. On PE1, configure PE1 to send both standard and extend communities to PE2.
3. On PE2, activate neighbor PE1.
4. On PE2, configure PE2 to send both standard and extend communities to PE1.

Answer to Lab 1.1

```
PE1#config t
Enter configuration commands, one per line. End with CNTL/Z.
PE1(config)#ip cef
PE1(config)#mpls ip
PE1(config)#interface serial 0/0
PE1(config-if)#mpls ip

P1#config t
Enter configuration commands, one per line. End with CNTL/Z.
P1(config)#ip cef
```

```
P1(config)#mpls ip
P1(config)#interface serial 0/0
P1(config-if)#mpls ip
P1(config-if)#exit
P1(config)#interface serial 0/1
P1(config-if)#mpls ip

P2#config t
Enter configuration commands, one per line. End with CNTL/Z.
P2(config)#ip cef
P2(config)#mpls ip
P2(config)#interface serial 0/0
P2(config-if)#mpls ip
P2(config-if)#exit
P2(config)#interface serial 0/1
P2(config-if)#mpls ip

PE2#config t
Enter configuration commands, one per line. End with CNTL/Z.
PE2(config)#ip cef
PE2(config)#mpls ip
PE2(config)#interface serial 0/0
PE2(config-if)#mpls ip
```

Answer to Lab 1.2

```
PE1#config t
Enter configuration commands, one per line. End with CNTL/Z.
PE1(config)#router bgp 65000
PE1(config-router)#no synchronization
PE1(config-router)#network 192.168.1.1 mask 255.255.255.255
PE1(config-router)#neighbor 192.168.1.4 remote-as 65000
PE1(config-router)#neighbor 192.168.1.4 update-source Loopback0
```

```
PE2#config t
Enter configuration commands, one per line. End with CNTL/Z.
PE2(config)#router bgp 65000
PE2(config-router)#no synchronization
PE2(config-router)#network 192.168.1.4 mask 255.255.255.255
PE2(config-router)#neighbor 192.168.1.1 remote-as 65000
PE2(config-router)#neighbor 192.168.1.1 update-source Loopback0
```

Answer to Lab 1.3

```
PE1#config t
Enter configuration commands, one per line. End with CNTL/Z.
PE1(config)#router bgp 65000
PE1(config-router)#address-family vpnv4
PE1(config-router)#neighbor 192.168.1.4 activate
PE1(config-router)#neighbor 192.168.1.4 next-hop-self
PE1(config-router)#neighbor 192.168.1.4 send-community both

PE2#config t
Enter configuration commands, one per line. End with CNTL/Z.
PE2(config)#router bgp 65000
PE2(config-router)#address-family vpnv4
PE2(config-router)#neighbor 192.168.1.1 activate
PE2(config-router)#neighbor 192.168.1.1 next-hop-self
PE2(config-router)#neighbor 192.168.1.1 send-community both
```

Challenge Lab 2

The following challenge lab tests your ability to configure tag switching, BGP, and MP-IBGP.

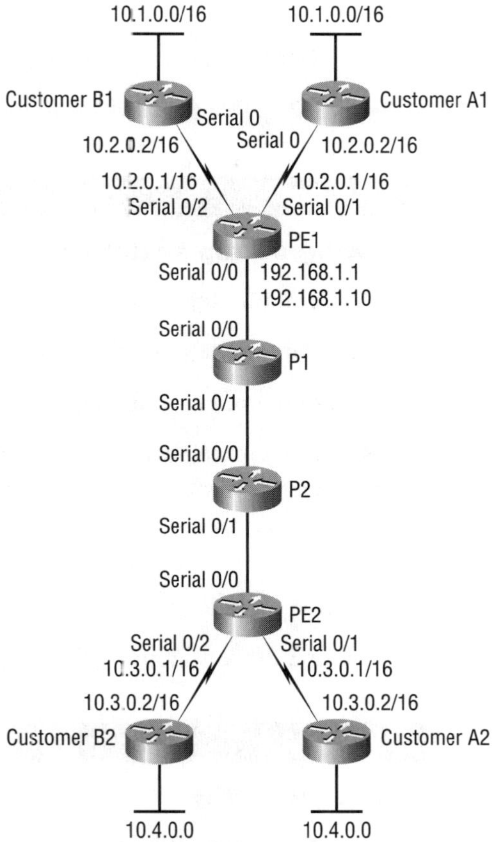

You need to know all the interfaces and IP addressing contained in the following table:

Device	Serial 0/0	Serial 0/1	Loopback 0
PE1	192.168.1.10		192.168.1.1
P1	192.168.1.9	192.168.1.14	192.168.1.2
P2	192.168.1.13	192.168.1.18	192.168.1.3
PE2	192.168.1.17		192.168.1.4

Tag Switching

This section includes the following lab exercise:

- Lab 2.1: Configure tag switching

LAB 2.1

Configure tag switching

1. Configure tag switching on PE1.
2. Configure tag switching on P1.
3. Configure tag switching on P2.
4. Configure tag switching on PE2.

BGP

This section includes the following lab exercise:

- Lab 2.2: Configure BGP

LAB 2.2

Configure BGP

1. Configure BGP AS 65000 on PE1.
2. Add an I-BGP neighbor statement for PE2 (use the Loopback 0 address).
3. Configure BGP AS 65000 on PE2.
4. Add an I-BGP neighbor statement for PE1 (use the Loopback 0 address).

MP-IBGP

This section includes the following lab exercise:

- Lab 2.3: Configure MP-IBGP

LAB 2.3

Configure MP-IBGP

1. On PE1, activate neighbor PE2.
2. On PE1, configure PE1 to send both standard and extend communities to PE2.
3. On PE2, activate neighbor PE1.
4. On PE2, configure PE2 to send both standard and extend communities to PE1.

Answer to Lab 2.1

```
PE1#config t
Enter configuration commands, one per line. End with CNTL/Z.
PE1(config)#ip cef
PE1(config)# tag-switching advertise tags
PE1(config)#interface serial 0/0
PE1(config-if)#tag-switching ip

P1#config t
Enter configuration commands, one per line. End with CNTL/Z.
P1(config)#ip cef
P1(config)# tag-switching advertise tags
P1(config)#interface serial 0/0
P1(config-if)# tag-switching ip
P1(config-if)#exit
P1(config)#interface serial 0/1
P1(config-if)# tag-switching ip

P2#config t
Enter configuration commands, one per line. End with CNTL/Z.
P2(config)#ip cef
P2(config)# tag-switching advertise tags
P2(config)#interface serial 0/0
P2(config-if)# tag-switching ip
```

```
P2(config-if)#exit
P2(config)#interface serial 0/1
P2(config-if)# tag-switching ip

PE2#config t
Enter configuration commands, one per line. End with CNTL/Z.
PE2(config)#ip cef
PE2(config)# tag-switching advertise tags
PE2(config)#interface serial 0/0
PE2(config-if)#tag-switching ip
```

Answer to Lab 2.2

```
PE1#config t
Enter configuration commands, one per line. End with CNTL/Z.
PE1(config)#router bgp 65000
PE1(config-router)#no synchronization
PE1(config-router)#network 192.168.1.1 mask 255.255.255.255
PE1(config-router)#neighbor 192.168.1.4 remote-as 65000
PE1(config-router)#neighbor 192.168.1.4 update-source
  Loopback0

PE2#config t
Enter configuration commands, one per line. End with CNTL/Z.
PE2(config)#router bgp 65000
PE2(config-router)#no synchronization
PE2(config-router)#network 192.168.1.4 mask 255.255.255.255
PE2(config-router)#neighbor 192.168.1.1 remote-as 65000
PE2(config-router)#neighbor 192.168.1.1 update-source
  Loopback0
```

Answer to Lab 2.3

```
PE1#config t
Enter configuration commands, one per line. End with CNTL/Z.
```

```
PE1(config)#router bgp 65000
PE1(config-router)#address-family vpnv4
PE1(config-router)#neighbor 192.168.1.4 activate
PE1(config-router)#neighbor 192.168.1.4 next-hop-self
PE1(config-router)#neighbor 192.168.1.4 send-community both

PE2#config t
Enter configuration commands, one per line. End with CNTL/Z.
PE2(config)#router bgp 65000
PE2(config-router)#address-family vpnv4
PE2(config-router)#neighbor 192.168.1.1 activate
PE2(config-router)#neighbor 192.168.1.1 next-hop-self
PE2(config-router)#neighbor 192.168.1.1 send-community both
```

Challenge Lab 3

The following challenge lab tests your ability to configure a VRF, a route distinguisher, a route target, RIPv2 as a PE-CE routing protocol, and RIPv2 redistribution into MP-BGP. Note that the network is already set up with MPLS and MP-BGP (AS 65000).

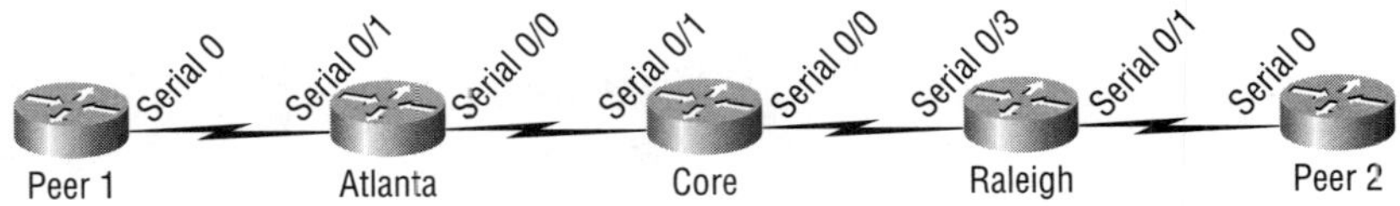

You need to know all the interfaces and IP addressing contained in the following two tables:

Customer Addressing

Device	Loopback 0	Serial 0
Peer1	192.168.1.1/32	192.168.3.5/30
Peer2	192.168.2.1/32	192.168.3.10/30

Service Provider Addressing

Device	Loopback 0	Serial 0/0	Serial 0/1	Serial 0/3
Atlanta	204.134.83.1/32	204.134.83.5/30	192.168.3.6/30	N/A
Core	204.134.83.2/32	204.134.83.9/30	204.134.83.6/30	N/A
Raleigh	204.134.83.3/32	N/A	192.168.3.9/30	204.134.83.10/30

VRF Configuration

This section includes the following lab exercise:

- Lab 3.1: Configure a VRF, a route distinguisher, and a route target

LAB 3.1

Configure a VRF, a route distinguisher, and a route target

1. On the Atlanta POP router, create a VRF called peer_vpn.
2. On the Atlanta POP router, assign a route distinguisher of 50:1.
3. On the Atlanta POP router, configure an import route target and an export route target of 50:1.
4. On the Atlanta POP router, associate the PE-CE interface with the VRF and assign the appropriate address from the table.
5. On the Raleigh POP router, create a VRF called peer_vpn.
6. On the Raleigh POP router, assign a route distinguisher of 50:1.
7. On the Raleigh POP router, configure an import route target and an export route target of 50:1.
8. On the Raleigh POP router, associate the PE-CE interface with the VRF and assign the appropriate address from the table.

RIPv2

This section includes the following lab exercise:

- Lab 3.2: Configure RIPv2 on peer and POP routers

LAB 3.2

Configure RIPv2 on peer and POP routers

1. Configure RIPv2 on Peer 1 for all networks.
2. Configure RIPv2 on Peer 2 for all networks.
3. Configure a RIPv2 context on the Atlanta POP router.
4. Configure a RIPv2 context on the Raleigh POP router.

Redistribution

This section includes the following lab exercise:

- Lab 3.3: Configure redistribution

LAB 3.3

Configure redistribution

1. Configure redistribution between MP-BGP and the RIPv2 context on the Atlanta POP router.
2. Configure redistribution between MP-BGP and the RIPv2 context on the Raleigh POP router.

Answer to Lab 3.1

```
Atlanta#conf t
Enter configuration commands, one per line. End with CNTL/Z.
Atlanta(config)#ip vrf peer_vpn
Atlanta(config-vrf)#rd 50:1
Atlanta(config-vrf)#route-target both 50:1
Atlanta(config-vrf)#exit
Atlanta(config)#int s 0/1
Atlanta(config-if)#ip vrf forwarding peer_vpn
% Interface Serial0/1 IP address 192.168.3.6 removed due
  to enabling VRF peer_vpn
Atlanta(config-if)#ip address 192.168.3.6 255.255.255.252
```

```
Raleigh#conf t
Enter configuration commands, one per line. End with CNTL/Z.
Raleigh(config)#ip vrf peer_vpn
Raleigh(config-vrf)#rd 50:1
Raleigh(config-vrf)#route-target both 50:1
Raleigh(config-vrf)#exit
Raleigh(config)#int s 0/1
Raleigh (config-if)#ip vrf forwarding peer_vpn
% Interface Serial0/1 IP address 192.168.3.9 removed due
  to enabling VRF peer_vpn
Raleigh(config-if)#ip address 192.168.3.9 255.255.255.252
```

Answer to Lab 3.2

```
Peer1#conf t
Enter configuration commands, one per line. End with CNTL/Z.
Peer1(config)#router rip
Peer1(config-router)#version 2
Peer1(config-router)#network 192.168.3.0
Peer1(config-router)#network 192.168.1.0
Peer1(config-router)#^Z
Peer1#

Peer2#conf t
Enter configuration commands, one per line. End with CNTL/Z.
Peer2(config)#router rip
Peer2(config-router)#version 2
Peer2(config-router)#network 192.168.3.0
Peer2(config-router)#network 192.168.2.0
Peer2(config-router)#^Z
Peer2#

Atlanta#conf t
Enter configuration commands, one per line. End with CNTL/Z.
Atlanta(config)#router rip
Atlanta(config-router)#version 2
```

```
Atlanta(config-router)#address-family ipv4 vrf peer_vpn
Atlanta(config-router-af)#network 192.168.3.0

Raleigh#conf t
Enter configuration commands, one per line. End with CNTL/Z.
Raleigh(config)#router rip
Raleigh(config-router)#version 2
Raleigh(config-router)#address-family ipv4 vrf peer_vpn
Raleigh(config-router-af)#network 192.168.3.0
```

Answer to Lab 3.3

```
Atlanta#conf t
Enter configuration commands, one per line. End with CNTL/Z.
Atlanta(config)#router rip
Atlanta(config-router)#address-family ipv4 vrf peer_vpn
Atlanta(config-router-af)#redistribute bgp 65000 metric
  transparent
Atlanta(config-router-af)#exit
Atlanta(config-router)#exit
Atlanta(config)#router bgp 65000
Atlanta(config-router)#address-family ipv4 vrf peer_vpn
Atlanta(config-router-af)#redistribute rip

Raleigh#conf t
Enter configuration commands, one per line. End with CNTL/Z.
Raleigh(config)#router rip
Raleigh(config-router)#address-family ipv4 vrf peer_vpn
Raleigh(config-router-af)#redistribute bgp 65000 metric
  transparent
Raleigh(config-router-af)#exit
Raleigh(config-router)#exit
Raleigh(config)#router bgp 65000
Raleigh(config-router)#address-family ipv4 vrf peer_vpn
Raleigh(config-router-af)#redistribute rip
```

Challenge Lab 4

The following challenge lab tests your ability to configure a VRF, a route distinguisher, a route target, OSPF as a PE-CE routing protocol, and OSPF redistribution into MP-BGP. Note that the network is already set up with MPLS and MP-BGP (AS 65000).

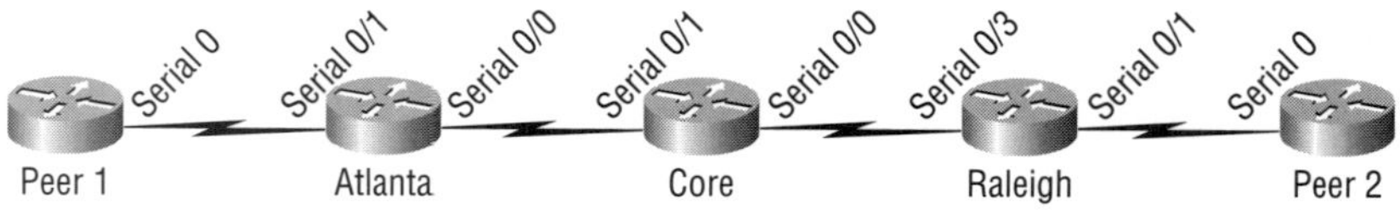

You need to know all the interfaces and IP addressing contained in the following two tables:

Customer Addressing

Device	Loopback 0	Serial 0
Peer1	192.168.1.1/32	192.168.3.5/30
Peer2	192.168.2.1/32	192.168.3.10/30

Service Provider Addressing

Device	Loopback 0	Serial 0/0	Serial 0/1	Serial 0/3
Atlanta	204.134.83.1/32	204.134.83.5/30	192.168.3.6/30	N/A
Core	204.134.83.2/32	204.134.83.9/30	204.134.83.6/30	N/A
Raleigh	204.134.83.3/32	N/A	192.168.3.9/30	204.134.83.10/30

VRF Configuration

This section includes the following lab exercise:

- Lab 4.1: Configure a VRF, a route distinguisher, and a route target

LAB 4.1

Configure a VRF, a route distinguisher, and a route target

1. On the Atlanta POP router, create a VRF called peer_vpn.
2. On the Atlanta POP router, assign a route distinguisher of 50:1.
3. On the Atlanta POP router, configure an import route target and an export route target of 50:1.
4. On the Atlanta POP router, associate the PE-CE interface with the VRF and assign the appropriate address from the table.
5. On the Raleigh POP router, create a VRF called peer_vpn.
6. On the Raleigh POP router, assign a route distinguisher of 50:1.
7. On the Raleigh POP router, configure an import route target and an export route target of 50:1.
8. On the Raleigh POP router, associate the PE-CE interface with the VRF and assign the appropriate address from the table.

OSPF

This section includes the following lab exercise:

- Lab 4.2: Configure OSPF on peer and PE devices

LAB 4.2

Configure OSPF on peer and PE devices

1. Configure OSPF Area 0 on the Peer 1 Serial 0 interface.
2. Configure OSPF Area 1 on the Peer 1 Loopback 0 interface.
3. Configure OSPF Area 0 on the Peer 2 Serial 0 interface.
4. Configure OSPF Area 1 on the Peer 2 Loopback 0 interface.
5. Configure OSPF on the Atlanta POP router for the VRF.
6. Configure OSPF on the Raleigh POP router for the VRF.

Redistribution

This section includes the following lab exercise:

- Lab 4.3: Configure redistribution

LAB 4.3

Configure redistribution

1. Configure redistribution between MP-BGP and the OSPF on the Atlanta POP router.
2. Configure redistribution between MP-BGP and the OSPF on the Raleigh POP router.

Answer to Lab 4.1

```
Atlanta#conf t
Enter configuration commands, one per line. End with CNTL/Z.
Atlanta(config)#ip vrf peer_vpn
Atlanta(config-vrf)#rd 50:1
Atlanta(config-vrf)#route-target both 50:1
Atlanta(config-vrf)#exit
Atlanta(config)#int s 0/1
Atlanta(config-if)#ip vrf forwarding peer_vpn
% Interface Serial0/1 IP address 192.168.3.6 removed due
  to enabling VRF peer_vpn
Atlanta(config-if)#ip address 192.168.3.6 255.255.255.252

Raleigh#conf t
Enter configuration commands, one per line. End with CNTL/Z.
Raleigh(config)#ip vrf peer_vpn
Raleigh(config-vrf)#rd 50:1
Raleigh(config-vrf)#route-target both 50:1
Raleigh(config-vrf)#exit
Raleigh(config)#int s 0/1
Raleigh(config-if)#ip vrf forwarding peer_vpn
% Interface Serial0/1 IP address 192.168.3.9 removed due
  to enabling VRF peer_vpn
Raleigh(config-if)#ip address 192.168.3.9 255.255.255.252
```

Answer to Lab 4.2

```
Peer1#conf t
Enter configuration commands, one per line. End with CNTL/Z.
Peer1(config)#router ospf 1
Peer1(config-router)#network 192.168.3.5 0.0.0.0 area 0
Peer1(config-router)#network 192.168.1.1 0.0.0.0 area 1
Peer1(config-router)#^Z
Peer1#

Peer2#conf t
Enter configuration commands, one per line. End with CNTL/Z.
Peer2(config)#router ospf 1
Peer2(config-router)#network 192.168.3.10 0.0.0.0 area 0
Peer2(config-router)#network 192.168.2.1 0.0.0.0 area 1
Peer2(config-router)#^Z
Peer2#

Atlanta#conf t
Enter configuration commands, one per line. End with CNTL/Z.
Atlanta(config)#router ospf 1 vrf peer_vpn
Atlanta(config-router)#network 192.168.3.6 0.0.0.0 area 0

Raleigh#conf t
Enter configuration commands, one per line. End with CNTL/Z.
Raleigh(config)#router ospf 1 vrf peer_vpn
Raleigh(config-router)#network 192.168.3.9 0.0.0.0 area 0
```

Answer to Lab 4.3

```
Atlanta#conf t
Enter configuration commands, one per line. End with CNTL/Z.
Atlanta(config)#router ospf 1 vrf peer_vpn
Atlanta(config-router)#redistribute bgp 65000 metric
  transparent
Atlanta(config-router-af)#exit
Atlanta(config-router)#exit
Atlanta(config)#router bgp 65000
```

```
Atlanta(config-router)#address-family ipv4 vrf peer_vpn
Atlanta(config-router-af)#redistribute ospf 1 vrf peer_vpn

Raleigh#conf t
Enter configuration commands, one per line. End with CNTL/Z.
Raleigh(config)#router ospf 1 vrf peer_vpn
Raleigh(config-router-af)#redistribute bgp 65000 metric
  transparent
Raleigh(config-router-af)#exit
Raleigh(config-router)#exit
Raleigh(config)#router bgp 65000
Raleigh(config-router)#address-family ipv4 vrf peer_vpn
Raleigh(config-router-af)#redistribute ospf 1 vrf peer_vpn
```

Challenge Lab 5

The following challenge lab tests your ability to configure a VRF, a route distinguisher, a route target, static routes as a PE-CE routing protocol, and static route redistribution into MP-BGP. Note that the network is already set up with MPLS and MP-BGP (AS 65000).

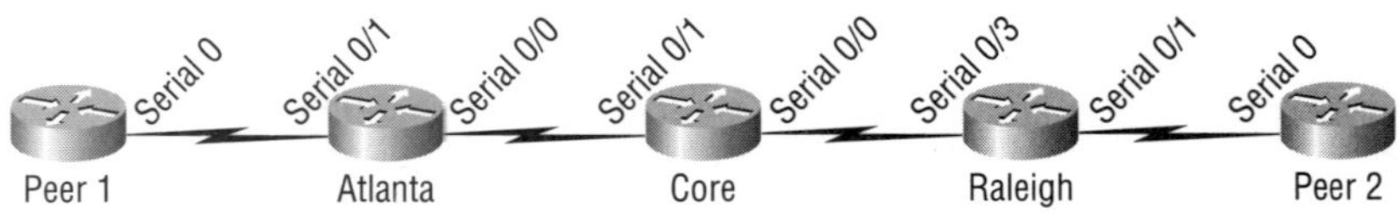

You need to know all the interfaces and IP addressing contained in the following two tables:

Customer Addressing

Device	Loopback 0	Serial 0
Peer1	192.168.1.1/32	192.168.3.5/30
Peer2	192.168.2.1/32	192.168.3.10/30

Service Provider Addressing

Device	Loopback 0	Serial 0/0	Serial 0/1	Serial 0/3
Atlanta	204.134.83.1/32	204.134.83.5/30	192.168.3.6/30	N/A
Core	204.134.83.2/32	204.134.83.9/30	204.134.83.6/30	N/A
Raleigh	204.134.83.3/32	N/A	192.168.3.9/30	204.134.83.10/30

VRF Configuration

This section includes the following lab exercise:

- Lab 5.1: Configure a VRF, a route distinguisher, and a route target

LAB 5.1

Configure a VRF, a route distinguisher, and a route target

1. On the Atlanta POP router, create a VRF called peer_vpn.
2. On the Atlanta POP router, assign a route distinguisher of 50:1.
3. On the Atlanta POP router, configure an import route target and an export route target of 50:1.
4. On the Atlanta POP router, associate the PE-CE interface with the VRF and assign the appropriate address from the table.
5. On the Raleigh POP router, create a VRF called peer_vpn.
6. On the Raleigh POP router, assign a route distinguisher of 50:1.
7. On the Raleigh POP router, configure an import route target and an export route target of 50:1.
8. On the Raleigh POP router, associate the PE-CE interface with the VRF and assign the appropriate address from the table.

Static Routes and Redistribution

This section includes the following lab exercise:

- Lab 5.2: Configure static routes on the peer and PE devices and configure redistribution static routes and connected interfaces

LAB 5.2

Configure static routes on the peer and PE devices and configure redistribution static routes and connected interfaces

1. On Peer 1, configure a default route using the Serial 0 interface.
2. On Peer 2, configure a default route using the Serial 0 interface.
3. On the Atlanta POP router, configure a static route to the Loopback 0 interface of Peer 1 for the VRF.
4. On the Atlanta POP router, configure redistribution of the static route and the VRF connected interface.
5. On the Raleigh POP router, configure a static route to the Loopback 0 interface of Peer 2 for the VRF.
6. On the Raleigh POP router, configure redistribution of the static route and the VRF connected interface.

Answer to Lab 5.1

```
Atlanta#conf t
Enter configuration commands, one per line. End with CNTL/Z.
Atlanta(config)#ip vrf peer_vpn
Atlanta(config-vrf)#rd 50:1
Atlanta(config-vrf)#route-target both 50:1
Atlanta(config-vrf)#exit
Atlanta(config)#int s 0/1
Atlanta(config-if)#ip vrf forwarding peer_vpn
% Interface Serial0/1 IP address 192.168.3.6 removed due
  to enabling VRF peer_vpn
Atlanta(config-if)#ip address 192.168.3.6 255.255.255.252

Raleigh#conf t
Enter configuration commands, one per line. End with CNTL/Z.
Raleigh(config)#ip vrf peer_vpn
Raleigh(config-vrf)#rd 50:1
Raleigh(config-vrf)#route-target both 50:1
```

```
Raleigh(config-vrf)#exit
Raleigh(config)#int s 0/1
Raleigh(config-if)#ip vrf forwarding peer_vpn
% Interface Serial0/1 IP address 192.168.3.9 removed due
  to enabling VRF peer_vpn
Raleigh(config-if)#ip address 192.168.3.9 255.255.255.252
```

Answer to Lab 5.2

```
Peer1#conf t
Enter configuration commands, one per line. End with CNTL/Z.
Peer1(config)# ip route 0.0.0.0 0.0.0.0 serial 0
Peer1(config)#^Z
Peer1#

Peer2#conf t
Enter configuration commands, one per line. End with CNTL/Z.
Peer2(config)#ip route 0.0.0.0 0.0.0.0 serial 0
Peer2(config)#^Z
Peer2#

Atlanta#conf t
Enter configuration commands, one per line. End with CNTL/Z.
Atlanta(config)# ip route vrf vpn_1 192.168.1.1
  255.255.255.255 Serial0/1 192.168.3.5
Atlanta(config)#router bgp 65000
Atlanta(config-router)#address-family ipv4 vrf peer_vpn
Atlanta(config-router-af)#redistribute connected
Atlanta(config-router-af)#redistribute static
Atlanta(config-router-af)#^Z
Atlanta#

Raleigh#conf t
Enter configuration commands, one per line. End with CNTL/Z.
Raleigh(config)# ip route vrf vpn_1 192.168.2.1
  255.255.255.255 Serial0/1 192.168.3.10
```

```
Raleigh(config)#router bgp 65000
Raleigh(config-router)#address-family ipv4 vrf peer_vpn
Raleigh(config-router-af)#redistribute connected
Raleigh(config-router-af)#redistribute static
Raleigh(config-router-af)#^Z
Raleigh#
```

Challenge Lab 6

The following challenge lab tests your ability to configure a VRF, a route distinguisher, a route target, and an E-BGP session between PE and CE routers. Note that the network is already set up with MPLS and MP-BGP (AS 65000). Both peer routers use AS 65001.

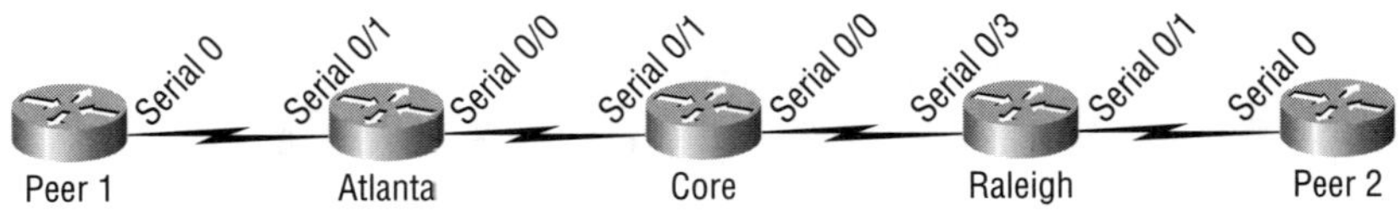

You need to know all the interfaces and IP addressing contained in the following two tables:

Customer Addressing

Device	Loopback 0	Serial 0
Peer1	192.168.1.1/32	192.168.3.5/30
Peer2	192.168.2.1/32	192.168.3.10/30

Service Provider Addressing

Device	Loopback 0	Serial 0/0	Serial 0/1	Serial 0/3
Atlanta	204.134.83.1/32	204.134.83.5/30	192.168.3.6/30	N/A
Core	204.134.83.2/32	204.134.83.9/30	204.134.83.6/30	N/A
Raleigh	204.134.83.3/32	N/A	192.168.3.9/30	204.134.83.10/30

VRF Configuration

This section includes the following lab exercise:

- Lab 6.1: Configure a VRF, a route distinguisher, and a route target

LAB 6.1

Configure a VRF, a route distinguisher, and a route target

1. On the Atlanta POP router, create a VRF called peer_vpn.
2. On the Atlanta POP router, assign a route distinguisher of 50:1.
3. On the Atlanta POP router, configure an import route target and an export route target of 50:1.
4. On the Atlanta POP router, associate the PE-CE interface with the VRF and assign the appropriate address from the table.
5. On the Raleigh POP router, create a VRF called peer_vpn.
6. On the Raleigh POP router, assign a route distinguisher of 50:1.
7. On the Raleigh POP router, configure an import route target and an export route target of 50:1.
8. On the Raleigh POP router, associate the PE-CE interface with the VRF and assign the appropriate address from the table.

E-BGP Configuration

This section includes the following lab exercise:

- Lab 6.2: Configure an E-BGP between the PE and CE routers

LAB 6.2

Configure an E-BGP between the PE and CE routers

1. On Peer 1, configure an E-BGP session to Atlanta and redistribute connected interfaces.
2. On Peer 2, configure an E-BGP session to Raleigh and redistribute connected interfaces.

LAB 6.2 *(continued)*

3. On the Atlanta POP router, configure Peer 1 as a neighbor, activate Peer 1, configure AS-override, and redistribute the connected VRF interface into BGP.

4. On the Raleigh POP router, configure Peer 2 as a neighbor, activate Peer 2, configure AS-override, and redistribute the connected VRF interface into BGP.

Answer to Lab 6.1

```
Atlanta#conf t
Enter configuration commands, one per line. End with CNTL/Z.
Atlanta(config)#ip vrf peer_vpn
Atlanta(config-vrf)#rd 50:1
Atlanta (config-vrf)#route-target both 50:1
Atlanta(config-vrf)#exit
Atlanta(config)#int s 0/1
Atlanta(config-if)#ip vrf forwarding peer_vpn
% Interface Serial0/1 IP address 192.168.3.6 removed due
  to enabling VRF peer_vpn
Atlanta(config-if)#ip address 192.168.3.6 255.255.255.252

Raleigh#conf t
Enter configuration commands, one per line. End with CNTL/Z.
Raleigh(config)#ip vrf peer_vpn
Raleigh(config-vrf)#rd 50:1
Raleigh (config-vrf)#route-target both 50:1
Raleigh (config-vrf)#exit
Raleigh (config)#int s 0/1
Raleigh (config-if)#ip vrf forwarding peer_vpn
% Interface Serial0/1 IP address 192.168.3.9 removed due
  to enabling VRF peer_vpn
Raleigh (config-if)#ip address 192.168.3.9 255.255.255.252
```

Answer to Lab 6.2

```
Peer1#conf t
Enter configuration commands, one per line. End with CNTL/Z.
```

```
Peer1(config)#router bgp 65001
Peer1(config-router)#neighbor 192.168.3.6 remote-as 65000
Peer1(config-router)#redistribute connected
Peer1(config-router)#^Z
Peer1#

Peer2#conf t
Enter configuration commands, one per line. End with CNTL/Z.
Peer2(config)#router bgp 65001
Peer2(config-router)#neighbor 192.168.3.9 remote-as 65000
Peer2(config-router)#redistribute connected
Peer2(config-router)#^Z
Peer2#

Atlanta#conf t
Enter configuration commands, one per line. End with CNTL/Z.
Atlanta(config)#router bgp 65000
Atlanta(config-router)#address-family ipv4 vrf peer_vpn
Atlanta(config-router-af)#neighbor 192.168.3.5 remote-as
  65001
Atlanta(config-router-af)#neighbor 192.168.3.5 activate
Atlanta(config-router-af)#neighbor 192.168.3.5 as-override
Atlanta(config-router-af)#redistribute connected
Atlanta(config-router-af)#^Z
Atlanta#

Raleigh#conf t
Enter configuration commands, one per line. End with CNTL/Z.
Raleigh(config)#router bgp 65000
Raleigh(config-router)#address-family ipv4 vrf peer_vpn
Raleigh(config-router-af)#neighbor 192.168.3.10 remote-as
  65001
Raleigh(config-router-af)#neighbor 192.168.3.10 activate
Raleigh(config-router-af)#neighbor 192.168.3.10 as-override
Raleigh(config-router-af)#redistribute connected
Raleigh(config-router-af)#^Z
Raleigh#
```

Appendix B

Service Provider Tag Switching with OSPF and IS-IS

Chapter 2, "Frame-Mode MPLS," introduced you to MPLS and tag switching deployment in service provider networks. In Chapter 2, I used RIPv2 as an IGP for the service provider network. Although RIPv2 works from an instructional standpoint, IS-IS and OSPF are real-world protocols used by service providers. In this appendix, a sample network is configured with BGP between the PE and CE routers. In the first example, OSPF is configured as the service provider IGP. In the second example, IS-IS is configured as the service provider IGP.

Service Provider Network Configuration with OSPF

Figure B.1 illustrates the service provider network you'll be using in this section.

FIGURE B.1 A service provider network to be configured with OSPF

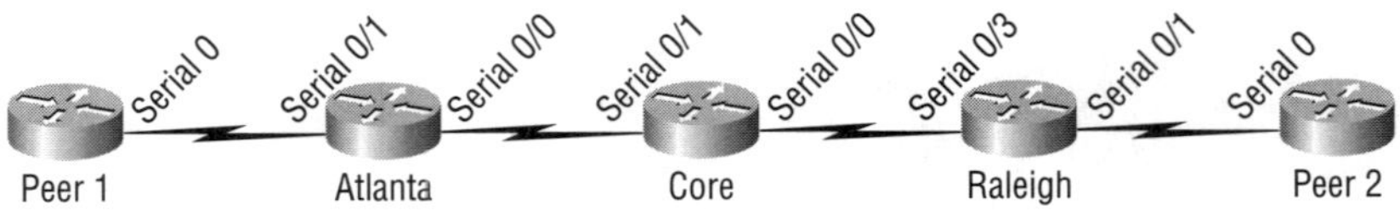

Figure B.2 illustrates the routing protocol utilization for the service provider network illustrated in Figure B.1.

FIGURE B.2 Network protocol utilization

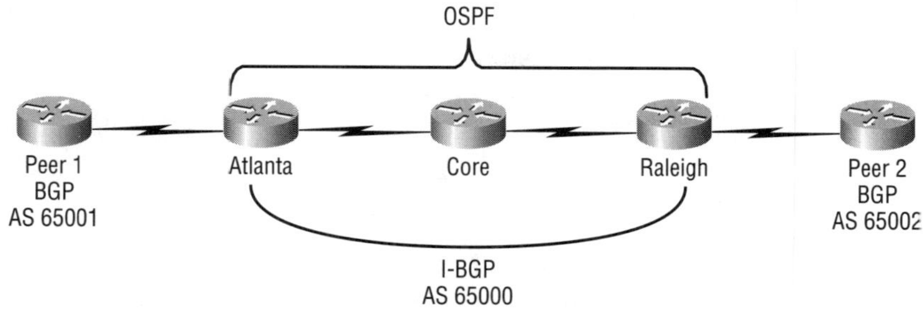

Table B.1 lists the IP addresses and interfaces of the CE devices in Figure B.1.

TABLE B.1 Customer Addressing

Device	Loopback 0	Serial 0
Peer 1	192.168.1.1/32	192.168.3.5/30
Peer 2	192.168.2.1/32	192.168.3.10/30

Table B.2 lists the IP addresses and interfaces of the service provider devices in Figure B.1.

TABLE B.2 Service Provider Addressing

Device	Loopback 0	Serial 0/0	Serial 0/1	Serial 0/3
Atlanta	204.134.83.1/32	204.134.83.5/30	192.168.3.6/30	N/A
Core	204.134.83.2/32	204.134.83.9/30	204.134.83.6/30	N/A
Raleigh	204.134.83.3/32	N/A	192.168.3.9/30	204.134.83.10/30

Router Configuration

This section shows the configuration of all the network devices. The peer routers run BGP, the Atlanta and Raleigh POP routers run OSPF and BGP, and the Core router runs only OSPF.

Peer 1 Router Configuration

On the Peer 1 router, MPLS is not enabled; only standard BGP is enabled.

```
Peer1#show running-config
Building configuration...

Current configuration : 914 bytes
!
version 12.1
service timestamps debug uptime
service timestamps log uptime
no service password-encryption
!
hostname Peer1
!
enable password cisco
!
!
!
!
!
ip subnet-zero
ip tcp synwait-time 5
no ip domain-lookup
!
!
!
!
interface Loopback0
 ip address 192.168.1.1 255.255.255.255
!
interface Ethernet0
 no ip address
 shutdown
!
```

```
interface Serial0
 description *** Link to Atlanta POP ***
 ip address 192.168.3.5 255.255.255.252
 no fair-queue
!
interface Serial1
 no ip address
 shutdown
!
router bgp 65001
 no synchronization
 bgp log-neighbor-changes
 redistribute connected
 neighbor 192.168.3.6 remote-as 65000
 no auto-summary
!
ip classless
no ip http server
!
!
line con 0
 exec-timeout 0 0
 privilege level 15
 logging synchronous
 transport input none
 ip netmask-format decimal
line aux 0
line vty 0 4
 privilege level 15
 password cisco
 logging synchronous
 login
 ip netmask-format decimal
!
end
```

Atlanta POP Router Configuration

On the Atlanta POP router, standard OPSF is configured as the IGP. I-BGP is set up between the Atlanta and Raleigh POP routers. An E-BGP session is set up between the Atlanta POP router and Peer 1. Tag switching is enabled only on the internal service provider link.

```
Atlanta#show running-config
Building configuration...

Current configuration : 1572 bytes
!
version 12.1
service timestamps debug uptime
service timestamps log uptime
no service password-encryption
!
hostname Atlanta
!
enable password cisco
!
!
!
!
!
memory-size iomem 25
ip subnet-zero
ip tcp synwait-time 5
no ip domain-lookup
!
ip cef
cns event-service server
!
!
!
!
!
```

```
interface Loopback0
 ip address 204.134.83.1 255.255.255.255
!
interface Serial0/0
 description *** Link to Core Router ***
 ip address 204.134.83.5 255.255.255.252
 tag-switching ip
 no fair-queue
 clockrate 64000
!
interface Serial0/1
 description *** Link to Peer1 ***
 ip address 192.168.3.6 255.255.255.252
 clockrate 64000
!
interface Serial0/2
 no ip address
 shutdown
 clockrate 64000
!
interface Serial0/3
 no ip address
 shutdown
 clockrate 64000
!
interface Ethernet1/0
 no ip address
 shutdown
!
interface Ethernet1/1
 no ip address
 shutdown
!
interface Ethernet1/2
 no ip address
 shutdown
!
```

```
interface Ethernet1/3
 no ip address
 shutdown
!
router ospf 1
 log-adjacency-changes
 network 204.134.83.1 0.0.0.0 area 0
 network 204.134.83.5 0.0.0.0 area 0
!
router bgp 65000
 no synchronization
 bgp log-neighbor-changes
 neighbor 192.168.3.5 remote-as 65001
 neighbor 204.134.83.3 remote-as 65000
 neighbor 204.134.83.3 update-source Loopback0
 neighbor 204.134.83.3 next-hop-self
 no auto-summary
!
ip classless
no ip http server
!
!
!
line con 0
 exec-timeout 0 0
 privilege level 15
 logging synchronous
 transport input none
 ip netmask-format decimal
line aux 0
line vty 0 4
 privilege level 15
 password cisco
 logging synchronous
 login
 ip netmask-format decimal
!
end
```

Core Router Configuration

On the Core router, standard OPSF is configured as the IGP. Tag switching is enabled on the two service provider links.

```
Core#show running-config
Building configuration...

Current configuration : 1353 bytes
!
version 12.1
service timestamps debug uptime
service timestamps log uptime
no service password-encryption
!
hostname Core
!
enable password cisco
!
!
!
!
!
memory-size iomem 25
ip subnet-zero
ip tcp synwait-time 5
no ip domain-lookup
!
ip cef
cns event-service server
!
!
!
!
!
interface Loopback0
 ip address 204.134.83.2 255.255.255.255
!
```

```
interface Serial0/0
 description *** Connection to Raleigh POP ***
 ip address 204.134.83.9 255.255.255.252
 tag-switching ip
 no fair-queue
!
interface Serial0/1
 description *** Connection to Atlanta POP ***
 ip address 204.134.83.6 255.255.255.252
 tag-switching ip
!
interface Serial0/2
 no ip address
 shutdown
!
interface Serial0/3
 no ip address
 shutdown
!
interface Ethernet1/0
 no ip address
 shutdown
!
interface Ethernet1/1
 no ip address
 shutdown
!
interface Ethernet1/2
 no ip address
 shutdown
!
interface Ethernet1/3
 no ip address
 shutdown
!
```

```
router ospf 1
 log-adjacency-changes
 network 204.134.83.2 0.0.0.0 area 0
 network 204.134.83.6 0.0.0.0 area 0
 network 204.134.83.9 0.0.0.0 area 0
!
ip classless
no ip http server
!
!
!
line con 0
 exec-timeout 0 0
 privilege level 15
 logging synchronous
 transport input none
 ip netmask-format decimal
line aux 0
line vty 0 4
 privilege level 15
 password cisco
 logging synchronous
 login
 ip netmask-format decimal
!
end
```

Raleigh POP Router Configuration

On the Raleigh POP router, standard OPSF is configured as the IGP I-BGP is set up between the Raleigh and Atlanta POP routers. An E-BGP session is set up between the Raleigh POP and Peer2. Tag switching is enabled only on the internal service provider link.

```
Raleigh#show running-config
Building configuration...
```

```
Current configuration : 1599 bytes
!
version 12.1
service timestamps debug uptime
service timestamps log uptime
no service password-encryption
!
hostname Raleigh
!
enable password cisco
!
!
!
!
!
memory-size iomem 25
ip subnet-zero
ip tcp synwait-time 5
no ip domain-lookup
!
ip cef
cns event-service server
!
!
!
!
!
interface Loopback0
 ip address 204.134.83.3 255.255.255.255
!
interface Serial0/0
 no ip address
 shutdown
 no fair-queue
 clockrate 64000
!
```

```
interface Serial0/1
 description *** Link to Peer2 ***
 ip address 192.168.3.9 255.255.255.252
 clockrate 64000
!
interface Serial0/2
 no ip address
 shutdown
 clockrate 64000
!
interface Serial0/3
 description *** Link to Core Router ***
 ip address 204.134.83.10 255.255.255.252
 tag-switching ip
 clockrate 64000
!
interface Ethernet1/0
 no ip address
 shutdown
!
interface Ethernet1/1
 no ip address
 shutdown
!
interface Ethernet1/2
 no ip address
 shutdown
!
interface Ethernet1/3
 no ip address
 shutdown
!
router ospf 1
 log-adjacency-changes
 network 204.134.83.3 0.0.0.0 area 0
 network 204.134.83.10 0.0.0.0 area 0
!
```

```
router bgp 65000
 no synchronization
 bgp log-neighbor-changes
 neighbor 192.168.3.10 remote-as 65002
 neighbor 204.134.83.1 remote-as 65000
 neighbor 204.134.83.1 update-source Loopback0
 neighbor 204.134.83.1 next-hop-self
 no auto-summary
!
ip classless
no ip http server
!
!
!
line con 0
 exec-timeout 0 0
 privilege level 15
 logging synchronous
 transport input none
 ip netmask-format decimal
line aux 0
line vty 0 4
 privilege level 15
 password cisco
 logging synchronous
 login
 ip netmask-format decimal
!
end
```

Peer 2 Router Configuration

On the Peer 2 router, MPLS is not enabled; only standard BGP is enabled.

```
Peer2#show running-config
Building configuration...
```

```
Current configuration : 951 bytes
!
version 12.1
service timestamps debug uptime
service timestamps log uptime
no service password-encryption
!
hostname Peer2
!
enable password cisco
!
!
!
!
!
ip subnet-zero
ip tcp synwait-time 5
no ip domain-lookup
!
!
!
!
interface Loopback0
 ip address 192.168.2.1 255.255.255.255
!
interface Ethernet0
 no ip address
 shutdown
!
interface Serial0
 description *** Link to Raleigh POP ***
 ip address 192.168.3.10 255.255.255.252
 no fair-queue
!
interface Serial1
 no ip address
 shutdown
!
```

```
router bgp 65002
 no synchronization
 bgp log-neighbor-changes
 redistribute connected
 neighbor 192.168.3.9 remote-as 65000
 no auto-summary
!
ip classless

no ip http server
!
!
line con 0
 exec-timeout 0 0
 privilege level 15
 logging synchronous
 transport input none
 ip netmask-format decimal
line aux 0
line vty 0 4
 privilege level 15
 password cisco
 logging synchronous
 login
 ip netmask-format decimal
!
end
```

Routing Tables

This section shows you the routing tables of each network device in the example network. Notice that the Core router has no knowledge of the peer router subnets and the peer routers have no knowledge of the core service provider networks. The Atlanta and Raleigh POP routers have full knowledge of all the subnets in the network.

Peer 1 Routing Table

On the Peer 1 router, internal service provider routes do not show up in the routing table:

```
 Peer1#show ip route
.
. Output Omitted
.
Gateway of last resort is not set

     192.168.1.0 255.255.255.255 is subnetted, 1 subnets
C       192.168.1.1 is directly connected, Loopback0
     192.168.2.0 255.255.255.255 is subnetted, 1 subnets
B       192.168.2.1 [20/0] via 192.168.3.6, 00:08:15
     192.168.3.0 255.255.255.252 is subnetted, 2 subnets
B       192.168.3.8 [20/0] via 192.168.3.6, 00:08:15
C       192.168.3.4 is directly connected, Serial0
```

Atlanta Routing Table

On the Atlanta POP router, all routes (both peer and service provider) are displayed in the routing table:

```
Atlanta#show ip route
.
. Output Omitted
.
Gateway of last resort is not set

     204.134.83.0 255.255.255.0 is variably subnetted, 5
        subnets, 2 masks
O       204.134.83.8 255.255.255.252
          [110/1562] via 204.134.83.6, 00:10:08, Serial0/0
C       204.134.83.1 255.255.255.255 is directly
   connected, Loopback0
O       204.134.83.3 255.255.255.255
          [110/1563] via 204.134.83.6, 00:10:08, Serial0/0
```

```
O       204.134.83.2 255.255.255.255
         [110/782] via 204.134.83.6, 00:10:08, Serial0/0
C       204.134.83.4 255.255.255.252 is directly
  connected, Serial0/0
     192.168.1.0 255.255.255.255 is subnetted, 1 subnets
B       192.168.1.1 [20/0] via 192.168.3.5, 00:22:47
     192.168.2.0 255.255.255.255 is subnetted, 1 subnets
B       192.168.2.1 [200/0] via 204.134.83.3, 00:09:24
     192.168.3.0 255.255.255.252 is subnetted, 2 subnets
B       192.168.3.8 [200/0] via 204.134.83.3, 00:09:24
C       192.168.3.4 is directly connected, Serial0/1
```

Core Routing Table

On the Core router, only internal service provider routes show up in the routing table:

```
Core#show ip route
.
. Output Omitted
.
Gateway of last resort is not set

     204.134.83.0 255.255.255.0 is variably subnetted, 5
        subnets, 2 masks
C       204.134.83.8 255.255.255.252 is directly
  connected, Serial0/0
O       204.134.83.1 255.255.255.255
         [110/782] via 204.134.83.5, 00:10:51, Serial0/1
O       204.134.83.3 255.255.255.255
         [110/782] via 204.134.83.10, 00:10:51, Serial0/0
C       204.134.83.2 255.255.255.255 is directly
  connected, Loopback0
C       204.134.83.4 255.255.255.252 is directly
  connected, Serial0/1
```

Raleigh Routing Table

On the Raleigh POP router, both service provider and peer routers are displayed in the routing table:

```
Raleigh#show ip route
.
. Output Omitted
.
Gateway of last resort is not set

     204.134.83.0 255.255.255.0 is variably subnetted,
       5 subnets, 2 masks
C       204.134.83.8 255.255.255.252 is directly
  connected, Serial0/3
O       204.134.83.1 255.255.255.255
          [110/1563] via 204.134.83.9, 00:11:17, Serial0/3
C       204.134.83.3 255.255.255.255 is directly
  connected, Loopback0
O       204.134.83.2 255.255.255.255
          [110/782] via 204.134.83.9, 00:11:17, Serial0/3
O       204.134.83.4 255.255.255.252
          [110/1562] via 204.134.83.9, 00:11:17, Serial0/3
     192.168.1.0 255.255.255.255 is subnetted, 1 subnets
B       192.168.1.1 [200/0] via 204.134.83.1, 00:10:33
     192.168.2.0 255.255.255.255 is subnetted, 1 subnets
B       192.168.2.1 [20/0] via 192.168.3.10, 00:24:05
     192.168.3.0 255.255.255.252 is subnetted, 2 subnets
C       192.168.3.8 is directly connected, Serial0/1
B       192.168.3.4 [200/0] via 204.134.83.1, 00:10:34
```

Peer 2 Routing Table

On the Peer 2 router, no service provider routes are displayed in the routing table:

```
Peer2#show ip route
.
. Output Omitted
.
```

```
Gateway of last resort is not set
     192.168.1.0 255.255.255.255 is subnetted, 1 subnets
B       192.168.1.1 [20/0] via 192.168.3.9, 00:11:45
     192.168.2.0 255.255.255.255 is subnetted, 1 subnets
C       192.168.2.1 is directly connected, Loopback0
     192.168.3.0 255.255.255.252 is subnetted, 2 subnets
C       192.168.3.8 is directly connected, Serial0
B       192.168.3.4 [20/0] via 192.168.3.9, 00:11:45
```

Tags

In this section, the mapping of tags to IP prefixes shows that a complete LSP exists between the loopback addresses on the Atlanta and Raleigh POP routers. With an end-to-end LSP, the Core router only needs to examine the label, and therefore does not require full knowledge of the peer subnets.

Atlanta POP Forwarding Table

In the following output from the Atlanta POP router, you can see that a full LSP exists between the Atlanta and Raleigh POP routers:

```
Atlanta#show tag-switching forwarding-table
Local Outgoing Prefix             Bytes tag    Outgoing   Next Hop
tag   tag or VC or Tunnel Id      switched     interface
26    Pop tag   204.134.83.2 255.255.255.255 0  Se0/0      point2point
27    26        204.134.83.3 255.255.255.255 0  Se0/0      point2point
28    Pop tag   204.134.83.8 255.255.255.252 0  Se0/0      point2point
```

Core Forwarding Table

On the Core router, labeled packets between the Atlanta and Raleigh POP routers will be label-switched, as indicated in the forwarding table:

```
Core#show tag-switching forwarding-table
Local Outgoing Prefix             Bytes tag       Outgoing  Next Hop
tag   tag or VC or Tunnel Id      switched        interface
26    Pop tag   204.134.83.3 255.255.255.255 1753  Se0/0     point2point
27    Pop tag   204.134.83.1 255.255.255.255 1812  Se0/1     point2point
```

Raleigh POP Forwarding Table

In the following output from the Raleigh POP router's forwarding table, you can see that a full LSP exists between the Raleigh and Atlanta POP routers:

```
Raleigh#show tag-switching forwarding-table
Local Outgoing  Prefix            Bytes tag     Outgoing   Next Hop
tag   tag or VC or Tunnel Id      switched      interface
26    Pop tag   204.134.83.2 255.255.255.255 0  Se0/3      point2point
27    Pop tag   204.134.83.4 255.255.255.252 0  Se0/3      point2point
28    27        204.134.83.1 255.255.255.255 0  Se0/3      point2point
```

Service Provider Network Configuration with IS-IS

In this section, a sample network is configured with BGP between the PE and CE routers. IS-IS is configured as the service provider IGP. Figure B.3 illustrates this network.

FIGURE B.3 A service provider network to be configured with IS-IS

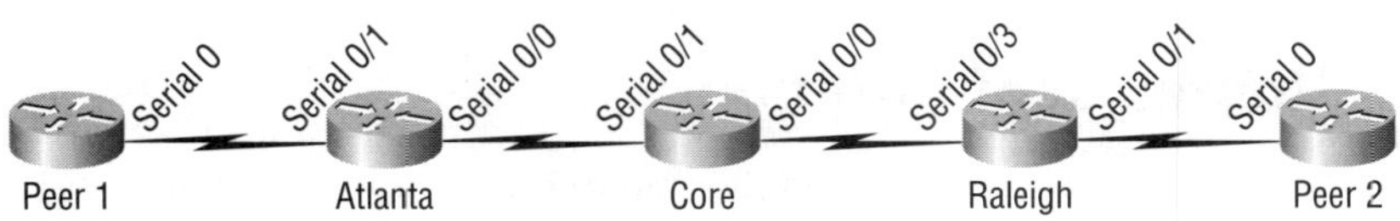

Figure B.4 illustrates the routing protocol utilization in the service provider network illustrated in Figure B.3.

FIGURE B.4 Network protocol utilization

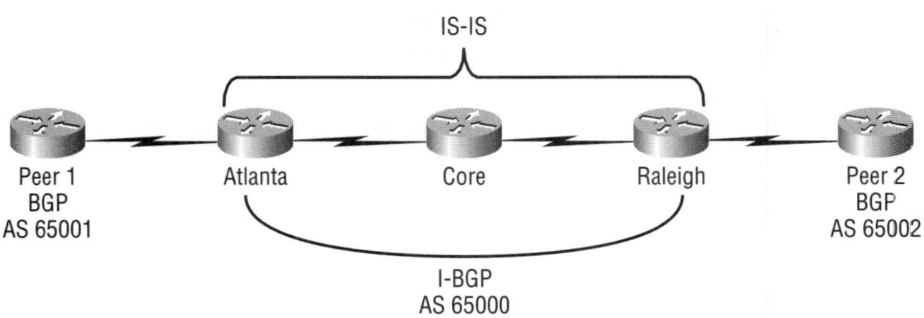

Table B.3 lists the IP addresses and interfaces of the CE devices in Figure B.3.

TABLE B.3 Customer Addressing

Device	Loopback 0	Serial 0
Peer 1	192.168.1.1/32	192.168.3.5/30
Peer 2	192.168.2.1/32	192.168.3.10/30

Table B.4 lists the IP addresses and interfaces of the service provider devices in Figure B.3.

TABLE B.4 Service Provider Addressing

Device	Loopback 0	Serial 0/0	Serial 0/1	Serial 0/3
Atlanta	204.134.83.1/32	204.134.83.5/30	192.168.3.6/30	N/A
Core	204.134.83.2/32	204.134.83.9/30	204.134.83.6/30	N/A
Raleigh	204.134.83.3/32	N/A	192.168.3.9/30	204.134.83.10/30

Router Configuration

This section shows the configuration of all the network devices in the example network. The peer routers run BGP, the Atlanta and Raleigh POP routers run OSPF and BGP, and the Core router runs only OSPF.

Peer 1 Router Configuration

On the Peer 1 router, MPLS is not enabled; only standard BGP is enabled.

```
Peer1#show running-config
Building configuration...

Current configuration : 914 bytes
!
```

```
version 12.1
service timestamps debug uptime
service timestamps log uptime
no service password-encryption
!
hostname Peer1
!
enable password cisco
!
!
!
!
!
ip subnet-zero
ip tcp synwait-time 5
no ip domain-lookup
!
!
!
!
interface Loopback0
 ip address 192.168.1.1 255.255.255.255
!
interface Ethernet0
 no ip address
 shutdown
!
interface Serial0
 description *** Link to Atlanta POP ***
 ip address 192.168.3.5 255.255.255.252
 no fair-queue
!
interface Serial1
 no ip address
 shutdown
!
```

```
router bgp 65001
 no synchronization
 bgp log-neighbor-changes
 redistribute connected
 neighbor 192.168.3.6 remote-as 65000
 no auto-summary
!
ip classless
no ip http server
!
!
line con 0
 exec-timeout 0 0
 privilege level 15
 logging synchronous
 transport input none
 ip netmask-format decimal
line aux 0
line vty 0 4
 privilege level 15
 password cisco
 logging synchronous
 login
 ip netmask-format decimal
!
end
```

Atlanta POP Router Configuration

On the Atlanta POP router, standard IS-IS is configured as the IGP. I-BGP is set up between the Atlanta and Raleigh POP routers. An E-BGP session is set up between the Atlanta POP router and Peer 1. Tag switching is enabled only on the internal service provider link.

```
Atlanta#show running-config
Building configuration...

Current configuration : 1556 bytes
!
```

```
version 12.1
service timestamps debug uptime
service timestamps log uptime
no service password-encryption
!
hostname Atlanta
!
enable password cisco
!
!
!
!
!
memory-size iomem 25
ip subnet-zero
ip tcp synwait-time 5
no ip domain-lookup
!
ip cef
cns event-service server
!
!
!
!
!
interface Loopback0
 ip address 204.134.83.1 255.255.255.255
 ip router isis
!
interface Serial0/0
 description *** Link to Core Router ***
 ip address 204.134.83.5 255.255.255.252
 ip router isis
 tag-switching ip
 no fair-queue
 clockrate 64000
!
```

```
interface Serial0/1
 description *** Link to Peer1 ***
 ip address 192.168.3.6 255.255.255.252
 clockrate 64000
!
interface Serial0/2
 no ip address
 shutdown
 clockrate 64000
!
interface Serial0/3
 no ip address
 shutdown
 clockrate 64000
!
interface Ethernet1/0
 no ip address
 shutdown
!
interface Ethernet1/1
 no ip address
 shutdown
!
interface Ethernet1/2
 no ip address
 shutdown
!
interface Ethernet1/3
 no ip address
 shutdown
!
router isis
 net 49.0001.1111.1111.1111.00
 is-type level-1
!
```

```
router bgp 65000
 no synchronization
 bgp log-neighbor-changes
 neighbor 192.168.3.5 remote-as 65001
 neighbor 204.134.83.3 remote-as 65000
 neighbor 204.134.83.3 update-source Loopback0
 neighbor 204.134.83.3 next-hop-self
 no auto-summary
!
ip classless
no ip http server
!
!
!
line con 0
 exec-timeout 0 0
 privilege level 15
 logging synchronous
 transport input none
 ip netmask-format decimal
line aux 0
line vty 0 4
 privilege level 15
 password cisco
 logging synchronous
 login
 ip netmask-format decimal
!
end
```

Core Router Configuration

On the Core router, standard IS-IS is configured as the IGP. Tag switching is enabled on the two service provider links.

```
Core#show running-config
Building configuration...

Current configuration : 1317 bytes
!
```

```
version 12.1
service timestamps debug uptime
service timestamps log uptime
no service password-encryption
!
hostname Core
!
enable password cisco
!
!
!
!
!
memory-size iomem 25
ip subnet-zero
ip tcp synwait-time 5
no ip domain-lookup
!
ip cef
cns event-service server
!
!
!
!
!
interface Loopback0
 ip address 204.134.83.2 255.255.255.255
 ip router isis
!
interface Serial0/0
 description *** Connection to Raleigh POP ***
 ip address 204.134.83.9 255.255.255.252
 ip router isis
 tag-switching ip
 no fair-queue
!
```

```
interface Serial0/1
 description *** Connection to Atlanta POP ***
 ip address 204.134.83.6 255.255.255.252
 ip router isis
 tag-switching ip
!
interface Serial0/2
 no ip address
 shutdown
!
interface Serial0/3
 no ip address
 shutdown
!
interface Ethernet1/0
 no ip address
 shutdown
!
interface Ethernet1/1
 no ip address
 shutdown
!
interface Ethernet1/2
 no ip address
 shutdown
!
interface Ethernet1/3
 no ip address
 shutdown
!
router isis
 net 49.0001.2222.2222.2222.00
 is-type level-1
!
ip classless
```

```
no ip http server
!
!
!
line con 0
 exec-timeout 0 0
 privilege level 15
 logging synchronous
 transport input none
 ip netmask-format decimal
line aux 0
line vty 0 4
 privilege level 15
 password cisco
 logging synchronous
 login
 ip netmask-format decimal
!
end
```

Raleigh POP Router Configuration

On the Raleigh POP router, standard IS-IS is configured as the IGP. I-BGP is set up between the Raleigh and Atlanta POP routers. An E-BGP session is set up between the Raleigh POP router and Peer 2. Tag switching is enabled only on the internal service provider link.

```
Raleigh#show running-config
Building configuration...

Current configuration : 1582 bytes
!
version 12.1
service timestamps debug uptime
service timestamps log uptime
no service password-encryption
!
```

```
hostname Raleigh
!
enable password cisco
!
!
!
!
!
memory-size iomem 25
ip subnet-zero
ip tcp synwait-time 5
no ip domain-lookup
!
ip cef
cns event-service server
!
!
!
!
!
interface Loopback0
 ip address 204.134.83.3 255.255.255.255
 ip router isis
!
interface Serial0/0
 no ip address
 shutdown
 no fair-queue
 clockrate 64000
!
interface Serial0/1
 description *** Link to Peer2 ***
 ip address 192.168.3.9 255.255.255.252
 clockrate 64000
!
```

```
interface Serial0/2
 no ip address
 shutdown
 clockrate 64000
!
interface Serial0/3
 description *** Link to Core Router ***
 ip address 204.134.83.10 255.255.255.252
 ip router isis
 tag-switching ip
 clockrate 64000
!
interface Ethernet1/0

 no ip address
 shutdown
!
interface Ethernet1/1
 no ip address
 shutdown
!
interface Ethernet1/2
 no ip address
 shutdown
!
interface Ethernet1/3
 no ip address
 shutdown
!
router isis
 net 49.0001.3333.3333.3333.00
 is-type level-1
!
router bgp 65000
 no synchronization
 bgp log-neighbor-changes
```

```
 neighbor 192.168.3.10 remote-as 65002
 neighbor 204.134.83.1 remote-as 65000
 neighbor 204.134.83.1 update-source Loopback0
 neighbor 204.134.83.1 next-hop-self
 no auto-summary
!
ip classless
no ip http server
!
!
!
line con 0
 exec-timeout 0 0
 privilege level 15
 logging synchronous
 transport input none
 ip netmask-format decimal
line aux 0
line vty 0 4
 privilege level 15
 password cisco
 logging synchronous
 login
 ip netmask-format decimal
!
end
```

Peer 2 Router Configuration

On the Peer 2 router, MPLS is not enabled; only standard BGP is enabled.

```
Peer2#show running-config
Building configuration...

Current configuration : 951 bytes
!
```

```
version 12.1
service timestamps debug uptime
service timestamps log uptime
no service password-encryption
!
hostname Peer2
!
enable password cisco
!
!
!
!
!
ip subnet-zero
ip tcp synwait-time 5
no ip domain-lookup
!
!
!
!
interface Loopback0
 ip address 192.168.2.1 255.255.255.255
!
interface Ethernet0
 no ip address
 shutdown
!
interface Serial0
 description *** Link to Raleigh POP ***
 ip address 192.168.3.10 255.255.255.252
 no fair-queue
!
interface Serial1
 no ip address
 shutdown
!
```

```
router bgp 65002
 no synchronization
 bgp log-neighbor-changes
 redistribute connected
 neighbor 192.168.3.9 remote-as 65000
 no auto-summary
!
ip classless

no ip http server
!
!
line con 0
 exec-timeout 0 0
 privilege level 15
 logging synchronous
 transport input none
 ip netmask-format decimal
line aux 0
line vty 0 4
 privilege level 15
 password cisco
 logging synchronous
 login
 ip netmask-format decimal
!
end
```

Routing Tables

This section shows the routing tables of each network device in the example network. Notice that the Core router has no knowledge of the peer router subnets, and the peer routers have no knowledge of the core service provider networks. The Atlanta and Raleigh POP routers have full knowledge of all the subnets in the network.

Peer 1 Routing Table

On the Peer 1 router, no service provider routes are displayed in the routing table:

```
Peer1#show ip route
.
. Output Omitted
.
Gateway of last resort is not set

     192.168.1.0 255.255.255.255 is subnetted, 1 subnets
C       192.168.1.1 is directly connected, Loopback0
     192.168.2.0 255.255.255.255 is subnetted, 1 subnets
B       192.168.2.1 [20/0] via 192.168.3.6, 00:04:31
     192.168.3.0 255.255.255.252 is subnetted, 2 subnets
B       192.168.3.8 [20/0] via 192.168.3.6, 00:04:31
C       192.168.3.4 is directly connected, Serial0
```

Atlanta Routing Table

The Atlanta POP router, running BGP and IS-IS, has knowledge of peer and service provider routes:

```
Atlanta#show ip route
.
. Output Omitted
.
Gateway of last resort is not set

     204.134.83.0 255.255.255.0 is variably subnetted,
       5 subnets, 2 masks
i L1    204.134.83.8 255.255.255.252 [115/20] via
  204.134.83.6, Serial0/0
C       204.134.83.1 255.255.255.255 is directly
  connected, Loopback0
i L1    204.134.83.3 255.255.255.255 [115/30] via
  204.134.83.6, Serial0/0
```

```
i L1    204.134.83.2 255.255.255.255 [115/20] via
  204.134.83.6, Serial0/0
C       204.134.83.4 255.255.255.252 is directly
  connected, Serial0/0
     192.168.1.0 255.255.255.255 is subnetted, 1 subnets
B       192.168.1.1 [20/0] via 192.168.3.5, 00:53:19
     192.168.2.0 255.255.255.255 is subnetted, 1 subnets
B       192.168.2.1 [200/0] via 204.134.83.3, 00:04:51
     192.168.3.0 255.255.255.252 is subnetted, 2 subnets
B       192.168.3.8 [200/0] via 204.134.83.3, 00:04:51
C       192.168.3.4 is directly connected, Serial0/1
```

Core Routing Table

The Core router, only enabled with IS-IS, has only internal service provider routes in its routing table:

```
Core#show ip route
.
. Output Omitted
.
Gateway of last resort is not set

     204.134.83.0 255.255.255.0 is variably subnetted,
       5 subnets, 2 masks
C       204.134.83.8 255.255.255.252 is directly
  connected, Serial0/0
i L1    204.134.83.1 255.255.255.255 [115/20] via
  204.134.83.5, Serial0/1
i L1    204.134.83.3 255.255.255.255 [115/20] via
  204.134.83.10, Serial0/0
C       204.134.83.2 255.255.255.255 is directly
  connected, Loopback0
C       204.134.83.4 255.255.255.252 is directly
  connected, Serial0/1
```

Raleigh Routing Table

The Raleigh POP router, running both BGP and IS-IS, has knowledge of peer and service provider routes:

```
Raleigh#show ip route
.
. Output Omitted
.
Gateway of last resort is not set

     204.134.83.0 255.255.255.0 is variably subnetted,
       5 subnets, 2 masks
C       204.134.83.8 255.255.255.252 is directly
  connected, Serial0/3
i L1    204.134.83.1 255.255.255.255 [115/30] via
  204.134.83.9, Serial0/3
C       204.134.83.3 255.255.255.255 is directly
  connected, Loopback0
i L1    204.134.83.2 255.255.255.255 [115/20] via
  204.134.83.9, Serial0/3
i L1    204.134.83.4 255.255.255.252 [115/20] via
  204.134.83.9, Serial0/3
     192.168.1.0 255.255.255.255 is subnetted, 1 subnets
B       192.168.1.1 [200/0] via 204.134.83.1, 00:05:27
     192.168.2.0 255.255.255.255 is subnetted, 1 subnets
B       192.168.2.1 [20/0] via 192.168.3.10, 00:54:04
     192.168.3.0 255.255.255.252 is subnetted, 2 subnets
C       192.168.3.8 is directly connected, Serial0/1
B       192.168.3.4 [200/0] via 204.134.83.1, 00:05:27
```

Peer 2 Routing Table

The Peer 2 router does not have any knowledge of service provider routes:

```
Peer2#show ip route
.
. Output Omitted
.
```

```
Gateway of last resort is not set

     192.168.1.0 255.255.255.255 is subnetted, 1 subnets
B       192.168.1.1 [20/0] via 192.168.3.9, 00:05:43
     192.168.2.0 255.255.255.255 is subnetted, 1 subnets
C       192.168.2.1 is directly connected, Loopback0
     192.168.3.0 255.255.255.252 is subnetted, 2 subnets
C       192.168.3.8 is directly connected, Serial0
B       192.168.3.4 [20/0] via 192.168.3.9, 00:05:43
```

Tag Switching Forwarding Tables

In this section, the mapping of tags to IP prefixes shows that a complete LSP exists between the loopback addresses on the Atlanta and Raleigh POP routers. With an end-to-end LSP, the Core router only needs to examine the label, and therefore does not require full knowledge of the peer subnets.

Atlanta POP Router Forwarding Table

The Atlanta POP router will label-switch packets to the Raleigh POP router, as you can see in its forwarding table:

```
Atlanta#show tag-switching forwarding-table
Local Outgoing Prefix             Bytes tag    Outgoing    Next Hop
tag   tag or VC or Tunnel Id      switched     interface
26    Untagged 204.134.83.2 255.255.255.255 0  Se0/0       point2point
27    26       204.134.83.3 255.255.255.255 0  Se0/0       point2point
28    Untagged 204.134.83.8 255.255.255.252 0  Se0/0       point2point
```

Core POP Router Forwarding Table

The Core router will label-switch labeled packets between the POP routers, as you can see in its forwarding table:

```
Core#show tag-switching forwarding-table
Local Outgoing  Prefix             Bytes tag        Outgoing    Next Hop
tag   tag or VC or Tunnel Id       switched         interface
26    Untagged  204.134.83.3 255.255.255.255 1417   Se0/0       point2point
27    Untagged  204.134.83.1 255.255.255.255 321    Se0/1       point2point
```

Raleigh POP Router Forwarding Table

The Raleigh POP router will send labeled packets to the Atlanta POP router, as you can see in its forwarding table:

```
Raleigh#show tag-switching forwarding-table
Local Outgoing  Prefix            Bytes tag     Outgoing   Next Hop
tag   tag or VC or Tunnel Id      switched      interface
26    Untagged  204.134.83.4 255.255.255.252 0  Se0/3      point2point
27    Untagged  204.134.83.2 255.255.255.255 0  Se0/3      point2point
28    27        204.134.83.1 255.255.255.255 0  Se0/3      point2point
```

Glossary

A

ABR See *area border router.*

address-family A sub-configuration command allowing for MPLS-specific configuration in BGP and RIPv2.

area border router (ABR) An OSPF router that has interfaces configured for two or more areas.

ASBR See *autonomous system boundary router.*

ATM label switch router (ATM-LSR) An ATM switch that is capable of forwarding packets based on labels.

ATM-LSR See *ATM label switch router.*

ATM-LSR domain A series of ATM-LSRs connected together with LC-ATM interfaces.

autonomous system boundary router (ASBR) An OSPF router that has at least one interface in the OSPF domain and one interface connecting to an external network.

B

backbone are The OSPF Area 0.

backbone router An OSPF router that has at least one interface in Area 0.

C

CEF See *Cisco Express Forwarding.*

Central Services MPLS VPN topology A Central Services MPLS VPN topology is a network where there is some central service, such as data storage facilities or media content, that is being accessed by different sites. These different sites have no access to each other, only to the central service site.

Cisco Express Forwarding (CEF) CEF creates an optimized, "cached" version of the routing table. CEF is a requirement for MPLS and tag switching.

control plane A component of the MPLS architecture that is responsible for binding a label to network routes and distributing those bindings among other MPLS-enabled routers.

D

data plane A component of the MPLS architecture where information that is created and maintained from the control plane is actually used. Also known as the *forwarding plane*.

dedicated router In a peer-to-peer VPN, a dedicated router is a service provider router that is connected to a single customer.

down bit The down bit is used to prevent routing loops between customer routes and the service provider OSPF super-backbone. When a route is redistributed from MP-IBGP into OSPF, the down bit is set in the Options field of the OSPF LSA header. Another PE router, receiving an LSA with the down bit set, does not redistribute the route into MP-IBGP.

downstream A term used when discussing MPLS label binding. Downstream refers to an originating or neighboring router that advertises a route.

downstream-on-demand Downstream-on-demand occurs when an upstream LSR, using the Label Request message, requests a label from its downstream neighbor.

E

edge label switch router (edge-LSR) An edge router that is also an LSR.

edge-LSR See *edge label switch router*.

egress router An edge router where packets leave the network.

export route target An export route target is applied by a PE router when VRF routes are redistributed into MP-BGP.

extranet A VPN category where sites from different companies are connected together.

F

FEC See *forwarding equivalence class.*

FIB See *forwarding information base.*

forwarding equivalence class (FEC) An FEC is a grouping of IP packets that are all treated the same way. For unicast-based routing, an IP prefix is the equivalent of an FEC.

forwarding information base (FIB) A FIB is essentially a cached version of the IP routing table that eliminates the need for a route-cache.

forwarding plane A component of the MPLS architecture where information that is created and maintained from the control plane is actually used. Also known as the *data plane.*

full-mesh topology A VPN topology where each site has a connection to every other site.

H

hub-and-spoke topology A VPN topology where spoke sites are all connected to a central hub site but not to each other.

I

import route target Used by a PE router to select, in conjunction with redistribution, which routes from MP-BGP to redistribute into a particular VRF.

independent control Independent control means to immediately bind a label to an FEC.

ingress router An edge router where packets enter the network.

internal router An OSPF router that has all configured interfaces in the same OSPF area.

intranet A class of VPNs where all connected sites are associated with the same company.

L

Label Distribution Protocol (LDP) The Label Distribution Protocol (LDP) is the IETF version of Cisco's TDP. LDP is used to bind labels to network routes.

label forwarding information base (LFIB) The LIB is built in the control plane, and only those labels in use reside in the LFIB. The LFIB is a subset of the LIB.

label imposition The point in the transit of a packet through a service provider network where the label is applied by a router and used by subsequent devices to label-switch the packet.

label information base (LIB) A mapping of incoming labels to outbound labels, along with outbound interface and link information.

label stacking An MPLS feature where more than one label can be carried. Label stacking is useful for applications such as traffic engineering and VPNs.

label switch controller (LSC) An external controller that, when added to an ATM switch, enables the switch to exchange routes and labels with its neighbors.

label-switched path (LSP) A unidirectional set of LSRs that the labeled packet must flow through to get to a particular destination.

label switch router (LSR) A router that is capable of forwarding packets based on MPLS labels.

LC-ATM A label-switching-controlled ATM interface where the VPI/VCI is assigned through MPLS or tag switching (LDP or TDP).

LDP See *Label Distribution Protocol.*

leased lines A dedicated private link through a service provider network. See also *point-to-point connection.*

LFIB See *label forwarding information base.*

LIB See *label information base.*

link state advertisement (LSA) Advertisements used by OSPF to exchange routing information with other OSPF-enabled routers.

LSA See *link state advertisement.*

LSC See *label switch controller.*

LSP See *label-switched path.*

LSR See *label switch router.*

M

MP-BGP See *Multi-Protocol BGP.*

MP-BGP backbone When Multi-Protocol BGP is deployed through a service provider network, the service provider backbone is referred to as the MP-BGP backbone.

MPLS See *Multi-Protocol Label Switching.*

MPLS label stack Another way of referring to the MPLS label or to a stack of MPLS labels.

MPLS VPN A VPN made possible with MPLS.

Multi-Protocol BGP (MP-BGP) An expanded BGP that has extensions used to carry MPLS-specific attributes through a network.

Multi-Protocol Label Switching (MPLS) A technology where labels are used to switch packets instead of route them. MPLS, as a technology, evolved from early attempts to glue the IP world and ATM world together. What we know as MPLS today is, for the most part, a standardized version of Cisco's proprietary tag switching.

N

Network Layer Reachability Information (NLRI) A way of referring to an IP prefix in BGP.

NLRI See *Network Layer Reachability Information.*

O

optimal routing Optimal routing is the process of a router selecting the best path for sending traffic.

ordered control Ordered control occurs when an upstream LSR must wait on a label to be received from its downstream LSR. Ordered control takes longer to set up a label-switched path (LSP) and is used by MPLS-enabled ATM label switch routers (ATM-LSRs).

OSPF domain A set of OSPF routers belonging to the same autonomous system.

OSPF super-backbone When running OSPF in an MPLS VPN, the service provider MP-BGP backbone is the OSPF super-backbone. The OSPF super-backbone eliminates the OSPF Area 0 requirement.

overlay A type of connection that uses an underlying technology to facilitate connections.

overlay MPLS VPN topology An MPLS VPN topology where a site participates in more than one MPLS VPN.

P

partial-mesh topology A VPN topology where some sites are connected to all other sites and some sites do not connect to every other site.

peer-to-peer VPNs A type of VPN where customer routers connect to service provider routers instead of having virtual circuits between sites.

penultimate hop popping A process by which the next-to-last router in an LSP removes a label and forwards it as unlabeled IP.

point-to-point connections A dedicated private link through a service provider network. See also *leased lines*.

popping The process of removing the MPLS label.

pushing The process of applying the MPLS label.

R

RD See *route distinguisher*.

redistribution The process of importing routes from another routing protocol or process.

redundant hub-and-spoke topology A VPN topology where spoke sites have more than one connection to a central site. The redundant hub-and-spoke topology usually uses more than one service provider for spoke site connectivity.

route distinguisher (RD) A 64-bit value that is used to keep possibly overlapping address from actually doing so in MP-IBGP.

routing bit A Cisco IOS mechanism used to ensure proper path selection. When a route is received by a PE with the down bit set, the routing bit is cleared. With the routing bit cleared, the route never shows up in the routing table of the PE, even if it is the best route as determined by OSPF.

routing context A VRF-specific set of configurations for a routing protocol.

S

shared router In a peer-to-peer VPN, a shared router is a service provider router that is connected to by different customers.

shim header Another way of referring to the MPLS label.

simple MPLS VPN topology An MPLS VPN where all sites are part of the same single MPLS VPN.

static routes Manually configured non-dynamic routes. In MPLS, static routes must always have the outbound interface specified. The next hop IP address is optional.

T

Tag Distribution Protocol (TDP) Cisco's proprietary protocol that is used to bind tags (which are the same as MPLS labels) to network routes in the routing table.

tag field A field, not used by the OSPF protocol, that the service provider AS number is mapped into. The mapping of the AS number into the tag field is used to prevent routing loops.

tag switching router (TSR) A router capable of switching packets based on tags instead of routing them.

TDP See *Tag Distribution Protocol*.

TLV See *Type-Length-Value*.

traffic engineering A process by which traffic is optimized to follow certain paths based on specified requirements.

TSR See *tag switching router*.

Type-Length-Value (TLV) The Type-Length-Value (TLV) is the LDP hop-count object. When an ATM-LSR receives a Label Request message with the TLV, it increments the hop-count value by 1.

U

unsolicited downstream A condition where a downstream router advertises a new binding without waiting for the neighbors to send a request.

upstream A term used when discussing MPLS label binding. Upstream refers to a route that was learned from the originating or neighboring router.

V

VCI See *virtual circuit identifier.*

VC merge See *virtual circuit merge.*

virtual circuit identifier (VCI) The address contained in the ATM cell header that is used to designate the virtual channel within the virtual path on the physical ATM link.

virtual circuit merge (VC merge) Used to solve cell-interleaving problems and allows the ATM-LSR to preserve label space. VC merge is enabled by default on an ATM-LSR.

virtual path identifier (VPI) An identifier in the ATM cell header that is used to designate the virtual path on the ATM physical link.

virtual private network (VPN) A virtual private network is a network that overlays public network infrastructure and that provides its own routing, security, and quality of service configuration.

virtual router A condition where a single router appears to be many routers to customers. Customer routing tables are kept separate even though they all connect to the same router.

virtual routing and forwarding (VRF) table A dedicated routing table, with routing table mechanisms, for a particular customer on a PE router.

VPI See *virtual path identifier.*

VPN See *virtual private network.*

VPNv4 routes A term for MP-BGP routes where the route distinguisher is prepended to the NLRI.

VRF See *virtual routing and forwarding tables.*

Index

Note to the Reader: Throughout this index **boldfaced** page numbers indicate primary discussions of a topic. *Italicized* page numbers indicate illustrations.

A

B

C

D

E

F

O

P

Q

R

S

T

U

V

W

X

T

U

V

W

X